A FUTURE BEYOND GROWTH

There is a fundamental denial at the centre of *why* we have an environmental crisis – a denial that ignores that endless physical growth on a finite planet is impossible. Nature provides the ecosystem services that support our civilization, thus making humanity unavoidably dependent upon it. However, society continues to ignore and deny this dependence.

A Future Beyond Growth explores the reasons why the endless growth economy is fundamentally *un*sustainable and considers ways in which society can move beyond this to a steady state economy. The book brings together some of the deepest thinkers from around the world to consider how to advance beyond growth. The main themes consider the deep problems of the current system and key aspects of a steady state economy, such as population; throughput and consumerism; ethics and equity; and policy for change. The policy section and conclusion bring together these various themes and indicate how we can move past the growth economy to a truly sustainable future.

This volume will be of great interest to students and scholars of economics, sustainability and environmental studies in general.

Haydn Washington is a Visiting Fellow in Interdisciplinary Environmental Studies (Science) at UNSW (University of New South Wales) Australia.

Paul Twomey is a Senior Research Fellow in the faculty of Built Environment at UNSW (University of New South Wales) Australia.

A FUTURE BEYOND GROWTH

Towards a steady state economy

Edited by Haydn Washington and Paul Twomey

First published 2016
by Routledge
2 Park Square, Milton Park, Abingdon, Oxon OX14 4RN

and by Routledge
711 Third Avenue, New York, NY 10017

Routledge is an imprint of the Taylor & Francis Group, an informa business

© 2016 selection and editorial matter, Haydn Washington and Paul Twomey; individual chapters, the contributors

The right of the editors to be identified as the authors of the editorial material, and of the authors for their individual chapters, has been asserted in accordance with sections 77 and 78 of the Copyright, Designs and Patents Act 1988.

All rights reserved. No part of this book may be reprinted or reproduced or utilised in any form or by any electronic, mechanical, or other means, now known or hereafter invented, including photocopying and recording, or in any information storage or retrieval system, without permission in writing from the publishers.

Trademark notice: Product or corporate names may be trademarks or registered trademarks, and are used only for identification and explanation without intent to infringe.

British Library Cataloguing-in-Publication Data
A catalogue record for this book is available from the British Library

Library of Congress Cataloging-in-Publication Data
Names: Washington, Haydn, 1955- editor. | Twomey, Paul, editor.
Title: A future beyond growth : towards a steady state economy / edited by Haydn Washington and Paul Twomey.
Description: Abingdon, Oxon ; New York, NY : Routledge, 2016.
Identifiers: LCCN 2015042068| ISBN 9781138953017 (hb) | ISBN 9781138953024
(pb) | ISBN 9781315667515 (ebook)
Subjects: LCSH: Stagnation (Economics) | Economic development--Environmental aspects. | Sustainable development.
Classification: LCC HD82 .F87 2016 | DDC 338.9/27--dc23
LC record available at http://lccn.loc.gov/2015042068

ISBN: 978-1-138-95301-7 (hbk)
ISBN: 978-1-138-95302-4 (pbk)
ISBN: 978-1-315-66751-5 (ebk)

Typeset in Bembo and Stone Sans
by Saxon Graphics Ltd, Derby

Printed and bound in the United States of America by Publishers Graphics, LLC on sustainably sourced paper.

Dedication

For Herman Daly, whose clarity of thought on the steady state economy has led the way.

"Ours is a world in potentially fatal overshoot; human consumption of living resources already exceeds the regenerative capacity of the ecosphere. If all that were needed for decision-makers to 'fix' the problem is a set of evidence-based briefing notes, they need look no further than *A Future Beyond Growth*. The remaining question is whether our political leaders can rise above collective denial, defy entrenched economic elites and (re)turn to serving humanity's collective interest in survival with dignity."

— *William E. Rees, Professor Emeritus (human ecology and ecological economics), UBC School of Community and Regional Planning, Canada and Fellow of the Post-Carbon Institute, USA*

"The age of growth is over. If humanity is to prosper in the years to come, then we must develop a new economics that does not rely on increasing GDP to deliver economic prosperity. *A Future Beyond Growth* makes an important contribution to the post-growth literature. It tackles tough topics such as the need to stabilise population, the subversive nature of a 'green' or 'circular' economy, and the conflict between capitalism and a steady-state economy. Its essays should be required reading for all those who are serious about sustainability."

— *Dan O'Neill, Lecturer in Ecological Economics, University of Leeds, UK, and co-author of 'Enough Is Enough' (2013)*

"Economic growth is in decline everywhere. Mainstream economists and politicians hope to reverse this trend. Others concerned about humanity's impacts on the planet look to a future beyond growth. What might such a future be like? This book provides some answers. Now if only those economists and politicians would read it!"

— *Peter A. Victor, Faculty of Environmental Studies, York University, Canada*

CONTENTS

List of illustrations	xi
List of contributors	xiii
Acknowlegements	xx

Foreword: Setting things straight for the steady state   xxi
Brian Czech

Introduction: Why the growth economy is broken   1
Haydn Washington

SECTION 1
Population: the heresy of numbers   15

1   A population perspective on the steady state economy   17
   Herman E. Daly

2   Population: better not bigger   21
   Ian Lowe

3   Nine population strategies to stop short of 9 billion   32
   Robert Engelman

4   Choosing a planet of life   43
   Eileen Crist

SECTION 2
Throughput and consumerism: a key elephant in the room — 57

5 Re-engineering cultures to create a sustainable civilization — 59
   Erik Assadourian

6 Sustainable business: what should it be? Circular economy and the 'business of subversion' — 70
   Helen Kopnina

7 Peak mining: stepping down from high resource use — 83
   Simon Michaux

SECTION 3
Key aspects of a steady state economy — 95

8 What is the steady state economy? — 97
   James Magnus-Johnston

9 The physical pathway to a steady state economy — 112
   Graham Turner

10 Relating the steady state economy to the green, circular and blue economies — 129
   Paul Twomey and Haydn Washington

11 Sustainable, equitable, secure: getting there? — 146
   Frank Stilwell

12 The Genuine Progress Indicator: an indicator to guide the transition to a steady state economy — 158
   Philip Lawn

13 Capitalism and the steady state: uneasy bedfellows — 176
   Joshua Farley

SECTION 4
Ethics and a message from the future — 193

14 Sustainable development vs. sustainable biosphere — 195
    Holmes Rolston III

15 A message from the future about the steady state economy — 200
    Geoff Mosley

SECTION 5
Policy for change — 211

16 Degrowth as a transition strategy — 213
    Robert Perey

17 Strategies for transition to a future beyond growth — 223
    Mark Diesendorf

    Conclusion: The endless growth myth: simplicity and complexity — 239
    Haydn Washington and Paul Twomey

Index — 252

ILLUSTRATIONS

Figures

0.1	The relationships between ecosystem health and human well-being	5
3.1	World population growth in the twenty-first century	33
3.2	Annual population growth rates by world and region, 1950–2010	34
7.1	Production and consumption of metals has increased	84
7.2	Grade of mined minerals has been decreasing	86
7.3	International market metal prices became volatile in 2005	90
8.1	Materials used by society	99
8.2	Percentage 'very happy' versus GDP per capita	100
9.1	Schematic summary of physical flow connections of a modern economy like Australia's	114
9.2	Feedback processes applied to the ASFF modelling to establish economically healthy unemployment levels and international trade balance (relative to GDP)	115
9.3	Increasing efficiency of energy and resource use simulated in the ASFF scenarios results in the overall carbon intensity falling steadily for the next 50 years	117
9.4	Economic outcomes under alternative socio-economics systems	122
9.5	Environmental impacts simulated in the ASFF under alternative socio-economics systems: (a) net oil imports (i.e. imports less exports) and (b) greenhouse gas emissions aggregated from main sources and sinks	124

9.6 Environmental impacts simulated in the ASFF under alternative socio-economics systems: (a) aggregated water use and (b) river flow leaving the Murray River, including the effects of a 'business-as-usual' climate scenario (A1FI) — 125
10.1 Google search webpage hits for different terms ('000s), July 2015 — 131
10.2 Relative popularity of term in Google search — 131
12.1 The scale effect of rising real GDP on Australia's energy consumption — 161
12.2 The economic welfare generated by a growing economy — 162
12.3 A comparison of the GDP and GPI for six industrialised nations — 170

Tables

7.1 *Limits to Growth* study modelling approach — 90
9.1 Summary of scenario settings implemented in the ASFF — 120
10.1 Comparison of economic models — 140
12.1 Items used to calculate the Genuine Progress Indicator (GPI) for Australia, 2010 — 168

Boxes

5.1 What would a culture of sustainability look like? — 62

CONTRIBUTORS

Erik Assadourian is a Senior Fellow at the Worldwatch Institute. Over the past 14 years with Worldwatch, Erik has directed two editions of Vital Signs and four editions of *State of the World,* including *State of the World 2013: Is Sustainability Still Possible?* Erik also directs Worldwatch's Transforming Cultures project, and designed *Catan: Oil Springs,* a climate change scenario for the popular board game *Settlers of Catan.* Erik is currently working to produce *Yardfarmers,* a reality TV show that will follow six millennial Americans as they exit the consumer economy to live with their parents and become sufficiency farmers. He is also Contributing Editor with *Adbusters* and *FUTUREPERFECT,* and he is Adjunct Professor at Goucher College. Erik also spends much of his time raising his toddler son, preparing him for the ecological transition and civilizational collapse most likely in our future. He's chronicling this at www.raisinganecowarrior.net.

Eileen Crist received her bachelor's in sociology from Haverford College in 1982, and her PhD from Boston University in 1994, also in sociology with a specialization in life sciences and society. She has been teaching at Virginia Tech in the Department of Science and Technology in Society since 1997. She is author of *Images of animals: Anthropomorphism and Animal Mind.* She is also co-editor of a number of books, including *Gaia in Turmoil: Climate Change, Biodepletion, and Earth Ethics in an Age of Crisis*; *Life on the Brink: Environmentalists Confront Overpopulation*; and *Keeping the Wild: Against the Domestication of Earth.* She is author of numerous academic and popular papers, and she contributed to the late journal *Wild Earth.* Her work focuses on biodiversity loss and destruction of wild places and pathways to halt these trends. More information and publications can be found on her website www.eileencrist.com.

Brian Czech has a PhD in Renewable Natural Resources Studies from the University of Arizona with a minor in political science. The Founding President of the Center for the Advancement of the Steady State Economy (CASSE), Brian is also a Visiting Professor at Virginia Tech in the National Capitol Region, where he teaches ecological economics. A prolific author in a variety of venues, his scientific articles have appeared in dozens of peer-reviewed journals, dealing primarily with ecological and economic sustainability issues. His books include *Supply Shock: Economic Growth at the Crossroads*, released in May 2013; *Shoveling Fuel for a Runaway Train*, which calls for an end to uneconomic growth; and *The Endangered Species Act: History, Conservation Biology, and Public Policy*. Brian is a regular contributor to *The Huffington Post* and *The Daly News*, a blog devoted to advancing the steady state economy as a policy goal with widespread public support. Brian is also an Interdisciplinary Biologist in the national office of the US Fish and Wildlife Service, where he received a 2010 Star Award for outstanding performance. He has played a leading role in engaging the environmental sciences and natural resources professions in ecological economics and macroeconomic policy dialogue.

Herman E. Daly is Emeritus Professor at the University of Maryland's School of Public Affairs. From 1988 to 1994 he was Senior Economist in the Environment Department of the World Bank. Prior to 1988 he was Alumni Professor of Economics at Louisiana State University. His books include: *Steady-State Economics* (1977; 1991); *For the Common Good* (1989; 1994); *Beyond Growth* (1996); *Ecological Economics and Sustainable Development* (2007); and *From Uneconomic Growth to a Steady-State Economy* (2014). In 1996 he received Sweden's Honorary Right Livelihood Award and the Heineken Prize for Environmental Science, awarded by the Royal Netherlands Academy of Arts and Sciences. In 2001 he received the Leontief Prize for Advancing the Frontiers of Economic Thought, and in 2002 he was awarded the Medal of the Presidency of the Italian Republic. In 2010 the National Council for Science and the Environment gave him its Lifetime Achievement Award. In 2014 he received the Blue Planet Prize, awarded by the Asahi Glass Foundation of Japan.

Mark Diesendorf is Associate Professor in Interdisciplinary Environmental Studies at UNSW Australia. Previously, at various times, he was a Principal Research Scientist in Australia's national research organisation, CSIRO; Professor of Environmental Science and Founding Director of the Institute for Sustainable Futures at University of Technology Sydney; and Director of Sustainability Centre Pty Ltd. Currently his principal research is on rapid mitigation of global climate change and, in particular, integrating renewable energy on a large scale into electricity supply-demand systems. He also researches the assessment of energy technologies (environmental, economic and social equity impacts), energy policy and ecological economics, especially steady state economics. His most recent books are *Sustainable Energy Solutions for Climate Change* (2014) and *Climate Action:*

A Campaign Manual for Greenhouse Solutions (2009). His website can be found at http://www.ies.unsw.edu.au/our-people/associate-professor-mark-diesendorf.

Robert Engelman is a Senior Fellow at the Worldwatch Institute, an environmental think tank in Washington, DC, where he served as President from 2011 to 2014. He currently directs the Institute's Family Planning and Environmental Sustainability Assessment, an evaluation of recently published peer-reviewed scientific articles on connections among family planning, population and the environment. A former journalist, who for many years covered science, health and the environment, Engelman was founding secretary of the US Society of Environmental Journalists and has been on the teaching faculty of Yale University. His research focuses especially on demographic aspects of critical environmental issues such as climate change, water scarcity and biodiversity loss. He has written for *Nature*, the *Wall Street Journal*, *Scientific American* and the *Washington Post*. His book *More: Population, Nature, and What Women Want* won the US Population Institute's Global Media Award for reporting. A graduate of the University of Chicago and Columbia University, Engelman lives just outside of Washington, DC.

Joshua Farley is an Ecological Economist and Professor in community development and applied economics. He is a Fellow at the Gund Institute for Ecological Economics at the University of Vermont, and Special Visiting Researcher at the Universidade Federal de Santa Catarina. He holds degrees in biology (BA), international affairs (MIA) and economics (PhD). He has previously served as Program Director at the School for Field Studies, Centre for Rainforest Studies; as Executive Director of the University of Maryland International Institute for Ecological Economics; and as Visiting Professor at the Federal Universities of Santa Catarina (UFSC) and Bahia (UFBA), and the University of the West Indies, Cave Hill. His broad research interests focus on the design of economic institutions capable of balancing what is biophysically possible with what is socially, psychologically and ethically desirable. His most recent research focuses on agroecology, farmer livelihoods and ecosystem services in Brazil's Atlantic Forest, redesigning finance and monetary systems for a just and sustainable economy, the just distribution of wealth and resources, and transdisciplinary problem solving that integrates research and teaching. He has conducted problem-based courses in ecological economics on six continents. He is co-author with Herman Daly of *Ecological Economics: Principles and Applications*, 2nd ed. (2010).

Helen Kopnina (PhD Cambridge University, 2002) is a Researcher in the fields of environmental education and environmental social sciences. Helen is currently employed at both Leiden University and the Hague University of Applied Science (HHS) in the Netherlands. At the Leiden Institute of Cultural Anthropology and Development Sociology she is an Assistant Professor of environmental anthropology. At the HHS, she is a coordinator and lecturer in the Sustainable Business program. Kopnina is the author of over 60 peer reviewed articles and (co)author and (co)editor of twelve books, including *Sustainability: Key Issues* (2015); *Culture and Conservation: Beyond Anthropocentrism* (2015); and *Handbook of Environmental Anthropology* (2016).

Philip Lawn is an Ecological Economist who has produced eight books, around 40 book chapters and over 50 journal articles on sustainable development; green national accounting; international trade and the environment; ecological macroeconomics; and issues concerning the perceived conflict between environmental conservation and employment. His latest book is on the ecological economics of climate change. Philip is a member of the International Society for Ecological Economics (ISEE) and served on the executive of the Australia and New Zealand Society for Ecological Economics (ANZSEE) – a chapter of ISEE – from 2003 to 2008. During this period, Philip was involved in the organization of three ANZSEE conferences and a pre-conference workshop on sustainable development indicators for the Asia-Pacific region in New Delhi in 2006. In 2004, Philip became the inaugural editor of the *International Journal of Environment, Workplace, and Employment* (Inderscience) and currently serves on the editorial boards of a number of academic journals. Besides his academic duties, Philip provides advice to policy-makers and regularly offers his services as a speaker at public speaking forums.

Ian Lowe is Emeritus Professor of science, technology and society at Griffith University in Brisbane, as well as an Adjunct Professor at Flinders University and the University of the Sunshine Coast. He is a Fellow of the Australian Academy of Technological Sciences and Engineering. He has published 10 books, more than 60 book chapters and over 50 journal articles. He has been involved in a wide range of advisory bodies for all levels of government over the last 30 years, including chairing the advisory council that produced in 1996 the first Australian national report on the state of the environment. He directed the Commission of the Future in 1988, when he was made Australian Humanist of the Year. He was made an Officer of the Order of Australia in 2001 for services to science and technology, especially environmental science. He received in 2000 the Prime Minister's Environmental Award for Outstanding Individual Achievement and the Queensland Premier's Millennium Award for Excellence in Science. He was also awarded the 2002 Eureka Prize for Promotion of Science. In 2009 the International Academy of Sciences, Health and Ecology awarded him the Konrad Lorenz Gold Medal.

James Magnus-Johnston is the Canadian Director of the Center for the Advancement of the Steady State Economy (CASSE), an Instructor of Political Studies and Economics with Canadian Mennonite University, and a part-time entrepreneur. James promotes the transition to a steady state economy via low-impact living strategies, financial reform, and economic re-localization, spearheading enterprise development through community partners RISE Urban Incubator, Transition Winnipeg, and the Green Action Centre. He previously worked in finance, communications and public policy, and has an MPhil in land economy from Cambridge University.

Simon Michaux has a Bachelor of Applied Science in physics and geology (QUT) and a PhD in mining engineering (UQ). Currently he is working at the University of Liege in Europe in the area of industrial recycling. In particular, he is working on Urban Mining in the H_2O_0 Circular Economy. Previously, he worked in the mining industry for 18 years in various capacities. He has worked in industry-funded mining research, coal exploration and in the commercial sector in an engineering company as a consultant. His areas of professional technical interest include geometallurgy, mineral processing in comminution, flotation and leaching, mining geology, mining investment and industrial sustainability. In parallel to operating a professional mining career, Simon has done work in and developed capability in self-sufficiency and environmental areas, in particular the environmental fallout of industrial development.

Geoff Mosley grew up in the English Peak District, where he experienced firsthand the major social and economic adjustments of World War II and the birth of the English National Park system. After serving as an Education Officer in the Royal Air Force, he moved first to Canada and then to New Zealand to prepare regional reports for the Town and Country Planning Branch, arriving in Australia in 1960. Trained as a geographer, his masters and doctorate research both involved conservation topics. In 1966 at the Australian National University (ANU) he gave the first Australian yearlong lecture course on the conservation of natural resources. At different times Geoff has been a Research Fellow at the Universities of Newcastle, ANU and Melbourne. Between 1973 and 1986 he was CEO of the Australian Conservation Foundation and from 1981 to 1988 representative of Australasia and Oceania on the Council of IUCN. Since 2003 he has been involved in various capacities with SIT Study Abroad and since 2008 has been the Australian Director of CASSE. He has written over 20 books, including *Steady State: Alternative to Endless Economic Growth*. He was the 2008 winner of the United Nations Association of Australia individual award.

Robert Perey is a Researcher and Trainer with a background in management and organizational change and development. Robert has worked on projects ranging through biodiversity awareness in culturally and linguistically diverse communities (CALD); sustainability case study development for inclusion in MBA programs; and is currently working on the CSIRO Wealth from Waste Cluster led by the Institute of Sustainable Futures (ISF), investigating emerging business models that promote circular flows of resources that now include waste as a valuable product. His research interests centre on organizational and societal change, ecological sustainability, complexity, social imaginaries and aesthetics. In recent years he has run numerous workshops on the degrowth economy.

Holmes Rolston III is University Distinguished Professor and Professor of philosophy at Colorado State University. He has written eight books: *A New Environmental Ethics: The Next Millennium for Life on Earth; Three Big Bangs; Genes, Genesis and God; Philosophy Gone Wild; Environmental Ethics; Science and Religion: A Critical Survey*; and *Conserving Natural Value*. He gave the Gifford Lectures at the University of Edinburgh, 1997–1998. Often called the father of environmental ethics, Rolston has spoken as a distinguished lecturer on all seven continents. He gave the opening address at the Royal Institute of Philosophy's annual conference in Cardiff, Wales, 1993. He participated by invitation in pre-conferences and the United Nations Conference on Environment and Development in Rio de Janeiro, 1992, where he was an official observer. He spoke at the World Congress of Philosophy in Moscow, 1993 and again in Boston, 1998. He is the subject of an intellectual biography by Christopher Preston called *Saving Creation: Nature and Faith in the Life of Holmes Rolston III*. He was named Templeton Prize Laureate in 2003. He is past and founding president of the International Society for Environmental Ethics. He is a founding editor of the journal *Environmental Ethics* and has served on the *Zygon* editorial board for two decades. He is a founding member of the International Society for Science and Religion.

Frank Stilwell is Professor Emeritus in political economy at the University of Sydney. He is one of the leading figures in the political economy movement in Australia, challenging economics thinking and developing progressive alternatives. He has written 12 books on various aspects of political economy, economic theory, economic policy, urban and regional development and economic inequality. He has also co-edited six other volumes of political economic writing. He has taught at the University of Sydney for 45 years and was twice given that university's Award for Excellence in Teaching. For the last three decades he has been the Coordinating Editor of the *Journal of Australian Political Economy*. Politically, he is active in the Greens and is Vice President of the Evatt Foundation, a labour-oriented research organization. He is a Fellow of the Academy of Social Sciences in Australia.

Graham Turner is an Applied Physicist whose work involves whole-of-system analysis on the long-term physical sustainability of the environment and economy. With a background in applied physics, Graham develops and applies the Australian Stocks and Flows Framework to create 'what if' scenarios that quantify sustainability challenges and explore potential solutions. Past topics have included Australian agriculture, fisheries, transport, climate change impacts, water–energy systems, water accounting, distributed energy, and employment in a green economy. Current interests involve food security, environmental implications of immigration, and coupling physical and economic models of the national economy. At the global level, Graham's analysis examines the Limits to Growth, demonstrating that the infamous modelling of the 1970s is, somewhat alarmingly, on track. Graham was a principal research fellow with the Melbourne Sustainable Society Institute at the University of Melbourne. His sustainability research began when he joined CSIRO in 2000. Prior to that Graham was a policy analyst at the Australian Defence Force Head Quarters, researched vacuum glazings at the University of Sydney for use as ultra-insulating windows in buildings, and undertook experimental and simulation research on industrial plasma physics at IBM's T.J. Watson laboratory in NY, USA, and at the University of Sydney.

Paul Twomey is a Senior Research Fellow at the Faculty of Built Environment at the UNSW Australia. He is currently a principal researcher for a low-carbon transitions project called Visions and Pathways 2040, which is funded by the CRC for Low Carbon Living, a national research and innovation hub that brings together industry, government, universities and civil society to find ways of creating a globally competitive low-carbon built environment. He has worked on climate and energy policy and environmental economics at the University of Cambridge, European University Institute (Florence) and UNSW. His research interests include robustness in policy mixes, carbon policy interactions and renewable energy policy, and is currently focused on policies and governance structures for a more sustainable built environment.

Haydn Washington is an Environmental Scientist and a Visiting Fellow in interdisciplinary environmental studies (science) at UNSW Australia. He has a degree in ecology, an MSc in eco-toxicology (heavy metal pollution) and a PhD in social ecology (2007). Haydn has variously worked in CSIRO, as Director of the Nature Conservation Council of NSW, as an environmental consultant, and as Director of Sustainability in local government. He has had a four-decade involvement with environmental NGOs in Australia. Haydn is the author of six books on the environment: *Ecosolutions: Environmental Solutions for the World and Australia* (1991), *A Sense of Wonder* (2002), *The Wilderness Knot* (2009), *Climate Change Denial: Heads in the Sand* (2011), *Human Dependence on Nature* (2013) and *Demystifying Sustainability: Towards Real Solutions* (2015). Haydn is the Co-Director of the New South Wales chapter of CASSE and was a major organizer of the 2014 Fenner Conference on the Environment 'Addicted to Growth?' at UNSW.

ACKNOWLEDGEMENTS

The editors would like to thank Sue Midgley of UNSW and Anna Schlunke of CASSE NSW for their work to make the 2014 Fenner Conference on the Environment 'Addicted to Growth?' a success, from which this book originated. We would like to thank Hannah Champney, Production Editor at Routledge and Margaret Farrelly, Editorial Assistant at Routledge, for their work and interest in the book. Finally, we would like to thank all the authors of the book's chapters for their work and commitment to bringing this book into being.

FOREWORD

Setting things straight for the steady state

Brian Czech

PRESIDENT, CASSE INTERNATIONAL

Extremely dangerous political rhetoric has proliferated over the past several decades, seducing the masses onto a path that leads to the destruction of nature and civilization. This rhetoric is centered on the claim that there is no conflict between growing the economy and protecting the environment! Politicians are all about economic growth, but at the same time, none of them want to be seen as willful destroyers of the environment. Therefore they stretch, warp, and corrupt the truth with the win-win rhetoric that we can have our cake and eat it too.

Such is the world that CASSE – the Center for the Advancement of the Steady State Economy – was born into on May 1, 2004. In fact, the 'win-win' rhetoric about growing the economy while protecting the environment was the primary impetus for establishing CASSE. The CASSE position on economic growth sets the record straight that 'there is a fundamental conflict between economic growth and environmental protection', leading up to this fact with seven 'whereas' clauses and following it with eight other 'therefore' findings.

Those having a counter-reaction that there doesn't have to be a conflict or it's not a fundamental conflict should read the full CASSE position. The fundamentality of the conflict between economic growth and environmental protection stems from the first two Laws of Thermodynamics. 'Laws of Thermodynamics' might sound intimidating to the uninitiated, yet the first two laws can be summarized in such commonsensical terms as the following: Law 1) You can't get something from nothing; Law 2) You can't get 100% efficiency in the production process. These laws set up a limit to economic growth, and they create a conflict between economic growth and environmental protection even before any limits are hit, as evidenced most clearly by the erosion of biodiversity in lockstep with economic growth.

So read the CASSE position, and read this book. While the relationship between economic growth and environmental protection is not an overly simple matter, the key points are readily grasped by sober readers with the benefit of a clearly written book such as *A Future beyond Growth*. Among the 13,000 signatories of the CASSE position are some of the world's leading sustainability thinkers, including the authors featured in *A Future beyond Growth*. Over 200 organizations have endorsed the position. Despite growing support for its central position, CASSE has been David to the Goliaths of Wall Street, neoclassical economics, and mainstream politics worldwide. Economic growth remains the top domestic policy goal among nations and lesser states as well, even as it causes more problems than it solves in the twenty-first century.

Of course if you're going to be a responsible critic of economic growth, much less a long-lasting one, you'd better have an *alternative* to offer. Fortunately it is easy to identify the basic alternatives to growth. There are but two: economic degrowth and the steady state economy. The best way to summarize the alternatives is with a reminder of what, precisely, is meant by 'economic growth'.

Economic growth is simply increasing production and consumption of goods and services in the aggregate. It entails increasing population and/or per capita consumption. Economic growth is indicated by increasing gross domestic product, or GDP. It entails higher demand for materials and energy, because 'you can't get something from nothing'.

Economic growth should be distinguished from 'economic development', which refers to qualitative change regardless of quantitative growth. For example, economic development may refer to the attainment of a fairer distribution of wealth, or a different allocation of resources reflecting the evolution of consumer ethics.

Degrowth, then, is simply defined as decreasing production and consumption in the aggregate, as indicated by decreasing GDP. Decreasing population and/or per capita consumption is required. The word 'degrowth' tends to have political connotations in addition to meaning a smaller economy, especially in Western Europe where the degrowth movement originated as 'La Décroissance'. (Frankly, 'economic growth' also has marked political connotations, but society has gotten numb to them.) As with economic growth, degrowth in the sense of a shrinking economy is ultimately unsustainable.

The sustainable alternative to unsustainable growth and degrowth is the *steady state economy*, which has stabilized production and consumption of goods and services in the aggregate. 'Stabilized' in this context means mildly fluctuating. A steady state economy has stabilized population and per capita consumption. Energy and material demands are gradually stabilized – in the aggregate and per capita – as the limits to productive efficiency are reached. All else equal, a steady state economy is indicated by stabilized GDP. The 'all else equal' (as I described in *Supply Shock: Economic Growth at the Crossroads and the Steady State Solution*) includes level of technology, inflation, the propensity to use money relative to other means of exchange, and environmental conditions. But the bottom line, so to speak, is that GDP is a fine indicator of one thing: the pure size of the economy. Which makes it a good indicator of one other thing: environmental impact.

Obviously the pursuit of a steady state economy invokes a thousand devils in the details of political and cultural reforms. Macroeconomic goals, tax codes, budgets, interest rates, terms of trade: these are some of the aspects of statecraft to be dramatically overhauled with steady statesmanship. In the private sector, what about the sociology of consumption? Imagine the attitudes toward conspicuous consumption in a world that finally 'gets it' about limits to growth. A basic measure of justice, with an equally basic measure of logic, suggests that the place to start in moving toward a steady state economy on Earth is with the wealthiest nations. Impoverished nations need economic growth, almost by definition. We all know who the wealthiest nations are – look for example at nighttime lighting imagery – and concerned citizens from these countries have helped raise awareness of the perils of pursuing perpetual growth.

Which brings us back to CASSE, the uphill-fighting, philanthropically-disadvantaged, non-governmental organization pursuing the mission of advancing the steady state economy through stabilized population and consumption as a policy goal with widespread public support. CASSE is almost entirely a volunteer organization. Its 'business model' should be referenced in quotes, as 'business' tends to connote things like money, salaries, contracts, and related financial features that are rare in the context of CASSE. But CASSE has a volunteer model that includes international chapters unified by the CASSE position on economic growth.

CASSE's New South Wales Chapter, led by Haydn Washington and Anna Schlunke, has demonstrated the potential of this volunteer model. When they invited me to give the keynote address at the Australian Academy of Science's 2014 Fenner Conference on the Environment, with the conference's theme focusing on the steady state economy, I had to check if it was April Fool's Day. To convene a major academy on the steady state economy in the United States, where Big Money calls the shots even in 'academic' affairs, would have been inconceivable. The fact that the CASSE New South Wales Chapter (and its partners) managed to deliver the goods on a national academy conference for the steady state economy says a lot about the chapter, the Australian Academy of Science, and even Australia itself.

What exactly does it say? For starters, it says that Haydn Washington and Anna Schlunke are diligent scholars, determined organizers, and capable communicators. It says that the Australian Academy of Science is a faithful champion of its scientific communities. It suggests, too, that an inquisitive, open-minded spirit prevails, at least in Australia, which offers hope to the international community. Open minds in Australia have gleaned crucial insights from CASSE's tireless Australian National Director, Geoff Mosley (Melbourne), and from one of the world's leading steady state economists, Philip Lawn (Adelaide), and other Australians who presented at the 2014 Fenner Conference.

A Future beyond Growth grew out of the proceedings of the 2014 Fenner Conference on the Environment. Not everything from the conference made it to print. My own talk, for example, stays mostly in the pages of *Supply Shock*, plus the current prefatory remarks. But much of the highly memorable Fenner Conference is presented herein, and I feel delighted to preface the chapters with one more thing:

The next time you hear the win–win spin that 'there is no conflict between growing the economy and protecting the environment' or the equivalent in your regional culture, don't just throw up your hands in resignation to the rhetoric. Think instead about *a future beyond growth*. That's where there's no conflict with protecting the environment, national security, and international stability.

INTRODUCTION

Why the growth economy is broken

Haydn Washington

UNSW AUSTRALIA

The endless growth economy is in the process of breaking – the reason is because it is based on delusion and not reality. Most people, when asked 'Can endless physical growth continue on a finite world?', reply 'Obviously not'. Indeed, it is bizarre to think that it *could* continue forever. It may be fun as kids to believe in the 'Magic Pudding' as Norman Lindsay (1918) portrayed it, where the pudding could never be consumed and just grew back no matter how much you ate. But if we live in the real world, then we have to accept the way that world *truly* works. That means we are bound by physical laws such as the Second Law of Thermodynamics (Daly 1991). It means we are bound by ecological realities such as carrying capacity and ecosystem thresholds for which beyond a certain point they can change rapidly (collapse) (Washington 2013). It means we are bound by the ecosystem services nature provides for free, which are the underpinnings of our society (MEA 2005). These rely on the wealth of biodiversity that has evolved over many millions of years. It means that humanity is dependent on the great cycles of nature: the water cycle, carbon cycle and nutrient cycles. The reality is that humanity – like all species of life – is *dependent on nature*. It is 'obligate dependence', meaning we don't have a choice. We *think* the world works by human decisions and by the power of the economy – but this is just something we have made up, it cannot change the realities we must live with, and the limits we must live within to be 'sustainable' in any meaningful sense (Washington 2015).

Do we have a problem?

This question must be asked and answered, as surprisingly many commentators seem to think everything is just fine. During the twentieth century (most figures from Rees 2008) the following changes have taken place:

- Human population is up 4-fold (Rees 2008).
- Industrial pollution is up 40-fold (Rees 2008).
- CO_2 emissions are up 17-fold (Rees 2008).
- Fish catches are up 35-fold (Rees 2008).
- Mining of ores and minerals is up 27-fold (UNEP 2011).
- One quarter of coral reefs (Postel 2013), a third of mangroves (MEA 2005) and half of all wetlands were destroyed (Meadows et al. 2004, p. 85).

Today it continues:

- At least 60 per cent of ecosystem services are degrading or being used unsustainably (MEA 2005).
- We have exceeded three 'planetary boundaries' – extinction, climate change and nitrate pollution (Rockstrom et al. 2009).
- Earth's ecological footprint is more than 1.5 Earths (GFN 2014) and the Living Planet Index has dropped by 52 per cent (WWF 2014).
- Extinction is *at least* 1000-fold above the normal levels (MEA 2005) in the fossil record, and Peter Raven et al. (2011) estimate that without change in the way we do things, by 2100 *two-thirds* of life may be extinct.

Let us ponder this. Two-thirds of life extinct by 2100 due to *our* actions. As Eileen Crist (2012) observes: 'The scale of what we are doing, the sheer moral evil, is almost unimaginable'. So yes, the facts are in – we do indeed have a major problem. Society's interaction with the world that supports it is fundamentally *un*sustainable.

However, Western society pretends it has escaped such limits with its intelligence and technology. One TV series proudly proclaimed that this is the 'human planet', while some have named this geological era 'the Anthropocene'. The reason scientists have used this term is not 'praise' for human actions, but a recognition that humanity is changing the world incredibly rapidly – and not for the better. Causing the sixth mass extinction of life on Earth is nothing to be proud of (Kolbert 2014). However, let us examine more deeply the ways humanity is dependent on nature.

Human dependence on nature

I summarise these dependencies from my book *Human Dependence on Nature* (Washington 2013).

Food webs: Aldo Leopold (1949) characterised the economy of nature as a 'fountain of energy flowing through a circuit of soils, plants and animals' (p. 253). Energy is continually being added to ecosystems from the sun, being trapped by plants (producers), and these plants are eaten by herbivores, which may be eaten by carnivores. This flow of energy in an ecosystem is called a food or 'trophic' chain, and the flow of energy through a web of different species is a *food web*.

Energy is life: Our planet is bathed in a life-giving stream of energy from the Sun. This supplies the energy for our fields, farm animals, and our own bodies. The fossil fuels that power our civilisation are carbon compounds trapped by photosynthesis of past ecosystems and fossilised hundreds of millions of years ago. Plants trap 1–2 per cent of the sunlight that falls on them (Hall and Rao 1999). The net primary productivity (NPP) from plants powers Earth's ecosystems, so the ancient Egyptians had it right – the Sun *is* the font of life.

The Second Law of Thermodynamics tells us that energy goes from a usable form to an unusable form as 'entropy' (disorder) increases. Energy thus passes from a high energy state to a low energy state (waste heat). It goes in one direction, so unlike nutrients, you cannot 'recycle' energy. The direction can be reversed by human action (e.g. a fridge), but this takes added energy. Thus, ultimately, the amount of life is determined by the fixed amount of sunlight falling on Earth. Unlike our society's energy consumption, solar energy is not increasing exponentially.

The energy limits of Earth's ecosystems cannot be ignored. On a finite Earth we cannot keep increasing the amount of food, fibre and wood we consume. Energy is life, but the amount coming to Earth is fixed. Humanity is now using about 12,000 times as much energy per day as was the case when farming first started. Ninety per cent of this is due to industrialisation, 10 per cent to our huge growth in numbers (Boyden 2004). So how much energy is humanity's due? How much of Earth's productivity should be controlled by just one species? Vitousek *et al.* (1986) estimated that about 40 per cent of net primary productivity (NPP) in terrestrial ecosystems was being co-opted by humans each year. Rojstaczer *et al.* (2001) argued this could be as high as 55 per cent, while Haberl *et al.* (2007) estimated a figure of 24–29 per cent. Whatever figure one uses, this is a huge percentage of the planet's NPP. How much is enough, how much too much? If we actually tried for 100 per cent of NPP, then natural ecosystems would completely collapse everywhere, as would civilisation. The fact that 60 per cent of ecosystem services are now being degraded or used unsustainably (MEA 2005) shows our current appropriation of NPP is far too high. Clearly, we are way *beyond* what could be considered 'equitable' in terms of our fair share. The energy of all ecosystems cannot end up being 'just for us'.

Keystone species: Each species in a food web may not have equal impact on other species. Some species have more effect on how energy moves through a food web, and even on what species are present. These are known as *keystone species*, being important but little known parts of ecosystems (Washington 2013). There are three types: predators, mutualists and ecosystem engineers. It is critical we keep keystone species, the trouble is we don't know what many (perhaps most) actually are.

Nutrient cycles: Energy may flow through to us from the Sun, but Earth is finite, with material limits. All life on Earth requires water and minerals to survive. The water that makes up 70 per cent of our bodies; the phosphorus incorporated in our bones and the ATP molecule that powers our cells; the nitrogen in amino acids that form proteins; the potassium we need for cellular reactions and osmotic control. Even the very carbon we eat in food and breathe out as carbon dioxide. If we only used these once, then they would have run out long ago, and life would have faded away. Instead, they are part of the 'great cycles', where each is taken up and used by plants and animals and then returned to Earth.

Nitrogen is a key nutrient cycle, for it forms the basis of the amino acids that make up proteins. Nitrogen gas in the atmosphere is not biologically available, and must be turned into nitrates that plants can absorb. This can happen naturally by the action of lightning, or by nitrogen-fixing bacteria found mostly in plant root nodules (especially legumes). Animals take up nitrogen in proteins by eating food and their waste decomposes back into nitrates. There is thus a great cycle of nitrogen moving from the atmosphere to the land, into living things, then back to ecosystems and back to the atmosphere. Humans now want more for agriculture, so we produce vast amounts of nitrate fertilisers (using fossil fuels). These provide the nutrients required to boost production and create the 'ghost acreage' where more food can be produced – as long as you have the fossil energy to make the nitrate fertilisers (Catton 1982).

Producing massive amounts of nitrate fertiliser has consequences. Vitousek *et al.* (1997) concluded that human alterations have approximately *doubled* the rate of nitrogen input into ecosystems and increased concentrations of the potent greenhouse gas nitrous oxide. Over the past four decades, excessive nutrient loading has become one of the most important stresses on ecosystems. Nitrate pollution has already exceeded planetary limits (Rockstrom *et al.* 2009). Phosphorus is another key nutrient cycle, and is one of the key limiting elements for plant growth. Humanity has altered the cycle by mining phosphate-rich rocks and guano deposits. This has at least *doubled* the amount of phosphorus moving through ecosystems. This huge addition of phosphorus puts a major strain on aquatic ecosystems, where it is the key limiting nutrient. Phosphorus pollution can cause massive algae growth and eutrophication, killing fish and sometimes flipping ecosystems into alternative, less diverse but stable states (MEA 2005). Phosphorus pollution is also beyond planetary boundaries (Steffen *et al.* 2015). Nutrient cycles thus form a key backbone of the life processes that run our world. They deserve our respect, and we disturb them at our peril – yet we continue to do so.

Ecosystem services: Gretchen Daily (1997) explains that ecosystem services are conditions and processes through which natural ecosystems 'sustain and fulfil human life'. They maintain biodiversity and the production of ecosystem goods that include seafood, forage, timber, fibre and medicines. They embody the actual life-support functions, such as cleansing and recycling. They also confer important aesthetic, spiritual and cultural benefits. Ecosystem services are commonly defined as the direct and indirect contributions of ecosystems to human well-being (De Groot *et al.* 2010). The Millennium Ecosystem Assessment (MEA 2005) split ecosystem services into four parts: *provisioning services* (products obtained from ecosystems), *regulating services* (benefits obtained from regulation of ecosystem processes), *cultural services* (non-material benefits) and *supporting services* (those necessary for the production of all other ecosystem services).

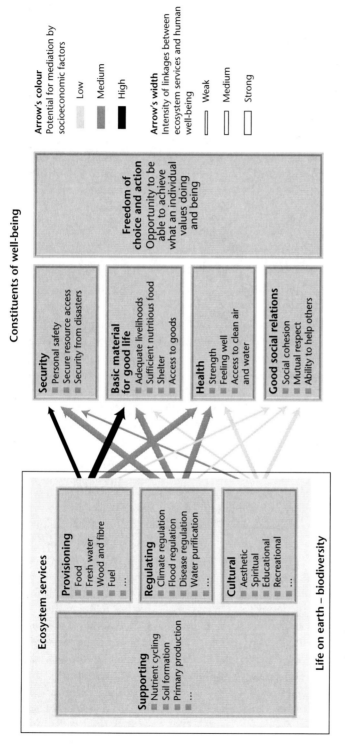

FIGURE 0.1 The relationships between ecosystem health and human well-being (MEA 2005)

The MEA (2005) noted that human use of all ecosystem services is growing rapidly. Overall it concluded that 60 per cent of ecosystem services are being degraded or used unsustainably. Many ecosystem services are being degraded primarily to increase food supply. Ecosystem collapse has been caused by: eutrophication; overfishing; species introduction; nutrient impact on coral ecosystems; regional climate change; unsustainable bushmeat trade; and loss of keystone species (MEA 2005). Should ecosystem collapse matter to us? There is a real (although unknown) possibility that net biodiversity loss will have catastrophic effects on human welfare (Gowdy et al. 2010). Certainly, we do know that humans are totally dependent on the ecosystem services that nature provides. If enough ecosystems collapse, this will have a big-time impact on human well-being. So humanity is dependent on nature, and we have ignored and denied this reality – to our (and nature's) great cost. Of course, as the old bumper sticker observed, given our obligate dependency, 'Nature bats last'.

Drivers of unsustainability

There are a number of drivers of unsustainability to discuss (Washington 2015):

- *Ecological ignorance* – much of society (and academia) remains determinedly ignorant of how the world works ecologically, and much of academia has a predilection to focus on theory rather than reality (Washington 2015).
- *Worldview and ideologies* such as modernism, anthropocentrism and resourcism. Modernism underlies the emergence of a profound anthropocentrism still dominant in the world, where nature is conceived of as 'nothing more than matter-in-motion' (Oelschlaeger 1991, p. 69). Resourcism sees nature as just a group of resources for human use (Crist 2012). Anthropocentrism in academia is insidious and widespread (Washington 2013) and can verge on 'human supremacy' (Crist 2012).
- *Overpopulation* – there are too many people on Earth, consuming at too high a level. World population is 7.3 billion and the UN (2012) indicates that by 2050 the population will reach a predicted medium figure of 9.6 billion, but it may be 10.9. Given that we know we have exceeded ecological limits, it would seem *obvious* that population increase is a driver for environmental degradation. Daily et al. (1994) argue that an ecologically sustainable world population is 2 billion or less. However, 'overpopulation' is still commonly ignored or even angrily denied.
- *Overconsumption* – as economist Paul Ekins (1991) has noted, a sustainable '*consumer*' society is actually a contradiction in terms. We cannot consume our world's ecosystems and be sustainable. Since 1960, population has grown by a factor of 2.2 while consumption has gone up *sixfold* (Assadourian 2010). Consumer expenditure per person has almost tripled. If the entire world were to adopt American (or Australian) lifestyles, we would need at least four more

planets to supply them (Graff 2010). This can't happen, hence why we are rapidly exceeding Earth's limits.
- The '*Endless Growth Myth*' – we as a society persist in believing this impossible myth. Overpopulation, overconsumption and even the critically serious problem of climate change are also really *symptoms* of a general malaise – the 'Endless Growth Myth' or what Boyden (2004) has called 'evermoreism'. Many environmental scientists and scholars believe that the fixation on growth and increasing consumption is precisely why we have an environmental crisis (Daly 1991).
- *Denial* of our predicament is possibly the biggest ongoing driver of unsustainability.

Believing in stupid things

Rees (2010) notes that humanity is a 'deeply conflicted species' torn between what reason and moral judgement tell us on the one hand, and what baser emotions tell us to do on the other, particularly in stressful circumstances. Yet society must deal with denial to have any chance of becoming sustainable in any meaningful way. Humanity is very good at believing in *stupid things* (Washington 2015), things that hold us back from reaching sustainability, such as:

1. The world and the universe are all about *us*.
2. Although we live on a finite planet, endless growth is somehow possible.
3. Population growth is not a problem ('more is better').
4. Endless growth in consumption and resource use is not a problem ('resource limits are in our mind').
5. The 'invisible hand' of the market is God and must not be regulated (neoliberalism).
6. Technology can solve everything (techno-centrism).
7. Greed is good.

The first is intensely anthropocentric (hubris); numbers 2–4 violate ecological reality and scientific laws (as well as common sense); the fifth is actually a religious myth (without scientific or ethical basis); the sixth is a modernist ideology that ignores ecological limits as well as ethics; while the seventh is unethical at so many levels, as noted by virtually every religious leader in history. Yet all of these are still espoused by various people in modern society. Indeed, many of them are still held by governments, the mass media, and by many of the public. Braungart and McDonough (2008, p. 117) note that 'insanity' is defined as doing the same thing over and over and expecting a different outcome. The environmental crisis tells us that belief in the above points has failed, yet we keep doing them. The fact that many of us still believe these stupid things, and continue to assert that they are true (or even 'good') shows why we must consider society's denial.

Denial blocking sustainability

Denial is arguably the greatest problem in the human psyche. Why? Because it makes us a 'seriously dumb species' (Soskolne 2008). It turns off our intelligence so we don't use our creativity to solve major problems. There are four huge 'elephants in the room' that society mostly doesn't see: overpopulation, overconsumption, the growth economy and climate change (Washington 2014). All of these have been ignored and denied by the majority of governments (and also 'we the people') over many decades. As a society, we continue to act as if there is no environmental crisis, no matter what the science shows. How is it possible for civilisations to be blind toward grave approaching threats to their security (D. Brown 2008)? We proceed often in a cultural trance of denial, where people and societies block awareness of issues too painful to comprehend. This human incapacity to hear 'bad news' makes it hard to solve the environmental crisis. We call ourselves *Homo sapiens*, but many of us seemingly are actually '*Homo denialensis*' (Washington 2014).

We deny some things as they force us to confront change, others because they are just too painful, or make us afraid. Sometimes we can't see a solution, so problems appear unsolvable. Thus many of us deny the root cause of the problem. Psychoanalysis sees denial as an 'unconscious defence mechanism for coping with guilt, anxiety or other disturbing emotions aroused by reality' (Cohen 2001). Zerubavel (2006) notes that the most public form of denial is *silence*, where some things are not spoken of. He posits that 'silence like a cancer grows over time', so that a society can collectively ignore 'its leader's incompetence, glaring atrocities and impending environmental disasters'. He concludes that denial is inherently *delusional* and inevitably distorts one's sense of reality.

Denial is as old as humanity. Examples of historical denial are: loss of wilderness; population; DDT; nuclear winter; tobacco; acid rain; the hole in the ozone layer; the biodiversity crisis; and climate change (Washington and Cook 2011; Washington 2014). There is far more involved than just 'confusion' about the science. There is a deliberate attempt to confuse the public so that action is delayed. Oreskes and Conway (2010) detail the support conservative think tanks give to denial. The link that united the tobacco industry, conservative think tanks and a group of denial scientists is that they were *implacably opposed to regulation*. They saw regulation as the slippery slope to socialism. They felt that concern about environmental problems was questioning laissez-faire economics and free market fundamentalism. These conservative bodies equate the free market with 'liberty', so if you attack the market then you attack liberty, and hence must be denied – and the science along with you (Oreskes and Conway 2010). The basis for much denial is thus not science but *ideology*.

The biggest elephant in the room – endless growth

When we confront endless growth, we face society's key denial, the biggest 'elephant in the room' – the one very few seem to want to see! Yet finding a 'future beyond growth' means we must confront the irrationality and denial at the core of modern society. We cannot keep growing physically on a finite world; it drives us towards collapse, as other civilisations discovered (Diamond 2005). We cannot continue to believe in 'magic', where we just keep using more and more resources, even when ecosystem services are in major decline. As Daly (1991) has eloquently pointed out, if growth is the cause of our problems, then we cannot keep suggesting that further growth is the cure. There is the added problem of the takeover of 'sustainable development' to essentially mean 'sustainable growth' – an oxymoron. Washington (2015) traces how both the UN and 'Our Common Future' (WCED 1987) were based on the idea of endless growth. For this reason, Washington (2015) concluded that any meaningful sustainability *cannot be the same* as the common meaning of 'sustainable development' as development has been co-opted to mean endless growth. This explains why after 28 years of 'sustainable development' since 'Our Common Future' came out, the world has become far less sustainable.

To have a future, we have to move past denial and delusion, we have to understand the reality of how this world works and that we have to live within the physical and ecological limits of Earth. We can grow our culture, ethics and wisdom, but we cannot keep growing the numbers of people and our use of resources. If we can start to *see* the elephant in the room then we can find ways to solve the problems it has caused. It is time to wake up, and break the denial dam.

Breaking the denial dam

Rees (2008) concludes that on the dark side of myth, our shared illusions converge on deep denial. Our best science may tell us that the consumer society is on a self-destructive path, but we successfully deflect the evidence by repeating in unison the mantra of perpetual growth. The first step toward a more sustainable world is to accept ecological reality and the socio-economic challenges it implies. While there is a tendency in society to deny things, there is also a tendency to challenge denial (Zerubavel 2006), and it is this we must foster. We can break the denial dam, and the first step is to *talk about it* – hence this book.

Denial has probably been with us since we first evolved. We let ourselves be duped, we let our consciences be massaged, and we let our desire for the 'safe and easy life' blot out unpleasant realities. We delude ourselves. It is time to wake up. If a large part of the public abandons denial, they can fairly quickly turn around corporate denial (especially if it costs them profits). If people tell our politicians that they want real action (not 'weasel words') then politicians will actually *act*. We are not powerless drones who cannot change things. En masse, if we accept the task of repairing Earth, we have the vision, the creativity and the power to solve the environmental crisis, and to move to a truly sustainable future.

What *should* 'economic sustainability' mean?

Sukhdev (2013) argues there is 'emerging consensus among governments and business leaders that all is not well with the market-centric economic model that dominates today' (p. 143). Economic sustainability in a finite world cannot be about endless economic growth. It must be an economy that is sustainable *over the long term*. This means not damaging the ecosystem services that underpin our society. Economic sustainability thus cannot mean 'business as usual' along the neoclassical model. It requires returning the economy to being a *servant* of society, not its master. It means questioning and abandoning most of the assumptions that underlie the neoclassical economic synthesis (Washington 2015). That means moving to a *steady state economy*, where population is stable and sustainable and throughput of materials is minimised. Ethically it arguably means *degrowth* in the developed world (Latouche 2010), with some further growth in the developing world (Daly 2012), where the final overall per capita resource use for everyone is lower. This might be at a level similar to what Australia had around 1960 (Lowe 2005). The reason for the distinction is due to the need to balance equity and reduce poverty. There is likely a need for growth in the developing world to meet 'basic needs' and pull people out of poverty. Growth in the overdeveloped world by contrast is not about this (Dietz and O'Neill 2013).

A new model of the economy would be based on the goal of 'sustainable well-being'. It would acknowledge the importance of ecological sustainability, social fairness, and real economic efficiency (Costanza *et al.* 2013). It would use measures of progress such as the Genuine Progress Indicator (GPI), not the GDP (see Lawn in this volume). Can we have a global economy that is not growing in material terms, but that is sustainable and provides a high quality of life for people? Costanza *et al.* (2013) argue the answer is 'yes', and list examples from past societies and current initiatives (e.g. Transition Towns, the Global Eco Village Network). Integrated modelling studies, such as World3 (Meadows *et al.* 2004), GUMBO, LowGrow (Victor 2008), and Turner (2011) also suggest economic sustainability via a no-growth economy *is* achievable (as noted by Costanza *et al.* 2013). The idea that we can change our economic system to ecological economics and a steady state economy is thus not a utopian fantasy. On the contrary, it is the neoclassical 'business as usual' that is the true fantasy (Costanza *et al.* 2013).

Solutions to overpopulation and overconsumption

To move to a steady state economy we have to tackle the difficult issues of overpopulation and overconsumption. Like the endless growth economy itself, these key drivers of unsustainability are largely denied. Overpopulation can be tackled by nine strategies (see Engelman in this volume). The fact that such strategies can work is attested to by the fact that Iran was able to halve its population growth rate from 1987 to 1994 (L. Brown 2011). Population Media (www.populationmedia.org) has also had great success through education in many nations.

Overconsumption is more difficult. The consumer ethic is actually a purposeful social construct (see Assadourian in this volume). Assadourian (2010) suggests three goals to tackle consumerism. First, consumption that undermines well-being has to be discouraged. Second, we need to replace private consumption of goods with *public* consumption of services (e.g. libraries, public transport). Third, necessary goods must be designed to last and be 'cradle to cradle' recyclable. Wilkinson and Pickett (2010) point out that if we improve *equality of income* in our societies, then consumer pressure will decline. To break free of consumerism, we will need to use all our social institutions: business, media, marketing, government, education, social movements, and social traditions (Assadourian 2013).

Conclusion

It is time for economics to serve society and accept limits and ecological realities. An ecologically sustainable biosphere has to be ranked higher than an endlessly increasing GDP. True economic sustainability will live within limits. It will be a steady state economy that is not based on endlessly growing numbers of people and resource use. Many may argue that the steady state economy is 'politically impossible'. It is true that it faces strong resistance, but increasingly, viable alternatives are being presented. There *is* another way, a way that accepts (even celebrates) the ecological limits of Earth. It is the task of true 'economic sustainability' to assist this transformation (Dietz and O'Neill 2013), where the politically impossible will become the politically inevitable. That nobody should deny.

References

Assadourian, E. (2010) 'The rise and fall of consumer cultures', in *2010 State of the World: Transforming Cultures from Consumerism to Sustainability*, eds. L. Starke and L. Mastny, London: Earthscan, pp. 3–20.

Assadourian, E. (2013) 'Re-engineering cultures to create a sustainable civilization', in *State of the World 2013: Is Sustainability Still Possible?*, ed. L. Starke, Washington, DC: Island Press, pp. 113–125.

Boyden, S. (2004) *The Biology of Civilisation: Understanding Human Culture as a Force in Nature*, Sydney: UNSW Press.

Braungart, M. and McDonough, W. (2008) *Cradle to Cradle: Remaking the Way We Make Things*, London: Vintage Books.

Brown, D. (2008) 'The ominous rise of ideological think tanks in environmental policy-making', in *Sustaining Life on Earth: Environmental and Human Health through Global Governance*, ed. C. Soskolne, New York: Rowman and Littlefield, pp. 243–256.

Brown, L. (2011) *World on the Edge: How to Prevent Environmental and Economic Collapse*, New York: W.W. Norton and Co.

Catton, W. (1982) *Overshoot: The Ecological Basis of Revolutionary Change*, Chicago: University of Illinois Press.

Cohen, S. (2001) *States of Denial: Knowing About Atrocities and Suffering*, New York: Polity Press.

Costanza, R., Alperovitz, G., Daly, H., Farley, J., Franco, C., Jackson, T., Kubiszewski, I., Schor, J., and Victor, P. (2013) 'Building a sustainable and desirable economy-in-society-in-nature', in *State of the World 2013: Is Sustainability Still Possible?*, ed. L. Starke, Washington, DC: Island Press, pp. 126–142.

Crist, E. (2012) 'Abundant Earth and the population question', in *Life on the Brink: Environmentalists Confront Overpopulation*, eds. P. Cafaro and E. Crist, Georgia: University of Georgia Press, pp. 141–151.

Daily, G. (1997) *Nature's Services: Societal Dependence on Natural Ecosystems*, Washington: Island Press.

Daily, G., Ehrlich, P., and Ehrlich, A. (1994) 'Optimum population size', *Population and Environment*, Vol 15, no 6, pp. 469–475.

Daly, H. (1991) *Steady State Economics*, Washington: Island Press.

Daly, H. (2012) 'Moving from a Failed Growth Economy to a Steady-State Economy', in *Towards an Integrated Paradigm in Heterodox Economics,* eds. J. Gerber and R. Stepacher, UK: Palgrave-Macmillan, pp. 176–189.

De Groot, R., Fisher, B. and Christie, M. (2010) 'Integrating the Ecological and Economic Dimensions in Biodiversity and Ecosystem Service Valuation', in *The Economics of Ecosystems and Biodiversity: Ecological and Economic Foundations*, ed. P. Kumar, London: Earthscan, pp. 9–40.

Diamond, J. (2005) *Collapse: Why Societies Choose to Fail or Succeed,* New York: Viking Press.

Dietz, R. and O'Neill, D. (2013) *Enough is Enough: Building a Sustainable Economy in a World of Finite Resources*, San Francisco: Berrett-Koehler Publishers.

Ekins, P. (1991) 'The sustainable consumer society: a contradiction in terms?', *International Environmental Affairs*, 3, pp. 243–257.

GFN (2014) 'World footprint: Do we fit on the planet?', Global Footprint Network, see: http://www.footprintnetwork.org/en/index.php/GFN/page/world_footprint/

Gowdy, J., Howarth, R. and Tisdell, C. (2010) 'Discounting, ethics and options for maintaining biodiversity and ecosystem integrity', in *The Economics of Ecosystems and Biodiversity: Ecological and Economic Foundations*, ed. P. Kumar, London: Earthscan, pp. 257–283.

GPI (2014) Genuine Progress Indicator website, see: http://genuineprogress.net/genuine-progress-indicator/

Graff, J. (2010) 'Reducing work time as a path to sustainability', in *State of the World 2010: Transforming Cultures from Consumerism to Sustainability*, eds. L. Starke and L. Mastny, New York: Worldwatch Institute/Earthscan, pp. 173–177.

Haberl, H., Erb, K., Krausmann, F., Gaube, V., Bondeau, A., Plutzar, C., Gingrich, S., Lucht, W. and Fischer-Kowalski, M. (2007) 'Quantifying and mapping the human appropriation of net primary production in earth's terrestrial ecosystems', *Proceedings of the National Academy of Sciences of the USA*, 104, pp. 12942–12947.

Hall, D.O. and Rao, K. (1999) *Photosynthesis*, 6th Edition, Cambridge, UK: Cambridge University Press.

Kolbert, E. (2014) *The Sixth Extinction: An Unnatural History*, New York: Holt and Company.

Latouche, S. (2010) 'Growing a degrowth movement' in *State of the World 2010: Transforming Cultures from Consumerism to Sustainability*, eds. L. Starke and L. Mastny, New York: Worldwatch Institute/Earthscan, p. 181 (Box 22).

Leopold, A. (1949) *A Sand Country Almanac, with Essays on Conservation from Round River*, New York: Random House (1970 printing).

Lindsay, N. (1918) *The Magic Pudding*, Sydney: Angus and Robertson.
Lowe, I. (2005) *A Big Fix: Radical Solutions for Australia's Environmental Crisis*, Melbourne: Black Inc.
MEA (2005) *Living beyond Our Means: Natural Assets and Human Wellbeing, Statement from the Board, Millennium Ecosystem Assessment*, United Nations Environment Programme (UNE), see: www.millenniumassessment.org.
Meadows, D., Randers, J., and Meadows, D. (2004) *The Limits to Growth: The 30-year Update*, Vermont: Chelsea Green.
Oelschlaeger, M. (1991) *The Idea of Wilderness: from Prehistory to the Age of Ecology*, New Haven/London: Yale University Press.
Oreskes, N. and Conway, M. (2010) *Merchants of Doubt: How a Handful of Scientists Obscured the Truth on Issues from Tobacco Smoke to Global Warming*, New York: Bloomsbury Press.
Postel, S. (2013) 'Sustaining freshwater and its dependents', in *State of the World 2013: Is Sustainability Still Possible?*, ed. L. Starke, Washington: Island Press, pp. 51–62.
Raven, P., Chase, J. and Pires, J. (2011) 'Introduction to special issue on biodiversity', *American Journal of Botany*, 98, pp. 333–335.
Rees, W. (2008) 'Toward Sustainability with justice: Are human nature and history on side?', in *Sustaining Life on Earth: Environmental and Human Health through Global Governance*, ed. C. Soskolne, New York: Lexington Books, pp. 13–25.
Rees, W. (2010) 'What's blocking sustainability? Human nature, cognition and denial', *Sustainability: Science, Practice and Policy* 6, no. 2 (ejournal). See: http://sspp.proquest.com/archives/vol6iss2/1001–012.rees.html
Rockström, J., Steffen, W., Noone, K., Persson, Å., Chapin III, F.S., Lambin, E., Lenton, T.M., Scheffer, M., Folke, C., Schellnhuber, H., Nykvist, B., De Wit, C.A., Hughes, T., van der Leeuw, S., Rodhe, H., Sörlin, S., Snyder, P.K., Costanza, R., Svedin, U., Falkenmark, M., Karlberg, L., Corell, R.W., Fabry, V.J., Hansen, J., Walker, B., Liverman, D., Richardson, K., Crutzen, P., and Foley, J. (2009) 'Planetary boundaries: Exploring the safe operating space for humanity', *Ecology and Society*, 14, no. 2, pp. 32–64. See: http://www.ecologyandsociety.org/vol14/iss2/art32/
Rojstaczer, S., Sterling, S., and Moore, N. (2001) 'Human appropriation of photosynthesis products', *Science*, 294, no. 5551, pp. 2549–2552.
Soskolne, C. (2008) 'Preface', in *Sustaining Life on Earth: Environmental and Human Health through Global Governance*, ed. C. Soskolne, New York: Lexington Books, pp. xvii–xviii.
Steffen, W., Richardson, K., Rockström, J., Cornell, S.E., Fetzer, I., Bennett, E.M., Biggs, R., Carpenter, S.R., de Vries, W., de Witt, C.A., Folke, C., Gerten, D., Heincke, J., Mace, G.M., Persson, L.M., Ramanathan, V., Reyers, B., and Sörlin, S. (2015) 'Planetary boundaries: Guiding human development on a changing planet', *Science*, 347 no. 6223, pp. 736–746. DOI: 10.1126/science.1259855
Sukhdev, P. (2013) 'Transforming the corporation into a driver of sustainability', in *State of the World 2013: Is Sustainability Still Possible?*, ed. L. Starke, Washington: Island Press, pp. 143–153.
Turner, G.M. (2011) 'Consumption and the environment: Impacts from a system perspective', in *Urban Consumption,* ed. P.W. Newton, Collingwood: CSIRO, pp. 51–70.
UN (2012) *World Population Prospects; The 2012 Revision*. See: http://esa.un.org/unpd/wpp/Documentation/pdf/WPP2012_HIGHLIGHTS.pdf
UNEP (2011) *Recycling Rates of Metals: A Status Report*, Nairobi: United Nations Environment Programme.

Victor, P. (2008) *Managing without Growth: Slower by Design, not Disaster*, Cheltenham, UK: Edward Elgar.
Vitousek, P., Ehrlich, A. and Matson, P. (1986) 'Human appropriation of the products of photosynthesis', *BioScience*, 36, no. 6, pp. 368–373.
Vitousek, P., Mooney, H., Lubchenco, J., and Melillo, J. (1997) 'Human domination of Earth's ecosystems', *Science*, 277, pp. 494–499.
Washington, H. (2013) *Human Dependence on Nature: How to Help Solve the Environmental Crisis*, London: Earthscan.
Washington, H. (2014) 'Denial as a key obstacle to solving the environmental crisis', in *Sustainable Futures: Linking Population, Resources and the Environment*, eds J. Goldie and K. Betts, Melbourne: CSIRO Publishing, pp. 159–166.
Washington, H. (2015) *Demystifying Sustainability: Towards Real Solutions*, London: Routledge.
Washington, H. and Cook, J. (2011) *Climate Change Denial: Heads in the Sand*, London: Earthscan.
WCED (World Commission on Environment and Development) (1987) *Our Common Future*, London: Oxford University Press.
Wilkinson, R. and Pickett, K. (2010) *The Spirit Level: Why Equality is Better for Everyone*, London: Penguin Books.
WWF (World Wide Fund for Nature) (2014) *Living Planet Report 2014: Species and Space, People and Places*. See: http://wwf.panda.org/about_our_earth/all_publications/living_planet_report/
Zerubavel, E. (2006) *The Elephant in the Room: Silence and Denial in Everyday Life*, London: Oxford University Press.

SECTION 1
Population
The heresy of numbers

1

A POPULATION PERSPECTIVE ON THE STEADY STATE ECONOMY

Herman E. Daly

UNIVERSITY OF MARYLAND

A steady state economy is defined by a constant population and a constant stock of physical capital. In a way it is an extension of the demographer's model of a stationary population to include non-living populations of artifacts, with production rates equal to depreciation rates and birth rates equal to death rates. The basic idea goes back to the classical economists and was most favorably envisioned by John Stuart Mill.

The population problem should be considered from the point of view of *all* populations – populations of both humans and their things (cars, houses, livestock, crops, cell phones, etc.) – in short, populations of all "dissipative structures" engendered, bred, or built by humans. Both human bodies and artifacts wear out and die. The populations of all organs that support human life, and the enjoyment thereof, require a metabolic throughput to counteract entropy and remain in an organized steady state. All of these organs are capital equipment that support our lives. Endosomatic (within skin) capital – heart, lungs, kidneys – supports our lives quite directly. Exosomatic (outside skin) capital supports our lives indirectly, and consists both of natural capital (e.g. photosynthesizing plants, structures comprising the hydrologic cycle), and man-made capital (e.g. farms, factories, electric grids).

In a physical sense, the final product of the economic activity of converting nature into ourselves and our stuff, and then using up or wearing out what we have made, is waste. What keeps this from being an idiotic activity – depleting and polluting, grinding up the world into waste – is the fact that all these populations of dissipative structures have the common purpose of supporting the maintenance and enjoyment of life. As John Ruskin said, "*There is no wealth but life.*"

Ownership of endosomatic organs is equally distributed, while the ownership of exosomatic organs is not, a fact giving rise to social conflict. Control of these external organs may be democratic or dictatorial. Our lungs are of little value without the complementary natural capital of green plants and atmospheric stocks of oxygen. Owning one's own kidneys is not enough to support one's life if one does not have access to water from rivers, lakes, or rain, either because of scarcity or monopoly ownership of the complementary exosomatic organ. Therefore all life-supporting organs, including natural capital, form a unity with a common function, regardless of whether they are located within the boundary of human skin or outside that boundary.

Our standard of living is traditionally measured by the ratio of man-made capital to human beings – that is, the ratio of one kind of dissipative structure to another kind. Human bodies are made and maintained overwhelmingly from renewable resources, while capital equipment relies heavily on non-renewable resources as well. The rate of evolutionary change of endosomatic organs is exceedingly slow; the rate of change of exosomatic organs has become very rapid. In fact the collective evolution of the human species is now overwhelmingly centered on exosomatic organs (Georgescu-Roegen 1971). We fly in airplanes, not with wings of our own. This exosomatic evolution is goal-directed, not random. Its driving purpose has become 'economic growth,' and that growth has been achieved largely by the depletion of non-renewable resources.

Although human evolution is now decidedly purpose driven, we continue to be enthralled by neo-Darwinist aversion to teleology and devotion to random. Economic growth, by promising more for everyone, becomes the *de facto* purpose, the social glue that keeps things from falling apart. But what happens when growth becomes uneconomic, when it begins to increase environmental and social costs faster than production benefits? How do we know that this is not already the case? If one asks such questions, one is told to talk about something else, like space colonies on Mars, or unlimited energy from cold fusion, or geo-engineering, or the wonders of globalization, and to remember that all these glorious purposes require growth, in order to provide still more growth in the future. Growth is the *summum bonum* – end of discussion!

In the light of these considerations, let us reconsider the idea of demographic transition. By definition this is the transition from a human population maintained by high birth rates equal to high death rates, to one maintained by low birth rates equal to low death rates, and consequently from a population with low average lifetimes to one with high average lifetimes. Statistically such transitions have often been observed as standard of living increases. Many studies have attempted to explain this correlation, and much hope has been invested in it as an automatic cure for overpopulation. 'Development is the best contraceptive' is a related slogan, partly based in fact and partly in wishful thinking.

There are a couple of thoughts I'd like to add to the discussion of demographic transition. The first and most obvious one is that populations of artifacts can undergo an analogous transition from high rates of production and depreciation to low ones. The lower rates will maintain a constant population of longer-lived, more durable artifacts. Our economy has a GDP-oriented focus on maximizing production flows (birth rates of artifacts) that keeps us in the pre-transition mode, giving rise to low product lifetimes, planned obsolescence, and high resource throughput, with consequent environmental destruction. The transition from a high maintenance throughput to a low one applies to both human and artifact populations independently. From an environmental perspective, lower throughput per unit of stock (longer human and product lifetimes) is desirable in both cases, at least up to some distant limit.

The second thought I would like to add is a question: Does the human demographic transition, when induced by rising standard of living, as usually assumed, increase or decrease the total load of all dissipative structures on the environment? Specifically, if Indian fertility is to fall to the Swedish level, must Indian per capita possession of artifacts (standard of living) rise to the Swedish level? If so, would this not likely increase the total load of all dissipative structures on the Indian environment, perhaps beyond capacity to sustain the required throughput?

The point of this speculation is to suggest that 'solving' the population problem by relying on the demographic transition to lower birth rates could impose a larger burden on the environment, rather than the smaller burden hoped for. Of course indirect reduction in fertility by automatic correlation with rising standard of living is politically easy, while direct fertility reduction is politically very difficult. But what is politically easy may be environmentally ineffective.

Also, even if a nation follows the demographic transition and achieves a balance between births and deaths, there is still the problem of immigration. In the US, Canada, and Western Europe, for example, nearly all population growth is due to net immigration. A mix of genuine humanitarianism and legitimate refugee needs on the one hand, with class-based cheap labor policies and ethnic politics on the other, has made immigration control politically divisive. If population pressure in pre-transition countries is eased by net emigration, while the benefits of population equilibrium in post-transition countries are erased by growth from net immigration, does that not weaken the basic causes of the demographic transition itself? In the face of increasingly open borders, high fertility seems less likely to be brought down by the automatic demographic transition. True, high-fertility immigrants into low-fertility countries eventually adopt the fertility behavior of the receiving country, but that takes a generation or more.

In a finite world, some populations grow at the expense of others. *Homo sapiens* and *Mechanistra automobilica* are now competing for land, water, and sunlight to grow either food or fuel. More nonhuman 'bodies' will at some point *force* a reduction in human bodies. This forced demographic transition is less optimistic than the voluntary one induced by chasing a higher standard of living by engendering fewer dependents. In an empty world, we saw the trade-off between products and people as motivated by desire for a higher standard of living. In the full world, that trade-off is forced by competition for limited resources.

The usual counter to such thoughts is that we can improve the efficiency by which resource throughput maintains dissipative structures. For example, a car that lasts longer and gets better mileage is still a dissipative structure, but with a more efficient metabolism that allows it to live on a lower rate of throughput. Likewise, human organisms might be genetically redesigned to require less food, air, and water. Indeed smaller people would be the simplest way of increasing metabolic efficiency (measured as the number of people maintained by a given resource throughput). To my knowledge no one has yet suggested breeding smaller people as a way to avoid limiting the number of births, and neither do I. We have, however, been busy breeding and genetically engineering larger and faster-growing plants and livestock, as well as building larger exosomatic organs, so that we become smaller relative to the other organisms we depend on, although we remain the same size absolutely. So far, in the empty world, the latter dissipative structures have been complementary with populations of human bodies, but in our finite and full world, the relationship has become competitive.

Indeed, if we think of population as the cumulative number of people ever to live over time, instead of those simultaneously living, then many artifact populations have long been competitive with the human population. That is, more consumption today of terrestrial low entropy in non-vital uses (Cadillacs, rockets, weapons) means less terrestrial low entropy available for tomorrow's vital use of capturing solar energy (plows, solar collectors, dams, windmills). The solar energy that will still fall on the earth for millions of years after the material structures needed to capture it are dissipated, will be wasted (Georgescu-Roegen 1971), just like the solar energy that currently shines on the barren moon.

If our ethical understanding of the value of 'sustainability' (longevity with sufficiency) is to 'maximize' cumulative lives ever to be lived, subject to a per capita consumption level sufficient for a good life, then we must limit the load we place on the earth at any one time. Fewer people, and lower per capita resource consumption, facilitated by more equitable distribution, mean more (and more abundant) lives for a longer, but not infinite, future. There is no point in maximizing the cumulative number of lives lived in misery, so the qualification 'sufficient for a good life' is important, and requires a deep rethinking of economics, and a shift of focus from growth to sufficiency, including sufficient habitat for other species. It also requires rethinking of the traditional pro-natalist dogmas of the fundamentalist branches of most religions, including Christianity, Islam, and Judaism. The modern secularist religions of Marxism and Scientism likewise proselytize for the Ecumenical Church of Growthism while ignoring population.

Note: This article originally appeared in: Daly, H. (2015).

References

Daly, H. (2015) 'A population perspective on the steady state economy', *Real-World Economics Review*, 70, pp. 106–109. See: http://www.paecon.net/PAEReview/issue70/Daly70.pdf

Georgescu-Roegen, N. (1971) *The Entropy Law and the Economic Process*, Cambridge, MA: Harvard University Press.

2
POPULATION
Better not bigger

Ian Lowe

GRIFFITH UNIVERSITY

Introduction

This chapter discusses the complex and controversial issues around overpopulation, a key driver of the environmental crisis. It considers the reasons why overpopulation must be considered and solved if we are to reach a *meaningful* sustainability. It lists the many misconceptions inherent in the debate, and debunks some of the myths involved. The chapter then discusses what an ecologically sustainable population might be for the Earth, and the humane and non-coercive strategies needed to move us there.

The problem

The fundamental reason for the environmental crisis is the total pressure of our human consumption on natural systems (Higgs 2014). This pressure is in turn the product of the number of people and their per capita consumption. The scale of consumption varies by about two orders of magnitude from the most wasteful society – the USA – to the poorest nations (Wilkinson and Pickett 2009), so we could make great strides toward achieving a balanced and sustainable future by reducing consumption levels and consequent environmental pressure in the most affluent countries. That simple statement ignores the obvious political problem: in every country in the world, not just the poorest and most frugal but also the richest and most profligate, elected politicians generally see economic growth as the highest priority, leading almost inevitably to increasing consumption. Even if we were able to achieve dramatic reductions in per capita consumption, those gains would be swallowed by increasing numbers if the human population were to continue growing. This is the basic point: no species can increase without limit in a closed system with finite resources. If the population is not stabilised by social measures at a level that can be sustainably supported, it will inevitably be reduced by the irresistible forces of starvation, disease and conflict.

There are only three models of species population over time in a closed system (Lowe 2012, pp. 22–24). The first, and most agreeable from our point of view, is that the population can increase until it stabilises at a sustainable level. The second, less appealing, is that it can increase beyond that before collapsing to a lower level, then recovering and oscillating above and below the scale that can be sustained. The third, disastrous, outcome is that the population can so greatly exceed the sustainable level that it collapses completely and the species becomes extinct. All three models give the same sort of graph of population against time in the early stages, the sort of exponential growth we have seen in the human population in recent centuries. The third model is extremely unlikely unless there were catastrophic events like a major meteorite impact or a global thermonuclear war. The most likely outcome on present trends is that the human population will so exceed the sustainable level that it will be significantly reduced by starvation, disease and conflict. I think it is fair to assume that most thoughtful people would prefer the alternative of stabilisation at a level that can be sustainably supported. Our collective decisions this century will determine which of these possible futures is the fate of *Homo sapiens*. Is the planet now overpopulated?

The question doesn't have a simple answer. As discussed earlier, the pressure of the human population on natural systems is the product of our numbers and our per capita consumption of resources. What is unarguable is that the natural systems cannot sustain the present population if everyone makes the same resource demands they do now; our current activity is reducing the capacity of natural systems to allow us to meet our basic needs for food, water, shelter and energy (see Washington in this volume), as well as degrading the experience of nature we used to take for granted (GFN 2013). It is even more obviously true that we can't expand the activities of the human population so that all use natural resources like an average Australian, let alone aspire to the consumption levels in more wasteful societies like the USA, where per capita energy use is nearly double the figure for Australia (Lowe 2005). It seems to be a local Australian political ambition to rival US resource use. As a specific example, the average new house in Australia is now the largest in the world, inevitably needing more energy and other resources for its use (James 2009). Sixty years ago, in 1955, the average per capita resource use in Australia was only about one-third of the figure it is today (Lowe 2005). Those of us who were alive then do not remember it as a time of Neolithic privation. On average, Australians lived quite comfortably, but much less wastefully than today. We were much more likely to travel by public transport. The cars that some people used were much smaller and used much less fuel. Frills like air conditioning and escalators were much less common. Scaling back per capita resource use to something like that of the 1950s in Australia would give a level of material consumption that could, at least in principle, be applied to *all* humans (Lowe 2005).

At one level, inequality and desperate poverty are a question of distribution rather than the total quantity of goods and services available. A recent calculation found that the Millennium Development Goals could be achieved, giving every human adequate food and water, secure shelter, basic health care and education for an amount of money equivalent to *less than 5 per cent* of the global military budget (Archer and Willi 2012). As a second example, if the current food production were distributed equally, it would amount to about two kilograms of food per person per day: about a kilogram of fruit and vegetables, about half a kilogram of cereals and pulses, and about half a kilogram of protein in the form of meat or eggs (Lowe 2009). While that would be a more than adequate diet for all, at the present time hundreds of millions of people are malnourished. In fact, cats and dogs in affluent countries are better fed than the poorest people of the world. A more equitable distribution could solve much of the deprivation we now see. The political problem is again that every society, from the poorest to the most affluent, aspires to *increase* their material consumption; most leaders would see reducing per capita resource use as a failure.

While the so-called demographic transition has seen birth-rates decline in many parts of the world, the human population is still increasing by about 80 million a year (UN 2012). The three factors that correlate consistently with a lower birth-rate are women being well educated, women being substantially in control of their fertility and families being financially secure. Where those three conditions apply, women consistently have about two children each, on average. The birth-rate could be significantly reduced if those conditions were to apply universally. However, there would still be an increasing population for the foreseeable future. The example of Australia illustrates the problem which has been called 'demographic inertia'. Most Australian women are well educated and financially secure. Since effective contraception became widely available about fifty years ago, the number of children per adult woman has fallen dramatically, from above four to below two. The number of children per adult woman is now slightly below the replacement rate. Despite this, there is a 'natural increase' – births minus deaths – of about 150,000 a year, so the Australian population would still be increasing rapidly if there were zero net migration (Lowe 2012). A small contribution to this figure has been a reduction in the death-rate; improving nutrition and general health combined with better medical care has increased the average life expectancy by about twenty years in the last century. The larger contribution is that the number of women of reproductive age is still increasing, as a result of migration and the past birth-rate. Demographic calculations show that the natural increase would decline to zero over the next twenty years or so if there were no net migration, giving Australia a stable population (Young and Day 1995).

Of course, there are still good reasons for accepting migrants, like our obligation to receive refugees and the need to allow family reunion. For low levels of net migration, the annual migrant intake adds to the population, so projections show that the population would stabilise later at a higher level. Christabel Young and Lincoln Day's calculations (1995) show that higher levels of migration push back the date at which the population would stabilise and increase the eventual stable population. This is true for levels of net migration between zero and about 70,000 a year, depending on the assumptions made about the age structure of the migrant group and the consequent differences in the probability that they will have children after they come here. At net migration levels above about 70,000, the population will continue to increase for the foreseeable future. Since the current levels of Australian net migration average about 250,000 a year, we have an implicit policy of allowing the population to keep increasing until its growth will eventually be curtailed by physical limits of water, food, etc.

Migration does not affect the global population, however, so it is clear that would be stabilised if the so-called demographic transition were to apply globally. In other words, if women all over the world were to be educated, secure and in control of their fertility. Even if this could be achieved universally in the very near future, however, we would still face the issue of inertia; the number of women in the fertile age range would continue to increase for about thirty years as a result of the past birth-rate, meaning the population would continue to increase. That is the fundamental reason why the UN projections of population give a range of future growth, but none shows the population stabilising below about 9 billion (UN 2012). Those projections assume that levels of malnutrition do not increase and that health care provision continues to improve. These are relatively optimistic assumptions, with many experts worrying about the world's capacity to maintain even the current level of food production. All the important indicators of food per person – grain per person, meat per person, fish per person – have peaked and are declining (Cribb 2014). The world's major fisheries are all either at peak production or in decline, while productive land is either being degraded by unsustainable practices or being lost to urban expansion. It is quite likely that the world's population will be curbed by food supply unless the existing production can be shared much more equally.

So there is no simple answer to the question of whether the world is already overpopulated? Washington (2015) has reviewed the various calculations of what would be a sustainable population. Biocapacity data suggest that if we made no change at all to consumption patterns, we could currently sustain a population of 4 to 5 billion. Our ecological footprint suggests no more than 4.7 billion people (Engelman 2013, p. 9), but not if every one of those lived at the US standard, where Earth could sustain only a quarter of today's population, or 1.75 billion people (Assadourian 2013, p. 115). This is similar to the 1.5 to 2 billion estimated by Daily et al. (1994). If everybody on Earth shared a modest standard of living, midway between the richest and the poorest, that figure would be around 3 billion (PM 2010). Those problems could be ameliorated by more equitable distribution of the food, water and shelter that is currently being produced. In the absence of the sort of social and economic changes that would enable more equitable distribution, the world *is* overpopulated. It is grossly overpopulated if we accept the implicit aim of development economics – for everyone on Earth to live as Australian or US citizens live today.

It is quite likely that the obstacles to equitable distribution will limit the future growth of population. Put bluntly, starvation and disease will continue to limit population growth in the poorest parts of the world. That reveals an obvious conundrum. If infant mortality is high because of malnutrition and disease, people are likely to continue to have large families in the hope that some of their children will survive. That produces a level of population growth that ensures malnutrition and disease, effectively preventing the demographic transition that would allow painless stabilising of population. It is difficult to be optimistic about the possibility of resolving this dilemma in the world of 2015, where freedom for international corporations is usually seen by elected politicians as a higher priority than equitable distribution that would achieve the Millennium Development Goals. While the population continues to increase, environmental degradation will also continue. More people means more natural vegetation being cleared for food production, more introduced species competing with native wildlife for food, more greenhouse gas production making climate change a worsening problem, more intensive exploitation of fisheries and so on. As the first report to the Club of Rome, *The Limits to Growth*, showed more than forty years ago, the only prospect of a sustainable future involves stabilising both the population and per capita consumption at levels that can be maintained for the indefinite future (Meadows *et al.* 1972).

Some critical myths

In most OECD nations, the average age of the population has increased significantly in recent decades (UN 2013). There are two reasons for this. First, women are having fewer children on average, so the number of new additions to the population has declined. Secondly, better nutrition and health care have improved life expectancy. In countries like Australia, the spectre of 'the ageing society' has been raised to suggest that a bleak future will inevitably result as fewer people of working age support increased numbers of retired people. This misconception has been used to argue that widespread misery will inevitably result if we stabilise the population (O'Connor *et al.* 2012).

There are three reasons why this fear is not valid. First, the entire pattern of work has changed in recent decades. In the 1950s, most people entered the workforce in their early teens or mid-teens. Most men worked full time until they were 60 or 65, while most women left the workforce when they married or had children. In 2015, most people do not take up full-time jobs until much later after a longer period of education, most women do not cease paid work when they have children, and many people continue working into their seventies or even eighties. Secondly, the nature of work has changed. Where there were once many jobs that demanded physical strength and youthful endurance, most of those jobs have been either replaced or radically transformed by technology. Where the agricultural workforce consisted of 600,000 people, almost all men, a hundred years ago, today it consists of about 100,000 and a significant fraction of them are women (Jones 1986). The jobs that once required physical strength, like mining or farming or stevedoring or road repair, are today heavily mechanised, so experience and wisdom are valued more than brute strength. A country like Australia is now overwhelmingly a service economy, with less than 20 per cent of the workforce engaged in the traditional productive areas of agriculture, fisheries, forestry, mining and manufacturing (ABS 2012). Finally, the burden on the community of health care for older people has been dramatically overestimated. The reason we have many more people living into their eighties and nineties is that we have become much healthier. I am alive, still writing book chapters (and playing serious cricket!) at an age when my father, both my grandfathers and indeed all my direct male ancestors were no longer alive. Analysis of health care costs shows that the greatest burden is in the last few years of life, but the ageing of the population has simply shifted those last years from the late sixties or early seventies to the eighties or nineties.

A second myth is that increasing the population is good for the economy, so stagnation and decline will inevitably result if the population stabilises. Since politicians generally believe that population growth is good for the economy, there is an implicit population policy in countries like Australia: effectively it is 'the more the better', in words once used by Bob Hawke when he was Prime Minister. At a superficial level, it is clearly true that a larger population requires more food, more housing, more clothes and more transport, so the growing population increases the overall level of economic activity. The economic question is not that simple. A growing population requires increasing investment in *infrastructure*: housing, power and water, waste management, transport services and so on. Some studies have concluded that there is a small net benefit, all things being considered, while others show a net cost to the community of population growth (Lowe 2012). The second issue is that individuals are only better off on average if the rate of economic growth is higher than the rate of population growth, thus increasing wealth per person.

There has been widespread support for the assumption that economic considerations demand growth since the 'Great Depression' of the 1930s, an economic slump that only ended with the massive public spending of World War II. Earlier economic thinkers such as Mill (1848) had argued for a steady state economy, a view also developed in the twentieth century by Daly (1991) as a professor and then as a senior economist at the World Bank. His writings had little impact on the orthodox economics profession, which almost universally believes in the necessity of growth. This is understandable, since debt financing of development implicitly requires growth to enable the repayments to be made; periods of low growth or recession cause serious economic problems as a result, so few question the need for economic growth. Since the simplest way to increase the overall scale of the economy is to have more people buying the goods and services produced, it is usually assumed that population growth is both inevitable and beneficial.

O'Sullivan (2012) has done detailed calculations of the economic impacts of growing population in Australian cities, concluding that each extra citizen (over their lifetime) requires public spending of about a quarter of a million dollars to provide electricity, water, transport, waste management and other essential services. So rapid population growth requires very large public investments to provide that infrastructure. This is effectively a public subsidy of those sections of the private economy that benefit, most obviously land development, housing and the retail sector.

Additionally, it is sometimes argued that increasing the workforce is necessary to meet the demands of the economy. At the overall level, Birrell et al. (2009) have shown that this is a circular argument. If you assume rapid population growth, you inevitably conclude that more workers are needed to meet the needs of the growing population. If you begin with the alternative hypothesis of a stable population or one which is growing slowly, the equally inevitable conclusion is that the main challenge is providing jobs for those who wish to work. It seems to be accepted by politicians that about 5 per cent of the workforce are unemployed and a larger group under-employed, but large numbers of people are being brought into Australia because of shortages of skilled workers, real or perceived. It is certainly true in many countries that recent migrants do jobs that members of the local population are reluctant to do, for one reason or another. I was in the UK when a politician said in response to a call to reduce immigration: 'The health service and public transport in London would collapse!'. From a local policy perspective, it is much less expensive to lure trained doctors and nurses from poor countries than to train them ourselves, but the practice has certainly caused resentment in some of those countries (Kanck 2011). I discuss the problematic issues arising from international migration in more detail below.

So how could the population be stabilised?

As discussed above, the factors that determine the size of the human population are the birth-rate and the death-rate. For the population to stabilise, these need to be equal. The only humane way to achieve this stabilised future is to find socially acceptable ways to lower the birth-rate.

In the late twentieth century, the leadership of China realised that their rapidly growing population posed a critical problem. Projecting the growth rate into the future, they concluded that it would be impossible to expand food production to meet the emerging needs. Though recognising that it would cause significant social and political pain, they proclaimed and ruthlessly enforced a 'One Child Policy'. It has slowed the rate of population growth, but serious problems have emerged from the newly developed capacity to determine the gender of unborn children. In a patriarchal society, which most still are in 2015, there is a preference for male children. The One Child Policy has led to a very large gender imbalance in the youthful Chinese population, with consequent serious social problems (UN 2013). For that reason alone, the Chinese approach is not seen as one that could be used more generally. It also involves a level of control and coercion that poses other social and cultural problems. The Chinese leadership is now loosening this policy in response to those problems, so it is reasonable to conclude that it could not be applied in societies that are less controlled.

As mentioned above, the three factors that consistently correlate with a reduced birth-rate are 1) women being well educated, 2) women being substantially in control of their fertility and 3) families being financially secure. That suggests an obvious way for OECD countries to speed up the achievement of population stability in poorer nations. The affluent world should recognise that it is in our collective self-interest to implement measures that will stabilise the population and potentially allow a sustainable future. So the UN overseas aid target of at least 0.7 per cent of GDP should be seen as a priority. At the time of writing, very few countries come close to this; the most recent budget in Australia slashed the already miserly aid allocation to an unprecedented low of 0.22 per cent. That should be seen as a national embarrassment. Even worse, a significant fraction of that budget is not genuine aid to poor countries, but effectively subsidises Australian corporations to make their businesses in those countries more profitable. Secondly, an explicit goal of aid to poor countries should be to enable them to stabilise their birth-rates. So educating women and ensuring they have control of their fertility should be seen as just as important as the short-term economic goals which are usually the focus of aid. There are some potential political problems in making it a priority in the most patriarchal societies to educate women and give them effective control over their fertility, but it is essential if we are serious about achieving a sustainable future. As the Chinese leadership recognised in the 1980s, political pain in the short term involves less human misery than mass starvation in future decades.

The issue of international migration raises complex problems. At a simplistic level, it could be argued that it makes no difference to the pressures on natural systems whether an individual lives in Bangladesh, Brisbane or Baltimore. In fact, it usually does make a difference, since the most common motivation for migration is to seek a more comfortable lifestyle. It requires a very strong belief in improvement to persuade people to leave their homeland and move to an unknown future in a new land. Some are driven from their homeland by violence, war or internal conflict, but most of the 2015 migrants are what have been called 'economic refugees'. People are moving in large numbers from poor areas to areas that are more affluent: from Africa to Europe, from Latin America to North America, from Asia to Australia, from the Pacific islands to New Zealand. While migrants continue to follow some of the habits of their homeland, they inevitably acquire some of the habits of their new home, while most studies show that the next generation move further down that path. In all these cases, that means greater resource use per person (Lowe 2012).

Some humanitarians argue that wealthy countries should be prepared to welcome migrants and extend to them the benefits of a more materially comfortable lifestyle. The problem is that this can only apply to relatively small groups of potential migrants. The annual increases in the populations of India and China are greater than the total population of Australia, so there is no way that Australia could open its doors to all those who might like to come. So other humanitarians argue that it would be better to improve the living conditions of people in poor countries, leading to them being more secure and content where they are, rather than sufficiently desperate to seek to migrate. It is much more practical to envisage raising the living standards generally in poorer nations than to allow anyone who so wishes to migrate.

A second issue relates to skills. In the 1950s and 1960s, under the Colombo Plan, Australia educated young people from our neighbouring countries, enabling them to play a greater role in helping their homelands to develop. So it was always an implicit condition, and sometimes an explicit condition, of their education that they should return home with their newly acquired skills and knowledge. In similar terms, countries like the UK and the USA tended to see education as the most concrete form of overseas aid, giving poorer nations the professionals they needed to develop. The results are there for all to see, with many of the leaders of development in relatively poor countries having benefited from education in wealthier nations. Today, the situation is radically different. Some educational institutions are explicitly marketing their courses as a back-door migration scheme, so overseas students are often encouraged to see their education as a path to permanent residence in a more affluent society. There is evidence that families send one member to a country like Australia to acquire a qualification which would entitle them to residence, in the hope that in turn they would be able to bring their relatives along later under family reunion schemes. Equally damaging to the prospects of development, countries like Australia, the USA and the UK have effectively recognised that it is cheaper to import skilled professionals like nurses, doctors and IT experts from poorer nations than to educate them. This is a brain drain which is reducing the capacity of poor nations to meet their own needs. A concrete form of aid to relatively poor countries would be to help them have a better educated workforce which would in turn lead to better infrastructure, more secure lifestyles and better public health.

Conclusion

The consumption of the human population is causing serious environmental problems: global climate change, loss of biodiversity, pollution of land and water, degradation of productive land. Unless consumption per person were to be radically reduced, which appears unlikely in the present political climate, the projected increase in human population will compound the pressure on natural systems, leading inevitably to widespread human misery. Even the World Economic Forum has recognised that 'business as usual' is no longer an option (WEF 2008). The only chance of a genuinely sustainable future requires stabilising the human population and significantly reducing the average per capita demand for natural resources. The affluent countries of the world should recognise that our collective self-interest demands a serious commitment to aid schemes that give women education, control over their fertility and economic security. While it is politically difficult, we should also be committed to reducing resource use dramatically by improving efficiency. The UN report 'Resource Efficiency and Economic Outlook for the Asia-Pacific Region' called for 'a new industrial revolution' which would enable us to meet material needs using one-quarter of the resources now used (UNEP 2008). Only such a huge change, the report argued, will allow us to meet the legitimate development aspirations of the region within the ecological constraints of natural systems. There have been other approaches along these lines, like Factor Four and the 'circular economy'. However, there still remains a fundamental problem, even if these sorts of technological and economic developments are embraced. Reducing per capita demand by a factor of four would allow the current population to live sustainably, but we will not have a sustainable society if the population continues to increase.

This seems to be an especially difficult case of selective blindness. Environmental activists and scientists recognise the need to limit greenhouse gas production to stabilise the atmosphere in a state that would allow us to continue to have a 'safe climate'. River ecologists recognise the need to limit the extraction of water to maintain the integrity of the riverine system. But discussion of what could be an ecologically sustainable population remains almost impossible. I have even been accused of advocating genocide for raising the question! Of course, there is a fundamental difference between advocating mass murder and advocating restraint of the birth-rate. It is reasonable to argue that the 1980s Chinese leadership actually prevented the untimely death of millions from starvation and disease by curbing the rate of population increase. Though the Chinese population is still growing, it may now be possible to provide for their needs, a task that would certainly have been impossible without the slowing of the birth-rate. The refusal to discuss the population issue, at a time when the demands of the current human population are degrading ecosystems and precipitating catastrophic biodiversity loss, is sentencing future generations to an impoverished existence. We owe it to our descendants to recognise the elephant in the room and discuss ways to prevent it trampling our own children.

References

ABS (2012) 'Fifty years of labour force: Now and then', in *Year Book Australia 2012*. See: http://www.abs.gov.au/ausstats/abs@.nsf/Lookup/1301.0Main+Features452012

Archer, C. and Willi, A. (2012) *Opportunity Costs: Military Spending and the UN's Development Agenda*, Geneva: International Peace Bureau.

Assadourian, E. (2013) 'Re-engineering cultures to create a sustainable civilization', in *State of the World 2013: Is Sustainability Still Possible?*, ed. L. Starke, Washington, DC: Island Press, pp. 113–125.

Birrell, B., Hawthorne, L.. and Richardson, S. (2009) 'Evaluation of the General Skilled Migration Categories Report', Canberra: Department of Immigration and Border Protection.

Cribb, J. (2014) *The Coming Famine: The Global Food Crisis and What We Can Do to Avoid It*, Oakland, CA: University of California Press.

Daily, G., Ehrlich, A., and Ehrlich, P. (1994) 'Optimum population size', *Population and Environment*, 15, no 6, pp. 469–475.

Daly H. (1991) *Steady State Economics*, Washington, DC: Island Press.

Engelman, R. (2013) 'Beyond sustainababble', in *State of the World 2013: Is Sustainability Still Possible?*, ed. L. Starke, Washington, DC: Island Press, pp. 3–16.

GFN (2013) World Footprint: Do we fit on the planet? See: http://www.footprintnetwork.org/en/index.php/GFN/page/world_footprint

Higgs, K. (2014) *Collision Course*, Cambridge, MA: MIT Press.

James, C. (2009) *Australian Homes Are Biggest in the World*, Commsec report, 30 November. See: http://commsec.com.au/ipo/UploaedImages/craigjames3f6189175551497fada1a4769f74do9c.pdf

Jones, B.O. (1986) *Sleepers, Wake! Technology and the Future of Work*, Melbourne: Oxford University Press.

Kanck, S. (2011) Personal communication from Sandra Kanck, National President of Sustainable Population Australia.

Lowe, I. (2005) *A Big Fix: Radical Solutions for Australia's Environmental Crisis*, Melbourne: Black Inc.

Lowe, I. (2009) *A Big Fix: Radical Solutions for Australia's Environmental Crisis*, 2nd edition, Melbourne: Black Inc.

Lowe, I. (2012) *Bigger or Better? Australia's Population Debate*, St Lucia: University of Queensland Press.

Meadows, D., Meadows, D.J., Randers, J., and Behrens III, W. (1972) *The Limits to Growth*, Washington, DC: Universe Books.

Mill, J.S. (1848) *Principles of Political Economy*, London: J.W. Parker.

O'Connor M., Hartwich, O., and Brown, J. (2012) *Why vs Why Population Growth*, Sydney: Pantera Press.

O'Sullivan, J.N. (2012) 'The burden of durable asset acquisition in growing populations', *Economic Affairs*, 32, no 1, pp. 31–37.

PM (2010) 'Capacity population', Population Matters leaflet. See: http://populationmatters.org/documents/capacity_leaflet.pdf

UN (2012) *World Population Prospects: The 2012 Revision*. See: http://esa.un.org/unpd/wpp/Documentation/pdf/WPP2012_HIGHLIGHTS.pdf

UN (2013) *World Population Ageing 2013*, New York: United Nations Department of Economic and Social Affairs, Population Division.

UNEP (2008) *Resource Efficiency and the Economic Outlook for the Asia-Pacific Region*, Bangkok: United Nations Environment Programme.

Washington, H. (2015) *Demystifying Sustainability: Towards Real Solutions*, London: Routledge.

WEF (2008) *Council on the Global Agenda*, Geneva: World Economic Forum.

Wilkinson, R. and Pickett, K. (2009) *The Spirit Level: Why Equality is Better for Everyone*, New York: Bloomsbury Press.

Young, C.M. and Day, L.H. (1995) 'Australia's demographic future: Determinants of our population', in *Population 2040*, ed. Australian Academy of Science, Canberra: Australian Academy of Science, pp. 19–46.

3
NINE POPULATION STRATEGIES TO STOP SHORT OF 9 BILLION

Robert Engelman

WORLDWATCH INSTITUTE

A promising sign for the future of the world's population appeared in 2014: some of the world's leading demographers disagreed publicly about it. There is no longer any expert consensus about the path of population growth from today's 7.3 billion human beings to 2050 and beyond, despite public perceptions to the contrary. And that underlines the simple reality that the actions of governments, civil society and individuals today might positively influence the world's demographic trajectory – and hence environmental and social ones – from today forward. I will explore nine such actions here that collectively could lead to an end of population growth before the 9-billion mark that is often seen as humanity's inevitable future.

But first the disagreement: in mid-2014, experts with the United Nations released a new assessment of population growth that suggested it would likely continue right through the twenty-first century and on into the twenty-second, with no particular end to the growth in sight (Gerland *et al.* 2014). Overturning the existing presumption that world population would peak at 9 billion in mid-century, the new projections expressed an 80 percent probability that population will reach 9.6 billion by 2050 and be between 9.6 billion and 12.3 billion in 2100. The projection posits that there is a 70 percent probability that the world's population will continue to grow after 2100. A main reason for this boosted assessment of likely future growth was not so much an 'expected future' as a surprising present: the UN authors had concluded that human fertility in parts of sub-Saharan Africa, in particular, was showing little sign of falling rapidly enough to allow human numbers to fall. Since that assessment was made, UN demographers revised their projections yet again, in mid-2015 stating with 80 percent probability that world population in 2100 will be between 10.5 billion and 12.5 billion (United Nations Population Division, 2015).

Demographers at the International Institute for Applied Systems Analysis in Austria begged to differ with their UN colleagues. In October of 2014 they released

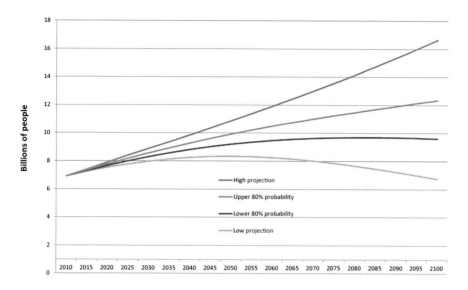

FIGURE 3.1 World population growth in the twenty-first century: four projections indicating range of possibilities and what is '80 percent probable,' according to the United Nations Population Division (2015)

their own projections indicating that the most likely future for world population, as they saw it, would be a peak at 9.4 billion in the year 2070 (Lutz et al. 2014a). They demonstrated strong correlations between the level of completed schooling and lifetime completed fertility among women worldwide in recent years – then projected these trends forward. They assumed that investment in education would continue worldwide as it has in recent decades, and that fertility would then come down faster than the UN demographers projected. While the differences were professional and anything but rancorous, some of the authors took it public with letters published in the journal *Science* and the newspaper *The Wall Street Journal* (Lutz et al. 2014b; Wilmoth 2014).

Despite their disagreement, neither set of demographers is wrong about world population. The numbers they assign to future dates are neither estimates (how can you estimate the size of something that has never been?) nor a prediction (how can anyone know enough about the future to predict how many of us will be living 35 or 85 years hence?). They are merely *projections*, and that makes all the difference. A projection is a conditional forecast of what will come about if various assumptions about declining human fertility and mortality prove true (Lutz et al. 1998; Bongaarts and Bulatao 2000).

No one, however, can be certain where birth or death rates will go in the coming years. Migration rates are even less certain, but they only influence global population if birth and death rates change because people move. And although policymakers and the news media rarely mention the possibility, societies can do a great deal to prompt an earlier peaking of world population at fewer than the 9 billion that many analysts mistakenly believe is still the expected future population peak.

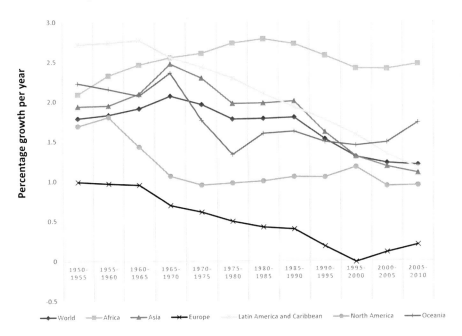

FIGURE 3.2 Annual population growth rates, world and region, 1950–2010

Ending population growth any time soon would accelerate population aging, which means a rising median age for people in a country or the world. That could challenge societies economically as smaller proportions of a population are working and contributing to the retirement and health care benefits of a growing number of older, non-working people. Yet that is all but certain to be a manageable trade-off in return for longer lives in a less crowded and environmentally stressed world. Humans have experience adjusting to changing population age structures; we have next to no experience addressing the environmental and social threats to our existence that our population growth may ultimately pose.

Ending population growth

The contribution that an end to population growth would make to environmentally sustainable prosperity is straightforward. The future of wealth and its distribution will be closely linked to the future of the global climate, the health of nature, and the availability of key natural resources. Since all descendants of today's low-income, low-consumption populations will anticipate and should expect consumption-boosting economic development, a lower future population would mean less pressure on climate, environment, and natural resources by future generations. It is a scenario without a downside for global well-being.

No ethical person would want an early end to population growth through rising death rates, though such an outcome cannot be ruled out given current trends in climate change, food production, and energy supplies. Similarly, who could rejoice about the possibility that, in a horrific example of negative feedback, human abuse of the environment might lead to increases in involuntary infertility? (Already there is some evidence this is possible (Chiu *et al.* 2015).) Nor is there any public support for policies that would impose reproductive limits on fecund couples and individuals. Abundant experience from around the world, however, demonstrates clearly how to reduce birth rates significantly through policies that not only respect the reproductive aspirations of parents and would-be parents but also support a healthy, educated, and economically active populace – especially women and girls. This chapter describes nine strategies that collectively would be likely, if implemented as fully as possible, to reverse human population growth before mid-century at a level below 9 billion. (See Figure 3.1 for world population projections from 2010 through 2100 and Figure 3.2 for population growth rates by world and region from 1950 through 2010.) Most of the policies are relatively inexpensive to put in place and implement, although some are culturally and, hence, politically sensitive in many or most countries (Bongaarts and Bulatao 2000).

Assure universal access to a range of safe and effective contraceptive options and family planning services for both sexes.
Since the early 1960s, the use of contraception has increased markedly, with most women of reproductive age around the world using it. This increasing contraceptive prevalence has closely tracked a comparable and opposite decrease in average family size worldwide. Nevertheless, based on survey work, an estimated 40 percent of all pregnancies are unintended, and a conservatively estimated 225 million women in developing countries alone are hoping to avoid pregnancy but not using effective contraception (Sedgh *et al.* 2012; Singh *et al.* 2014). Although physical access to contraception does not guarantee that all reproductive-age people will use it, it is essential for personal fertility control – especially where there is little or no access to safe abortion. Demographic evidence is growing that if all women could time their pregnancies according to their own desires, total global fertility would fall below effective replacement levels (two-plus-a-fraction children per woman), putting population immediately on a trajectory toward a peak and gradual decline, which could possibly be by the middle of the century (Engelman 2011).

An estimated $9.4 billion a year would pay for modern contraceptive services for all sexually active women in developing countries (Singh *et al.* 2014). By comparison, the world spends approximately $42 billion on pet food each year (Assadourian 2010). This step alone would cut global unintended pregnancies by an estimated 70 percent, from 74 million to 22 million annually. While cost estimates aren't available for the many other actions governments and societies can take, there is no question that wider use of long-acting reversible contraceptives (LARCs) – intra-uterine devices, sub-dermal implants and injectables are examples – would reduce such pregnancies even more by all but removing the chance of user error. Education, especially through secondary school and ideally including comprehensive sexuality education, reduces both unintended and intended pregnancy rates (Lutz *et al.* 2014a). While the research base is weaker for the other actions suggested in this chapter, logic and experience powerfully suggest they would reduce birth rates even further, especially in combination with greater educational attainment and universal access to effective family planning services.

Perhaps the dominant obstacle to making access to family planning universal is widespread ambiguity about human sexuality and the persistence of religious and cultural barriers to the principle that women, whether married or not, should be able to choose sexual expression without fear of unintended pregnancy. Surveys indicate that the vast majority of Americans, at least, believe that women should be able to choose the timing and frequency of childbearing by having access to contraception. Ensuring that all couples can make such choices will require much stronger public support in the face of ongoing opposition to family planning and marginalization of the links between women's reproductive choices, population dynamics, and social well-being (Campbell *et al.* 2006).

Guarantee education through secondary school for all, with a particular focus on girls.
Experts differ on whether contraceptive access or educational attainment more directly reduces fertility. In every culture surveyed, however, women who have completed at least some secondary school education have fewer children on average, and have them later in their lives, than women who have less education. Surveying literature on this connection, for example, Dina Abu-Ghaida and Stephan Klasen (2004) of the World Bank estimated that with each year of completed secondary schooling, women's average fertility rates around the world are 0.3–0.5 children lower than those of women without that amount of schooling.

Worldwide, according to calculations by demographers at the International Institute for Applied Systems Analysis, women with no schooling have an average of 3.9 children, whereas those with any amount of post-secondary education have an average of 1.6, a figure that over time would lead to a decreasing population (Eder *et al.* 2015). Education informs girls about healthy behavior and life options and hence motivates them to endeavor to postpone and minimize the frequency of childbearing so that they can more easily explore aspects of life beyond motherhood (Lutz *et al.* 2014a).

As with the increasing use of contraception, global progress in educating girls is already impressive. As of 2010, two-thirds of those 15 and older – or 1.8 billion girls and women – had finished at least some secondary school during their lifetimes (Eder *et al.* 2015). This proportion has risen from 36 percent in 1970 and from 50 percent in 1990 (Lutz *et al.* 2007). Girls as well as boys have benefited from this improvement. Yet a gender gap between female and male educational attainment remains (World Bank 2011), with the percentage of girls in school consistently about 9 percentage points lower than the percentage of boys in school. And there appears to be a long way to go before most young women have effective access to a complete and adequate secondary school education, especially in the least developed countries. These countries are generally the ones with the most stubbornly high fertility. Investing in education – not just to bring children into schoolrooms but to improve the quality of their schooling – is among the rare 'triple wins' that boost human well-being, economic development, and women's intentions and capacities to have fewer children later in their lives (KC *et al.* 2010).

Eradicate gender bias from law, economic opportunity, health, and culture.
While universal access to good contraceptive services and secondary school education in combination would be likely to reverse world population growth on its own, active efforts to foster legal, political, and economic gender equality would make both access and education much easier to achieve and would hasten the reversal of growth. Women who are able to own, inherit, and manage property, to divorce their husbands, to obtain credit, and to participate in civic and political affairs on equal terms with men are more likely to postpone childbearing and reduce the number of their children compared with women lacking such rights and capacities.

Research indicates that a number of specific indictors of women's empowerment result in reduced or later childbearing. A study in northern Tanzania, for example, found that women with an equal say to their husbands in household matters preferred to have significantly fewer children than those who had to defer to their husbands' decisions (Larson and Hollos 2003). This is particularly important because men, free of the physical hazards and discomforts of childbearing and usually investing much less time than women do in childrearing, tend in most countries to want more children than their partners do.

Demographic and health surveys over the past several decades for the U.S. Agency for International Development (DHS 2015) show that women in almost all developing countries express a desire for fewer children than they end up having, as well as fewer children than men want. The more children a woman has, the more likely she is to want fewer additional ones than her partner. How any specific indicator interacts with fertility intentions and outcomes remains unclear, but the broad connection of women's status and autonomy to later childbearing and smaller completed families adds to the reason to support laws and customs that institutionalize gender equality.

Offer age-appropriate sexuality education for all students.
A major obstacle to the prevention of unintended pregnancy is ignorance by young people about how their bodies work, how to abstain from unwanted sex, how to prevent pregnancy when sexually active, and how important it is to respect the bodies and sexual intentions of others. Education in all these matters would further reduce unintended pregnancies and hence slow population growth. This can begin in age-appropriate ways almost as soon as schooling does. Questions about sex typically arise early in children's lives and require appropriate responses from the adults around them. Children are sometimes the victims of sexual harassment or

violence and need to learn early in their lives how to recognize, protect themselves from, and report inappropriate sexual behavior.

Sexuality education differs significantly among countries and is absent from the curricula of many or most. In the United States, comprehensive sex education tends to stress the health and pregnancy-avoidance benefits of abstinence as well as the importance of contraception and safe sexual practices for those who choose not to be abstinent. U.S. data indicate that exposure to comprehensive programs tends to delay the initiation of sex and to increase the use of contraception among young people. Along with the other benefits provided, both of these trends would logically contribute to lower teen birth rates and probably lower completed fertility (Mueller, Gavin, and Kulkarni 2008).

End all policies that reward parents financially based on the number of their children.
There is no reason to believe that pro-natalist government policies that reward couples financially for each additional birth have significantly raised total fertility rates in any country. Nonetheless, it seems logical that at least on the margin such policies do boost birth rates at least to some extent. The policies may be as blatant as those in Russia and Singapore that directly pay couples for additional children. Or they may be couched as childcare tax credits that reduce a parent's taxes for each additional child under 18 without limit, as in the United States (Gross 2006; GOS 2015). Such policies subsidize 'super-replacement' fertility (rates well above two children per woman), contributing to populations larger than they would otherwise be.

Where it is clear that women and couples are forgoing childbearing because of social discouragement (for example in the workplace) or a lack of acceptable child care options, governments can address these issues directly. In some northern European countries, for instance, fertility rates rebounded from very low levels after governments made paid leave mandatory for new parents of either sex (Tsuyo 2003). Governments can preserve and even increase tax and other financial benefits aimed at helping parents by linking these not to the number of children but to parenthood status itself. A fixed benefit for all parents would allow couples to decide for themselves whether another child makes economic sense given that the benefit will not grow – just as the environment and its resources do not grow with any addition to the family.

Integrate teaching about population, environment, and development relationships into school curricula at multiple levels.
Although environmental science education is now well established, especially at the university level, few if any school systems around the world include curricula that teach young people how human numbers, the natural environment, and human development interact. Yet today's young people are very likely to spend most of their lives in densely populated human societies facing significant environmental and natural resource constraints. Eschewing advocacy or propaganda,

schools should help young people make well-informed choices about the impacts of their behavior, including their sexual and reproductive behavior, on the world in which they live.

In the United States, the organization Population Connection has an active education program (Population Connection 2015) that provides curricular material and training to teachers interested in awakening students of all ages to the dynamics and importance of population growth. It is not clear, however, how widespread the concept is either in the United States or in other countries. More education about human–environment interactions, including the influence of human numbers, nonetheless could become an important stimulus to a cultural transformation that can hasten an end to population growth.

Put prices on environmental costs and impacts.
Governments need to move toward environmental pricing – including taxes, fees, rebates, and so on – for many reasons as soon as politically feasible. Among the benefits of carbon and other green taxes is their value in reminding parents that each human being, including a new one, has impacts on the environment. In a crowded world of constrained resources, these impacts should be accounted and paid for so that large environmental footprints face economic constraints. These constraints could be government imposed, as in the case of carbon taxes or usage fees for waste removal services that are based on weight. Such environment-related governmental constraints on consumption are currently rare, however, and may not be feasible politically for some time. Free-market pricing may eventually play a similar role if the costs of food, energy, and various natural resources continue to rise due to scarcity and distribution challenges, as many analysts predict.

The rising financial costs of large families already discourage high fertility in countries where contraception is socially acceptable and readily available. If at some point governments opt to raise the costs of consumption that has negative impacts on the environment, couples and individuals will still be free to choose the timing and frequency of childbearing. Yet by translating into higher costs the impact of individuals, environmentally based pricing will tend to reduce fertility and birth rates as couples decide the cost of having an additional child is too high. This is hardly the reason to move toward environmental pricing, but it will be among its benefits.

Adjust to population aging rather than trying to delay it through governmental incentives or programs aimed at boosting childbearing.
Higher proportions of older people in any population are a natural consequence of longer life spans and women's intentions to have fewer children, neither of which societies should want to reverse. The appropriate way to deal with population aging is to make necessary social adjustments, increasing labor participation and mobilizing older people themselves to contribute to such adjustments, for instance, rather than urging or giving incentives to women to have more children than they think best.

Population aging is a short-term phenomenon that will pass before the end of this century, with impacts far less significant and long-lasting than ongoing population growth, a point policymakers need to understand better (Sanderson and Scherbov 2010). Even if today's policymakers could boost population growth through higher birth rates or immigration, future policymakers would have to grapple with the problems of aging at some later time – when higher population density and its associated problems only make boosting population growth less attractive and feasible.

Convince leaders to commit to ending population growth through the exercise of human rights and human development.
Several decades ago, it was not unusual for presidents and prime ministers in industrial and developing countries to declare their own commitment to slowing the growth of population in their countries. Today, with twice as many people worldwide seeking the good life, the need is more acute than ever for political leaders to find the courage to acknowledge the importance of ending population growth. For a variety of reasons, however, population has become a taboo topic in politics and in international affairs, though perhaps somewhat less so in the news media and in public discourse.

Speaking out on the importance of ending human population growth worldwide will be easier if leaders acquaint themselves with how the population field has evolved over the past few decades. They will then understand that human numbers are best addressed – in fact, can only be effectively and ethically addressed – by empowering women to become pregnant only when they themselves choose to do so. One irony of this is that slowing population growth needs to be seen not so much as the goal of some kind of crisis or emergency program – a vision that the public and politicians alike would find frightening – but merely as a recognized and lauded side benefit of a host of policies that improve the lives of women, men, and children. If, through the education strategies described here and a broader cultural transformation on the topic, more people recognize the value of an end to population growth, each of these policies will become more feasible and more effective in bringing about beneficial demographic and environmental change.

The impact of the nine strategies

To some extent most of these policies are already moving forward, albeit sluggishly, in different countries around the world. Powerful forces – in some cases religious and cultural, in others economic – oppose them, however. It may be years or decades before increasing environmental deterioration and resource shortages in an ever more crowded world arouse the public so much that people demand governmental action on root causes. A powerful momentum helps drive today's population growth. As long as many more people are in or approaching their childbearing years than are nearing the end of their lives, as is the case today, humanity will increase for some time even if families are quite small. It will take time for the smaller generations of children to become parents themselves and produce even smaller generations as the larger, older generations pass on. The longer governments delay policies such as those described here, the more likely the world is to face large and denser populations or increases in death rates – or both.

If, by contrast, each of these policies somehow could be put in place quickly and were well supported by the public and policymakers, population momentum itself would be slowed significantly, through later and fewer pregnancies, than ever witnessed in recorded history. Few demographers have attempted to quantify the population impact of various interventions beyond family planning access and education for girls on fertility. But based on what is known and can be logically conjectured, it seems likely that putting most of these policies together would lower desired family size and undermine population momentum. Through both mechanisms, along with bringing unintended pregnancies as close to zero as possible, such policies could produce a turn-around in population growth earlier than most demographers believe is likely or even possible. The fertility declines that could bring a population peak between 8 billion and 9 billion before mid-century, with no increases in death rates, are possible to imagine. If this were to occur, a truly prosperous and sustainable global society would be one long stride closer than ever before.

(Revised and updated with permission from *State of the World 2012: Moving Toward Sustainable Prosperity*, the Worldwatch Institute.)

References

Abu-Ghaida, D. and Klasen, S. (2004) 'The costs of missing the millennium development goal on gender equity', *World Development*, 32, no 7, pp. 1075–1107.
Assadourian, E. (2010) 'The rise and fall of consumer cultures', in *2010 State of the World: Transforming Cultures from Consumerism to Sustainability*, eds. L. Starke and L. Mastny, London: Earthscan, pp. 3–20.
Bongaarts, J. and Bulatao, R., eds. (2000) *Beyond 6 Billion: Forecasting the World's Population*, Washington, DC: National Academy Press.
Campbell, M., Sahin-Hodoglugil, N., and Potts, M. (2006) 'Barriers to fertility regulation: A review of the Literature', *Studies in Family Planning*, 37, pp. 87–98.
Chiu, Y.H., Afeiche, M.C., Gaskins, A.J., Williams, P.L., Petrozza, J.C., Tanrikut, C., Hauser, R., and Chavarro, J.E. (2015) 'Fruit and vegetable intake and their pesticide residues in relation to semen quality among men from a fertility clinic', *Human Reproduction* (advance access), doi:10.1093/humrep/dev064
DHS (2015) 'Family planning'. See: http://dhsprogram.com/Topics/Family-Planning.cfm
Eder, J., Goujon, A., Haplichnik, T., KC, S., Lutz, W., and Potančoková, M. (2015) *Global Human Capital Data Sheet 2015*, Vienna: Wittgenstein Centre for Demography and Global Human Capital.
Engelman, R. (2011) 'An end to population growth: Why family planning is key to a sustainable future', *Solutions*, 2, no 3, pp. 32–41.

Gerland, P., Raftery, A.E., Ševčíková, H., Li, N., Gu, D., Spoorenberg, T., Alkema, L., Fosdick, B.K., Chunn, J., Lalic, N., Bay, G., Buettner, T., Heilig, G.K., and Wilmoth, J. (2014) 'World population stabilization unlikely this century', *Science*, 346, issue 6206, pp. 234–237.

GOS (2015) 'Baby bonus', Government of Singapore website. See: http://www.babybonus.gov.sg/bbss/html/index.html

Gross, D. (2006) 'Children for sale: Would $36,000 convince you to have another kid?', *Slate*. See: http://www.slate.com/articles/business/moneybox/2006/05/children_for_sale.html

KC, S., Barakat, B., Goujon, A., Skirbekk, V., Sanderson, W., and Lutz, W. (2010) 'Projection of populations by level of educational attainment, age, and sex for 120 countries for 2005–2050', *Demographic Research*, 22, no 15, pp. 383–472.

Larson, U. and Hollos, M. (2003) 'Women's empowerment and fertility decline among the Pare of Kilimanjaro region, northern Tanzania', *Social Science & Medicine*, 27, pp. 1099–1115.

Lutz, W., Sanderson, W.C., and Scherbov, S. (1998) 'Expert-based probabilistic projections', *Population and Development Review*, 24, pp. 139–155.

Lutz, W., Goujon, A., KC, S., and Sanderson, W.C. (2007) 'Reconstruction of population by age, sex and level of educational attainment of 120 countries for 1970–2000', *Vienna Yearbook of Population Research*, vol. 2007, Laxenberg, Austria: International Institute for Applied Systems Analysis (IIASA), pp. 193–235.

Lutz, W., Butz, W.P., and KC, S. (eds) (2014a) *World Population & Human Capital in the Twenty-First Century*, London: Oxford University Press.

Lutz, W., Butz, W.P., KC, S., Sanderson, W.C., and Scherbov, S., (eds) (2014b) 'Population growth: Peak probability', *Science*, 346, issue 6209, p. 560.

Mueller T., Gavin L., and Kulkarni, A. (2008) 'The association between sex education and youth's engagement in sexual intercourse, age at first intercourse, and birth control use at first sex', *Journal of Adolescent Health*, 42, no 1.

Population Connection (2015) Population Education website. See: https://www.populationeducation.org/index.php?option=com_content&view=article&id=1&Itemid=2

Sanderson, W. and Scherbov, S. (2010) 'Remeasuring aging', *Science*, 10 September 2010, pp. 1287–1288.

Sedgh, G., Singh, S., and Hussain, R. (2012) 'Intended and unintended pregnancies worldwide in 2012 and recent trends', *Studies in Family Planning*, 45, no 3, pp. 301–314.

Singh, S., Darroch, J., and Ashford, L. (2014) *Adding It Up: The Costs and Benefits of Investing in Sexual and Reproductive Health 2014*, New York: Guttmacher Institute.

Tsuyo, N. (2003) 'Fertility and family policies in Nordic countries, 1960–2000', *Journal of Population and Social Security (Population), Supplement to Volume 1*, Tokyo: National Institute of Population and Social Security Research. See: http://www.ipss.go.jp/webj-ad/webjournal.files/population/2003_6/4.Tsuya.pdf (accessed 27/2/15)

United Nations Population Division (2015) *World Population Prospects, the 2015 Revision*. See: http://esa.un.org/unpd/wpp/

Wilmoth, J. R. (2014) 'The U.N.'s population projections are likely to be right' (letter), *Wall Street Journal*, 27–28 September 2014.

World Bank (2011) *Getting to Equal: Promoting Gender Equality through Human Development*, Washington, DC: World Bank.

4

CHOOSING A PLANET OF LIFE

Eileen Crist

VIRGINIA TECH

One of the commonplaces of environmental writing these days is a population forecast of 10 billion (or more) people by century's end (UN 2012). Indeed, this projection is endlessly repeated, as if it were as inevitable as the calculable trajectory of an asteroid hurtling through space. Besides being a facile 'meme' amenable to replication, this recurrent demographic report signals a widely shared fatalism: the coming growth has too much inertia behind it, and is far too politically sensitive, to question. At the same time, the projection reinforces a collective impression that nothing can be done to change it. Ironically, the incantation of '10 billion' seems at work as a self-fulfilling prophecy, for without urgent, concerted, and proactive intervention it is roughly the number to be expected. So do we hypnotize and propel ourselves in the predicted direction.

Environmental analysts have divergent responses to this particular figure (which is the latest United Nations estimate). Some are incredulous that such a number can be approached – let alone sustained – and contend that the consequences of moving in that direction will be disastrous (for example, Ehrlich and Ehrlich 2014; Brown 2011a). They suggest that a catastrophe or combination of catastrophes is bound to derail professional demographers' expectations, and humanity (after enduring much suffering, or perhaps experiencing some kind of wake-up call) will stabilize at lower numbers. But other environmental observers, describing themselves as more 'optimistic', are endeavouring to figure out strategies that might sustain the expected billions. They hope that with the right developments and innovations in crop genetics, irrigation technologies, fertilizer application ('responsible nutrient management'), efficiency gains (including closing 'yield gaps' and curbing food waste), requisite energy transitions, and other advances, the planet might feed, provide water for, house, educate, and medicate – at an acceptable standard of living for all – the coming 10 billion (Foley 2014; Shellenberger and Nordhaus 2011). There is reason to wager, optimists maintain, that humanity might succeed at the task, since people are resourceful, determined, and apt to get out of a tight spot even in the nick of time.

Thus where some see disaster on the immediate horizon, others submit that with another techno-managerial turn of the screw, humanity might avert grim penalties to population growth. Yet despite considerable divergence in outlook, all environmental analysts agree that (even as our global numbers continue to climb) we face gruelling challenges, each immense in its own right but dizzying in their unpredictable synergies: biodiversity destruction, climate change, freshwater depletion, ceilings on agricultural productivity, all manner of pollution, topsoil loss, and ocean acidification to mention some prominent examples.

Rather than taking sides between the forecast of impending tragedy versus optimism about feeding the world, there is another way to tell the near future's story. On that telling, the issue is not whether it is possible for 10 billion people to eat industrial food, commune with iPhones, and make a decent living on planet Earth (an outlying scenario, but perhaps stranger things have happened in the universe). The point to focus on instead is that a world of so many billions does not, in any case, turn out well: because such a world is only possible by taking a spellbindingly life-abundant planet and turning it into a human food plantation, gridded with industrial infrastructures, webbed densely by networks of high-traffic global trade and travel, in which remnants of natural areas – simulacra or residues of wilderness – are zoned for ecological services and ecotourism. In such a world, cruise ships with all-you-can-eat buffets will circumnavigate seas stripped of their plenitude of living beings, on waters awash with plastic refuse decomposing into bite-sized and eventually microscopic particles destined for incorporation into the worldwide food web.

What's more, a sustainable geopolitical status quo of 10 billion consumers will require comprehensive mega-technological support: offshore dike projects; more dams, which are already being constructed at 'a furious pace' (Biello 2009); desalinization plant construction with accompanying transport infrastructures; scaling-up of industrial aquaculture; genetic modification of crops and animals to adapt to climatic and consumer demands; cultivating so-called marginal lands to grow grasses and other plants for biofuels; the spread of the fracking scourge; climate engineering at global and regional scales; and the spread and normalization of factory farms. *The Economist* (2011) praises the efficiency of the latter institution over traditional husbandry, calling it – in apparent oblivion of the term's Orwellian malodour – 'the livestock revolution'.

In such a world, corporations are likely to continue reigning supreme, for the coming technological gigantism, not to mention the escalation of mass consumption, will make them indispensable. Corporate expertise and products will be required to keep the biosphere on permanent 'dialysis' – to borrow a fitting metaphor from James Lovelock (2007). Corporations will continue generating enormous revenues, via tax-based subsidies for their 'public works' and by catering their products to huge numbers of people. (Any doubt regarding the relationship between private-sector opulence and consumer population size is dispelled by taking note of the correlation between today's wealthiest companies and their bulging middle-class client base. Indeed, capitalism is quite partial to the twin perks of population growth: cheap labour and mass clientele.) Whatever relatively natural places remain will be slated as the real estate and vacation destinations of the most affluent – as they are to a large degree today. But regardless of whether or not corporations and the gilded class entrench their reign, everyone (including the rich) will be wretchedly dispossessed, hustling for happiness on a planet degraded to serve a bloated user-species.

In such a world – whatever it augurs for humanity, which seems bleak to say the least – the exuberance of Life will suffer a tremendous blow. This Life is barely hanging on in the present world; it will not survive a world that is a magnified version of the one we live in. I use the word Life, with a capital 'L', to mean something akin to what life scientists call 'biodiversity'. Unfortunately, though, the latter term is often mistakenly conflated with numbers of species on Earth. While numbers of species are a significant dimension of Life's fecundity, Life is far greater than a total species inventory – as extravagant as that inventory may be. Life is bewildering in its creative expressions, its beauty, strangeness, and unexpectedness, its variety of physical types and kinds of awareness, and its dynamic, burgeoning, and interweaving world-making.

Earth's story is about Life, whose phenomena emerge in each place uniquely and over the whole planet diversely, always contiguous and interconnected at local, regional, and global levels. Life fills niches and also creates them; life-forms accommodate other life-forms via niche construction and by their edible, breathable, or otherwise consumable waste by-products (including, ultimately, their own corpses). With the exception of mass extinction events, Life is always enabling more of itself to surge (Wilson 1999; Dirzo and Raven 2003). There's ceaseless feeding on one another and on each other's by-products, as well as a co-moulding of a physical and chemical environment in which more life is supported to flourish (see Crist 2010). Importantly, a vast array of life-forms – from all five kingdoms of life – are involved in building soil, which is not only Life's foundation but itself a living phenomenon. Through organism-mediated processes, the land brings nutrients to the seas, and the seas (through organism-mediated processes) return nutrients to the land. Forest canopies feed the life in the understory, and life in the forest understory feeds the trees and all who live in their canopies. Beings in the seas' upper layers sustain the strange menagerie of abyssal creatures, and organism-created nutrients in the depths well up and nourish fellow beings in the upper zones.

In the interdisciplinary dance of Life – where phenomena of physics, organismal biology, biochemistry, behaviour, awareness, and chaos jostle in established and spontaneous patterns – Life creates abundance. For example, hundreds of millions of eggs wash to the sea's edge, feeding multitudes before a fraction develop into the organisms that spawned them. Prey species proliferate wildly in response to the pressure of their predators – incalculable numbers of marine creatures once sustained the tens (and perhaps hundreds) of millions of sharks, seals, and whales who existed before their concerted extermination began. Enormous, ever-on-the-move ungulate herds do not decimate the lush grasslands that feed them, on the contrary the grasses grow because of them, and the animals and grasses (with other life-forms) together create more soil. Freely moving, pristine rivers teemed with fish even in recent history. Great flocks of birds graced skies, wetlands, and seashores. And land, sea, and air animal migrations have not only told the seasons' stories but contributed to bringing the seasons into being. The intermingled manifestations of Life on Earth – when Earth is allowed to manifest them – have no finitude.

As for a popularized claim that, alas, life is all about struggle, competition, and selfishness, it is best to turn away from such claptrap: for it is only within a planet of Life, a Life-world, that phenomena of struggle, competition, and selfishness arise and pass away in their relevant contexts (Rolston 1992; Margulis 1999). The Life-world itself is far more encompassing in the kinds of phenomena it manifests and cannot be reduced to a one-dimensional schema. Except for the one thing we know in the marrow of our bones and in our hearts: that the Life-world is All-good.

And here's the crux of the matter: humanity can choose to live on a planet of Life instead of haplessly plunging toward a human-colonized planet on dialysis ('wisely managed'). To live on a planet of Life it is necessary to *limit ourselves* so as to allow the biosphere freedom to express its ecological and evolutionary arts. For that, we in turn need to cultivate the breadth of imagination to give the concept of freedom wider scope – pushing its territory beyond the sheath of human exclusivity. In the name of a higher freedom that encompasses Earth and its entire community of beings, we can choose to let the world be the magnificence and wealth it was – and still can be. Borrowing words from nature writer Julia Whitty's 'Deep Blue Home', this path is about cultivating intimacy with the natural world, taking as our lover the way things really are and finding our way home (2011).

But the wisdom of limitations – of our numbers, economies, and places of habitation – is rarely entertained in mainstream thought for what it is: the elegant way home and the surest means for addressing the deepening (and likely self-endangering) problems of extinctions, ecosystem destruction and simplification, rapid climate change, freshwater and topsoil depletions, as well as (relatedly) mounting concerns about 'feeding the world'. The path of limitations is rarely entertained, for it is assumed to be unrealistic and thus politically inexpedient. But knowledge of the multiple stresses on the biosphere, along with an understanding of the adverse, volatile ways these may compound one another, yield the recognition that drastically scaling down the human project is the most realistic approach to imminent catastrophes (see Washington 2013). If political expediency cannot see that, then political expediency and those who speak for it need to be deposed so we can get on with the real work.

In the meantime, even as the available option of limitations is bypassed as ostensibly unrealistic, the prevailing question (voiced with increasingly shrill urgency) is: Can the Earth feed 10 billion people? By most expert accounts, because of population growth along with the rise of meat and animal product consumption, food production will have to essentially double by 2050 to meet demand (FAO 2011) – and the big question is: Can it be done? There is an effort underway to figure this out, by experimenting in research and development labs, working in research stations, and analyzing agricultural databases (see Anon 2010). And because it is well known that most (and certainly the most fertile) arable lands are already in cultivation, and that the areas where wild creatures live are already pushed to their limits, the effort to increase food production (to double it in about forty years and triple it by century's end) is invariably escorted by the caveat that it must be done without 'further damage to biodiversity' or 'taking over more uncultivated lands'.

Since at least the early 2000s, this 'ecologically correct' sound-bite has been activated in environmental writings, journalistic reports, and corporate web pages: we must produce more crops (for food, feed, and fuel), as well as more meat and animal products, by means of careful planning and management, with minimal additional ecological impacts (for example, Clay 2011). Oddly, the latter disclaimer is stated as if tropical forests are not today giving way to soybean monocultures, cattle ranches, and oil palm, sugar, tea, and other plantations; as if large-scale acquisitions recruiting land in Africa and elsewhere are not already underway in the name of 'food security'; as if marine life is not being chewed up by the industrial machine; and as if rivers are not today so taxed by damming, extraction, diversion, and pollution that the crisis of freshwater Life may well be the gravest extinction site on Earth (a big non-event as far as the public and its elected officials are concerned). Despite all these things happening already today (in a global economy of 7.3 billion), those at work to figure out if food production can be doubled and eventually tripled (to serve a world of 9, 10, or more billion in an intensified global economy) always add that it must be done 'without additional ecological damage'. When we encounter such pious declarations of intent we'd do well to recall Hamlet's sardonic response to the question, 'What do you read?'. *Words, words, words.*

Those endeavouring to figure out how to increase food production without more harm to nature may well be sincere; but they are in the throes of wishful thinking posing as optimism. For even if for a moment we ignore the fact that present-day industrial agriculture, industrial aquaculture, and industrial fishing constitute a mounting planet-wide disaster – which goes largely unremarked only because it is equalled by planet-wide unawareness – simply saying that we need to grow more food 'without further ecological destruction' is not going to stop hungry and acquisitive people from taking what they need and think they need: clearing more forests and grasslands, moving up slopes, overgrazing pasture and rangelands, decimating sea creatures, replacing mangrove forests with shrimp operations, or killing wild animals for cash or food.

Even so, the most pernicious thing about this formulaic mandate-plus-caveat – grow more food, don't damage more nature – has yet to be stated: namely, that it insinuates that the *current* damage our food system inflicts is acceptable and irreversible. Hands down, however, industrial food production is the most ecologically devastating enterprise on Earth. (More on this shortly.) Yet mainstream discourses do not tend to flag the food system's earth-shattering demands on the biosphere. Instead, the current ability to produce ample amounts of food – enough for all, including those not yet at the table – appears to merit a different cluster of conclusions: that humanity's food-producing capacity is not constrained by natural limits; that we may be able to stretch that productivity even further via managerial and technological innovations; and that *Homo sapiens* is unlike all other species, which are checked by nature whenever their numbers exceed the capacity of the environment to sustain them. Indeed, the belief that humans are exempt from any natural 'carrying capacity' is a cornerstone of the mission to continue expanding food production to support the coming billions (see Ellis *et al*. 2013 and Ellis 2013 for recent expositions of these views).

The demographic idea of carrying capacity refers to the maximal population of a species that its environment can support, without that environment becoming too degraded to support the species in the future. If a species, for some reason or other, does exceed its carrying capacity – with numbers mounting beyond what the natural setting can sustain – the consequences are implacable: starvation, disease, and death follow, until the population is brought back within a supportable range. While this natural law of the relationship between population size and sustenance appears broadly applicable in the animal kingdom, here's the key point regarding human exemption: it is widely believed that history has shown that it 'does not apply to us'.

At the turn of the nineteenth century Reverend Thomas Robert Malthus sought to apply the logic of natural limits, and the severe costs of transgressing them, to humanity. He predicted that because population grows faster than food production, human numbers would outstrip the available food supply and people would reap the woes of famine, disease, and war (Malthus 2008). But the two centuries following his analysis did not see a human population crash, as food production kept up with mounting numbers of people; in fact, during the last half of the twentieth century the rate of food production even outpaced the rate of population growth. So the Malthusian thesis came to be viewed as repudiated, and the doctrine of human *exemptionalism* from natural limits received a victorious boost.

Indeed, the foreboding forecast that the human population would inevitably exceed the amount of available food to (at least in principle) feed everyone did not come to pass. It was refuted by converting Earth's most fertile lands for agriculture (after being denuded of their Life-rich forests, grasslands, and wetlands); by taking over extensive swathes of natural areas for domestic animal grazing; by appropriating half the world's freshwater – with the biggest share diverted for agriculture; by applying enormous quantities of synthetic chemical and fertilizer pollutants; and by plundering untold numbers of wild fish. In other words, the prediction of human tribulation in the wake of unsustainable numbers was refuted by means of the near-conversion of the biosphere into a human food pantry.

The seemingly 'winning argument' that humanity is uniquely capable of keeping food production apace with (or ahead of) demographic growth reveals a profound lack of insight into the bigger picture of what stretching our food-producing capacity has really portended. It reveals an inability to appreciate – or even to entertain as a passing thought – that human carrying capacity (how many people the Earth can support) has been extended not simply because we are so clever at manipulating natural processes and inventing stuff, but through forcefully taking over the carrying capacity of other life-forms and, in the process, wiping them out regionally or globally. Moreover, the exemptionalism thereby displayed – that we are not bound by natural conditions like other species- beyond the superficial 'fact' that it seems to be, serves conveniently as an ideological handmaiden of human *expansionism*. For what the doctrine of exemptionalism tacitly conveys and inculcates is that because humanity is so special by comparison to all other creatures, it is proportionately that much more entitled; and thus the acts of war on the natural world that undergird human expansionism (for food production in particular) become unrecognizable as acts of war.

The question of whether ultimately there are (or not) natural limits to our food-producing ability, which will (or not) check human demographic growth, is not so interesting; the experiment required for the final verdict is an ugly one either way. Instead, I along with other deep ecologists, invite consideration of something far more enticing: that by choosing the wisdom of limitations and humility, humanity can reject life on a planet converted into a human food factory and allow for the rewilding of vast expanses of the biosphere's landscapes and seascapes. To drive home why the latter option is much more beautiful (as well as more prudent), I turn to the highlights of how food production is contributing the lion's share of anthropogenic ecological havoc.

Cropland uses a portion of the planet the size of South America, while land for grazing farm animals eats up an even larger share – an area the size of Africa (Foley 2012). Effectively, humanity has seized the temperate zone for agriculture, wiping out all or most former nonhumans and ecologies in order to mine the soil. (How did *they* get on top of *our* soil?) The raising of tens of billions of farm animals has exacted the eradication or displacement of wild animals from their former habitats, the persecution and slaughter of carnivores viewed as threats to domestic animals (themselves reduced to being 'live-*stock*'), and the erosion and degradation of lands from overgrazing. And the alternative to grazing – *The Economist's* so-called livestock revolution – constitutes a pollution nightmare and an egregious violation of basic decency in the treatment of animals. (Yet factory farming is a production method that today both supplements grazing and is swiftly spreading.) Regarding the seas, the human food factory has demanded that 98 percent of them be fishable. This reign of terror for marine species is partly underwritten by an institution called, without the slightest irony, 'the freedom of the seas'. As a consequence, only about 10 percent of the big fish are left and there is no end in sight to the demand on everything from krill to sharks (Jackson 2008). In the literal and figurative industrial mowing of the world's oceans, the countless beings who suffer and die in the name of mass consumption and profit are referred to as 'catch' and 'bycatch' (for a recent overview of the endangered oceans, see Danson 2011).

Industrial food production, and most especially the meat and animal products sector, contributes at least 30 percent of anthropogenic greenhouse gases – more than any other economic activity (Goodland and Anhang 2009; Gilbert 2012). These greenhouse gases are driving a climate change episode that (barring the energy transition everyone is still waiting for) could egg the planet to an average temperature increase in the ballpark of the Paleocene-Eocene Thermal Maximum. (If you have never heard of the Paleocene-Eocene Thermal Maximum, please Wiki it.) The food factory – the one often touted as a miracle of ingenuity bestowing the badge of exemptionalism on *Homo sapiens* – consumes upward of 70 percent of the freshwater taken from ecological watersheds, thus depriving the nonhumans who called that water home, and killing or driving them to extinction (in many cases even before we could meet them). Food production drives soil erosion and desertification, giving rise to ocean-spanning dust storms. It also depends on constant applications of fertilizers, pesticides, herbicides, and other biocides: indeed, many consumers and growers, alike, have been duped by corporate salesmen (and their government gofers) into believing that it is normal and necessary to poison the biosphere for the purpose of producing human nourishment. Streams, rivers, lakes, wetlands, and estuaries around the world are fouled or deadened by agricultural runoff and farm animal excrement – all just 'how things have to be' if we are to eat.

This unprecedented impact on the living world allows for the production of so much food as to seemingly demonstrate our ability to feed billions and, with some additional resourcefulness, perhaps feed even more. From a deep ecological perspective, however, the unprecedented ecological impact demanded for the production of so much food has demonstrated our capacity to take a magnificent planet – second to none in the known universe – and turn it into, or use it as, a human feedlot, and then muster the arrogance to call this act of pilfering and degradation an 'achievement'.

In his latest work, *Countdown* (2013), author Alan Weisman sums our current Green Revolution food system as involving 'fossil fuel gluttony', 'river fouling fertilizers', 'dependence on poisons', and 'monocultural menace to biodiversity'. So how is the amount of food we produce to be doubled or more without additional damage? Remarkably, one of the strategies being considered is to extend the productivity of Green Revolution methodologies to places they have not yet fully penetrated, such as Africa and Eastern Europe (see Foley 2012). Indeed, as the global population continues to grow, spreading the Green Revolution in order to feed the world will be the likely tack of the present-day policy framework, which is beholden to (in no particular order) corporate interests, institutional inertia, and acute anthropocentrism. Predictably, the call to extend the Green Revolution is cushioned by all the ecologically-correct pleas for wiser uses of water, more efficient application of fertilizers, prudent deployment of pesticides and herbicides, inclusion of no-till agriculture, and so forth: an appeal to 'greening' the Green

Revolution that not only is politic but also constitutes necessary re-tooling in a time of potential phosphate shortages, expanding dead zones, water wars, and fossil fuel price volatility. But making a destructive food model more efficient does not the model make 'good'. At best it yields a world – as Rachel Carson (1962) so cuttingly put it – that is *not quite lethal*.

I have digressed into the ecological discontents of humanity's current food production in order to submit the following: that the social mission to double or triple it is *madness*. But the proposal to move deliberately in the direction of more than halving our global population, and simultaneously radically changing our food system, is not.

If women (and their partners) today were voluntarily to choose having an average of one child (meaning many would choose none, many one, and others no more than two), then the world's population – instead of climbing toward 10 billion – would stabilize and then begin descending toward 2 billion (see Weisman 2007; Crist 2012). Were the current generation of child-bearing women to embrace this voluntary mandate for the sake of a living planet and the quality of life (perhaps even survival) of future people, how could this possibly be construed as a sacrifice? It is intelligent and compassionate action that many people would be willing to take if only they became properly informed and knowledgeable about the planetary emergency we are in. As for those who hear 'coercion' in such a proposal – and respond by defending 'human reproductive rights' – they should at least take a moment to acknowledge a fact that population experts have long been well aware of: that some of the grossest violations of human rights are perpetrated in societies that force women to start (involuntarily) having children when they are barely beyond childhood themselves, and to continue reproducing until their bodies give way or they are no longer fertile. The population question is indeed pressing in countries where patriarchal, polygamous, fundamentalist, and military cultures are keeping women handcuffed, and thus adding roadblocks to a restored future.

Yet population size is not strictly a 'developing world' problem but a global issue and task. One of the most effective and tangible ways to address climate disruption, as well as to curb the excessive consumption of everything (including food), is to move toward the substantial reduction of the number of consumers worldwide, meaning both the populations of the developed world and of 'emerging economies' in Asia, Southeast Asia, and Latin America. Concerning the developed world's responsibility in addressing overpopulation, it is also reasonable to insist that monetarily affluent nations and institutions should provision the financial backing and expertise for bringing state-of-the-art reproductive health services around the world – including their own home territories. For example, about half the pregnancies that occur in the United States are unintended – a statistic that speaks to a social, cultural, and educational failure, not just to a weakness of human nature. The important work of demographic expert Robert Engelman (2008; 2012) has shown that if unintended pregnancies (everywhere) were reduced to a humanly possible minimal, this alone would lead to a reduction in both population size and numbers of abortions.

Wherever concerted policies to lower birth rates have been implemented, birth rates have declined with alacrity (Potts 2009). By concerted policies I include the following: prominent, unembarrassed public discourse and campaigning on the issue; prioritizing the education of girls and women; establishing reproductive clinics that are accessible and affordable to all; training large numbers of health workers for grassroots education and support; making marriage counselling widely available; bringing sex education to school curricula; providing the full array of modern contraceptive methods for free or at minimal cost; and instituting legal, safe abortion services. (On the latter controversial point, it needs to be added that implementing all the above measures would significantly lower the number of abortions worldwide as well as the number of deaths from slipshod, illicit abortions.) Implementing these population policies worldwide, on a massive scale and in a rational manner, is what our predicament calls for. As Paul and Anne Ehrlich (2014) recently put it, 'only dramatic changes, on the scale of World War 2 mobilisations, hold out… hope'.

I expressly do not include immigration restrictions among the population policies sorely needed, because confronting overpopulation is a global environmental emergency that should not be bogged down or obfuscated by political sideshows. The restless, massive movement of poor people today is driven by economic suffering and environmental degradation, which are both (more often than not) causally tied to the activities of the global North. Attempting to restrict the emigration of people from South to North – in the name of an *ecological* cause – is incoherent and backfires against that very cause. The reason it is incoherent is that affluent nations cannot, on one hand, export environmental destruction while, on the other, refuse to import it. The reason calls for 'immigration restriction' (in the name of ecology) backfire against the imperative of bringing our global numbers down is that such calls understandably foment acrimony precisely for being incoherent. I regard overpopulation as a global problem that should be solved by means of the voluntary reduction of fertility rates below replacement *everywhere*. We live on one Earth and we are all one family, humans and nonhumans included.

The combination of heightened public awareness, the empowerment of women, and the availability and affordability of up-to-date reproductive information and services yields swift declines in birth rates (see Brown 2011b; Potts 2009). Such declines have nothing to do with the imposition of some top-down coercion, but follow from a straightforward bio-cultural cause: that the vast majority of women, when they attain free choice, rarely want more than one or two children, because numerous offspring are hard on the female organism and also take time away from self-realization pursuits. As the peerless work of population analyst Martha Campbell has shown, this natural female propensity for few offspring surfaces straight away once barriers to reproductive services are removed and freedom of choice becomes reality (see, for example, Campbell and Bedford 2009). If, additionally, today's fertile women were presented with the beautiful and compassionate mandate to help alleviate the world's most pressing ecological and social problems, then the average fertility rate might well shrink even further. Does this sound unreasonable? Certainly not more so than the unthinkable mission to double or triple food production, which augurs a colonized and ecologically impoverished biosphere, haunted by scarcity, extinctions, and human and animal starvations, and possibly marauded by nasty social mayhem to boot.

Bringing our global population down to, say, 2 billion will not be the magic bullet that solves every ecological and social problem. But we can rest assured that it will be *a* magic bullet for doing so. Significantly lowering our numbers facilitates a more harmonious way of life on Earth in at least two ways. First, many problems – from traffic jams, to health care budgets, to climate change – become more tractable as the dimension that magnifies them is curtailed. Lowering our numbers, in other words, helps downscale harms: for example, there is a yawning difference between a world of 1 billion vehicles (causing damage enough) versus a world of 2, 3, or 4 billion vehicles (the direction we are headed). There is also a vast difference between urban settlements beautified and balanced by an abundance of open, green spaces versus the nightmare of unending road, housing, and strip-mall construction to serve the glutton of sprawl.

The second way in which significantly lowering our global population supports the turn to what we might call 'beautiful human habitation' involves food production: a lower population will make possible the radical transformation of an industrial food regime that is currently bludgeoning ecologies, wild and domestic animals, and human wellness. (Four leading causes of disease and death are linked to industrial food, and especially to the consumption of mass-produced animal products: heart disease, diabetes, cancer, and stroke.) The whole world can indeed be fed: with organically grown, nutritious food; by prioritizing local and regional food economies; without mining, polluting, and dispersing the soil but by caring for it and building it; through diversified, smaller-scale farm operations modelled on natural ecosystems; in lovely and fecund interfaces with wild nature ('farming with the wild'); and by forsaking high quantities of animal foods, for the occasional consumption of such foods produced with due consideration to ethical and nutritional values. This wholesome turn only becomes possible if our global numbers are *far lower than today's*.

We need an authentic 'green revolution'. Instead of holding demographic growth as given, and a biosphere-wrecking food system as 'normal', let's imagine what the world could look like if we actively renounced both. Such a world would be dramatically more beautiful and sane following expansive rewilding – with abundant food, ecologically and ethically produced; with streams, rivers, lakes, and estuaries returned to being living waters; with deforestation halted and grassland ecologies reinstated; with the extinction crisis arrested and seas thriving again with Life; and with climate change made more manageable via carbon-sequestering forests and grasslands and decelerated emissions. If all these things can be achieved, what is keeping us from pursuing such a world? Indeed, what is detaining us from creating a civilization in harmony with wild Earth?

(This paper is a slightly modified version from its first publication as the Afterword of *Overdevelopment, Overpopulation, Overshoot*, edited by Tom Butler and published by the Foundation for Deep Ecology in 2015).

References

Anon (2010) 'News feature: Food', *Nature*, 466 (29 July), pp. 531–532, 546–560.
Biello, D. (2009) 'The dam building boom: Right path to clean energy?' *Yale Environment 360*. See: http://e360.yale.edu/feature/the_dam_building_boom_right_path_to_clean_energy/2119/
Brown, L. (2011a) 'The new geopolitics of food', *Foreign Policy*, May/June, pp. 54–62.
Brown, L. (2011b) *World on the Edge: How to Prevent Environmental and Economic Collapse*, New York: W.W. Norton and Co.
Butler, T. (2015) *Overdevelopment, Overpopulation, Overshoot*. San Francisco: Foundation for Deep Ecology.
Campbell, M. and Bedford, K. (2009) 'The theoretical and political framing of the population factor in development', *Philosophical Transactions of the Royal Society*, 364, pp. 3101–3113.
Carson, R. (1962) *Silent Spring*, Boston: Houghton Mifflin.
Clay, J. (2011) 'Freeze the footprint of food', *Nature*, 475(21 July), pp. 287–289.
Crist, E. (2010) 'Intimations of Gaia', in *Gaia in Turmoil: Climate Change, Biodepletion, and Earth Ethics in an Age of Crisis*, eds. E. Crist and B. Rinker, Cambridge: MIT Press, pp. 315–333.
Crist, E. (2012) 'Abundant Earth and the population question', in *Life on the Brink: Environmentalists Confront Overpopulation*, eds. P. Cafaro and E. Crist, Georgia: University of Georgia Press, pp. 141–151.
Danson, T. (2011) *Oceana: Our Endangered Oceans and What We Can Do to Save Them*, New York: Rodale.
Dirzo, R. and Raven, P. (2003) 'Global state of biodiversity and loss', *Annual Review of Environment and Resources*, 28, pp. 137–167.
The Economist (2011) 'A special report on feeding the world: The 9-billion-people question', 26 February, pp. 3–14.
Ehrlich, P. R. and Ehrlich, A. H. (2014) 'It's the numbers, stupid!', in *Sustainable Futures: Linking Population, Resources and the Environment*, eds. J. Goldie and K. Betts, Melbourne: CSIRO Publishing.
Ellis, E. (2013) 'Overpopulation is not the problem', *New York Times* (Op. Ed.), 13 September.
Ellis, E., Kaplan, J., Fuller, D., Vavrus, S., Klein Goldewijk, K., and Verburg, P. (2013) 'Used planet: A global history', *PNAS*, 110, no 20, pp. 7978–7985.
Engelman, R. (2008) *More: Population, Nature, and What Women Want*, Washington, DC: Island Press.
Engelman, R. (2012) 'Trusting women to end population growth', in *Life on the Brink: Environmentalists Confront Overpopulation*, eds. P. Cafaro and E. Crist, Georgia: University of Georgia Press, pp. 223–239.
FAO (2011) *The State of the World's Land and Water Resources for Food and Agriculture (SOLAW)*, Rome: Food and Agriculture Organisation.
Foley, J. (2012) 'How can we feed a growing world and still sustain the planet?', *3rd Annual Malthus Lecture* IFPRI, 22 May. See http://www.ifpri.org/event/3rd-annual-malthus-lecture
Foley, J. (2014) 'A five-step plan to feed the world', *National Geographic*, May, pp. 27–59.

Gilbert, N. (2012) 'One-third of our greenhouse gas emissions come from agriculture', *Nature*, 31 October. See http://www.nature.com/news/one-third-of-our-greenhouse-gas-emissions-come-from-agriculture-1.11708

Goodland, R. and Anhang, J. (2009) 'Livestock and climate change', *World Watch*, November/December, pp. 10–19.

Jackson, J. (2008) 'Ecological extinction and evolution in the brave new ocean', *PNAS* 105, 12 August, pp. 11458–11465.

Lovelock, J. (2007) *The Revenge of Gaia: Earth's Climate Crisis and the Fate of Humanity*. New York: Basic Books.

Malthus, T.R. (2008) *An Essay on the Principle of Population*, Oxford: Oxford Press.

Margulis, L. (1999) *Symbiotic Planet: A New Look at Evolution*, New York: Basic Books.

Potts, M. (2009) 'Where next?', *Philosophical Transactions of the Royal Society*, 364, pp. 3115–3124.

Rolston III, H. (1992) 'Disvalues in nature', *The Monist*, 75, no 2, pp. 250–280.

Shellenberger, M. and Nordhaus, T. (2011) 'Evolve', in *Love Your Monsters: Postenvironmentalism and the Anthropocene*, eds. M. Shellenberger and T. Nordhaus, Oakland, CA: The Breakthrough Institute, n.p.

UN (2012) *World Population Prospects; The 2012 Revision*. See: http://esa.un.org/unpd/wpp/Documentation/pdf/WPP2012_HIGHLIGHTS.pdf

Washington, H. (2013) *Human Dependence on Nature: How to Help Solve the Environmental Crisis*, London: Earthscan.

Weisman, A. (2007) *The World Without Us*, New York: Picador.

Weisman, A. (2013) *Countdown: Our Last, Best Hope For a Future on Earth?*, New York: Little, Brown & Company.

Whitty, J. (2011) *Deep Blue Home: An Intimate Ecology of Our Wild Ocean*, New York: Houghton Mifflin.

Wilson, E.O. (1999) *The Diversity of Life*, New York: Norton.

SECTION 2
Throughput and consumerism

A key elephant in the room

5

RE-ENGINEERING CULTURES TO CREATE A SUSTAINABLE CIVILIZATION

Erik Assadourian

WORLDWATCH INSTITUTE

Introduction

At the heart of how humans live their lives are the cultures they are part of. These cultures – and the norms, stories, rituals, values, symbols, and traditions that they incorporate – guide nearly all of our choices, from what we eat and how we raise our children to how we work, move, play, and celebrate. Unfortunately, consumerism – a cultural pattern that was nurtured by a nexus of business and government leaders over the past few centuries – has now spread around the globe, becoming the dominant paradigm across most cultures. More people are defining themselves first and foremost through how they consume and are striving to own or use ever more stuff, whether in fashion, food, travel, electronics, or countless other products and services (Assadourian 2010b).

But consumerism is not a viable cultural paradigm on a planet whose systems are deeply stressed and which is currently home to 7.3 billion people, let alone on a planet of 9.4–10 billion people, the population the United Nations projects for 2050 (UN 2015). Ultimately, to create a sustainable human civilization – one that can thrive for millennia without degrading the planet on which we all depend – consumer cultures will have to be re-engineered into cultures of sustainability, so that living sustainably feels as natural as living as a consumer does today.

Granted, this is no easy task. It will and is being resisted by myriad interests that have a huge stake in sustaining the global consumer culture – from the fossil fuel industry and big agribusiness to food processors, car manufacturers, advertisers, and so on. But given that consumerism and the consumption patterns it fuels are not compatible with the flourishing of a living planetary system, either we find ways to wrestle our cultural patterns out of the grip of those with a vested interest in maintaining consumerism, or Earth's ecosystems decline and bring down the consumer culture for the vast majority of humanity in a much crueler way.

Consuming the planet

In 2008, people around the world used 68 billion tons of materials, including metals and minerals, fossil fuels, and biomass. That is an average of 10 tons per person – or 27 kilograms each and every day (Dittrich et al. 2012). That same year, humanity used the biocapacity of 1.5 planets, consuming far beyond what the Earth can sustainably provide (WWF 2012).

Of course, not every human consumes at the same level. While the average Southeast Asian used 3.3 tons of materials in 2008, the average North American used 27.5 tons – eight times as much. And the spread of consumerism has driven many regions to dramatically accelerate material consumption. Asia used 21.1 billion tons of materials in 2008, up 450 percent from the 4.7 billion tons that the region used in 1980 (Dittrich et al. 2012).

This vast differentiation in consumption is often explained as simply a difference in development levels – with growth in consumption trends routinely celebrated by leading newspapers, policymakers, and economists, regardless of the current size of the host economy. In reality, however, such high levels of consumption often undermine the well-being of high-income consumers themselves, while also deeply undermining humanity's long-term well-being and security. The United States, for example, now suffers from an obesity epidemic in which two-thirds of Americans are overweight or obese (RWJF 2008). This leads to significant increases in mortality and morbidity from a variety of chronic, diet-related diseases like diabetes, heart disease, and several forms of cancer (Brown 2011). Worse, obesity has reached a point that it is affecting children and even shortening the average American lifespan, not to mention costing the United States $270 billion a year in additional health care costs and lost productivity (Olshansky et al. 2005).

Beyond the personal impact, this obesity epidemic – which has spread around the world, with 1.9 billion people now overweight or obese globally and suffering similar health impacts – adds significantly to the demands humanity puts on Earth. Obesity has added an extra 5.4 percent of human biomass to the planet – 15.5 million tons of human flesh – which means that people are eating enough extra food each year to feed an additional 242 million people of healthy weight (Weil 2011; Walpole et al. 2012). And obesity is just one manifestation of the ills of overconsumption, to which we could add urban sprawl, traffic, air pollution from automobiles and factories, and dependence on a growing number of pharmaceutical drugs like antidepressants (Assadourian 2012).

Consuming at such high levels is depleting the capacity of Earth to provide vital ecosystem services – from a stable climate, due to the profligate use of fossil fuels and consumption of meat, to provision of freshwater and fish, through pollution by chemicals and plastics (MEA 2005). And as high consumption levels are promoted as ways to increase well-being, development, and economic growth, these pressures only increase. Indeed, if all humans consumed like Americans, Earth could sustain only about one quarter of the human population without undermining the planet's biocapacity. But even if everyone only consumed like the average Chinese person, the planet could sustain just 84 percent of today's population (WWF 2012).

Why are people consuming so much? The answer cannot be simply because they can afford to. In short, it stems from decades of the engineering of a set of cultural norms, values, traditions, symbols, and stories that make it feel natural to consume ever larger amounts – of food, of energy, of stuff. Policymakers changed laws, marketers and the media cultivated desires, businesses created and aggressively pushed new products, and over time 'consumers' deeply internalized this new way of living (Assadourian 2010b).

In a majority of societies today, consumerism feels so natural that it is hard to even imagine a different cultural model. Certain goods and services – from air conditioning and large homes to cars, vacation travel, and pets – are seen as a right, even an entitlement. Yet it is these and countless other lifestyle choices that in the aggregate are undermining the well-being of countless humans, today and for centuries into the future (Assadourian 2010b). Moving away from consumerism – now propped up by more than $500 billion in annual advertising expenditures (ZOM 2012), by hundreds of billions of dollars in government subsidies and tax breaks, billions more in lobbying and public relations spending (Assadourian 2010b), and the momentum of generations of living the consumer dream – will undoubtedly be the most difficult part of the transition to a sustainable society. Especially if, as analysts predict, an additional 1 billion consumers join the global consumer class by 2025 (McKinsey 2012).

But ultimately consumerism will decline whether people act proactively or not, as human society has far transcended Earth's limits. Our profligate use of fossil fuels has all but guaranteed an increase in average global temperatures of 2 degrees Celsius, and current projections suggest that unless a dramatic shift in policies and behaviors occurs, an increase of 4 degrees Celsius or more by the end of this century, or even mid-century, is possible (New et al. 2011; Potsdam 2012).

These vast climatic changes will bring unprecedented heat waves, megastorms, massive droughts, dramatic floods, population displacements, and the deaths of tens, even hundreds of millions of people – not to mention political instability and conflict (DARA 2012). None of these are conducive to the perpetuation of a global consumer culture, though surely a small elite will still be able to maintain the materialistic version of 'the good life'. Ideally, however, we will not accept this as our likely future but instead will grapple with the main challenge of our times: re-engineering human cultures to be inherently sustainable (see Box 5.1 on the following page).

BOX 5.1: WHAT WOULD A CULTURE OF SUSTAINABILITY LOOK LIKE?

When discussing the transition beyond consumerism, opponents often conjure up a return to hunting and gathering and living in caves. In reality, if proactive – that is, if we do not wait until Earth's systems are irrevocably degraded – humanity can maintain a decent quality of life for all (and not just current consumers) at a much lower level of impact.

Stulz and Lütolf (2006) of 'Novatlantis' looked at what an equitable and sustainable consumption level would look like. They found that from an energy perspective – with a commitment to move to a sustainable energy paradigm based on renewables (admittedly a big qualifier) – the average human could continuously use 2,000 watts of energy (or 17,520 kilowatt-hours per year) for all of his or her needs, including food, transportation, water, services, and possessions. This is the current global average energy use – but it is unequally divided, with people in industrial countries using far more, such as in the United States, which uses six times this amount per person. What does living off this amount of energy look like?

One Australian researcher and inventor, Saul Griffith (2009), analyzed a 2,000-watt lifestyle at a personal level and found that he would need to own one-tenth as much stuff and make it last 10 times as long, that he would have to fly rarely, drive infrequently (and mostly in efficient vehicles fully loaded with passengers), and become six-sevenths vegetarian. Put simply, a 2,000-watt lifestyle looks like the way much of the world lives today, or better, but gone are the celebrated entitlements of the high-income lifestyle – 79 kilograms of meat a year (2.5 servings a day (Nierenberg and Reynolds 2012)), nearly daily access to a private car (often with only one passenger), air-conditioned homes, family pets, and unfettered access to flights around the world. In truth, these luxuries will no longer be routinely accessible to the vast majority of people in a truly sustainable society, though they may be available as rarer treats, like the once-every-three-years flight to visit his parents that Griffith (2009) factored into his new energy allowance.

Sometimes these lost consumer luxuries will be difficult sacrifices to accept after a lifetime with free access to them, though rarer consumption of luxuries may actually make them more enjoyable, like escaping to a cool café on a very hot day or enjoying meat on special occasions. But offsetting these lost consumer luxuries will in all likelihood be improved health, more free time, less stress, a strengthening of community ties (as people rely on each other instead of on privatized services) (Schor 2010), and – most important – a stop to the decline of major ecosystems on which a stable human civilization depends.

Learning from past greatness

Keep in mind that cultures are always changing in large ways and small – sometimes organically and other times intentionally with a push in certain directions, whether driven by religious, political, technological, or other forces. There have been many spectacular beneficial cultural shifts in recent history: slavery was abolished in the United States, apartheid disappeared in South Africa, women have equal representation in many societies, fascism was defeated in Western Europe. Of course, some of these shifts required military power, not just 'people power', and none of the victories is guaranteed to stay with us indefinitely without vigilance. But perhaps the biggest cultural transformation of all – one often overlooked but in reality one to draw inspiration from – was the initial engineering of consumerism.

At first there was resistance to the introduction of some elements of consumerism. For example, the first generation of factory workers typically chose to work fewer hours when receiving raises, not buy more stuff. The purpose of life, after all, was not to spend most of a person's waking hours in hot, dangerous conditions, away from family and community (Stearns 2001). This resistance could be seen over and over: to disposable goods that were introduced in the 1950s, which went against the cultural norm of thrift that had been so important to family survival; even to the switch from oil lamps to gas lights, which to some seemed unnaturally bright and 'glaring' (*The Economist* 2010). But over time people got used to new products, some of which did indeed improve life quality and many of which were at least marketed as such by clever entrepreneurs and a new advertising industry. Eventually we could hardly imagine life without an abundance of products. Three sectors deserve special recognition for so effectively shifting (and continuing to shift) cultural norms around transportation, food, and even relationships – and in turn, even if unintentionally, helping to engineer a global consumer culture (Cohen 2003).

The automobile industry offers an excellent case study on how to change cultural norms. Car companies used nearly every societal institution to shift transportation norms and even our understanding of the street, which before cars came along was understood as multimodal – shared by humans, horses, carts, and trolleys. A combination of tactics shifted this norm.

Automobile companies bought up city trolley systems and dismantled them. They distributed propaganda (disguised as safety educational materials) in schools, teaching children from an early age that the street was built for cars, not them. Companies helped create and finance citizen groups to oppose people who were concerned with the spread of cars and the accidents they were causing. They even helped local police forces fine, arrest, or shame pedestrians who crossed streets wherever they wanted to (known today as 'jaywalkers' – a word that was intentionally spread by car companies and their allies), helping to further establish the car as the dominant user of streets (Dauvergne 2008; Norton 2008). And of course, they spent huge sums marketing cars as sexy, fun, and liberating (Williams 2012). Today the car industry spends $31 billion a year just in the United States on advertising and has effectively exported car culture to developing countries – like China, where the automobile fleet has grown from less than 10 million to 73 million in just 11 years – using lessons learned in earlier successes (Renner 2012).

The fast-food industry provides another good example. Serving over 69 million people around the world every day, McDonald's is a global power. So it may come as a surprise that less than a century ago the hamburger – today's iconic American meal – was a taboo food, unsafe, unclean, and eaten only by the poor. But technological changes, including the assembly line and the automobile, helped make the conditions right for a transformation in how we eat: quickly, on the go, and out of the home. McDonald's not only seized on this, it accelerated the transformation, retraining the palates of entire generations of Americans and now the 119 countries in which the company operates. To do this, the company used a clever set of complementary strategies including advertising to children, toys given out with kid's meals, restaurant playgrounds, and even the creation of a lovable clown to peddle the company's food (Schlosser 2005).

The third relevant case study is the pet industry. In India, dog ownership has grown significantly in recent years. In part this has been driven by demographic changes that include later marriages and increasing social isolation, but the obvious solution to this did not have to be pet ownership. Yet a global pet industry, recognizing an opportunity to grow, worked to stoke this enormous potential new market. It is part of the larger industry effort to transform pets into family members so that more people will buy pets and owners will spend more on them (which industry and many owners call their 'children') (Polgreen 2009).

And it has worked. People spend more than $58 billion on pet food each year around the world, and billions more on veterinarian care, toys, clothes, and other pet supplies (TMR 2012). Considering the ecological impact of the millions of dogs and cats (133 million dogs and 162 million cats in just the top five dog- and cat-owning countries in the world), this is not just another curious consumer trend. Two German Shepherds have a larger ecological footprint from their food requirements alone than a person in Bangladesh does in total (Vale and Vale 2009). And unfortunately it is Bangladeshis – whose country is one of the most vulnerable to climate change – not wealthier people's pets, who will bear the brunt of climate change.

These products and countless others are supported by $16,000 of advertising every single second somewhere in the world (Assadourian 2010b). So how do we transform the world's cultures so that living sustainably becomes as natural as living as a consumer has been made to feel today? Just as consumer interests learned over the decades as they worked to stimulate markets and, intentionally or inadvertently, engineer cultural norms, it will be essential to use the full complement of societal institutions to shift cultural norms – business, media and marketing, government, education, social movements, even traditions.

First attempts to pioneer cultures of sustainability

While consumerism is being spread more aggressively every year, many cultural pioneers are working to spread a culture of sustainability, in both bold and subtle ways, locally and globally, and often in ways they may not even recognize as culture changing. The most effective of these pioneers tend to use dominant societal institutions to normalize an alternative set of practices, values, beliefs, stories, and symbols (Assadourian 2010b).

Within the business sector, a handful of executives are using their companies to transform broader consumption norms. The clothing company Patagonia, for instance, recognizing that its continued success depends on Earth and that 'the environmental cost of everything we make is astonishing', has taken the bold step of encouraging its customers to not even buy its products unless truly needed, encouraging them to instead either buy used Patagonia products or do without. The company even worked with eBay to create a ready supply of used Patagonia gear (Nudd 2011; Aston 2011).

While some change will be driven by large corporations – which have significant capital and influence at their disposal – the real drivers of a culture of sustainability in the business sector are entrepreneurs and business leaders working to transform the sector's mission altogether, with a positive social purpose being first and foremost and with revenue generation simply being the means to achieve that. The good news is that an increasing number of business leaders, when creating new businesses, are establishing these 'social enterprises' with the specific goal of using their businesses, and the profits they generate, to improve society.

And today, more social enterprises like these are flourishing and even locking their beneficial missions directly into their corporate charters. Many businesses are now legally incorporating or getting certified as 'B' or 'benefit' corporations. By fall of 2013, there were 855 certified B corporations in 27 countries, with annual revenues of an estimated $6.3 billion and employing some 33,000 people (Cordes 2014).

Within government, more policymakers are recognizing the need to use this institution to help steer citizens toward consuming less and living more sustainably, editing out unsustainable options like supersized sodas in New York City (Lerner 2012) and plastic bags in San Francisco (Riley 2012). And some are supporting sustainable choices like mass transit, bicycle lanes, even super accessible libraries, as with the series of library kiosks that Madrid placed in its subway system (Maniates 2010; Assadourian 2010a).

A few governments are starting to lead even bolder transformations – such as expanding fundamental rights to the planet itself. Just as the introduction of human rights transformed the legal realm and was a catalyst for social change around the world, Earth's rights could have the same potential. In recent years, Ecuador and Bolivia have both incorporated Earth's rights into their constitutions, in turn empowering people to legally defend Earth's interest even when no humans are directly harmed – for example, by stopping mining projects in an uninhabited area (Cullinan 2010; Olson 2011).

Beyond governance, local communities are organizing themselves to both reinforce sustainability norms locally and inspire others to do the same. There are now hundreds of ecovillages around the world modeling sustainable and low-consumption lifestyles. And hundreds of Transition Towns are working to transform existing communities to be both more sustainable and more resilient. While all these efforts are small in scale and scope, their potential to inspire and experiment with new cultural norms is exponentially larger (Assadourian 2008; 2012).

A number of schools and universities are also working to embed sustainability directly into their school cultures, including integrating environmental science, media literacy, and critical thinking into their curricula. In Europe, 39,500 schools have now been awarded a 'Green Flag' for greening their curricula, empowering students to make their schools more sustainable, and articulating the schools' ecological values alongside their educational values. Some schools are also modeling a sustainable way of living, from integrating gardening programs and renewable energy production onto school grounds to changing what is served in the cafeteria (Jensen *et al.* 2012). In Rome, a leader in school food reform, two-thirds of food served in cafeterias is organic, one quarter is locally sourced, and 14 percent is certified Fair Trade (Morgan and Sonnino 2010).

Like education, cultural and religious traditions play a central role in shaping our understandings of the world. Fortunately, more religious communities are starting to draw attention to practices and teachings that reinforce our sustainable stewardship of Creation (Gardner 2010). Storytelling and myth building also have tremendous potential to help transform cultures, from efforts like 'Big History', which is working to incorporate sustainability into cultural creation stories, to a plethora of films and television shows that wrestle with sustainability themes. Finally, given that media – and the marketing now embedded at its every level – play such a powerful role in shaping modern cultures, social marketing and 'ad jamming' will be a powerful means to harness marketing energy for positive ends. Examples include social marketing efforts like 'The Story of Stuff' project, which uses short, catchy videos to build political support for reduced consumption, and ad jamming efforts by Adbusters, the Billboard Liberation Front, and the Yes Men. The Yes Men, for example, uses fake ads and press conferences to draw attention to hypocritical positions of businesses and global institutions. With few resources – leveraged in aikido-like fashion – these efforts garner significant attention and undermine the public relations efforts of those spending millions on advertising to shape the public's view of the company, their products, and, more generally, progress.

Just as water can erode rock into a grand canyon, the continuing pursuit of culture-changing efforts can add up to much more than their constituent parts. And the seeds that pioneers like these sow today, even if they fail to take root while consumerism dominates the landscape, may sprout as humanity desperately reaches for a new set of norms, symbols, rituals, and stories to rebuild a semblance of normality once Earth's systems unravel under the unbearable burden of sustaining a global consumer economy.

Tilting at cultural norms?

When the dominant institutions of most societies are primarily still promoting consumerism, and probably will not stop anytime soon, how will upstart efforts to engineer cultures of sustainability have any chance of success? Ultimately, if Don Quixote had just waited long enough, the passage of time would have brought down his windmill giants. The same is true for the consumer culture giants, which depend completely on the bounty of the energy embedded in fossil fuels, abundant resources, and a stable planetary system provided to humanity at this stage in its development.

Given Earth's weakening capacity to absorb greenhouse gases and other wastes generated in pursuit of the consumer dream, the end of the consumer culture will come – willingly or unwillingly, proactively chosen or not – and sooner than we would like to believe. The only question is whether we greet it with a series of alternative ways of orienting our lives and our cultures to maintain a good life, even as we consume much less. Every culture-changing effort, whether small or large, will help facilitate this transition and lay the foundation for a new set of cultural norms – quite possibly only implemented when humanity has no other choice.

While some will argue until the bitter end that letting go of certain consumer luxuries is a step backwards – as North Face apparel company co-founder and environmentalist Doug Tompkins notes: 'What happens if you get to the cliff and you take one step forward or you do a 180-degree turn and take one step forward? Which way are you going? Which is progress?' – Patagonia founder Yvon Chouinard answered that the solution for a lot of the world's problems may be 'to turn around and take a forward step. You can't just keep trying to make a flawed system work' (Magnolia Pictures 2010).

The challenge will be convincing more individuals that further efforts to spread a consumer culture are truly a step in the wrong direction and that the faster we use our talents and energies to promote a culture of sustainability, the better off all of humanity will be.

(We would like to acknowledge that this chapter is edited and updated from Assadourian, E. (2013) 'Re-engineering cultures to create a sustainable civilization', in *State of the World 2013: Is Sustainability Still Possible?*, ed. L. Starke, Washington: Island Press, pp 113–125. We thank the Worldwatch Institute for permission to use this material.)

References

Assadourian, E. (2008) 'Engaging Communities for a Sustainable World' in, *State of the World 2008*, Worldwatch Institute, New York: W. W. Norton & Company, pp. 151–165.

Assadourian, E. (2010a) 'The Mallport and the Bibliometro', in *Transforming Cultures Blog*, 30 March 2010. http://blogs.worldwatch.org/transformingcultures/bibliometro/

Assadourian, E. (2010b) 'The Rise and Fall of Consumer Cultures', in *2010 State of the World: Transforming Cultures from Consumerism to Sustainability*, eds. L. Starke and L. Mastny, London: Earthscan, pp. 3–20.

Assadourian, E. (2012) 'The Path to Degrowth in Overdeveloped Countries', in *State of the World 2012*, Washington, DC: Island Press, pp. 22–37.

Aston, A. (2011) 'Patagonia Takes Fashion Week as a Time to Say: "Buy Less, Buy Used"', *GreenBiz*, 8 September.

Brown, D. (2011) 'Life Expectancy in the U.S. Varies Widely by Region, in Some Places Is Decreasing', *Washington Post*, 15 June.

Cohen, L. (2003) *A Consumer's Republic: The Politics of Mass Consumption in Postwar America*, New York: Alfred A. Knopf.

Cordes, C. (2014) 'The Rise of Triple-Bottom-Line Businesses', in *State of the World 2014: Governing for Sustainability*, ed. L. Mastny, Washington: Island Press, pp. 203–214.

Cullinan, C. (2010) 'Earth Jurisprudence: From Colonization to Participation', in *2010 State of the World: Transforming Cultures from Consumerism to Sustainability*, eds. L. Starke and L. Mastny, London: Earthscan, pp. 143–148.

DARA (2012) *Climate Vulnerability Monitor: A Guide to the Cold Calculus of a Hot Planet*, 2nd ed., Washington, DC: DARA International.

Dauvergne, P. (2008) *The Shadows of Consumption: Consequences for the Global Environment*, Cambridge, MA: MIT Press.

Dittrich, M., Giljum, S., Lutter, S., and Polzin, C. (2012) *Green Economies Around the World?*, Vienna: Sustainable Europe Research Institute.

The Economist (2010) 'Not Such a Bright Idea: Making Lighting More Efficient Could Increase Energy Use, Not Decrease It', 26 August 2010.

Gardner, G. (2010) 'Engaging Religions to Shape Worldviews', in *2010 State of the World: Transforming Cultures from Consumerism to Sustainability*, eds. L. Starke and L. Mastny, London: Earthscan, pp. 23–29.

Griffith, S. (2009) 'Climate Change Recalculated', presentation at The Long Now Foundation, San Francisco, 16 January 2009.

Jensen, T.S., Glyki, E., Hayles, A., and Normander, B. (2012) *From Consumer Kids to Sustainable Childhood*, Copenhagen: Worldwatch Institute Europe.

Lerner, G. (2012) 'New York Health Board Approves Ban on Large Sodas', *CNN*, 14 September 2012.

Magnolia Pictures (2010) *180° South*, film about Jeff Johnson, who founded the Patagonia company. See: http://www.magpictures.com/profile.aspx?id=69f442d0–8f47–46c4-ac5d-d91c11deb605

Maniates, M. (2010) 'Editing Out Unsustainable Behavior', in *2010 State of the World: Transforming Cultures from Consumerism to Sustainability*, eds. L. Starke and L. Mastny, London: Earthscan, pp. 119–26.

McKinsey (2012) *Urban World: Cities and the Rise of the Consuming Class*, Washington, DC: McKinsey & Company.

MEA (2005) *Ecosystems and Human Well-Being: Synthesis*, Millennium Ecosystem Assessment, Washington, DC: Island Press.

Morgan, K. and Sonnino, R. (2010) 'Rethinking School Food: The Power of the Public Plate', in *2010 State of the World: Transforming Cultures from Consumerism to Sustainability*, eds. L. Starke and L. Mastny, London: Earthscan, pp. 69–74.

New, M., Liverman, D., Schroder, H., Anderson, K. (2011) 'Four Degrees and Beyond: The Potential for a Global Temperature Increase of Four Degrees and Its Implications', *Philosophical Transactions of the Royal Society A*, January, pp. 6–19.

Nierenberg, D. and Reynolds, L. (2012) 'Disease and Drought Curb Meat Production and Consumption', *Vital Signs Online*, 23 October 2012.

Norton, P. (2008) *Fighting Traffic: The Dawn of the Motor Age in the American City*, Cambridge, MA: MIT Press.

Nudd, T. (2011) 'Ad of the Day: Patagonia', *Ad Week*, 28 November.

Olshansky, S.J., Passaro, D.J., Hershow, R.C., Layden, J., Carnes, B.A., Brody, J., Hayflick, L., Butler, R.N., Allison, D.B., and Ludwig, D.S. (2005) 'A Potential Decline in Life Expectancy in the United States in the 21st Century', *New England Journal of Medicine*, 17 March, pp. 138–45.

Olson, G. (2011) 'Bolivia's Law of Mother Earth', *Common Ground*, July.

Polgreen, L. (2009) 'Matchmaking in India: Canine Division', *New York Times*, 17 August, p. A5.

Potsdam Institute for Climate Impact Research and Climate Analytics (2012) *Turn Down the Heat: Why a 4°C Warmer World Must Be Avoided*, Washington, DC: World Bank.

Renner, M. (2012) 'Auto Production Roars to New Records', *Vital Signs Online*, 11 September.

Riley, N. (2012) 'Expanded Plastic Bag Ban Takes Effect Monday', *SFGate*, 29 September.

RWJF (2008) *F as in Fat: How Obesity Policies Are Failing in America*, Washington, DC: Robert Wood Johnson Foundation.

Schlosser, E. (2005) *Fast Food Nation*, New York: Harper Perennial Company.

Schor, J. (2010) *Plenitude: The New Economics of True Wealth*, New York: Penguin Press.

Stearns, P. (2001) *Consumerism in World History: The Global Transformation of Desire*, New York: Routledge, pp. 34–35.

Stulz, R. and Lütolf, T. (2006) 'What Would Be the Realities of Implementing the 2,000 Watt Society in Our Communities?' presentation, Novatlantis, 23–24 November.

TMR (2012) 'Global Pet Food Market is Forecasted to Reach USD 74.8 Billion by 2017', press release, 10 August, Albany, NY: Transparency Market Research.

United Nations, Department of Economic and Social Affairs, Population Division (2015) *World Population Prospects: The 2015 Revision, Key Findings and Advance Tables*. Working Paper No. ESA/P/WP.241.

Vale, R. and Vale, B. (2009) *Time to Eat the Dog: The Real Guide to Sustainable Living*, London: Thames & Hudson, pp. 235–38.

Walpole, S., Prieto-Merino, D., Edwards, P., Cleland, J., Stevens, G., and Roberts, I. (2012) 'The Weight of Nations: An Estimation of Adult Human Biomass', *BMC Public Health*, 12, pp. 439–45.

Weil, R. (2011) 'Levels of Overweight on the Rise', *Vital Signs Online*, 14 June.

Williams, S. (2012) 'Report Predicts Auto-Ad Spending Will Grow 14% This Year', *Advertising Age*, 30 April.

WWF, GFL, and ZSL (2012) *Living Planet Report 2012*, Gland, Switzerland: WWF.

ZOM (2012) 'ZenithOptimedia Releases September 2012 Advertising Expenditure Forecasts', press release, 1 October, London: ZenithOptimedia.

6

SUSTAINABLE BUSINESS: WHAT SHOULD IT BE?

Circular economy and the 'business of subversion'

Helen Kopnina
LEIDEN UNIVERSITY AND THE HAGUE UNIVERSITY OF APPLIED SCIENCE

Introduction

According to the critics of conventional sustainability models, particularly within the business context, it is questionable whether the objective of balancing the social, economic and environmental triad is feasible, and whether human equality and prosperity (as well as population growth) can be achieved with the present rate of natural degradation (Rees 2009). The current scale of human economic activity on Earth is already excessive, finding itself in a state of unsustainable 'overshoot' where consumption and dissipation of energy and material resources exceed the regenerative and assimilative capacity of supportive ecosystems (Rees 2012). Conceptualizing the current 'politics of unsustainability' reflected in mainstream sustainability debates, Blühdorn (2011) explores the paradox of wanting to 'sustain the unsustainable', noting that the socio-cultural norms underpinning unsustainability support denial of the gravity of our planetary crises. This denial concerns anything from the imminence of mass extinctions to climate change. As Foster (2014) has phrased it: 'There was a brief window of opportunity when the sustainability agenda might, at least in principle, have averted it'. That agenda, however, has failed. Not *might fail*, nor even *is likely to fail* – but *has already* failed. Yet, instead of acknowledging this failure and moving on from realization of the catastrophe to the required radical measures, the optimists of sustainable development and ecological modernization continue to celebrate the purported 'balance' between people, profit, and planet.

Critics have found that the stated goal of maintaining economic growth – creating more wealth while simultaneously keeping the health of the ecosystems intact – is oxymoronic (Rees 2010; Foster 2014; Washington 2015). Critiques have noted that programs to promote 'economic development' may have caused more harm than good in promoting a system of production and consumption that is essentially unsustainable (e.g. Washington 2015). The most prominent (as well as constructive) critique was voiced by the proponents of alternative economic systems such as the steady state economy (e.g. Daly 1991), and closed loop production systems such as 'Cradle to Cradle' or 'C2C' (e.g. McDonough and Braungart 2002), and the circular economy (e.g. Webster 2007; Huckle 2012). The steady state economy is based on a steady sustainable population and a minimized throughput of resources. The former is not inherent in the term 'closed loop' process, while C2C aims to reduce throughput.

This reduction of throughput requires deconstruction of the mainstream sustainability approaches. Within these 'mainstream' approaches, the 'eco-efficiency' (doing more with less) was criticized for leaving the existing destructive system of industrial production intact. McDonough and Braungart (2002) have argued that industrialization has unintentionally created a system that has resulted in an alarming amount of toxic materials discharged into the air, water, and soil, as well as an ever-increasing amount of waste disposed of in landfills or incinerators.

The closed-loop systems and circular frameworks are often discussed as hopeful alternatives to the mainstream eco-efficiency which essentially makes a bad thing (design, or form of energy) last longer. Cradle to Cradle and circular economy frameworks call not for 'small steps' and reducing the damage, but for a radical re-evaluation of the methods of production that is fully good, not a bit less bad. Basically, the circular economy and C2C emphasize that the biggest danger of resilience, adaptation, or mediation thinking that is so prominent in sustainability discourse makes the bad system literally more sustainable, as resilience through eco-efficiency or recycling allows for relative durability of a bad design.

Indeed, as Crist (2012: 148–149) has reflected, perceiving nature as a human resource base that can be easily modified by being more efficient allows one to speak of the malleability of resources without perceiving the great damage done to the long-term survival or health of the natural systems:

> More serious than modern society's potential ability to technologically fix or muddle through problems of its own making is people's apparent willingness to live in an ecologically devastated world and to tolerate dead zones, endocrine disruptors, domestic animal torture (aka CAFOS), and unnatural weather as unavoidable concomitants of modern living … What is deeply repugnant about such a civilization is not its potential for self-annihilation, but its totalitarian conversion of the natural world into a domain of resources to serve a human supremacist way of life, and the consequent destruction of all the intrinsic wealth of its natural places, beings, and elements.

In fact, empirical evidence of mass extinctions in the last few decades as well as population growth illustrates that the human population is much more resilient to pollution, climate change, desertification, and deforestation than flora and fauna is (Shoreman-Ouimet and Kopnina 2016).

The steady state economy perspective also calls for the recognition of twin forces of population and consumption growth, and the need to address difficult questions in relation to the moral responsibility of humans to the natural world (Daly 1991; Dietz and O'Neill 2013). Translated into educational practice, this means putting an emphasis on ecologically-benign models of production and consumption (e.g. McDonough and Braungart 2002; Webster 2007; Huckle 2012; Kopnina 2012, 2013a, 2013b, 2013c). As an educational charity, the Ellen MacArthur Foundation promotes debate and discussion around the possibilities inherent in just one of these models: a transition from today's predominately linear 'throughput' economy to one which, reflecting insights from living systems, is a circular or 'roundput' economy. However, while the Ellen MacArthur Foundation is the champion of the circular economy, it sees this as a 'new engine of growth'. Many ad hoc circular economy educational activities have sprung up in different universities, including a few in the Netherlands.

While the closed loop and circular economy models have a significant role to play in sustainable resource management, they are not without limitations. As Washington (2015) notes, sustainability should not be allowed to be subverted and hijacked to justify further 'business-as-usual' growth. Even hopeful alternative frameworks can be subject to subversion. For example, the 'pioneers' of the circular economy, or Cradle to Cradle, have indeed sometimes profited from setting up certification systems, limiting the global applicability of their concepts, or sometimes cooperating closely with companies that do not strictly adhere to these frameworks (Brennan et al. 2015).

This chapter explores how students can be taught to distinguish between more helpful sustainability frameworks (in terms of their ability to avoid environmental harm), and how the pitfalls of subversion of these helpful frameworks can be avoided. The following sections will explore the closed loop sustainability frameworks, discuss the areas in which subversion is possible, and discuss its implications for teaching these frameworks using the case study of bachelor's students of 'Circular Economy in the Cloud', an experimental online course piloted by vocational schools in Rotterdam, Utrecht and The Hague universities in the Netherlands.

Closed loop sustainability frameworks

The circular economy model argues that the functioning of ecosystems is an exemplar for industrial processes and systems, emphasizing a shift towards ecologically-sound products and renewable energy, and highlighting the role of diversity as a characteristic of resilient and productive systems (Ellen MacArthur Foundation; Brennan et al. 2015). Diesendorf (2014) has demonstrated that appropriate technologies such as renewable energy, energy conservation, and sustainable building are both economically and socially feasible.

The ideas of a circular economy were adopted by the American architect William McDonough and the German chemist Michael Braungart. The idea behind their critique of the current system is that production remains linear, a 'cradle to grave' process that, despite efforts at eco-efficiency, still results in waste. The Cradle to Cradle framework criticizes eco-efficiency and recycling, stating that they enable the bad system to last longer. In this view, a bad thing (such as fossil fuel motors in cars) should not be 'efficient', rather they should not be there in the first place. Even the conventional eco-efficiency approach and well-intentioned practice of recycling lead to mostly 'down-cycling', where materials are reused to make products of lower quality, which require a new application of energy to produce a new product.

The application of the idea of a production system that does not produce unproductive or unusable waste at an economic level was propelled forward by reports by the Ellen MacArthur Foundation and other initiatives stimulated by both government and business stakeholders (Brennan et al. 2015). Thus, proponents of both circular economy and the closely related 'C2C' share their support for the forms of production that support an endless cycle of materials that mimics nature's 'no waste' nutrient cycles. These frameworks basically adhere to the 'waste = food' principle. This principle is well illustrated by the metaphor of the cherry tree, which produces 'waste' (berries, leaves, etc.) that actually serves as food for other species and for formation of the soil.

C2C proposes that only biodegradable materials (biological nutrients) and non-compostable materials (technical nutrients) should be used, so that a product can be disassembled and the two kinds of materials can be either left to disintegrate and be used for agricultural fertilization (although other uses are also possible), or reused without the loss of quality and energy for a different product. Inspired by such frameworks, some companies have noted that the closed loop model is in line with traditional 'business sense' through its potentially immense savings.

The risks of subversion

However, there are trade-offs that need to be considered when it comes to implementing circularity ideas, in terms of design and business implications. Closed-loop frameworks need to be understood in terms of their strengths and their weaknesses. Brennan et al. (2015) reflect: 'Keeping a product in use for longer implies that direct sales of new products decrease, impacting on-going profits that could otherwise be made. This is a challenge to mainstream business operations that rely on repeat purchases by challenging the popular "planned obsolescence" approach' (p. 234).

Critical observers have noted that companies that get certified as C2C (http://www.c2ccertified.org/get-certified/product-certification) or placed on the list of 'good practice' case study examples on the circular economy (see the website of Ellen MacArthur Foundation: http://www.ellenmacarthurfoundation.org/case_studies), though they are not necessarily following the ideal principles as originally explained. Some of the companies listed, for example Coca-Cola, have indeed taken some steps toward reducing material use in each stage of the packaging chain (materials, design, disposal, recovery and recycling). It has a modest aim of 'reducing 25 per cent of material used by 2020' and 'to improve the overall recyclability of their packs'. Clearly, however, recycling rather than upcycling is still used as the key concept, and the goal of reduction of 25 per cent of material leaves questions about the other 75 per cent. It also makes one wonder about why such reductions cannot be accomplished *before* 2020. Their current re-use is about 7 per cent (http://www.ellenmacarthurfoundation.org/case_studies/coca-cola-enterprises).

Critics have noted that some of these companies improve one small part of their operation without the needed overhaul of the *entire* supply chain, mode of operation, and radical change in product materials. Nevertheless, despite such problems they were able to obtain an expensive certificate or placement on the C2C and circular economy websites. Many critics have pointed out that endless economic growth is simply incompatible with sustainability and social equality, and have pointed out that aspirations of most commercial companies (such as those listed on the Ellen MacArthur website) still tend to be supportive of the endless growth model. Instead, the steady state economy approach has been proposed.

The key parts of the steady state economy are fixed population (at an ecologically sustainable level) and a constant sustainable throughput of resources (Daly 1991; 1996). The steady state economy espouses the vision that the economy is an open subsystem of a finite and non-growing ecosystem, the environment. The economy lives by importing low-entropy matter-energy (raw materials) and exporting high-entropy matter-energy (waste). It is suggested that any subsystem of a finite non-growing system must itself at some point also become non-growing. Additionally, critical authors have emphasized that environmental, social, and economic problems are caused by the growth economy, and that 'growthism' itself is an unsustainable ideology (Washington 2015). 'Growthism', as well as innovation without clear aim, is likely to result in the same effects discussed by McDonough and Braungart in relation to eco-efficiency. By softening the blow of *un*sustainability by resorting to 'eco-friendly' technologies and scientific innovations, we might be discovering that unsustainability can in fact be sustained for very considerable – even though not unlimited – periods of time. In Blühdorn's (2011:44) words:

> It can be maintained if (and as long as) ways can be found to reduce their environmental side effects, that is, the physical referent of social problem perceptions (e.g., by means of technomanagerial fixes or policies of displacement), if (and as long as) there are strategies for managing their social impact, be it reduced or not (e.g., by means of displacement, externalisation, or enhanced security systems), and if (and as long as) social norms and expectations can be adapted in such a way that the social and ecological side effects are no longer perceived as unacceptable.

Thus, optimistic prescriptions and the apparently 'simple and easy' approach need to be treated with caution. Also, without strict measures counteracting population growth, any efforts at innovation in production, including that of circular economy, are likely to fail (Rees 2010). If social and particularly economic equality is taken as *the* central departure point for sustainability and ethics (as it is often formulated in the mainstream sustainability literature), the underlying limits to growth are likely to be forgotten. In their focus on the dynamics of social exploitation and inequality, those who are drawn to the social equality aspects of the mainstream sustainability approach tend to place the exclusive culpability for unsustainability (and unethical consumption) on the neoliberal, industrial or political elites who are reaping the multigenerational benefits of unjust and unsustainable lifestyles. Yet, proponents of social equality, while correct in assuming that unfair distribution of environmental risks and benefits is permitted by fundamentally unsustainable socio-economic relations, tend to ignore another significant dimension of unsustainability – population growth. Many authors think about population not as a global issue, but as an issue that concerns only the increasing numbers of a highly privileged and highly exploitative minority, by which they normally mean the overconsumptive North. One of the persistent claims is that resource use by marginal human communities, those of the 'victimized South', is either 'relatively benign' or 'environmentally innocuous' (Robbins 2012). This position is well illustrated by Fletcher *et al.* (2014), who argue that the focus on overpopulation in the developing world focuses attention away Western consumption; obscures inequality in Western consumption; and ignores the fact that the capitalist system encourages unsustainable overconsumption *everywhere*.

Simultaneously with this blaming the rich (Western) consumers, the questions associated with human population growth are often ignored in politically correct academic circles – perhaps due to the geopolitics and political correctness (Smail 2003; Campbell 2012). Yet, the fact remains that the basic causes of unsustainability lie in the *combined* action of (a) technological advance; (b) population increase; and (c) conventional (but wrong) ideas about the nature of man and his relation to the environment (Bateson 1972). If we assume that social justice concerns are valid (and we want *everybody* in this world to live 'decent' lives), expansion of wealth will necessarily cause greater pressure on the planet (Wijkman and Rockström 2012). Having many children in the poorest countries also further impoverishes people (*The Economist* 2009; 2014). Furthermore, although the rich countries have been responsible for causing issues such as climate change, the poor countries are rapidly 'catching up' as evidenced by the designation 'developing' countries. As Crist and Cafaro (2012:6) summarize it:

> To scrutinize the global North and see only the variable of consumption is to remain blind to that mass that qualifies it. A major factor underlying destructive consumerism is population size: the sheer numbers of consumers around the globe. To propagate the myth that population growth is not itself a problem and to lament, instead, the harmful effects of unsustainable production and consumption bypasses one leading reason that production and consumption are unsustainable.

Another significant issue is the fact that a growing population serves capitalist, industrial, and expansionist interests as population creates a 'demographic dividend' which is good for the growth economy (e.g. Forbes 2009). It is not just defenders of human rights and proponents of the 'every (human) life is sacred' mantra, but also corporate and political elites might see population growth as an opportunity for bigger markets (Blowfield 2013). Thus tackling population growth would go against the grain of capitalist industrialist expansionism and be opposed by the elites on 'humanitarian' grounds (Washington 2015). It is a worrisome trend that academics seem to have bought into this deception. When human populations increase in number, they consume more; when human populations increase their socio-economic level, they consume more, especially more meat (http://www.worldwatch.org/global-meat-production-and-consumption-continue-rise). Thus, unless we assume that poor people will always stay poor, and unless it is assumed that somehow the consumer ideology is going to spontaneously give way to much more ecologically benign practice, the insistence that population is not a problem seems at best naïve. Denying the problem of a growing population – whose appetites, material aspirations, and life expectancy have greatly increased – seems detrimental to the aims of achieving sustainable development in the long term.

Thus, considering the questions of social justice, the need for critically addressing production and consumption systems everywhere appears even more urgent. Without adaptation of production and consumption, which in effect implies radical re-orientation of existing models, population growth threatens to – and already does – exacerbate sustainability challenges globally, and indeed leaves large parts of the human population dispossessed – not just of natural resources for today, but of future prospects.

As the case study below will illustrate, subversion of C2C and circular economy models is a real danger that needs to be considered if C2C and the circular economy are to be useful parts of a steady state economy and tools to reduce the environmental crisis.

The case study

This case study is based on 'Circular Economy in the Cloud', an experimental online course piloted by universities of applied science (vocational schools) in Rotterdam, Utrecht, and The Hague business departments. The course was initiated in September 2014 by the Rotterdam Business School, and the author was a tutor/assessor.

The main objective of this minor course, given between September 2014 and February 2015, was to teach students what the circular economy is, and how small and medium-sized enterprises (SMEs) could make the transition from a linear business model to a circular economy business model. 68 students were initially enrolled in the minor course, with 39 completing it. The course had a strong practical component, which meant that the sponsor company was supposed to implement all or a part of the changes recommended by the students. International knowledge and experience-sharing through The Cloud were seen as being key to the quality of the student deliverables. The students were supposed to improve the ability to combine knowledge, skills, and attitude to show expected behavior when performing a professional task in a European/international business context. Prior to the start of the course, SMEs were contacted by lecturers to ask for their participation. A total of 17 SMEs were selected to participate and students chose which company to work with. Students carried out the follow-up with the selected company. SMEs were willing to participate because they expected to benefit from the practical solutions the teams would offer.

It was assumed that the companies would benefit from relevant information in order to keep up-to-date with the most efficient and effective techniques, like in procurement and inbound logistics. They would be able to select and develop the technologies that would give them competitive advantage, and decide if it is relevant to make some changes in their action plan. The project groups were supposed to make a valuable input into the overall strategic planning for their sponsor company, producing a proposal that would serve as a guideline for the company to take important decisions related to the supply value chain that would allow the company to transit to the circular model. Overall, the aim of the course was to critically consider the aspects of 'added value' to product or service.

Findings: company M

The two teams that the author supervised did their project with a company that makes bridges (company M). Company M was founded in 2012. The student group worked on 'bridge division'. The aim was to advise the company to transit from linear to circular model of production, as well as to help the company gain access to other European countries. The students provided the client a value chain analysis of two of its biggest competitors. Another purpose of the report was to make a comparison between wooden bridges and composite bridges, and provide the client with an analysis with a focus on sustainability.

Students researched the materials used for making bridges and their alternatives, primarily using the sources Gkaidatzis (2014). In their report, they specified that the bridges are manufactured from steel, plastic, resins, and fiber. Most natural fibers have different specifications and functions that highly depend on the plant environment. According to student research, the baste family (hemp, flax and jute) may have specific strength and material properties that compete with glass fiber. This family of natural fibers has a higher elongation-to-break ratio than glass or carbon fibers. This can improve the performance of the composite if used for reinforcement (Gkaidatzis 2014). Based on this information, the students proposed the use of these fibers to their sponsor company.

The group pitched a proposal to their sponsors after four weeks. After evaluating the working processes of company M's competitors, the students reported that the competitors are more mature and have been in business longer. This would be helpful to analyze current practices in the industry. At the end of the project, the company responded that the change of materials for production was not feasible due to financial constraints. The students reported that they had begun to doubt the feasibility of the transition as well as the company's willingness to undertake the necessary steps. In their final report, the obstacles to successful implementation as reported by students included the lack of top manager commitment to the project and the unwillingness of the company to change its business model.

Reflection

Students in some cases were refused information about materials used by the company, or about the whole supply chain or parts of it. Hence it seems the student study was largely unsuccessful. There appears to be a degree of mismatch between expectations of the company and those of the students. There also seemed to be a mismatch between theory and practice in the sample of companies that the student teams approached. The original aim was for student teams to help the company to make a business plan transition from a linear economy model to a circular one. However, subversion of the original aim of the project may be due to a number of factors.

First, the mismatches had to do with the recruitment method, as the companies were told that they would be working with business students who are interested in sustainability. The companies were not explicitly informed about the circular economy model (and did not seem to have a good understanding of what this was). Rather, most companies in the sample asked the students to help them with 'business-as-usual' projects – marketing, branding, finance – assuming that the company was already 'green enough' and that business students could help them to spread their 'green' credentials.

Second, there were a number of practical constraints that companies experienced when examining financial viability and the radical overhaul of established practices within the *entire supply chain* of the company's product or service. Many companies realized halfway through the project that they either could not (or did not want to) undergo the transition away from linear models – because it was seen as impractical, expensive, or altogether impossible (given the nature of their product). Another mismatch observed was between what students learn in macro-economic theory and the application through micro-economic scenarios in small companies. As a result, the students were disappointed regarding the outcome.

Despite these difficulties, it is important not to 'throw the baby out with the bathwater' here. Cradle to Cradle and circular economy frameworks do deserve support, as ideally they go way beyond mainstream sustainability strategies – but they do have a long way to go in practice. It is thus crucial to make a distinction between ideal practice, possible practice, and subverted practice. In the context of this case study, it did not appear that students made a meaningful contribution to the companies, but they did gain critical learning experience. Progress towards workable C2C transitions, however, may not happen unless a number of adjustments are made.

The big challenge is how to find something applicable and practical at BA-level, with enough 'good' companies willing to participate, and how to match the macro-theory and ideals to the actual practice. Following from this, a more successful integration of theory and practice and alignment of expectations should include:

1. A concise summary about the circular economy and the expectations of the student study should be given to the participating companies *before* they agree to participate
2. Another way of approaching the challenge of transition to a circular economy is to embrace economic and social pragmatism. In the context of sustainability, this could mean doubting not only the linear and existing models of production, but also scrutinizing the alternatives and seeing what works best in each case. In this case, the 'best' would imply being workable, feasible, with least impact – even if not a totally closed-loop model. For example, while it might be all but impossible to build a 100 per cent sustainable bridge using organic fibers, a compromise between the use of acceptable, desirable, and perhaps less-desirable materials might need to be made.

Discussion

Despite the difficulties reported, it should be emphasized that the models that support Cradle to *Grave* production are not an alternative, however great the obstacles to circular economy or C2C realization. Good examples of production that eliminates unproductive waste altogether are not hard to find, as they can historically be found everywhere in the form of pre-industrial production systems. Until very recently, shoppers took their own glass bottles to be refilled at the shops (or the proverbial milkman distributed those same washed bottles by horse and cart). In India, the author has witnessed a production of clay cups created from the mud at hand, filled with tea, and smashed back into the ground to form a new material for a new cup instantaneously. The movement of the wrist used for spinning the clay pot platform was no more labor-intensive or strenuous than that of a barman serving drinks.

This does not mean that producers and consumers should revert back to pre-industrial lifestyles, nor that producers should sell 'retrogressive' design products. Intelligent marketing has been known for generations to sell old ideas as new (Blowfield 2013). Besides, many truly innovative technologies – particularly in the area of solar and wind energy – have indeed offered attractive and forward designs. For example, solar power has spread to many applications in the past decades, from space to military technology, to multiple civilian appliances, to transport and consumer electronics. Solar power used for military drones and space technology means economic and practical benefits as the electrically powered drones (or unmanned aerial vehicles) or shuttles do not have to transport fuel or carry recharging equipment. To take the example of drones, these small airplanes can survey pipelines and power cables; perform aerial filming, including detection of poachers in protected conservation areas; monitor fires; and assist in search-and-rescue operations. Other applications includes a Sunkseeker solar airplane, designed by Solar Flight. At the moment of writing, a solar airplane called Solar Impulse is making its way around the world (http://www.solarimpulse.com/).

More generally, one does not even have to admit that humanity made a mistake 200 years ago during the intense love affair with the 'progress' engendered by the industrial revolution, but just move on in the direction of the new ecologically benign revolution. After all, many corporate leaders are known for their optimism, and their ability to turn consumers' non-existent needs into persistent desires. If one such desire is for a sustainable future, perhaps the power of corporate leaders to transform the world could indeed be used for a more long-term progress. What is 200 years in the course of the human history of production? It is time to go back to the 'tried and true' circular systems our ancestors understood.

Conclusion

Based on this reflection, we can recommend that in the teaching of the circular economy one should be aware of the pitfalls and risks, such as the case of subversion of good intentions (and greenwashing). To be meaningful, 'sustainable business' must be based on an understanding of the environmental crisis we face, and the need to change the consumer throwaway culture and vastly reduce the throughput of materials. The circular approach is potentially highly useful within a steady state economy – provided it remains true to the original idea and is not subverted to the cause of continuing an unsustainable, business-as-usual model.

References

Bateson, G. (1972) 'The Roots of Ecological Crises'. In G. Bateson (ed.), *From Steps to an Ecology of the Mind*, Chicago: University of Chicago Press, pp. 494–499.

Blowfield, M. (2013) *Business and Sustainability*. Oxford: Oxford University Press.

Blühdorn, I. (2011) 'The Politics of Unsustainability: COP15, Post-Ecologism, and the Ecological Paradox'. *Organization Environment*, 24(1): 34–53.

Brennan, G., Tennant, M., and Blomsma, F. (2015) 'Business and Production Solutions: Closing the Loop'. In H. Kopnina and E. Shoreman-Ouimet (eds), *Sustainability: Key Issues*. New York: Routledge, pp. 219–240.

C2C (n.d.) Get-Certified Product-Certification. See: c2ccertified.org/get-certified/product-certification

Campbell, M. (2012) 'Why the Silence on Population?' In P. Cafaro and E. Crist (eds). *Life on the Brink: Environmentalists Confront Overpopulation*. Athens: University of Georgia Press, pp. 41–56.

Coca Cola (n.d.) Case Studies. See: http://www.ellenmacarthurfoundation.org/case_studies/coca-cola-enterprises

Crist, E. (2012) 'Abundant Earth and Population'. In P. Cafaro and E. Crist (eds), *Life on the Brink: Environmentalists Confront Overpopulation*. Athens: University of Georgia Press, pp. 141–153.

Crist, E. and Cafaro, P. (2012) 'Human Population Growth as If the Rest of Life Mattered'. In P. Cafaro and E. Crist (eds). *Life on the Brink: Environmentalists Confront Overpopulation*. Athens: University of Georgia Press, pp. 3–15.

Daly, H. (1991) *Steady State Economics*. Washington, DC: Island Press.

Daly, H. (1996) *Beyond Growth*. Boston, Beacon Press.

Diesendorf, M. (2014) *Sustainable Energy Solutions for Climate Change*. London: Earthscan.

Dietz, R. and O'Neill, D. (2013) *Enough is Enough: Building a Sustainable Economy in a World of Finite Resources*. New York: Berrett-Koeler Publishers.

The Economist (2009) 'The Baby Bonanza: Is Africa an Exception to the Rule That Countries Reap a "Demographic Dividend" as They Grow Richer?' See http://www.economist.com/node/14302837

The Economist (2014) 'Fertility Treatment: Birth Rates Are Not Falling in Africa as Fast as They Did in Asia. More Contraception Would Help'. See: http://www.economist.com/news/leaders/21598648-birth-rates-are-not-falling-africa-fast-they-did-asia-more-contraception-would

Ellen MacArthur Foundation (n.d.) See: http://www.ellenmacarthurfoundation.org/

Fletcher, R., Breitlin, J., and Puleo, V. (2014) 'Barbarian Hordes: The Overpopulation Scapegoat in International Development Discourse'. *Third World Quarterly*, 35(7): 1195–1215.

Forbes (2009) 'You Worry. You Shouldn't. Part 1: Overpopulation and Resource Exhaustion'. See: http://www.forbes.com/sites/artcarden/2012/06/15/you-worry-you-shouldnt-part-1-overpopulation-and-resource-exhaustion/

Foster, J. (2014) 'After Sustainability: Life Beyond the End of Pretending?' (Blog post). See http://www.routledge.com/sustainability/articles/after_sustainability_life_beyond_the_end_of_pretending

Gkaidatzis, R. (2014) *Bio Based FRP Structures*. Master Graduation Thesis, Delft University of Technology.

Huckle, J. (2012) 'Even More Sense and Sustainability: A Review Essay. Sense and Sustainability: Educating for a Circular Economy'. *Environmental Education Research*, 18(6): 845-858. See: http://john.huckle.org.uk/download/2954/EER2012MSandS.pdf

Kopnina, H. (2012) 'Education for Sustainable Development (ESD): The Turn Away from 'Environment' in Environmental Education?' *Environmental Education Research*, 18(5): 699–717.

Kopnina, H. (2013a) 'Schooling the World: Exploring the Critical Course on Sustainable Development through an Anthropological Lens'. *International Journal of Educational Research*, 62: 220–228.

Kopnina, H. (2013b) 'Evaluating Education for Sustainable Development (ESD): Using Ecocentric and Anthropocentric Attitudes toward the Sustainable Development (EAATSD) scale'. *Environment, Development and Sustainability*, 15(3): 607–623.

Kopnina, H. (2013c) 'An Exploratory Case Study of Dutch Children's Attitudes towards Consumption: Implications for Environmental Education'. *Journal of Environmental Education*, 44(2): 128–144.

McDonough, W. and Braungart, M. (2002) *Cradle to Cradle: Remaking the Way We Make Things*. New York: North Point Press.

Rees, W. (2009) 'The Ecological Crisis and Self-Delusion: Implications for the Building Sector'. *Building Research and Information*, 37(3): 300–311.

Rees, W. (2010) 'What's blocking sustainability? Human nature, cognition, and denial'. *Sustainability: Science, Practice, & Policy*, 6(2):13–25.

Rees, W. (2012) 'On the Use and Misuse of the Concept of Sustainability: Including Population and Resource Macro-Balancing in the Sustainability Dialog'. A paper for the 8th International Conference on Environmental, Cultural, Economic, and Social Sustainability, University of British Columbia, Vancouver, Canada. See: http://www.environicfoundation.org/GSS/recognition/On%20the%20Use%20and%20Misuse%20of%20the%20Concept%20of%20Sustainability-Vancouver2012%20(1).pdf

Robbins, P. (2012) *Political Ecology: A Critical Introduction*, 2nd ed. Malden, MA: Wiley & Sons.

Shoreman-Ouimet, E. and Kopnina, H. (2016) *Conservation and Culture: Beyond Anthropocentrism*. New York: Routledge/Earthscan.

Smail, K. (2003) 'Remembering Malthus III: Implementing a Global Population Reduction'. *American Journal of Physical Anthropology*, 123(2): 295–300.

Washington, H. (2015) *Demystifying Sustainability: Towards Real Solutions*. London: Routledge.

Webster, K. (2007) 'Hidden Sources: Understanding Natural Systems Is the Key to an Evolving and Aspirational ESD'. *Journal of Education for Sustainable Development*, 1(1): 37–43.

Wijkman, A. and Rockström, J. (2012) *Bankrupting Nature: Denying Our Planetary Boundaries*. New York: Routledge.

World Watch Institute. (n.d.) 'Global Meat Production and Consumption Continue to Rise.' http://www.worldwatch.org/global-meat-production-and-consumption-continue-rise

7

PEAK MINING

Stepping down from high resource use

Simon Michaux
UNIVERSITY OF LIEGE

Introduction

Society is in the throes of a fundamental transformation. We are seeing the initial reactions to the shift in fundamentals that support our society. It could be argued that what we are seeing is merely another cycle. A case can be made to show that the supporting raw materials that make the modern world possible are now depleting and will soon not be able to meet the required demand. This has serious implications for the continued method of operation of our civilisation at a fundamental level (Diamond 2005).

Mining provides a fundamental support for our industrial civilisation

Everything we have built as a society has been dependent on non-renewable natural resources. Raw metals supply our industrial manufacture. Without this, real work and tangible goods cannot be produced. Metals support our current civilisation and our industrial technology in a similar fashion to food, water and energy. As this is a finite planet, there will come a point when these natural resources will deplete. Rates of production will decrease as humanity is forced to extract the low-quality reserves that require more energy to exploit. There is now data available to show that almost all of our natural resources have either already peaked in rates of extraction, or soon will.

Consumption of natural resource is increasing exponentially

While all our natural non-renewable resources are depleting, demand for manufactured goods of all kinds is exponentially increasing. Each of the human-managed systems on the planet follow this profile (Bartlett 1994; 1996). The problem with this is that the first half of the resources is consumed over a comparatively long time, while the last half is consumed in a very short time. By the time it is recognised that there is a serious supply problem, there is very little time to respond effectively. Our culture's fundamental belief that there are no limits and growth is good seems to be based on the belief that all resources are infinite. As this is a finite planet, and our exploitation of these natural resources is exponential in form, there will come a point where resource scarcity will become a reality. As we also seem incapable of understanding the long-term consequences of our actions, humanity has developed some very shortsighted methods of managing our natural resources.

We are addicted to the manufactured short-term use of material goods (Hamilton and Denniss 2005). Not only does this deplete our resources inefficiently, it generates environmental pollution and degrades the planet's ecosystems. We are a wasteful society that must change the way we think and how we manage our environment. The development of industrialisation has required the ever-increasing demand of consumption of metal resources (Figure 7.1).

Figure 7.1 shows another exponential consumption profile of a finite natural resource. Copper annual global demand in 2010 was 17 million tonnes, which at an ore grade of 0.5 per cent (global average for 2010) represents 3.4 billion tonnes of rock mined. It is projected that, by the year 2100, annual copper demand will be 100 million tonnes. I have calculated that if the average copper ore grade stayed at 0.5 per cent, this would represent 20 billion tonnes of rock mined. If average ore grade dropped to 0.2 per cent, this would represent 50 billion tonnes of rock mined. Next-generation mine feasibility studies are already considering copper

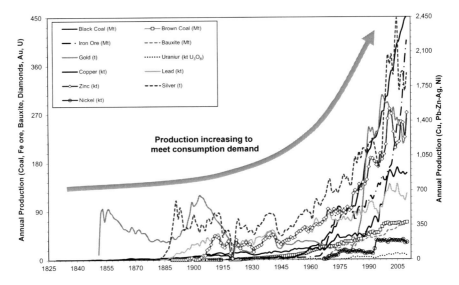

FIGURE 7.1 Production and consumption of metals has increased (Mudd 2009)

grade cut-offs at 0.1 per cent. There will come a point where our wants and desires will be overrun by harsh reality. The cost of processing and storing the waste will outweigh the value of the extracted target metal.

Peak mining

The Australian mining boom has clearly moved into a contraction cycle. The mining industry has seen mass layoffs and large operation shutdowns, resulting in troubled economic predictions for the Australian economy. Demand for iron ore and coal in particular has dropped. Economies of scale have been used to mine and process more ore to meet demand targets. This can be shown across the mining industry, where the Productivity Index for mining fell by 48 per cent between 2001 and 2010 (ABARES 2011). This means it now takes 48 per cent more work to extract the same unit of metal from the ground compared to the year 2000–01. Mining is no longer the financial bonanza it used to be. There are a number of technical reasons for this, which have exacerbated other global-scale issues, which could be seen as a marker for fundamental change in how our industrial sector functions. These are (Michaux 2014):

- Decreasing grade
- Increasing rock hardness
- Higher strip ratio
- Increase in penalty elements
- Increase in required energy vs. peak energy production
- Decreasing grind size
- Increase in required potable water
- Much greater environmental impact (Unger et al. 2015).

The primary driver of the trend shown in Figure 7.2 is lowering grade of deposits. All of the high-grade, easy-to-work and easy-to-access deposits have been mined out first, leaving the difficult low-grade deposits in increasingly remote and difficult locations (Giuro et al. 2010). Figure 7.2 shows the decrease in ore grade of several minerals over the last 150 years or so, as well as the decrease in production of metal.

Rates of mining have decreased. A case can be made that globally, peak mining has already happened – sometime in the early 1990s. The only region left on the planet that is increasing rates of mining is China (ICMM 2012). What has facilitated this inefficient and wasteful state of affairs is our sources of energy. Oil, coal and gas have accounted for the vast amount of industrial development over the last 160 years. Rates of metal extraction through mining will perforce peak and decline (Frimmel and Muller 2011; Foran and Poldy 2002). It is postulated that insecurity in energy reserves will be the cause when this happens.

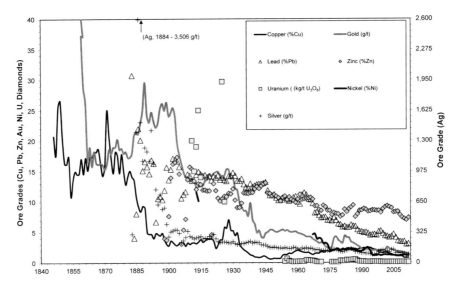

FIGURE 7.2   Grade of mined minerals has been decreasing (Mudd 2009)

Energy is the defining resource

Energy is the decisively significant resource for industrialisation, as it has allowed us to empower technology at ever increasing economies of scale. This has allowed us to extract ever lower-quality resources, which in turn has delayed the need for development or sustainable alternatives. The majority of our energy consumption has come from the nonrenewable resources of oil, gas and coal.

Peak Oil

Currently, we are a petroleum-based society (Ruppert 2004; Martenson 2011; Morse and Jaffe 2001). Petroleum products and petrochemicals derived from oil provide goods and services for most of the vital requirements of our industrial civilisation. Everything from food production to plastics manufacture is dependent on oil in some form (there are some synthetic alternatives but they are costly and not as effective as natural crude oil as a raw feed product). When crude oil was first discovered and production started in the late 1880s, extraction was much easier than it is now. All that was required was to drill to a depth as shallow as 70 metres (400 metres was about standard for the time), and light, sweet crude oil would gush out under pressure. All that was required was to capture the oil and store it. Very little refining was needed to produce usable petroleum products (Heinberg 2003; Hughes 2013).

Now, most conventional crude oil is extracted from under the ocean, which has required engineering technology at the very limits of what humanity has been capable of. As time has passed, the size of these deep-water oil rigs has increased in scale and expense. Increasingly, conventional sources of crude oil have been difficult to discover and exploit. The easy-to-get, -extract and -process deposits have all been discovered and exploited. Most oil discovered was mapped out several decades ago, with its peak in rate of discovery in the 1960s (Morse and Jaffe 2001). Conventional peak crude oil production is now understood to have happened in 2006, as defined by the International Energy Agency (IEA 2014; Staniford 2010). It is to be recognized that this does not mean we have run out of oil. Peak oil production is the *peak rate of production*. Approximately half of total oil reserves are still in the ground, but now oil takes more time and effort to extract (IEA 2014).

As conventional oil has peaked and plateaued in rates of production, demand has continued to grow in line with a growing population and expanding technological complexity. To make up the supply gap to meet the required oil demand, unconventional sources of oil are now being extracted. One example of this is tar sands in Alberta, Canada. The oil is coated and embedded in the sands. Large quantities of natural gas are used to generate steam, which is used to separate the oil from the sand. This is an expensive method that requires a massive process plant (Goodman and Rowan 2014). The environmental fallout of tar sands mining is considerable and far-reaching (Mech 2011). Shale oil is an unconventional oil produced from oil shale rock fragments by pyrolysis, hydrogenation or thermal dissolution (Hughes 2013), where the refined products can be used for the same purposes as those derived from crude oil. The Energy Watch Group report (Zittel *et al.* 2013) shows total oil production by region, using data to the year 2012, with future projections based on existing resource data and exploration trends. Peak oil production (conventional and unconventional) is projected to have happened around the year 2012.

This is supported by US petroleum imports, which show a sharp contraction of petroleum products in the US economy from mid-2006 (EIA 2015a). Also, US retail gas sales from refineries have contracted sharply from August 2006 (EIA 2015b). The United States was the largest economy on the planet, accounting for approximately 20–25 per cent of global oil consumption (Morse and Jaffe 2001). A significant contraction in the consumption of oil in the largest oil consumer can be used as a temporal marker to demonstrate that we have indeed passed peak total oil, and that our industrial civilisation is now coming down the declining side of the peak. Peak oil has come and gone. Australia has only 3 days of petroleum products in storage and is dependent on just-in-time supply from Singapore (Blackburn 2013). As Australia does not refine its own petroleum products, a peak and decline in supply would have very serious implications very quickly.

Peak gas

Gas as a commodity is important to society's industrialisation. As industrial sites require large quantities of power, a gas-fired power station is often installed. Acquiring data for gas production has been difficult but it has been argued that conventional production of natural gas peaked in the year 2011 (Hughes 2013). To meet industrial demand, unconventional sources of gas like 'fracking' (hydraulic fracturing) Coal Seam Gas (CSG) and shale seam gas have been developed. Unconventional gas supply has been touted as a replacement for conventional sources of gas (Hughes 2013). Fracking is an extraction technique in which rock is fractured by a hydraulically pressurized liquid made of water, sand and chemicals. When the hydraulic pressure is removed from the well, small grains of hydraulic fracturing 'proppants' (a solid granular material, either sand or aluminium oxide) hold the fractures open. Gas then bubbles out of the fractured rock and up to the well rig. Production from shale gas 'fracked' wells typically declines 80 to 95 per cent in the *first 36 months* of operation, which is much less productive than conventional gas wells (which typically last 10–15 years). For the US shale gas industry to maintain 2013 production rates, it needs to drill approximately 7200 new wells *each year*. Industry insiders have referred to this requirement as 'the treadmill to hell'. This engineering limitation means that fracking is not as beneficial as suggested by the gas industry and will not be able to meet future requirements of gas demand.

There are significant concerns associated with hydraulic fracturing, including the potential to contaminate potable water sources (Lowe 2013), concerns such as the contamination of artesian aquifers from the chemicals added to fracking fluid, as well as the contamination of water supplies from fugitive gas after fracking. Large amounts of saline water are left on the surface, where it has the potential to pollute arable land. CSG projects in Australia have been rushed through the legislative feasibility system and almost all of them were accepted. If existing due process was properly followed, then the majority of CSG projects should have been rejected, due to the unknown nature of the environmental fallout of this technology (Michelmore and Agius 2013). Concerns of the local people are the loss of drinking water and environmental pollution in their regions. Global peak total gas production is projected to be approximately in the year 2018 (Zittel *et al.* 2013). The true answer may well be three years away.

Peak coal

Coal is another energy resource that both our domestic power grid and industrial capability depends upon. In many areas in the world, the domestic power grid that supplies electricity is dependent on coal. Peak global coal production is projected to happen in approximately the year 2020 (Zittel *et al.* 2013).

Peak total energy

Each energy source often serves different purposes, so one resource cannot necessarily directly replace another (Heinberg 2011). For the purposes of comparison, though, all energy sources discussed have been put onto one graph, where each energy source is quantified using million tonnes of oil equivalent (Zittel *et al.* 2013), where all known energy resources are used. Summing all fossil fuels and nuclear uranium fuel together shows total quantity of energy is projected to peak sometime between 2015 and 2020 (Zittel et al. 2013).

As energy is directly correlated with the ability to do physical work, this means that industrialisation in a global context will soon start to contract in activity as opposed to continuing to grow (as per current corporate objectives). Thus, the end of growth-based economics would be observed on a global scale for the first time since the beginning of the industrial revolution.

Each energy source supports a different part of our industrialisation. To meet the difficult challenge of energy depletion and to engineer and produce an alternative system will take time. To replace the petroleum product system that supports our oil-dependent economy currently would take 20 years at a comfortable pace in any of the Western, developed economies (once a viable one has been presented) (Hirsch et al. 2005). It would take 10 years to replace petroleum products at the rate of industrialisation seen in World War II in the United States (Hirsch et al. 2005). The heavy energy consumption that some forms of industrialization require, like aluminum smelting, is dependent on gas. Replacing gas as an energy source would be easier than oil, as there is less complexity in the distribution network. That being stated, the scale of engineering required would have a similar time frame to deploy. As the projected date for peak total energy is only a few years away, the implications of Figure 7.3 are quite serious. Even if the projection were incorrect by 10 years, our industrial society would still be faced with an unprecedented challenge.

Change is upon us

When will things change and society be forced to act? A compelling case can be made that the change is already happening. The data suggests that the year 2005 (a few years before the GFC) was decisive. Figure 7.3 shows metal prices blowing out in the year 2005.

The data shown in Figure 7.3 is the international metal price as released by the Australian Bureau of Statistics (ABARES 2011), adjusted where the price of each of these metals has been indexed to the number 100 in the year 2000–2001. The price of metals was relatively stable for the years 1990–2005. During 2005, prices doubled and tripled in magnitude in a structurally different signature. The GFC was in 2008, which can be seen on this graph. Years after this, the same volatility seen prior to 2008 can be observed. This means that, whatever the underlying cause to this price volatility, a major global economic correction did not resolve the structural issues. The year 2005 was also when the Energy Index and the Metal Index, as used by the World Bank to monitor the global economy, structurally changed their behaviour. Prior to the year 2000, these indices showed fundamentally different profiles. After the year 2000 they converged for the first time, and in 2005, they sharply increased.

Figure 7.3 demonstrates that arguably a fundamental structural change in both our real economy and in the supporting industrial manufacturing sector occurred

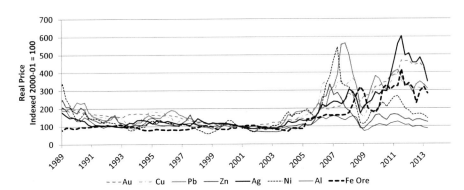

FIGURE 7.3 International market metal prices became volatile in 2005 (graph based on public domain data from ABARES 2011)

in the year 2005. To date, that change is still in progress and has not been resolved. We are 10 years into an era of *industrial transformation*. The GFC was a symptom, not a cause, and the underlying issues are still in play. This implies that a much worse correction is inevitable when those underlying issues are forced into mainstream consciousness.

Limits to growth

In 1972, a global think tank called the Club of Rome, which examines a variety of international political issues, released its findings from a four-year study of the trends in our society at the time (Meadows *et al.* 1972). This was a systems-based approach that used the following as inputs to model past and future trends (Table 7.1).

TABLE 7.1 *Limits to Growth* study modelling approach

Modelled Structural Problem	Modelled Applied Solution
• Natural resources • Food production • Human population • Generated pollution • Industrial output per capita	• 'unlimited' resources • pollution controls • increased agricultural productivity • 'perfect' birth control

In addition to this, several alternative scenarios were modelled, based around radical change applied to some of the system inputs. The conclusions of the study were as follows:

- The existing trends resulted in the complete depletion of natural resources, which seriously hampered fundamental reform.
- The basic behaviour model of the world system is exponential growth of population and capital followed by collapse.

- Application of technology to the apparent problem of resource depletion or pollution or food shortages has no impact on the essential problem of exponential growth.
- Population crisis and crash could be postponed, but not indefinitely.

Turner (2008) from the CSIRO examined the conclusions put forward by the original study in the context of data collected for the 30 years after the 1972 report was released. This showed that for 30 years, world data has tracked close to the original Limits to Growth models. These seem to be symptoms of a world in 'overshoot' (Catton 1982), where we are drawing on the world's resources faster than they can be restored, and we are releasing wastes and pollutants faster than the Earth can absorb them or render them harmless (see Washington in this volume). It would seem they are leading us toward global environmental and economic collapse.

Evolution of human civilisation

Every non-renewable natural resource we depend upon is now depleting to the point of peak extraction, or will do so soon. Industrial systems that are heavily dependent on energy reserves and metal resources are now at serious risk of collapse as production of those raw materials will soon not be able to meet demand. All living systems on the planet are in serious stress and are also being heavily degraded (MEA 2005). Natural ecosystems of all kinds are being depleted in the name of uncontrolled economic development. The planet's climate is also undergoing rapid change, while entire regions of the planet are heavily polluted. As the Earth's natural bio systems are being devastated by human industrialisation, the planet has been forced to absorb the environmental fallout while economic targets have been pursued. Thus, economic performance has been seen as important, and environmental pollution has been ignored. While humanity has been able to do this to date, there will soon come a time when planetary environmental degradation will mean that industrialisation will not be feasible, therefore neither will our global society or the global economy.

As our economic and financial systems are volatile and virtual in form (with a foundation of consumer confidence and administered as electronic data as opposed to being based on physical assets), the economic system would be the first system put under functional stress in a fashion that would impact the industrial society to operate normally. Our financial institutions and nation state economies are saturated with debt (US Debt Clock 2015) and are not in a position to engage in industrial reform. A fundamental problem is the exponential growth of the human population, in conjunction with industrial technological development consuming more resources per capita as time progresses. All of the activities that describe human development can be modelled using an exponential function. As this is a finite planet, there will come a point where resource scarcity will override economic development. We are reaching such a point, or it's possible we may have *passed it already*.

The fundamental challenge that faces humanity is a choice between our consciousness and our ability to learn from our mistakes, or our cultural conditioning from our past. Are we driven to consume everything in our path? Or can our intelligence and understanding help us evolve to become a respectfully sustainable society? If we wish to take our place on this planet as a genuinely sustainable species, 'we the people' have to decide what kind of world we wish to live in. This choice is now upon us. Peak mining is a symptom of an unsustainable worldview, ethics and a 'shop till you drop' consumer culture (pushed along by massive advertising spending) (see Assadourian in this volume). The limits of the Earth are becoming more apparent – and peak mining and energy demonstrate this as well as other indicators such as an unsustainable ecological footprint. In terms of a steady state economy, Daly (1991) made it clear that a key aspect was low, sustainable resource use. Peak mining shows the essential need for such a commitment, and also shows us that low resource use is not just a good idea philosophically and ethically (which it is), it is essential for very *practical* reasons. The world is finite, so endless physical use of non-renewable resources cannot work. Our culture needs to accept that reality, and evolve and transform.

References

ABARES (2011) 'Australian Mineral Statistics ABS 1350.0 Financial Markets – Long term. See: http://www.abs.gov.au/AUSSTATS/abs@.nsf/DetailsPage/1350.0Jul%202012?OpenDocument

Bartlett, A. (1994) 'Reflections of Sustainability, Population Growth and the Environment', *Population & Environment*, Vol. 16, No. 1, pp 5–35.

Bartlett, A. (1996) 'The Exponential Function, XI: The New Flat Earth Society', *The Physics Teacher*, Vol. 34, pp 342–343.

Blackburn, J. (2013) 'Australia's Liquid Fuel Security', Report for NMRA Motoring and Services (NRMA). See: http://www.mynrma.com.au/media/Fuel_Security_Report.pdf

Catton, W. (1982) *Overshoot: The Ecological Basis of Revolutionary Change*, Champaign, IL: University of Illinois Press.

Daly, H.E. (1991) *Steady-State Economics: Second Edition with New Essays*, Washington, DC: Island Press.

Diamond, J. (2005) *Collapse: How Societies Choose to Fail or Survive*, Australia: Penguin Group.

EIA (US Energy Information Administration) (2015a) 'Weekly US Net Imports of Crude Oil and Petroleum Products'. See: http://www.eia.gov/dnav/pet/hist/LeafHandler.ashx?n=PET&s=WTTNTUS2&f=W

EIA (2015b) 'US Total Gasoline Retail Sales by Refiners' . See: http://www.eia.gov/dnav/pet/hist/LeafHandler.ashx?n=PET&s=A103600001&f=M

Foran, B. and Poldy, F. (2002) 'Future Dilemmas: Options to 2050 for Australia's Population, Technology, Resources and Environment', CSIRO (Commonwealth Scientific and Industrial Research Organisation) Sustainable Ecosystems, Working paper series 02/01. See: http://resourcelists.lib.deakin.edu.au/items/4D882196-5FF1-8E33-BC50-08D1F1D9900F.html

Frimmel, H. and Muller, J. (2011) 'Estimates of Mineral Resources Availability – How Reliable Are They?', *Akad. Geowiss. Geotechn., Veröffentl.*, Vol. 28, pp. 39–62.

Giuro, D., Prior, T., Mudd, G., Mason, L., and Behrisch, J. (2010) 'Peak Minerals in Australia: A Review of Changing Impacts and Benefits', Cluster Research Report 1.2, Institute of Sustainable Futures, Sydney University and Department of Civil Engineering Monash University, CSIRO. See: http://www.researchgate.net/publication/241406336_Peak_Minerals_in_Australia_A_review_of_changing_impacts_and_benefits

Goodman, I. and Rowan, B. (2014) 'Economics of Transporting and Processing Tar Sands Crudes in Quebec', Goodman Group Ltd. in Collaboration with Équiterre and Greenpeace Canada. See: http://www.greenpeace.org/canada/Global/canada/report/2014/06/Goodman%20report.pdf

Hamilton, C. and Denniss, R. (2005) *Affluenza*, Australia: Allen & Unwin.

Heinberg, R. (2003) *The Party's Over: Oil, War, and the Fate of Industrial Society*, Canada: New Society Publishers.

Heinberg, R. (2011) *The End of Growth – Adapting to Our New Economic Reality*, Canada: New Society Publishers.

Heinberg, R. (2013) *Snake Oil – How Fracking's False Promise of Plenty Imperils Our Future*, USA: Post Carbon Institute.

Hirsch, R., Bezdek, R., and Wending, R. (2005) *Peaking of World Oil Production: Impacts, Mitigation & Risk Management*, US Department of Agriculture Report. See: http://www.netl.doe.gov/publications/others/pdf/oil_peaking_netl.pdf

Hughes, D. (2013) *Drill, Baby, Drill – Can Unconventional Fuels Usher in a New Era of Energy Abundance?*, Post Carbon Institute Report. See: http://www.netl.doe.gov/publications/others/pdf/oil_peaking_netl.pdf

ICMM (International Council on Mining and Metals) (2012) 'Trends in the Mining and Metals Industry – Mining's Contribution to Sustainable Development'. See: http://www.icmm.com/document/4441

IEA (International Energy Agency) (2014) *World Energy Outlook 2014*. See: http://www.worldenergyoutlook.org/publications/weo-2014/

Lowe, D. (2013) 'Fractured Country – An Unconventional Invasion: Lock the Gate Alliance'. See: http://www.lockthegate.org.au/films

Martenson, C. (2011) *The Crash Course: The Unsustainable Future Of Our Economy, Energy, And Environment*, New Jersey: Wiley and Sons.

MEA (Millennium Ecosystem Assessment) (2005) *Ecosystems and Human Well-Being: Opportunities and Challenges for Business and Industry*. See: http://www.millenniumassessment.org/documents/document.353.aspx.pdf

Meadows, D., Meadows, G., Randers, J., and Behrens III, W. (1972) *The Limits to Growth*, New York: Universe Books.

Mech, M. (2011) *Comprehensive Guide to Alberta Tar Sands – Understanding the Environmental and Human Impacts, Export Implications, and Political, Economic, and Industry Influences*, Global Oil Watch Report. See: http://tarsandsoilmobile.com/wp-content/uploads/2013/09/A-Comprehensive-Guide-to-the-Alberta-Oil-Sands-may-2011.pdf

Michaux, S. (2014) 'The Coming Radical Change in Mining Practice', in Goldie, J. (ed), *Sustainable Futures – Linking Population, Resources and the Environment*, Canberra: CSIRO Publishing, pp. 73–84.

Michelmore, K. and Agius, C. (2013) 'Critical Information Missing from LNG Approvals', *ABC News*, 1 April. See: http://www.abc.net.au/news/2013-04-01/key-information-missing-from-lng-approvals/4603026

Morse, E. and Jaffe, A. (2001) *Strategic Energy Policy – Challenges for the 21st Century*, A Report of an Independent Task Force Cosponsored by the James A Baker III Institute and the Council of Foreign Relations. See: http://www.cfr.org/energy-policy/strategic-energy-policy-challenges-21st-century/p3942

Mudd, G. (2007/2009) *The Sustainability of Mining in Australia – Key Production Trends and Their Environmental Implications for the Future*, Report for the Department of Civil Engineering, Monash University and the Mineral Policy Institute (revised 2009). See: http://users.monash.edu.au/~gmudd/files/SustMining-Aust-Report-2009-Master.pdf

Ruppert, M. (2004) *Crossing the Rubicon – the Decline of the American Empire at the End of the Age Of Oil*, Canada: New Society Publications.

Staniford, S. (2010) 'IEA Acknowledges Peak Oil'. See: http://www.resilience.org/stories/2010-11-11/iea-acknowledges-peak-oil

Turner, G. (2008) 'A Comparison of *The Limits to Growth* with Thirty Years of Reality'. Socio-Economics and the Environment in Discussion (SEED), CSIRO Working Paper Series. See: http://www.sciencedirect.com/science/article/pii/S0959378008000435

Unger, C., Lechner, A., Kenway, J., Glenn, V., and Walton, A. (2015) 'A Jurisdictional Maturity Model for Risk Management, Accountability and Continual Improvement of Abandoned Mine Remediation Programs', *Resources Policy*, Vol. 43, pp. 1–10.

US Debt Clock (2015) See: http://usdebtclock.org/world-debt-clock.html

Zittel, W., Zerhusen, J., Zerta, M., and Arnold, N. (2013) *Fossil and Nuclear Fuels – The Supply Outlook*, Energy Watch Group Report. See: http://energywatchgroup.org/wp-content/uploads/2014/02/EWG update2013_short_18_03_2013.pdf

SECTION 3
Key aspects of a steady state economy

8

WHAT IS THE STEADY STATE ECONOMY?

James Magnus-Johnston

CANADIAN MENNONITE UNIVERSITY AND CASSE CANADA

As we witness the declining health of the planet and worsening social inequality, there is considerable skepticism that economic growth in high-income countries will continue to transform lives for the better or deliver modest social gains like a reduction in poverty. Meanwhile, the singular pursuit of economic growth continues to exacerbate threats to human life, including climate disruption, mass extinction, and other symptoms of decline in the planet's carrying capacity. We are facing a choice: reduce the scale of economic activity or risk irreversible ecological damage and unimaginable future costs. How can societies organize their economic affairs with the goal of improving well-being and restoring the health of the planet?

The two sides of the growth debate

The answer you get depends on who you ask.[1] The conventional neoclassical economist would be inclined to tell you that there have always been measurable efficiency, income, and quality of life improvements under conditions of economic growth. If the economy continues to grow, so their theory goes, ecological limits will be overcome with technological solutions and a structural shift towards a post-industrial knowledge economy.[2] In economic jargon, this ideal trajectory is called 'decoupling growth from material input' or 'dematerialization,' as each unit of GDP requires fewer and fewer material inputs. Some theorists, such as Voluntary Simplicity proponent Samuel Alexander, call this view 'techno-optimism,' and this issue remains the crux of the growth debate (Alexander 2014).

Many other economists and an increasing number of thinkers across the arts and sciences argue that economic growth is the proverbial 'elephant in the room'. The economy's aggregate material footprint, especially in high-income regions, continues to climb despite technological innovation, efficiency gains, and structural economic changes, and marches in lockstep with growth in GDP. Moreover, growth doesn't necessarily improve well-being, and the gains aren't shared equitably with those who could benefit from them the most, especially in the world's poorest regions. This in turn means that we should do what many economists would consider the unthinkable: actually produce and consume less, strive for a more fulfilling and less materialistic life, and tailor policies to address specific ecological, social, and financial challenges. This scenario would require that we foster social and technological innovation without growth, and transition to a steady state economy (SSE).

What is growth?

Before we define a steady state economy in more detail, we should put to rest any confusion about what is meant by 'growth'. The rhetoric of growth is everywhere in our news and politics, and has many positive associations, like the growth of a garden or that of a young child. Constant and unyielding growth beyond sufficiency, however, bears negative associations with cancer, or with indulgent obesity. When economists refer to *economic* growth, we are referring to an increase in the production and consumption of goods and services (as measured by GDP), resulting in the quantitative material expansion of the economy. Growth, as defined by Daly and Farley (2004, p. 28) in *Ecological Economics*, is:

> an increase in throughput, which is the flow of natural resources from the environment, through the economy, and back to the environment as waste. It is a quantitative increase in the physical dimensions of the economy or of the waste stream produced by the economy. This kind of growth, of course, cannot continue indefinitely, as the Earth and its resources are not infinite. While growth must end, this in no way implies an end to development, which we define as qualitative change, realization of potential, evolution toward an improved but not larger structure or system.

The perspective that GDP reflects physical economic expansion is contentious, but empirically sound. The only time the world has seen an aggregate reduction in material economic scale was during periods of economic upheaval, such as after the collapse of the Soviet Union or very briefly following the World Wars (Krausmann *et al.* 2009). Since GDP reflects rates of production and consumption, steady state theorists largely accept that GDP is a suitable analogue for physical economic growth (Czech 2008). To put the point succinctly, even financiers and software engineers have to eat, wear clothes, and use transportation.

Environmental impact is often expressed in terms of the well-known formula I=PAT (Impact=Population x Affluence x Technology), which draws attention to yet another inconvenient truth (Ehrlich *et al.* 1977). The key factors influencing economic growth include *population* and *consumption*, the latter of which is expressed in terms of affluence, or the ability to purchase goods and services. The final variable, technology, can serve to improve or worsen environmental pressure,

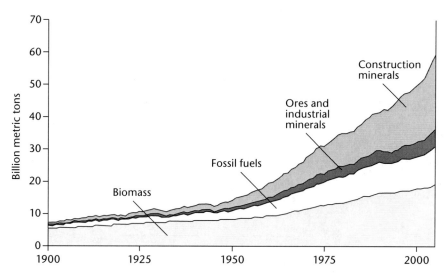

FIGURE 8.1   Materials used by society (Dietz and O'Neill 2013)

depending on whether or not efficiency gains are paired with a decline in resource use, rather than an increase in consumption. Nevertheless, if it is true that our economy is exceeding the carrying capacity of the biosphere (see Washington in this volume), it is also therefore true that either the human population is too great in number or that the population is consuming too much (or *both*). In order to make planetary room for the poorest two-thirds of humanity to improve their material living standards, levels of consumption must decline in high-income regions (Meyer 2000).

Does growth improve well-being?

A growing economy may improve well-being, or it may feature *un*economic growth, in which rates of natural resource use increase without a corresponding increase in a population's quality of life (Daly 1991). In my home country of Canada, our economy has grown while our ranking on the human development index (HDI) has toppled from 1st to a low of 11th place in 2013, due to Canada's relative decline in income equality, education, and life expectancy.[3] For every $100 of global economic growth that occurred between 1990 and 2001, Woodward and Simms (2006) estimate that only 60 cents went to people who make less than a dollar a day.

While many neoclassical economists attribute improved life conditions – from healthcare to communication technologies – to an increase in production and consumption, steady state theorists attribute these innovations instead to the human drive for qualitative improvement (see Lipsey *et al.* 2005).[4] Innovation, after all, has been a feature of all human civilizations, including those that existed prior to the industrial revolution. Like the unyielding growth of the cancer cell, contemporary

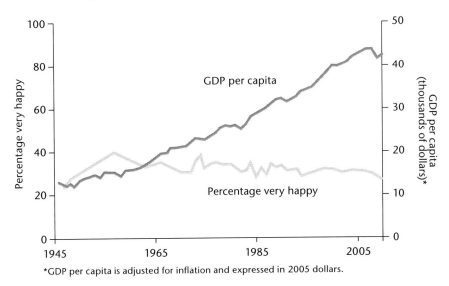

FIGURE 8.2 Percentage 'very happy' versus GDP per capita (Dietz and O'Neill 2013)

economic growth in high-income countries has also fostered mass consumerism, sedentary lifestyles, an obesity epidemic, and an overall decline in emotional and spiritual fulfillment. In the US, the percentage of people that report being 'very happy' has modestly declined since 1955, despite a steady rise in GDP per capita (see Figure 8.2). Several studies now suggest that beyond a limit (ranging from $20,000 to $35,000 per person), income does not improve happiness (Dietz and O'Neill 2013). Can we transition away from a singular neoliberal focus on increased production and consumption, and rather implement changes to improve development and stabilize the biosphere?

What is a steady state economy?

A steady state economy (SSE) is a dynamic market economy that efficiently allocates goods and services but uses the lowest feasible rates of natural capital depletion to achieve a high quality of life. An SSE features a sustainable population size for the carrying capacity of a particular bioregion, and a distribution of wealth which is fair and equitable on an intergenerational basis. The term may apply to a city, region, nation, or to a global economy that fits within the carrying capacity of the planet's biosphere. Daly and Farley (2004, p. 20) summarize the three objectives of an SSE as optimal scale, fair distribution, and efficient allocation, in that particular order.

Contrast these three steady state objectives with the rather narrow scope of neoclassical economics, which is the efficient allocation of goods. Questions related to scale are left *almost entirely unconsidered* in conventional economics and public policy, while the question of fair distribution is a secondary consideration. Steady state proponents don't see how it's possible to avoid questions of economic scale and wealth distribution in the context of present-day social, economic, and ecological challenges. Towards the end of this chapter, we will very briefly examine some of the policies that may already signal the glimmerings of a transition towards a steady state economy.

How can it be measured?

While some contend that there is no agreed-upon metric to measure progress towards a steady state economy, there are a variety of metrics that any government could adopt in addition to GDP. Metrics such as the Genuine Progress Indicator (see Lawn in this volume) incorporate a variety of environmental and social factors, which gives a fuller picture of a population's well-being. Many governments already use dedicated instruments to monitor social and ecological outcomes in addition to standard economic metrics.

While measuring progress towards a steady state economy is undoubtedly important, Daly suggests that ongoing debates over the most appropriate methodology should not delay our transition to an SSE. He explains that 'as important as empirical measurement is, it is worth remembering that when one jumps out of an airplane, a parachute is more beneficial than an altimeter' (Daly 2007, p. 22).

As scientists continue to ring the alarm over the rapidly declining health of the biosphere, we have enough information to know that we need to alter course sooner rather than later. Ceballos *et al.* (2015) argue the Earth has entered a sixth mass extinction period, demonstrating that the rate of species loss is the worst in 65 million years. Likewise, climate scientists suggest that some aspects of climate change, such as sea-level rise, are exceeding worst case scenarios (Dutton *et al.* 2015), echoed by studies that we are on track for a catastrophic three-to-six degree rise in the Earth's temperature by the end of this century (Sherwood *et al.* 2014). The generally conservative IPCC is actually starting to consider geoengineering to bring the climate back to stability (Klein 2014). Under these dire conditions, 'more precise information, though not to be disdained, is not necessary, and waiting for it may prove very costly' (Daly 2007, p. 22).

An economics that respects the physical sciences

While the term 'steady state' has been criticized for sounding technical, it bears a particular significance and history that respects physics and ecology (Cato 2010).[5] Herman Daly, building upon the foundational work of his mentor Nicholas Georgescu-Roegen, integrated the term 'steady state' into economics from the empirical sciences. It reflects the laws of thermodynamics, the finite nature of the earth, and the characteristics of an economy as a complex adaptive system.

The concept of thermodynamic irreversibility was applied to economics initially by Nobel Prize-winning chemist Frederick Soddy, and then by Nicholas Georgescu-Roegen, the latter of whom is credited for identifying that neoclassical economic theory either fails or avoids the satisfaction of the first and second thermodynamic laws. These two laws include (1) mass balance and (2) the entropy law. Mass balance refers to the condition that matter and energy are never destroyed, they merely change state. The entropy law states that when matter-energy changes state through an irreversible chemical conversion, it degrades. The implications for the economy are fairly straightforward: each industrial conversion begins with a higher-quality natural resource input and spits it out as lower-quality material, in the form of waste. Daly and Farley (2004, p. 38) clarify:

> we do not use up matter and energy per se (the first law of thermodynamics), but we do irrevocably use up the quality of its usefulness as we transform matter and energy to achieve our purposes (second law of thermodynamics). All technological transformations require a before and after, a gradient or metabolic flow from concentrated source to dispersed sink, from high to low temperature. The capacity for entropic transformations of matter-energy to be useful is reduced both by the depletion of finite sources and by the pollution of finite sinks.

The principle of *irreversibility* has important implications for seeing the whole environment–economy system as one that is materially unified, and of complete thermodynamic integrity. It is also important to note that, given the principles of thermodynamics, a circular economy such as the supply chain management system proposed by the World Economic Forum (2014) is not infinitely possible for all materials, or in all jurisdictions. Since the amount of available material from recycled goods degrades over time, an economy will always require significant flows of new resources (see Victor 1991). The economy–environment system therefore cannot be described in mechanical terms borrowed from Newtonian physics, which is the conceptual language of neoclassical economics (Homer-Dixon 2007; Beinhocker 2007).

Second, the term 'steady state' also accurately reflects the characteristics of an economy in a complex adaptive system. The economy has traditionally been considered a closed equilibrium system, which is balanced, predictably deterministic, and in a state of rest. However, the economy–environment system in fact fits the characteristics of an open, complex adaptive far-from-equilibrium system. Open, complex systems such as the economy–environment system cannot reach 'equilibrium', which is the term used by neoclassical economists (as in 'general equilibrium theory'). Complex systems can only mimic a state of equilibrium by reaching a 'steady state', or they can exhibit complex, unpredictable behaviour, including exponential growth, radical collapse or oscillations (Beinhocker 2007).

The terms and concepts of neoclassical economics were imported from Newtonian physics, long before important discoveries had been made in ecology, physics, and systems sciences. The term 'steady state' modernizes our economic vocabulary to respect a century of developments in the empirical sciences. It more accurately reflects the characteristics of an economy in a finite and complex economy–environment system of unified thermodynamic integrity.

Locating steady state theory in ecological economics

Daly and Georgescu-Roegen are among the foundational theorists of ecological economic discourse, which explores the intersections between economics and ecology, as well as politics, ethics, and philosophy. The field was influenced by the earlier foundational work of thinkers such as Frederick Soddy, E.F. Schumacher, and Kenneth Boulding, all of whom emphasized the need for an alternative to the growth paradigm.

The term 'steady state' has a number of related concepts in the discourse of ecological economics, including 'degrowth'; H.T. Odum's 'Prosperous Way Down' (Odum and Odum 2001); Peter Victor's description of an economy that is 'slower by design, not disaster' (Victor 2008); Andrew Simms' 'dynamic equilibrium' (Simms *et al.* 2010); or the even more general 'new economy', as promoted by the New Economy Coalition. The latter, however, is sometimes confused with a post-industrial service economy rather than a low- or non-growing economy.

In their textbook *Ecological Economics*, Herman Daly and Joshua Farley label the field a 'transdiciphne' which accepts factual knowledge across disciplines. They argue that 'the disciplinary structure of knowledge is a problem of fragmentation, a difficulty to be overcome rather than a criterion to be met' (Daly and Farley 2004, p. 10). 'Ecological economics' is an economics that acknowledges the ecological limits of the planet and considers interactions between economic systems and ecological systems. The emerging field is defined by its focus on nature, justice, and time. Issues of intergenerational equity, irreversibility of environmental change, uncertainty of long-term outcomes, and sustainability all guide the research of ecological economics. Ecological economics can therefore be delineated from *environmental* economics, the latter of which is a sub-branch of standard neoclassical growth economics. Environmental economists emphasize optimal pricing for waste and emissions and are more inclined to embrace the conventional techno-optimist perspective on growth.

Given the transdisciplinary breadth of ecological economics, however, there is still quite a bit of room for debate over questions related to growth and scale. For one to embrace the term 'steady state economy' would be to reflect some acceptance of Daly's theoretical synthesis and the key points defined earlier, though like-minded proponents of 'degrowth' emphasize a more radical reduction in the scale of economic activity and a shift away from capitalism and mass consumerism. Degrowth, a term that has been attributed to Georgescu-Roegen, is a largely European social movement and emerging body of literature that explores 'a downscaling of production and consumption that increases human well-being and enhances ecological conditions' (Schneider *et al.* 2010).

While steady state theorists accept the need to shrink the economy so that it fits within the limits of the biosphere, they note that degrowth is sustainable in the long run. Degrowth of production and consumption has a limit, just as growth has a limit. Canadian economist Peter Victor points out that 'it is not intended that degrowth continue indefinitely; rather that it is a transformative path leading to a steady-state at a reduced level of economic output' (Victor 2008, p. 5).

Earliest theoretical proponents

The earliest glimmers of steady state thinking can be found in the writings of John Stuart Mill, one of the most prominent philosophers of the nineteenth century. Mill predicted that growth would be followed by what he called a 'stationary state'. In *Principles of Political Economy* (Mill 1848), he writes:

> the increase of wealth is not boundless. The end of growth leads to a stationary state... a stationary condition of capital and population implies no stationary state of human improvement. There would be as much scope as ever for all kinds of mental culture, and moral and social progress; as much room for improving the art of living, and much more likelihood of it being improved, when minds ceased to be engrossed by the art of getting on.

Likewise, John Maynard Keynes, the influential twentieth-century economist, considered the day when society could focus on desirable ends such as happiness and well-being, rather than economic means, including economic growth and individual pursuit of profit. Keynes writes:

> the day is not far off when the economic problem will take the back seat where it belongs, and the arena of the heart and the head will be occupied or reoccupied, by our real problems – the problems of life and of human relations, of creation and behavior and religion.
>
> (Keynes 1945)

Keynes also noted that in a post-growth economy, the rate of return (or interest) must consequently be minimized. He said that a person 'would still be free to accumulate his earned income with a view to spending it at a later date. But [the] accumulation would not grow' (Keynes, 1936, p. 199). This is an especially poignant remark today, as investments in assets like fossil fuels and real estate require growth in order to provide a return, but neither investment is sustainable in the long run (Rubin 2012).

Each of these foundational thinkers emphasizes the need to move beyond economics in the narrowest sense, towards moral and social progress, increased happiness, well-being, and human fulfilment. Indeed, many ecological economists emphasize growth in culture, knowledge, and goodness, rather than growth in materialism and consumption.[6]

Efficiency vs. sufficiency: the crux of the growth debate

At present, the growth debate is mired not in questions over 'well-being' – which should arguably top any society's agenda – but in questions over how to decrease the scale of the economy relative to the planet's carrying capacity. It's therefore worth revisiting my introductory points to consider this debate in greater detail.

Techno-optimists argue that ecological limits will be overcome with efficiency improvements and a structural shift towards a post-industrial 'knowledge' economy. Techno-skeptics, including many ecological economists, argue for a reduction in economic scale through an emphasis on sufficiency, and the qualitative improvement of well-being without growth. While evidence shows that economies have achieved some success at relative decoupling in a precious few sectors of the economy, the global economy requires more resources than ever, and only countries that have deliberately elected to reduce waste, like Germany, have seen notable improvement.

Ecological economist Tim Jackson (2009) writes that increasing fossil fuel efficiency hasn't even compensated for the growth in population, let alone growth in incomes. Instead, CO_2 emissions have grown by 2 per cent per year, leading to a 40 per cent emissions increase in just under two decades. Global carbon emissions from fossil fuels have increased by 80 per cent since 1970. The even more important point, however, is that efficiency improvements are not beneficial enough to improve climate stability or any other planetary life-supporting process. The only periods of declining emissions and resource use were during periods of recession.

Increasing efficiency isn't reducing overall resource use

Krausmann *et al.* (2009, p. 7) note that the only short periods which have actually witnessed aggregate 'dematerialization' were periods of economic recession or very limited growth. Dematerialization is the theoretical process whereby economic value is *decoupled* from its matter-energy requirement, enabling an increase in economic growth without a corresponding increase in materials use. The authors explain:

> Throughout [the 20th century] materials use has reacted sensitively to recessions and even to slowdown in economic growth: Whenever the global economy experienced decline or stagnation, materials and energy use slumped. The only periods of absolute global dematerialisation occurred after the two World Wars and during the World economic crisis in the late 1920ies [sic] and following the oil-price peaks in the 1970s.

Behrens *et al.* (2007) estimate that global resource use will continue to accelerate, with an expected increase of almost a third by 2020. During the twentieth century, the global population grew by a factor of four, while industrial output grew by a factor of forty, more than ten times that of the population. The gap between population growth and industrial output would widen even more significantly if it could be adjusted for waste sink and life support degradation. The balance of evidence suggests that decoupling holds little promise in reducing economic scale, leading many ecological economists to conclude that planetary environmental degradation is an inevitable consequence of economic growth.

Daly writes that 'ecological economics sees this coupling as by no means fixed, but not nearly as flexible as neoclassicals believe it to be – in other words, the "dematerialisation" of GNP and the "information economy" will not save growth economics' (Daly 2007, p.88). The hopes of many techno-optimists, as reflected in the UNEP's 'green economy' initiative, are predicated on 100 per cent decoupling, but it is becoming increasingly apparent that this is virtually impossible. While there has been relative decoupling in some sectors, there is no empirical evidence that absolute decoupling has ever taken place.

Knowing that continued absolute material input at exponential rates place unparalleled strain on biophysical and economic systems, the very difficult question of how to reduce throughput in absolute terms must take its place within twenty-first century economic theory and practice despite a prevailing political and academic propensity for growth.

Key initiatives for a steady state economy

If economic growth is failing and no longer materially feasible, how can we transition to a prosperous steady state economy? There is an inherent difference gearing our institutions for impossible growth, and gearing institutions for a steady state economy by design. As Victor (2008) aptly calls it, the SSE is an economy that's 'slower by design, not disaster'. While Diesendorf briefly covers key ideas in this volume, I would like to cover three catalyst initiatives that may be politically feasible within our lifetime.

Many initiatives can be introduced painlessly, and some are being considered seriously due to a confluence of factors, including tax-shifting to environmental 'bads', and establishing a guaranteed annual income. Other initiatives are well-understood imperatives among ecological economists, like developing 'cost' and 'benefit' categories for GDP, stabilizing population and throughput levels with a combination of policies (see Diesendorf in this volume), limiting the use of non-renewable resources, and reforming international trade institutions.[7] Currently, the World Bank, the IMF, and the World Trade Organization have too much power to block the kind of development that is necessary for a steady state economy.

Limit income inequality

Growth is said to improve income inequality because it provides new opportunities for the poorest members of society, but over the last decade, growth has not been shared equitably with our poorest citizens and is starting to grow out of control. Reducing poverty and ensuring social cohesion and stability require meaningful income redistribution. By permitting wealth disparities where some of the richest members of society earn 500 times more than the poorest earners, the sense of community necessary to foster a just and democratic society is impossible. Daly notes that 'rich and poor separated by a factor of 500 have few experiences or interests in common, and are increasingly likely to engage in violent conflict' (Daly 2013).

In the United States, the civil service and academia manage with a limited range of inequality, by a factor of 15 or 20 times the minimum, while corporate America has a range of 500 or more. Many industrial nations are below a factor of 25. Czech (2013) argues for an upper limit of 15 times the minimum earners, citing the example of professional league 'salary caps', as well as the Mondragon cooperative, which has a maximum pay of 9 times the minimum (Dietz and O'Neill 2013). Daly argues that even starting at a limit of 100 would be better than present-day, which means that while a minimum of twenty thousand dollars per year would make subsistence, a maximum of two million per year would be allowed to reward initiative. Those who enjoy their work at a minimum level of income could live simply – as many do today – and devote their extra time to personal enjoyment or public service (Daly 2013).

Increase work flexibility

While full-time employment for all might be hard to provide without growth, it's also true that growth already provides too much employment for some, and not enough for others. Intergenerationally, baby boomers maintain high-income jobs and continue accumulating earnings while the next generation explores the virtues of working less, partly due to concerns over income stagnation, poor employment prospects, high debt loads, and fears that climate change will interfere catastrophically with the economy in their retirement years. More millennials are abandoning the rat race and consuming less, in favour of indulging more life-affirming and creative pursuits.

The industrialized world's 'forty-hour work week' and the 'nine-to-five' workday are relatively recent inventions that many of us see as a norm rather than a variable that we have freedom and control over. An international study found that 41 per cent of workers would prefer to spend less time working and earn less rather than the inverse (Dietz and O'Neill 2013). There are examples of successful alternatives. Germany's Kurzabeit job-sharing program, which saw 1.4 million workers and 63,000 employers participate in 2009, has lowered unemployment rates while effectively reducing the number of hours worked per person. There are similar success stories in France, the Netherlands, and the US state of Utah. By creating greater work flexibility, people are likely to consume less, which simultaneously improves their quality of life and takes some pressure off the biosphere.

Reform banks and reduce debt

One of the greatest *institutional* barriers to the steady state economy is a banking system that has been foolishly engineered to collapse if it does not grow. Since the 1970s, the percentage of money created as debt by private banks (rather than by national governments) has been steadily increasing. Today, about 97 per cent of money is created electronically as debt by private banks, which in turn means that interest needs to accrue on 97 per cent of all money. Thus, the economy must grow through either inflation (increasing prices) or expansion (increasing production and consumption) simply to finance growth in the money supply. The only way debt can be 'paid' is by increasing prices or increasing production, but debt must always outpace income growth!

What can we do to fix the financial mess? First, we have to put control of the money supply back into the hands of central banks. Until recently, the dividends that private banks now cash out to corporate interests were used by governments to invest in schools, hospitals, and roads. Second, we have to rebuild our financial system to thrive on savings rather than debt by requiring banks to gradually increase the amount of money they have in reserve.

Currently, banks may have as little as 1 per cent of the money they claim to 'lend out', because money is simply created electronically when a borrower applies for a loan or buys a house. With 100 per cent reserves, every dollar loaned to a borrower would be a dollar previously saved by a depositor, thereby re-establishing the balance between savings and investment. In a savings-based financial system, borrowing would be done more carefully, and there would be fewer systemic risks to banks. Gradually, inflation rates and prices would become lower and more stable. Your savings would hold their value and assets like homes would become more affordable, which would also have the effect of reducing the gap between the richest and poorest citizens.

This is how the banking system functioned during the prosperous post-war period, and the principle remains in operation in Islamic banking institutions and through savings banks, including the JAK Members Bank of Sweden.

Conclusion

Much of the discourse surrounding the steady state economy sounds policy-oriented and technical, but the real initiating factors are much more profound than mere economics. As John Stewart Mill (1848) foreshadowed, a steady state economy needs to be initiated by a cultural, spiritual, and political value shift towards simplicity, sufficiency, sharing, community, and a deep respect for the natural world. Change like that will take time, and unfortunately – as steady state theorists are well aware – time is not on our side.

Nevertheless, signals of *meaningful change* are as present as the alarms of decline, including the rise of the 'benefit corporation' and not-for-profit economy in business; the rise of planet-restoring permaculture and agro-ecology; and the emergence of voluntary simplicity and neighbourhood-based transition initiatives. Taken together, the paradigm shift towards a steady state economy may seem like a difficult one in the context of today's planet-ravaging economic framework, and the SSE will also undoubtedly need further development and study. However, none of these ideas are exactly 'radical', and some refinements simply can't be studied without implementation in the real world. On the bright side, the vast majority of the initiatives listed above have already been tested, and are being suggested precisely because they work.

For some, mere knowledge of severe climate instability and mass extinction will be enough to impel them to action; others need to bear witness to the consequences. Still others will always have trouble understanding cause-and-effect. In the rich world, we are beginning to witness the costs of growth outpacing benefits, ushering in an era of 'uneconomic' growth (Daly 1991). However events unfold over the coming years and decades, it's clear that the status quo is less realistic and potentially more violent than a mindful transition to a steady state economy. While it may be too late to avoid the inevitable consequences of growth, while we endure a long period of large-scale changes and potential decline, we should meditate on the principles that might help guide the reinvention of our future.

Notes

1 In this chapter, I'll emphasize the perspective of the steady state economist since the conventional neoclassical economist is well represented in existing economic discourse and policy. To some extent, these hard positions are constructions in order to provide a fair level of contrast. In reality, there is plenty of ambiguity, and healthy academic debate between the concrete positions outlined in this chapter.
2 The information economy has several synonyms and related concepts, including *angelized growth*, as well as the *value-added, ethereal, ephemeral, post-industrial*, or simply *new* economy.
3 There is some disagreement about whether the changes reflect shifts in HDI methodology rather than changes in Canadian society. See http://www.theglobeandmail.com/globe-debate/sorry-but-canada-was-never-the-no-1-place-to-live/article9942689/
4 For a techno-optimist perspective of the growth debate, see 'Economic Transformations: General Purpose Technologies and Long-Term Economic Growth' by Richard Lipsey et al. (2005).
5 Cato (2010), for instance, argues that the phrase 'steady state economy' 'implies a state of stagnation that is neither appealing nor compatible with nature's way of creative evolution'.
6 See Czech (2000, 2013); Victor (2008); Jackson (2009); Simms *et al.* (2010); Heinberg (2011); and Dietz and O'Neill (2013).
7 For a more substantive policy list, see Daly (1991); Layard (2005); Czech (2000, 2013); Victor (2008); Jackson (2009); Simms *et al.* (2010); Heinberg (2011); Dietz and O'Neill (2013); Sukhdev (2013); and Costanza *et al.* (2013).

References

Alexander, S. (2014) *A Critique of Techno-Optimism*. Melbourne: Melbourne Sustainable Society Institute.
Behrens, A., Giljum, S., Kovanda, J., and Niza, S. (2007) 'The material basis of the global economy: Worldwide patterns of natural resource extraction and implications for sustainable resource use policies', *Ecological Economics*, vol. 64, pp. 444–453.
Beinhocker, E. (2007) *The Origin of Wealth: Evolution, Complexity, and the Radical Remaking of Economics*. London: Random House.

Cato. M. S. (2010) 'We Scare People off by Talking about 'Degrowth'', *Ecologist*, 14 July. See: http://www.theecologist.org/blogs_and_comments/commentators/Molly_Scott_Cato/538745/we_scare_people_off_by_talking_about_degrowth.html.

Ceballos, G., Ehrlich, P., Barnosky, A., Garcia, A., Pringle, R., and Palmer, T. (2015) 'Accelerated modern human-induced species losses: Entering the sixth mass extinction', *Science Advances*, vol. 1, e1400253.

Costanza, R., Alperovitz, G., Daly, H., Farley, J., Franco, C., Jackson, T., Kubiszewski, I., Schor, J., and Victor, P. (2013) 'Building a sustainable and desirable economy-in-society-in-nature', in *State of the World 2013: Is Sustainability Still Possible?*, ed. L. Starke. Washington, DC: Island Press, pp. 126–142.

Czech, B. (2000) *Shoveling Fuel for a Runaway Train: Errant Economists, Shameful Spenders, and a Plan to Stop them All*. Berkeley: University of California Press.

Czech, B. (2008) 'Prospects for reconciling the conflict between economic growth and biodiversity conservation with technological progress', *Conservation Biology*, vol. 22, no. 6, pp. 1389–1398.

Czech, B. (2013) *Supply Shock: Economic Growth at the Crossroads and the Steady State Solution*. Vancouver, British Columbia: New Society Publishers.

Daly, H. E. (1991) *Steady-state economics*. Washington, DC: Island Press.

Daly, H. E. and Farley, J. C. (2004) *Ecological economics principles and applications*. Washington, DC: Island Press.

Daly, H.E. (2007) *Ecological economics and sustainable development: Selected essays of Herman Daly*. Massachusetts: Edward Elgar Publishing.

Daly, H.E. (2013) 'Top 10 Policies for a Steady-State Economy', *The Daly News*, 29 October. See: http://steadystate.org/top-10-policies-for-a-steady-state-economy/

Dietz, R. and O'Neill, D. (2013) *Enough Is Enough: Building a Sustainable Economy in a World of Finite Resources*. San Francisco: Berrett-Koehler Publishers.

Dutton, A., Carlson, A.E., Long, A.J., Milne, G.A., Clark, P.U., DeConto, R., Horton, B.P., Rahmstorf, S., and Raymo, M.E. (2015) 'Sea-level rise due to polar ice-sheet mass loss during past warm periods', *Science*, vol. 349, aaa4019.

Ehrlich, P., Ehrlich, A., and Holdren, J. (1977) *Ecoscience: Population, Resources, Environment*. New York: W. H. Freeman and Co.

Heinberg, R. (2011) *The End of Growth: Adapting to Our New Economic Reality*. Vancouver, British Columbia: New Society Publishers.

Homer-Dixon, T. F. (2007) *The Upside of Down: Catastrophe, Creativity and the Renewal of Civilization*. London: Souvenir.

Jackson, T. (2009) *Prosperity Without Growth: Economics for a Finite Planet*. London: Earthscan.

Keynes, J. M. (1936) *The General Theory of Employment Interest and Money*. New York: Harcourt, Brace.

Keynes, J. M. (1945) *First Annual Report of the Arts Council England (1945–1946)*. London: Arts Council. See http://www.artscouncil.org.uk/who-we-are/history-arts-council/

Klein, N. (2014) *This Changes Everything: Capitalism vs. the Climate*. New York: Simon and Schuster.

Krausmann, F., Gingrich, S., Eisenmenger, N., Erb, K. H., Haberl, H., and Fischer-Kowalski, M. (2009) 'Growth in global materials use, GDP and population during the 20th century', *Ecological Economics*, vol. 68, pp. 2696–2705.

Layard, R. (2005) *Happiness: Lessons from a New Science*. New York: Penguin Press.

Lipsey, R.G., Carlaw, K.I., and Bekar, C.T. (2005) *Economic transformations, general purpose technologies and long-term economic growth*. Oxford: Oxford University Press.

Meyer, A. (2000) *Contraction and Convergence: The Global Solution to Climate Change*. Totnes, Devon: Green Books (for the Schumacher Society).

Mill, J. S. (1848) 'Of the Stationary State', Book IV, Chapter VI in *Principles of Political Economy: With Some of Their Applications to Social Philosophy*. London: J.W. Parker. See: http://www.econlib.org/library/Mill/mlP61.html#Bk.IV,Ch.VI

Odum, H. T. and Odum, E. C. (2001) *A Prosperous Way Down: Principles and Policies*. Colorado: University Press of Colorado.

Rubin, J. (2012) *The End of Growth*. Toronto: Random House Canada.

Schneider, F., Kallis, G., and Martinez-Alier, J. (2010) 'Crisis or opportunity? Economic degrowth for social equity and ecological sustainability. Introduction to this special issue', *Journal of Cleaner Production*, vol. 18, pp. 511–518.

Sherwood, S. C., Bony, S. and Dufresne, J. -L. (2014) 'Spread in model climate sensitivity traced to atmospheric convective mixing', *Nature*, vol. 505, pp 37–42. DOI:10.1038/nature12829

Simms, A., Johnson, V., and Chowla, P. (2010) *Growth Isn't Possible: Why We Need a New Economic Direction*. London: New Economics Foundation. See: www.neweconomics.org/publications/growth-isnt-possible

Sukhdev, P. (2013) 'Transforming the corporation into a driver of sustainability', in *State of the World 2013: Is Sustainability Still Possible?*, ed. L. Starke. Washington, DC: Island Press, pp. 143–153.

Victor, P. (1991) 'Indicators of sustainable development: some lessons from capital theory', *Ecological Economics*, vol. 4, pp. 191–213.

Victor, P. (2008) *Managing without Growth: Slower by Design Not Disaster*. Cheltenham: Edward Elgar.

Woodward, D. and Simms, A. (2006). *Growth Isn't Working: The Unbalanced Distribution of Benefits and Costs from Economic Growth*. London: New Economics Foundation.

World Economic Forum (2014) *Towards the Circular Economy: Accelerating the Scale-Up across Global Supply Chains*. Isle of Wight: Ellen MacArthur Foundation.

9

THE PHYSICAL PATHWAY TO A STEADY STATE ECONOMY

Graham Turner

UNIVERSITY OF MELBOURNE

Background

When contemplating a steady state economy or sustainable future it's common to invoke the IPAT equation. The well-known IPAT equation introduced by Ehrlich and Holdren in the 1970s contends that environmental impacts (I) are determined by population size (P), affluence (A, or consumption, i.e. products or services per capita) and economic throughput (T, resources or wastes per product or service) multiplied together (Lutz *et al.* 2002).

This IPAT formulation gives the somewhat misleading impression that environmental impacts can be lowered or eliminated simply by suitable reduction in one or more of population, consumption and throughput. A common suggestion is that the use of technology (especially efficiency) can lower material and energy flows (i.e. throughput), and thereby offset the effects of growth in population and consumption. The concepts of dematerialisation, Factor-4 and decoupled economies are essentially founded on this assumption.

These simple views, however, are not supported by more detailed modelling and analyses which employ system perspectives. This chapter presents system analysis to examine the environmental impact of population, technology and common societal or economic goals. An outcome of this examination was the simulation of a steady state economy. This focuses on the Australian economy, but the issues are global phenomena, as well illustrated by the *Limits to Growth* modelling from the 1970s – recently shown to be an accurate reproduction of the last three decades of the twentieth century (thereby dispelling malicious claims to the contrary) (Turner 2008, 2012b).

The analysis in this chapter shows that reducing environmental impacts toward sustainable levels is likely to require very substantial changes to a range of social and economic factors. It is not simply a matter of reducing consumption, or of exploiting technological progress, though both of these factors are important or perhaps even crucial. Population size also has significant environmental impact, with smaller populations easing the environmental burden without necessarily being economically disadvantageous. But even stable or diminishing populations do not ensure environmental sustainability. The system analysis identifies that a crucial further ingredient to sustainability is how our societies deal with economic growth, material wealth, unemployment and the 'work-life balance'.

Simulating the economy's physical activity and its environment

The Australian Stocks and Flows Framework (ASFF) is a highly disaggregate simulation of all physically significant stocks and flows in the Australian socio-economic system (Figure 9.1). Stocks are the quantities of physical items at a point in time, such as land, livestock, people and buildings. Flows represent the rates of change resulting from the operation of physical processes over a time period, such as the (net) additions of agricultural land, immigration and birth rates, new and discarded vehicles, etc. The ASFF models the processes of the physically significant elements of each sector of the Australian economy, including some service aspects. Natural resources (land, water, air, biomass and mineral resources) are also represented explicitly.

The ASFF categorises population in terms of age-cohort demographics, household size and location. Lifestyle-related parameters such as various product consumption rates per capita, transport mode shares and household characteristics collectively represent affluence. Economic throughput is modelled in detail in the ASFF, and incorporates technological efficiency parameters, substitution options (e.g. different fuels) and stock dynamics to simulate infrastructure turnover, for example.

Geographically, the ASFF covers continental Australia, including the marine area within Australia's economic exclusion zone. Within specific sectors of the framework different geographic resolutions are used, e.g. agriculture is resolved at the 58 statistical divisions across Australia. The temporal extent of the ASFF is long-term: scenarios over the future are calculated to 2100, and the model is also run over an historical period from 1941. In some sectors such as agriculture it is necessary to provide data substantially prior to 1940 due to the lengthy lifetime of important agricultural land stocks, e.g. of different quality. The time step used is five years, coinciding with Australian Bureau of Statistics census years.

An indicative measure of GDP has been calculated in the ASFF based on the physical stocks of capital and labour. This indicative GDP is an approximation for an income-based GDP (ABS 2000). (An alternative is expenditure-based GDP.) To calculate the income-based GDP, the labour numbers in the ASFF are combined with salary and wages data to calculate the 'compensation of employees' component of GDP; and to estimate the 'gross operating surplus' component, the new stocks of productive physical capital in the ASFF are combined with calibrated data on the cost of capital and a rate of return upon investment for all sectors. The

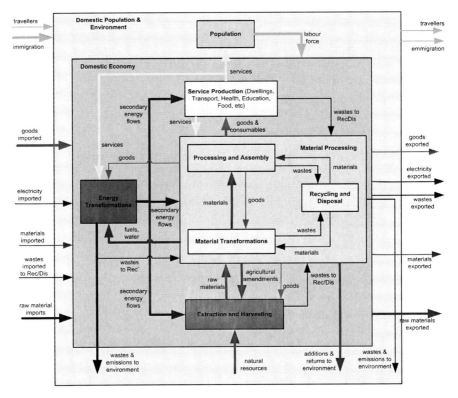

FIGURE 9.1 Schematic summary of physical flow connections of a modern economy like Australia's. Flows of people, energy and materials may enter and exit the economy, principally as imports and exports on the left and right respectively. Within the domestic economy, natural resources are extracted or harvested from the environment (shown at the centre-bottom of the diagram). Materials are transformed progressively (going upward in the diagram) with the use of suitable energy to eventually provide goods and services for the population. The population provides a labour force (at the top) for all the economic sectors. Wastes and emissions are generated by the economic activity, and may be recycled, exported or returned to the environment. Other flows occur between economic sectors (Turner 2011).

new stocks are those items of physical capital that contribute to economic output. They incorporate machinery, commercial vehicles and commercial buildings in the primary, secondary, transport and service sectors covered in the ASFF.

The first application of the ASFF was for the Australian Government's Immigration Department to explore the environmental implications of potential alternative immigration scenarios (Foran and Poldy 2002). In subsequent years, the ASFF has been applied and refined in a number of areas, including: agricultural land (Dunlop et al. 2002) and cropping systems (Dunlop and Turner 2003); fisheries (Kearney and Foran 2002, Lowe et al. 2003); state of the environment reporting (Lennox and Turner 2005); rail transport (Turner et al. 2002); resource use trajectories (Schandl *et al.* 2008); 'green collar' jobs (Hatfield-Dodds *et al.* 2008); and national dematerialisation potential (Schandl and Turner 2009). The effects of different immigration rates on the environment was recently revisited for the Immigration Department (Sobels *et al.* 2010). The ASFF has recently been expanded in detail and scope, and its historical calibration updated, to examine Australian food security (following a pilot project for the state of Victoria (Turner *et al.* 2012)).

Simulating a healthy economy

Recent development in the ASFF incorporates economic settings within the scenario simulations. This means that economic growth can be made endogenous to the simulations – it can be an outcome rather than an assumption of the simulation. In this approach, both production (primary and secondary industry output) and final demand consumption are adjusted to simultaneously maintain a target unemployment rate and a target trade balance relative to GDP (Figure 9.2).

The level of (un)employment is a result of the population size, its age profile, the participation rate, labour productivity, and the various economic activities requiring labour. If no other change is made to the ASFF inputs, then increased productivity (labour input per unit output and other efficiencies) leads to increased unemployment due to the simple fact that the same economic output can be achieved with fewer workers. With typical productivity growth rates of about 1 per cent per annum (p.a.), mass unemployment of the order of 50 per cent would occur after several decades.

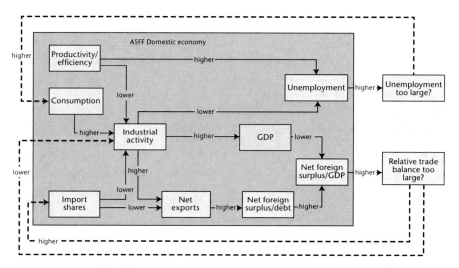

FIGURE 9.2 Feedback processes applied to the ASFF modelling to establish economically healthy unemployment levels and international trade balance (relative to GDP). The arrows indicate the direction of feedback adjustments on aggregate modules of the ASFF to correct poor economic outcomes (Turner 2011).

To achieve a stable unemployment level and replicate past economic conditions, a reference scenario incorporates re-employment of displaced labour through increased economic activity. It was assumed that the trends in labour participation rates are not changed from their background settings. Consequently, in the reference scenario, final demand consumption was increased (or decreased) in order to lower (or raise) the unemployment rate. The modelling calculations allow for service workers supporting the physically productive sectors of the economy.

The other key macro-economic indicator simulated is the international trade debt/surplus (relative to gross domestic product, GDP). High rates of debt (and surplus) are considered to be contrary to a stable national economy. In one measure of the economy, the net foreign debt (NFD) is compared with the nation's GDP in order to judge whether an economy is overstretched to pay its international debt.

The net foreign debt in the ASFF was adjusted by changes to exports and imports, international travel (inbound visitors and outbound Australians) and investment. It is possible to achieve the same NFD through different combinations of changes to exports, imports and investment. Adjustments to exports were made by altering activity in both primary and secondary industry, after allowing for domestic requirements to be met from these industries (where Australian exports are a large fraction of Australian production). International travel and investment were adjusted by the same proportion as exports. Imports were adjusted by changing the fraction of the domestic demand for goods/commodities that is obtained from overseas. These changes also alter GDP, so that an iterative feedback calculation is necessary to achieve the specified NFD:GDP ratio.

Making comparisons on the role of consumption and other factors

The analysis in this chapter draws on an examination of the effect of various drivers or factors in the economy. This approach is somewhat different from one based on creating and comparing qualitatively different scenarios, where the emphasis is on different plausible views or storylines of the future. Instead, the analysis presented here focuses on changes to specific factors (though these could be construed as 'sub-scenarios'), such as population or technological innovations, to identify those factors that are key to achieving sustainability or that are deleterious.

The next section describes the reference scenario assumptions for the economy modelled in the ASFF. This includes how economic growth is an outcome of the desire to avoid mass unemployment. The subsequent section examines several variations on this standard economy, including size of the population and what type of economy a nation might pursue.

Simulating a standard growth paradigm for a reference scenario

This section describes a background or reference scenario, in terms of the conditions or assumptions that are used in the ASFF. These conditions have been chosen as generally representative of business as usual, though this is not an attempt to be predictive. The initial conditions imposed on the model are to varying degrees arbitrary; their intended purpose is to provide insight into the general function of the economy and its impacts on the environment and resources, and to enable subsequent alternatives to be compared.

The future population of Australia in the reference scenario has been drawn from one of the trajectories recently provided by the Australian Bureau of Statistics (ABS) (ABS 2008). The ABS created population projections from collections of alternative assumptions about immigration (net overseas immigration, NOM), fertility rates and life expectancies. The 'Series B' projection incorporates a NOM level of 180,000 persons per year, a total period fertility of 1.8 births per female and slight increases to life expectancy, all of which are consistent with recent rates. This results in an Australian population of about 35 million by 2051, which is a significant increase on the recent figure of some 22 million.

Technological progress is also a key feature of human endeavour and economic performance. This has been embodied in the reference scenario in broad changes to labour productivity, and efficiency of energy and material use. Consequently, as an example, the aggregate carbon intensity of the economy (i.e. the volume of carbon per dollar of GDP) decreases steadily throughout the scenario period (Figure 9.3).

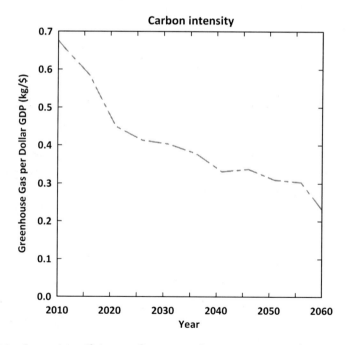

FIGURE 9.3 Increasing efficiency of energy and resource use simulated in the ASFF scenarios results in the overall carbon intensity falling steadily for the next 50 years (Turner 2011).

Labour productivity was assumed to increase at a typical rate of 1 per cent pa in all of the economic sectors. Efficiencies of resource use were assumed to increase by 20 per cent over the 20-year period to 2031, based on common aspirations or suggestions from a wide range of commentators, rather than specific individual technological assessments. Nevertheless, such a change is likely to be deemed feasible in most cases. The reference scenario did not incorporate transitions to alternative systems, such as renewable electricity generation or electric vehicles.

Rather than leave unemployment increasing continuously as a result of the conditions above, personal and household consumption rates were adjusted until the unemployment rate had stabilised at acceptable levels. For the reference scenario, the target rate of 5 per cent unemployment was used since this is considered to foster minimum inflationary effects (Swan 2010).

The simulation shows that, in general, per capita consumption rates (such as cars per household, dwelling size, or consumables per person) increase over time, though some cycles occur due to the dynamics associated with the introduction of productive physical capital. New capital is required to replace aging plant and to satisfy demand created by consumption. Capital turnover is also affected by the degree of domestic manufacturing compared with importing goods, which is determined by the objective of establishing a stable foreign balance.

A reference level of the net foreign debt (relative to GDP) was simultaneously established at about 50 per cent, to be consistent with recent levels. The NFD:GDP has increased over recent decades, to 52 per cent in 2006 (Kryger 2009). The reference level was achieved by adjustments to exports, imports, travel and other international transactions as described above.

Consequently, the simulated Australian economy shifts to increased domestic manufacturing of goods, and decreased proportions that are imported. Even so, with growth in both population and per capita consumption, import volumes increase steadily. This is approximately matched by growth in exports, mostly in final demand goods associated with the resurgent domestic manufacturing, while exports of primary products roughly stabilise or fall somewhat. These outcomes contrast with recent economic development in Australia; it should be recognised that they are not predictions per se of Australia's economic trajectory, but reflect conditions that achieve the macro-economic goals of stable unemployment and trade balance imposed on the simulations. Other economic developments could and might occur, but these would affect the macro-economic goals potentially in negative ways.

The scenarios simulated also generally excluded the impacts of climate change, except in the case of water resources. In this case, a simple hydrological model (Preston and Jones 2008) is used to estimate the change in water volume runoff based on regional climate change data for rainfall and evapo-transpiration rates (CSIRO and BoM 2007). A 'business-as-usual' type climate scenario was used, i.e. the IPCC A1FI scenario based on further global population and economic growth, increasing efficiencies and fossil fuels for energy. This was chosen since climate impacts are likely to continue to grow (even if commonly proposed carbon reduction schemes are implemented) due to the inertia in the climate system and recent observations that greenhouse gas emissions and anticipated climate impacts have exceeded the A1FI trajectory.

Environmental and economic outcomes of alternative scenarios, including a steady state economy

Having established a reference scenario in the ASFF, which embodies endogenous economic growth, we now examine how various factors could be introduced as alternative scenarios for environmental and economic sustainability. Debates about sustainability typically hinge around the issues of population, consumption and technology – but usually with a focus on one issue at a time rather than more nuanced combinations. The association between consumption and employment is not often recognised in the sustainability literature. Notable exceptions include qualitative arguments in *The Upside of Down* (Homer-Dixon 2006), modelling of the Canadian economy (Victor and Rosenbluth 2007; Victor 2008), system analysis presented in *Prosperity without Growth* (Jackson 2009) and policies and plans in *Enough is Enough* (O'Neill et al. 2010). Thomas Homer-Dixon describes how the Great Depression delivered the lesson to the major economies on how important consumption was to avoid mass social unrest from high levels of unemployment (2006). The LOWGROW system dynamics model of Canadian economist Peter Victor (2008) explicitly incorporates employment effects among other economic outcomes and some environmental impacts. Tim Jackson has utilised this modelling and placed it within a wide descriptive account of economic and social systems behaviour (2009). Based on these works, *Enough is Enough* provides a policy blueprint for a steady state economy (O'Neill et al. 2010).

These studies clearly point to the need to explore further the possibility for lifestyle and other changes to achieve desired environmental outcomes, while recognising the inherent innovation of humans (leading to ongoing productivity and efficiency, among other things). Consequently, a set of scenarios were developed in the ASFF building on the earlier standard growth reference scenario, as described in the following (and specific settings summarised in Table 9.1).

Major 'lifestyle change' is introduced, firstly through a 50 per cent reduction in personal and household consumption. In order to maintain the unemployment level at 5 per cent at lower consumption levels, this is accompanied by a second major lifestyle (and structural) change to a shorter working week. In the modelling this is implemented as reduced labour participation rates.

Further 'technology/investment' advances are then implemented. Material and energy efficiencies are doubled over the period to 2040 simultaneously across numerous sectors. The physical feasibility of this efficiency change has not been considered in this scenario analysis – there may be thermodynamic limits to some efficiency gains.

TABLE 9.1 Summary of scenario settings implemented in the ASFF

Scenario element	Components of change	Description of overall change	Specific components affected
Business as usual			
	Population growth	Reaches about 35 million by 2050 (Series B of ABS projections)	Net immigration is 180,000 p.a.; Total period fertility rate is 1.8; Medium life expectancy
	Labour productivity increases	Continual 1% p.a. increase in productivity	Applied to all sectors
	Increased material and energy efficiency	20% increase over 20 years	All buildings, vehicles and industrial sectors
Lifestyle change			
	Reduced household and personal consumption	Per capita (and per household) consumption rates reduced by 50% by 2041	Consumables (e.g. paper, plastics, etc.); food; personal vehicles; dwelling floor space (and contents); international travel rate
	Lower labour participation rates (mimicking a reduced working week)	Reduced by approximately 40% by 2050 to maintain unemployment at 5%; this equates to achieving a 3-day working week by 2050	Applied to all sectors, including service workers
Technology/Investment			
	Increased material and energy efficiency	Double efficiency, i.e. 100% increase achieved over 30 years	All buildings, vehicles, and industrial sectors
	Electricity generation shifts to low GHG emission technologies	Power delivered by equal contributions from wind, solar (PV) and gas combined cycle (with hydro contributing ~5%)	Centralised power plant (no distributed generation); installed capacity is larger to account for variability of renewable generation and typical load factors
Stabilised population			
		Approximately stabilised population of 21 million by 2050 (Series D of ABS projections)	Net immigration is zero; Total period fertility rate is 1.6; Medium life expectancy

Source: Turner 2011

Also, the portfolio of electricity generation is transitioned away from mainly coal-based thermal power stations to a mix of renewable generators and gas-powered combined cycle stations. The transition occurs as coal power stations are decommissioned at the end of their life (assumed on average to be 40 years), avoiding stranded assets.

A final scenario variant introduces a stable population (Series D). Consequently, in the following discussion of economic and environmental outcomes, four scenario variants are compared: three with medium (Series B) population growth, comparing business as usual (BAU), lifestyles changes, and combined lifestyle and technology/investment changes; and the low/stable population (Series D) with the combined lifestyle and technology/investment changes.

Following the simulation of these scenario variants, some key measures of environmental outcomes and economic performance have been selected from the large number of outputs that can be derived from the ASFF. Economic performance is represented by GDP and GDP per capita (complementing the background condition of stabilised unemployment and international foreign debt). The environmental outcomes are represented by net imports of oil, greenhouse gas emissions, water use and remaining river flow (for the Murray River). These indicators have been aggregated over their many contributing components, and commonly indexed here to highlight the relative change occurring in the scenarios. This set of environmental indicators covers critical issues for sustaining a national economy, namely energy, water and food security, and contribution to climate change.

Overall, the combination of low/stable population with both lifestyle and technology/investment changes yields substantial environmental benefits, while managing to maintain individual wealth at contemporary levels (Figure 9.4b), i.e. a steady state economy that has the highest level of energy, water, food and climate security (Figures 9.5 and 9.6).

A substantial contribution to this outcome derives from lifestyle changes – the reduced consumption and shorter working week. For example, growth in GDP is substantially less than in BAU, increasing by 80 per cent compared with some 250 per cent for BAU (Figure 9.4a). While the changes are ultimately substantial, such as moving to a three-day working week, they can be introduced incrementally, e.g. decreasing the working week by half a day every five years or so. This compares favourably with (larger) reductions in labour hours by Victor's LOWGROW modelling, which also features stabilised population and large reductions in GHG emissions (Victor 2010).

Not only do these two factors (consumption and working time) go hand in hand to ensure low, stable unemployment, but they are also consistent in that a shorter working week implies lower income and hence consumption. In approximate terms, material wealth in the modelling returns to about 1970 levels. This does not necessarily mean a reduced standard of living – in fact potentially the opposite, since progress can still continue in delivery of health, education and communication services, for example. Meaningful take-up of these services may also be facilitated by increased leisure time, as well as other benefits (NEF 2010).

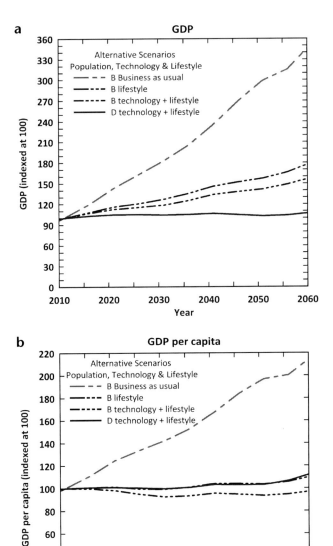

FIGURE 9.4 Economic outcomes under alternative socio-economics systems. Three scenarios use Series B population (34m in 2050), and compare the effects of typical growth (business as usual) with substantial lifestyle changes and then combined with further substantial technological change. A fourth scenario incorporates low/stable population (Series D, 21m in 2050) along with lifestyle and technological change. (a) aggregate Australian and (b) average individual wealth (represented by GDP and GDP per capita respectively) simulated in the ASFF (Turner 2011).

In the scenarios implemented here, 'technology/investment' makes its largest relative contribution in the area of energy and climate security (Figure 9.5). Nevertheless, long-term oil imports are about double recent levels, and while GHG emissions are substantially reduced they remain above suggested targets for developed countries of 90 per cent reduction on 1990 levels. Also, individual wealth is slightly reduced relative to contemporary levels (down about 10 per cent) and is the lowest of all four scenarios (Figure 9.4b).

To achieve the best environmental outcomes it is necessary to maintain a low/stable population on top of lifestyle and technology/investment changes. Oil imports are less than double recent levels, in the long-term. This would significantly facilitate moves to transition to alternative transport fuels/systems, such as electric vehicles or hydrogen fuel cells. GHG emissions appear to be reduced to the very low levels suggested for developed countries.

Water use volumes are reduced by almost 60 per cent by 2060, resulting in river outflow (of the MDB) that is slightly lower than recent averages. This alleviates one pressure on domestic food production, though potential supply constraints on fertilisers may remain an issue (Turner et al. 2012).

The scenario analysis here shows that it may be technically plausible to achieve a sustainable steady state economy, through the combination of low/stable population, reduced consumption and working hours, and technology and investment. Other approaches that do not employ such a comprehensive combination of strategies are unlikely to lead to sustainability. The combination of strategies required in the national analysis bears considerable similarity to the insight of the *Limits to Growth* modelling at the global level, where the 'stabilised world' scenarios employed population, consumption and technological strategies.

Despite the apparent technical feasibility for a steady state economy and sustainable future, there are a range of issues that would need to be addressed to achieve this sustainable future. Among the considerable governance, institutional and societal issues to be addressed are: the simultaneity of numerous changes and considerable speed of change that would require global/national effort and coordination; funding the transformational investment at a time of global debt burden; providing the workforce for research, development and construction while also shifting to shorter working weeks; ensuring equitable distribution of labour force changes; displacing GDP growth as a measure of societal progress; and likewise the perception of continual growth in material wealth as a personal indicator. Since many of these present substantial and unprecedented challenges for modern economies, the realistic likelihood of a transition to a sustainable future is, unfortunately, vanishingly small (Turner 2012a).

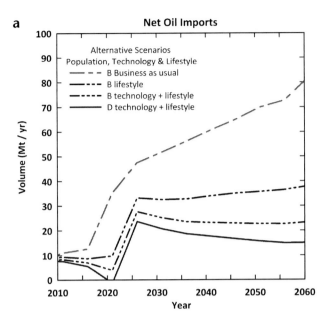

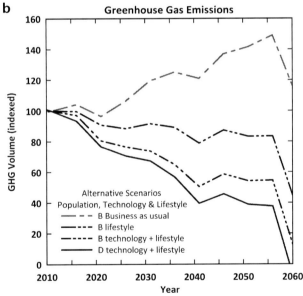

FIGURE 9.5 Environmental impacts simulated in the ASFF under alternative socio-economics systems. Three scenarios use Series B population (34m in 2050), and compare the effects of typical growth (business as usual) with substantial lifestyle changes and then combined with further substantial technological change. A fourth scenario incorporates low/stable population (Series D, 21m in 2050) along with lifestyle and technological change. (a) Net oil imports (i.e. imports less exports) and (b) greenhouse gas emissions aggregated from main sources and sinks (Turner 2011).

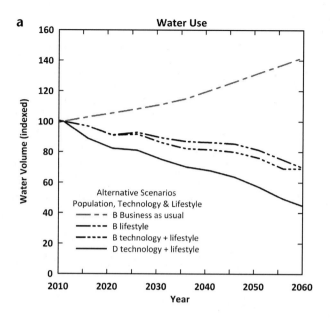
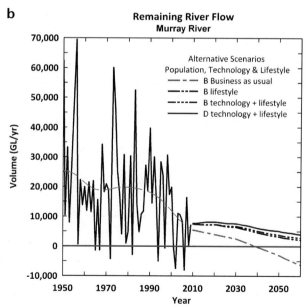

FIGURE 9.6 Environmental impacts simulated in the ASFF under alternative socio-economics systems. Three scenarios use Series B population (34m in 2050), and compare the effects of typical growth (business as usual) with substantial lifestyle changes and then combined with further substantial technological change. A fourth scenario incorporates low/stable population (Series D, 21m in 2050) along with lifestyle and technological change. (a) Aggregated water use and (b) river flow leaving the Murray River, including the effects of a 'business-as-usual' climate scenario (A1FI) (Turner 2011).

Conclusions

Both global and national level analyses highlight the significant and detrimental impacts of consumption on the environment. The modelling shows that the 'business as usual' practice of buying ever-more things and discarding them is undermining energy, water, food and climate security to such an extent that an economic and societal collapse is likely if substantial changes are not made.

But it is also clear that simply shifting to a low-consumption lifestyle is not sufficient for a sustainable future. Much wider changes are needed, particularly to circumvent the unacceptably large unemployment rate that would otherwise occur.

Implementing other partial strategies may also result in surprising and limited outcomes. For instance, increasing efficiency and productivity within standard modern economies does not yield the expected environmental benefits because higher consumption and economic growth is encouraged in order to avoid deleterious unemployment caused by the technological progress.

Alternatively, lower population levels can ease environmental pressures somewhat, but not eliminate them, since in standard economic conditions stable or small populations can achieve virtually the same economic growth of growing or large populations. This growth diminishes the environmental relief of a small population.

Achieving sustainability requires a combination of substantial strategies. Independent modelling at the global and national levels, based on *The Limits to Growth* and the Australian Stocks and Flows Framework respectively, shows that a comprehensive suite of changes can, technically, yield a steady state economy and sustainable system. Typically what is required is: stabilised or lower population; reduced household consumption (say to 1970 material standards in developed countries) along with shorter working weeks (e.g. reaching three-day weeks by mid-century); and large material and energy efficiency improvements and investment in 'green' infrastructure. This is a formidable challenge, to say the least.

(This publication was derived with permission from CSIRO Publishing from: Turner, G. M. (2011) 'Consumption and the environment: Impacts from a system perspective'. In Newton, P. W. (ed.) *Urban Consumption*. Collingwood: CSIRO Publishing. http://www.publish.csiro.au/pid/6472.htm)

References

ABS (2000) *Australian System of National Accounts – Concepts, Sources and Methods*, Canberra: Australian Bureau of Statistics.

ABS (2008) *Population Projections: Australia, 2006 to 2101*, Canberra: Australian Bureau of Statistics.

CSIRO and BoM (2007) *Climate Change in Australia: Technical Report 2007*, Canberra: CSIRO, Australian Bureau of Meteorology.

Dunlop, M. and Turner, G. (2003) *Future Sustainability of the Australian Grains Industry*, Report for the Grains Council of Australia, Canberra: CSIRO Sustainable Ecosystems, Resource Futures Program, National Futures.

Dunlop, M., Turner, G., Foran, B., and Poldy, F. (2002) *Decision Points for Land and Water Futures*, Canberra: CSIRO Sustainable Ecosystems, Resource Futures Program, National Futures.

Foran, B. and Poldy, F. (2002) *Future Dilemmas: Options to 2050 for Australia's Population, Technology, Resources and Environment*, Report to the Department of Immigration and Multicultural and Indigenous Affairs, Canberra: CSIRO Sustainable Ecosystems.

Hatfield-Dodds, S., Turner, G. M., Schandl, H., and Doss, T. (2008) *Growing the Green Collar Economy: Skills and Labour Challenges in Reducing Our Greenhouse Emissions and National Environmental Footprint*, Canberra: Report to the Dusseldorp Skills Forum.

Homer-Dixon, T. (2006) *The Upside of Down – Catastrophe, Creativity and the Renewal of Civilization*, Washington, DC: Island Press.

Jackson, T. (2009) *Prosperity without Growth? The Transition to a Sustainable Economy*, London: Sustainable Development Commission.

Kearney, B. and Foran, B. (2002) *Policy Implications of the FRDC Fish Futures Project*, Canberra: CSIRO Sustainable Ecosystems, Resource Futures Program, National Futures.

Kryger, T. (2009) *Australia's Foreign Debt – Data and Trends*, Canberra: Department of the Parliamentary Library.

Lennox, J. A. and Turner, G. (2005) *State of the Environment Report on Human Settlements: Stocks and Flows Indicators*, Canberra: CSIRO Sustainable Ecosystems, Resource Futures.

Lowe, D. B., Poldy, F., Foran, B., Kearney, R. E., and Turner, G. (2003) *Australian Fisheries Futures: 2020 and Beyond*, Canberra: CSIRO Sustainable Ecosystem, Resource Futures Program, National Futures.

Lutz, W., Prskawetz, A., and Sanderson, W. C., eds. (2002) *Population and Environment: Methods of Analysis*, New York: Population Council.

NEF (2010) *21 Hours. Why a Shorter Working Week Can Help Us All Flourish in the 21st Century*, London: New Economics Foundation.

O'Neill, D. W., Dietz, R., and Jones, N. (2010) *Enough Is Enough: Ideas for a Sustainable Economy in a World of Finite Resources*, Leeds, UK: Center for the Advancement of the Steady State Economy and Economic Justice for All.

Preston, B. L. and Jones, R. (2008) 'A National Assessment of the Sensitivity of Australian Runoff to Climate Change', *Atmospheric Science Letters*, 9(4), 202–208.

Schandl, H., Poldy, F., Turner, G. M., Measham, T. G., Walker, D., and Eisenmenger, N. (2008) 'Australia's Resource Use Trajectories', Special Issue on Material Use across World Regions: Inevitable Pasts and Possible Futures, *Journal of Industrial Ecology*, 12(5), 669–685.

Schandl, H. and Turner, G. M. (2009) 'The Dematerialization Potential of the Australian Economy', *Journal of Industrial Ecology*, 13(6), 863–880.

Sobels, J., Richardson, S., Turner, G., Maude, A., Tan, Y., Beer, A., and Wei, Z. (2010) *Research into the Long-Term Physical Implications of Net Overseas Migration*, Adelaide, SA: National Institute of Labour Studies, Flinders University School of the Environment, and CSIRO Sustainable Ecosystems.

Swan, W. (2010) *Intergenerational Report 2010 – Australia to 2050: Future Challenges*, Canberra: Treasury, Australian Government.

Turner, G., Foran, B., and Poldy, F. (2002) *Demography to 2051: Impacts of the VHST Development – Phases Two & Three*, Report for the Department of Transport and Regional Services, Canberra: CSIRO Sustainable Ecosystems, Resource Futures Program, National Futures.

Turner, G. M. (2008) 'A Comparison of *The Limits to Growth* with 30 Years of Reality', *Global Environmental Change*, 18(3), 397–411.

Turner, G. M. (2012a) 'Energy Shocks and Emerging Alternative Technologies', Special Issue, *Australian Journal of International Affairs*, 66(5), 606–621.

Turner, G. M. (2012b) 'On the Cusp of Global Collapse? Updated Comparison of *The Limits to Growth* with Historical Data', *GAiA – Ecological Perspectives for Science and Society*, 21(2), 116–124.

Turner, G. M., Larsen, K. A., Ryan, C., and Lawrence, M. (2012) 'Australian Food Security Dilemmas – Comparing Nutritious Production Scenarios and Their Environmental, Resource and Economic Tensions' in Farmar-Bowers, Q., Higgins, V., and Millar, J., eds., *Food Security in Australia*, New York: Springer.

Victor, P. A. (2008) *Managing without Growth: Slower by Design, Not Disaster*, Cheltenham, UK: Edward Elgar.

Victor, P. A. (2010) 'Keynote Presentation – Steady State Economy Conference, Leeds', [online], available at: http://steadystate.org/learn/leeds2010/videos/

Victor, P. A. and Rosenbluth, G. (2007) 'Managing without Growth', *Ecological Economics*, 61, 492–504.

10
RELATING THE STEADY STATE ECONOMY TO THE GREEN, CIRCULAR AND BLUE ECONOMIES

Paul Twomey and Haydn Washington

UNSW AUSTRALIA

Introduction

Alternative discourses to the traditional growth economy model have existed for many decades. One such concept, the theme of this book, is the steady state economy, most commonly associated with Herman Daly (e.g. Daly 1991). In the 1970s Daly provided a high-level set of criteria as to what constitutes a steady state economy, acknowledging that there was – and still is – much to debate and learn as to the best ways of achieving it. Alongside this concept, recently there has emerged a number of other discourses that would appear to be closely related to the steady state economy (SSE), including the green economy, the circular economy and the blue economy. A cursory look at these different terms indicates a significant overlap in the type of policies and strategies recommended by the four approaches. Furthermore, the green economy and circular economy concepts, in particular, have been successfully gaining prominence with governments and businesses. They are even being adopted by some businesses in their strategic planning (see Kopnina in this volume), something that the steady state economy has mostly failed to achieve to date (Charonis 2012).

Therefore, attempts at building greater collaboration and integration among these discourses would seem to be a sensible strategy for those who are alarmed by the fragility of our ecological, social and economic systems. Such a strategy could increase the chances of building a strong and widely supported coalition that mainstreams a viable alternative to the traditional growth economy model, which is seen by many as one of the primary causes of these problems.

However, important questions remain as to how closely these alternative models relate to an SSE. In particular, from an SSE perspective, there are concerns that these new discourses, while providing many valuable innovative ideas as well as an attractive, positive ethos, may be mistaking elements of a long-term solution with the entirety of the solution. At worst, they may be so closely aligned with a traditional growth agenda that they can accommodate (and perhaps support) a 'business as usual' paradigm. The history of the much debated concept of sustainable development parallels such concerns (Washington 2015).

The aim of this chapter, therefore, is to describe some key features of the green economy, the circular economy and the blue economy, and to discuss how they relate to the steady state economy. We will focus our attention on these three concepts as they have probably been the most prominent in recent government and business forums. These concepts are also closely linked to a cluster of related concepts such as Factor 5 (von Wieszacker *et al.* 2009), Cradle-to-Cradle (Braungart and McDonough 2008) and the performance economy (which will also be briefly mentioned here). There is also another related grouping of concepts, including 'degrowth', 'post-growth', 'voluntary simplicity' and 'transition' movements, which particularly focus on the problematics of growth. They will only be briefly discussed here, as Perey (this volume) discusses degrowth more thoroughly.

The outline of this chapter is as follows: The next section examines the green economy concept, particularly as outlined by UNEP (2011). The following section turns to the currently topical circular economy concept, which has adopted and extended Cradle-to-Cradle ideas, and has most recently been associated with the Ellen MacArthur Foundation. Another current but perhaps less known concept is the blue economy, which has been proposed and promoted by entrepreneur and economist Gunter Pauli and is then outlined. We then discuss how these three models compare to the steady state economy, including how they address the issues of population and consumption growth, which are core issues in the steady state economy model. The conclusion reviews the different economic models and how they relate to the steady state economy.

The green economy

The term 'green economy' and its sister term 'green growth' have become popular among policy makers and sustainability organizations around the world in recent years. They were particularly prominent in the rhetoric of responses to the global recession of 2008, and in the lead up to and following the UN Rio+20 Summit in 2012. The terms were embedded into a number of framework documents that were intended to reinvigorate support for sustainable development. These documents included UNEP (2011), OECD (2012) and World Bank (2012) as well as charters for new organizations and initiatives such as the Green Economy Coalition, Global Green Growth Institute, the Green Growth Knowledge Platform and the Green Growth Best Practice Initiative.

Figures 10.1 and 10.2 show how the term 'green economy' returns far more webpages (as of July 2015) and over the past eight years has been a much more popular Google search term than compared to the three other models discussed in this paper.

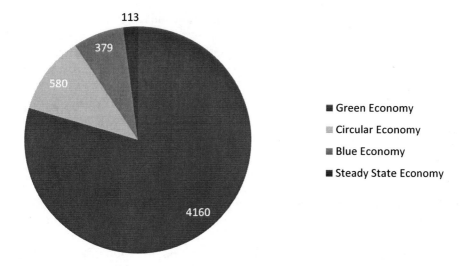

FIGURE 10.1 Google search webpage hits for different terms ('000s), July 2015

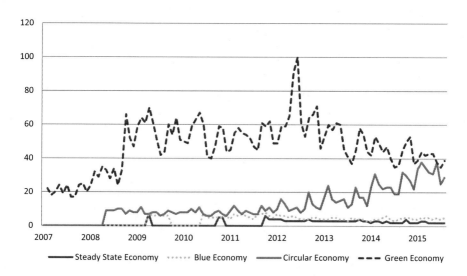

FIGURE 10.2 Relative popularity of term in Google search (Google Trends. Note: the levels represent relative popularity of search terms and not absolute levels.)

While there is no globally accepted definition of the green economy (or indeed green growth), perhaps the most commonly used definition is that of UNEP (2011), which defines the green economy as:

> one that results in improved human well-being and social equity, while significantly reducing environmental risks and ecological scarcities ... one which is low carbon, resource efficient and socially inclusive.

Their definition maintains the three dimensions of the WCED (1987) *Our Common Future* usage of 'sustainable development' (economic, environmental and social sustainability) and shows that the green economy does not seek to replace sustainable development, but rather is intended to serve as the tool for achieving it.

Compared to the circular and blue economies, the green economy has a stronger focus on the whole economy, including issues such as national or global employment and emissions. For example, the UNEP (2011) report uses a global macroeconomic model to demonstrate the benefits of shifting from a 'brown economy' (fossil fuel-based economy) to a green economy. The approach is also not shy of proposing economy-wide aspirational goals. They make an economic and social case for investing 2 per cent of global GDP in greening ten central sectors of the economy in order to shift development onto a low-carbon, resource-efficient path.

To make the transition to a green economy, UNEP (2011) points to a number of specific enabling conditions. For governments, this would include phasing out fossil fuel subsidies; improving environmental rules and regulations; strengthening market and legal infrastructure; employing new market-based mechanisms; redirecting public investment; and greening public procurement. For the private sector, this would involve recognizing the opportunities offered by the transition to the green economy and responding to price signals and policy reforms.

New ways of measuring progress are also a prominent aspect of the green economy literature. The inadequacy of conventional economic indicators, such as GDP, are readily apparent and acknowledged in the literature, including the failure to account for environmental degradation and depleting resources. A number of green economy reports point towards alternative natural capital and full cost accounting systems, such as the UN's System of Environmental and Economic Accounting (SEEA 2012) and the World Bank's Adjusted Net National Savings method (World Bank 2007).

Green growth is a concept closely related in academic discussion to that of the green economy (Charonis 2012). Though not specifically mentioned as a term in UNEP (2011), the document makes clear on page 3 that the green economy is a 'new engine of growth'. OECD (2011) defines green growth as follows:

> Green growth means fostering economic growth and development, while ensuring that natural assets continue to provide the resources and environmental services on which our well-being relies.

The UNSD (2015a) acknowledges that there are at least 13 separate definitions for green growth. The two terms of green economy and green growth, however, are often used interchangeably in academia and government (UNESCAP 2015). However, it could be argued that the concepts are distinct. UNSD (2015b) states:

> Despite the growing international interest in green economy, negotiations between Member States on the concept in the lead up to Rio+20 were challenging. This was partly due to the lack of an internationally agreed

definition or universal principles for green economy, the emergence of interrelated but different terminology and concepts over recent years (such as green growth, low carbon development, sustainable economy, steady-state economy etc.)

Raouf and Luomi (2015) argue that the difference between the green economy and green growth relate to the scope of the two concepts. The green economy, they argue, relates to governance systems and promotes a shifting in the *whole* of the economy towards a transformation beyond the brown economy. Green growth refers to increasing the quantity of goods and services in the economy in an environmentally friendly manner, but does not require that all the economy be green. However, it is most often the case that the major proponents of the green economy also endorse green growth (even if this is not precisely defined).

The circular economy

The circular economy is a term that has recently become fashionable among the business community and a number of governments (see Kopnina in this volume). The term has been particularly popularized by a series of reports by the Ellen MacArthur Foundation, an independent charity established in 2010 (EMF 2012). As Figure 10.2 indicates, the term circular economy has now become equally as popular as the green economy as a search term. The circular economy now regularly headlines as a theme of the business conference circuit. Similarly in policy circles, the European Commission has announced that it will be presenting an ambitious circular economy strategy in late 2015 (EC 2015).

Compared to the broad set of goals and enabling policies of the green economy, the circular economy has a more narrow focus on the diagnosis and solutions for a more sustainable world. The particular focus is on the traditional industrial model of production and the wasteful style of daily consumption (if not especially challenging consumerism as such). This linear model of 'take, make and dispose' arose in an era of (apparently) cheap and abundant resources, which is no longer the case. By contrast, in a circular economy, products are *eco-designed* and *eco-effective* such that they use as little energy and materials as possible. Product design involves forming a 'closed loop' so that all waste is accounted for and put to good use. Designed objects can have multiple life cycles and renewable energy systems can be used to power the circular cycle. This 'designing out' of waste should be differentiated from current disposal and recycling methods, which can themselves require significant resources to implement.

The generic idea behind the circular economy is not new: how can we create better industrial design, business models and consumer practices that use the Earth's resources more efficiently and productively? For example, the idea of circular material flows as a model for the economy traces back to at least 1966 with Kenneth Boulding, one of the forefathers of ecological economics, in his paper 'The Economics of the Coming Spaceship Earth' (Boulding 1966). The concept can also been seen as an application of the Cradle-to-Cradle design philosophy which was coined by Walter Stahel (e.g Stahel and Reday 1976) and popularized by Michael Braungart and William McDonough in their book *Cradle to Cradle* (2008).

The banner of the circular economy can therefore be seen as a reinvigoration of these earlier ideas. In addition to various new materials recovery methods, two of the more interesting business and social practices which are being promoted by the circular economy are *service orientated business models* and *sharing economy networks*. Both of these innovations, which have also been around for many years (but are only now finding their moment), involve a rethinking of the importance of private ownership of the things we use in the economy.

In the circular economy, businesses will more likely be orientated towards selling services or leasing products, rather than selling products outright (Wijkman and Rockström 2012). The producer would thus take responsibility for the product over its whole life-cycle, and replace it when it wears out, making sure its materials are reused or recycled. Thus the circular economy seeks to eradicate the 'planned obsolescence' business strategy which is arguably very common in the business world. The idea of selling goods as services as a key strategy of the circular economy has been particularly associated with the work of Walter Stahel, who used the term 'the performance economy' as the title of his 2006 book (Stahel 2006). He currently works closely with the Ellen MacArthur Foundation on promoting this idea.

A famous pioneering example of a service-orientated approach is Interface, a carpet company that was built on the conventional retail model of selling carpets to customers. The owner, being concerned over how much used carpet was unnecessarily becoming landfill after the customers installed new carpets, was inspired in 1995 to develop the Evergreen Lease program, which aimed to sell a floor covering service rather than the carpets. The carpet was modularized so that only the worn carpet would be replaced and the replaced carpet could be reclaimed, repaired and reused by Interface. It has developed into being an economically and ecologically successful idea (Anderson 1999).

An example of dramatic savings that could arise from using circular economy principles has been estimated for the market for mobile phones (which are in fact often leased to customers on services agreements, but are usually not reclaimed by the phone provider). If the industry made handsets that were easier to take apart, improved the reverse cycle and offered incentives to return devices that are no longer needed, modelling suggests that costs (and similarly the ecological impact) of handsets could be reduced by 50 per cent (WEforum 2015).

Different ideas of ownership are also present in what is best called the 'sharing economy' (Friedman 2013) or 'collaborative economy' but is closely aligned and embraced by the circular economy (WEforum 2015). In the sharing economy, technology has enabled those who have assets with 'idle capacity' (e.g. bicycles, cars, household tools, unoccupied rooms) to lend, swap, barter or sell that spare capacity. Unlocking the untapped value of underutilized assets means that a smaller stock of such assets is required in the economy. Recent famous examples exploiting this new model for profit are the car-riding Uber services and the room-sharing Airbnb, but similar not-for-profit ventures also exist.

The blue economy

The blue economy is another idea that has close links to the green economy and circular economy. The term was coined by Belgian economist Gunter Pauli. His 2010 book, *The Blue Economy*, was commissioned as a report for the Club of Rome think tank. Note that the use of the term blue economy as outlined by Pauli should be distinguished from an alternative meaning, namely in relation to the conservation and sustainable management of oceans and ensuring small island developing states benefit from their marine resources (e.g. UN 2012).

Like the circular economy, the blue economy includes the aim of achieving radical resource efficiency and minimal waste. This includes incorporating concepts such as cradle-to-cradle products, closed loop production, industrial ecology, renewable energy and the sharing economy. However, the blue economy claims to distinguish itself from green and circular economy practices by claiming to be (i) more *systemic* in its perspective; (ii) focused on novel ways for businesses to create *new ecological and social value* (in addition to finding core efficiencies); (iii) strong in presenting *inspirational case studies*; and (iv) having an emphasis on *local development* (Jewel 2014).

The blue economy has partly framed itself in opposition to the standard green economy paradigm, which is perceived as a linear, piecemeal, incremental, diminishing-return process, where the endpoint is simply one of making something 'less bad' (Jewell 2014). Disappointing outcomes of many green projects, where unintended consequences have resulted in suboptimal environmental outcomes, have produced a 'green fatigue'. The green building industry is given as an example of where one sees a range of technologies being put into a building and then given a high green certification (and much praise) but only later sees evidence that the building is not performing as intended due to various integration issues and other unintended outcomes. The blue economy approach claims to adopt an holistic, complex adaptive system approach that can more reliably construct 'win-win-win' scenarios, where the economy, the local community and the environment all do well (Jewell 2014).

Another emphasis of the blue economy is that it shifts the emphasis away from business models that focus on core competences in a specific sector or industry, where the strategies are about endless cost cutting or sales growth as the only means to increase profits. Instead, the blue economy advocates a more systemic perspective where new value is *created* across a portfolio of businesses. In particular, the focus of the blue economy is on the ways that businesses can create and promote business activities that are both environmentally beneficial and which have financial and wider social benefits, including job creation, reduced energy use and more diversified revenue streams (Pauli 2010).

As compared to the other models, the blue economy is also primarily an open-source solutions-based approach for inspiring and creating a more sustainable economy, rather than one which sets out high-level sustainability goals or theories of a sustainable economy. The primary Blue Economy website (www.theblueeconomy.org) provides over a hundred case studies of projects which have demonstrated ecological and social benefits through connecting and combining seemingly disparate environmental problems with open-source scientific solutions based upon physical processes common in the natural world. One example is of a coffee company which generates income from coffee (its core business), but which can now also generate revenue from the mushrooms farmed on the waste, and for which the residuals after harvesting the protein-rich fungi can also be used as animal feed. A one revenue model is now transformed into a three revenue model with a raft of environmental benefits (Pauli 2010).

The blue economy also has a strong entrepreneurial spirit, and Pauli admits that the blue economy is not tailored to large corporations, which have established business models that are resistant to change. Pauli (2010) imagines that the blue economy model can inspire entrepreneurial minds by providing a broad platform of innovative ideas that have been implemented somewhere in the world to demonstrate what may be possible if we move beyond the conventional business models.

Comparing the models: relating the green, circular and blue economies to the steady state economy

A summary comparison of the three models, along with the steady state economy model, is presented in Table 10.1. We do not provide a fuller description of the steady state economy here, as this is covered thoroughly by Magnus-Johnston in this volume.

As the table shows, one of the clearest differences between the steady state economy model and the other models is the broadness of scope of what the former is attempting to achieve. The steady state economy tackles the question of the scale of the entire economy in relation to ecological limits. This is aligned with one of the central themes of ecological economics and contrasts with much of conventional 'environmental' economics, which focuses more on issues of efficiency and substitution, to the neglect of concern with scale (van den Bergh 2000). The green economy is closest (if not very close) to the steady state economy in terms of addressing sustainability in a number of different sectors. The circular economy and blue economy are limited to mostly focusing on industrial activities and particularly the role of business, including new models of business and industrial activity.

The difference in concern with scale and the entire economy is also apparent in terms of the scope of policies and strategies that the steady state economy suggests. These include ideas ranging from reforming the financial system to reshaping values and the work-life balance. This contrasts with a narrower (but deeper and nuanced) set of policies and strategies in the other models.

Another useful way of comparing and untangling some key differences between the SSE and the other models is through the use of the I=PAT framework (Ehrlich et al. 1977). The I=PAT entity is a simple conceptual entity for describing environmental impact (I) as a product of three factors: (i) population (P); (ii) affluence (A) or average consumption per person; and (iii) technology (T) or how resource-, energy- and waste-intensive the production of affluence is.

A key difference of all three models compared to the SSE is highlighted in the first factor, population, in that *none of them tackle the population issue*. Population is a central concern for the SSE (Daly 1991). One of the core principles of the SSE is a stable population, which means zero net population growth. However, in all of the three other models above the question of ongoing population growth is usually absent (indeed ignored) or explicitly allowed.

For example, the UNEP (2011) discussion of the green economy, while acknowledging population growth a number of times, makes no mention of policies orientated towards moderating population growth. Similarly, *Towards the Circular Economy* (EMF 2012) only mentions population in passing, noting that it will rise. There is no discussion that the Earth may already be overpopulated in terms of humanity exceeding ecological limits (see Washington in this volume). Braungart and McDonough (2008, p.5) in *Cradle to Cradle* state that stabilizing the population is 'like looking into the eyes of a child and saying "It would be better if you were not here"'. They state on p. 66 that those concerned about population believe that humans should stop having children (without quoting what such groups actually say). *The Blue Economy* (Pauli 2010) is also mostly silent on the issue of population.

The second factor in the I=PAT entity, affluence, is also barely touched on in the green, circular and blue economy models. Indeed, continued growth in consumption (as well as population) appears to be *taken for granted* as both possible and desirable. Consumerism, as such, is not challenged by any of the three, nor is the predominance of advertising, while Daly (2008) actually suggests an advertising tax to control this.

This is seen very clearly in UNEP's green economy, which is still very much promoted as a *growth economy* (though it mostly calls this 'progress') (UNEP 2011, p. 2). At the same time, it acknowledges that 'economic growth of recent decades has been accomplished mainly through drawing down natural resources ... allowing widespread ecosystem degradation and loss'. UNEP argues that 'greening' not only generates increases in wealth (in particular gains in natural capital), but also produce a higher rate of GDP growth. They point to an inextricable link between poverty eradication and better conservation of nature. Similarly, in a transition to a green economy, new jobs are created, which over time exceed the losses in 'brown economy' jobs. However, there is a period of job losses in transition, which requires investment in re-skilling and re-education. UNEP (2011, p. 22) concludes that moving towards a green economy has the potential to achieve sustainable development and poverty eradication on a scale and speed 'not seen before'.

Braungart and McDonough (2008, p.4) in *Cradle to Cradle* argue that calling for change in endless growth is somehow anti-human. They note that '[i]f the assumption is that human beings are bad for the planet, surely the best thing is for us not to be here at all'. They then discuss the 'guilt language' of environmentalism. The idea that endless growth on a finite planet is highly problematic, if not absurd, is not recognized.

Now it can be said that 'growth' is possibly compatible with SSE *if* the growth is non-material (and not caused by population growth). Indeed, it may be fairly said that the key feature of the green, circular and blue economy models is that they are advocating a 'decoupling' of the economy from material use. UNEP (2011, p. 16) says that 'the central challenge … as we transition to a resource and carbon constrained world, is to decouple growth absolutely from material and energy intensity'. Similarly, in advocating the circular economy, Ellen MacArthur also clearly highlights the central role of decoupling:

> The concept of the Circular Economy is rapidly capturing attention as a way of decoupling growth from resource constraints. It opens up ways to reconcile the outlook for growth and economic participation with that of environmental prudence and equity.
> *(quoted in WEforum 2015, p. 3)*

The idea of achieving sustainability entirely through significant increases in resource efficiency is also behind the concept of 'Factor 5', described in a 2009 book of that title by Ernst Ulrich von Weizsäcker and an Australian team at The Natural Edge Project (von Weizsaker *et al.* 2009). They argue for an 80 per cent improvement in resource efficiency (i.e. Factor 5) as a panacea to resource and ecological constraints, apparently without requiring significant changes in current consumption levels or population growth.

However, is decoupling realistic or even possible? Almost all economic production requires the transformation of raw materials (Costanza *et al.* 2013). Thus, the scope for de-coupling growth in production and consumption from environmental degradation is not boundless, and the decoupling is unable to keep up with unlimited growth (Næss 2011). Victor (2008) notes that decoupling slows down the rate at which things get worse, but *does not turn them around*. He notes further that some modest decoupling of material flows occurred in some industrialized countries from the mid-1970s to mid-1990s, but total material throughput still increased. Despite increases in efficiency, decoupling GDP and throughput has yet to manifest itself as an increase in GDP combined with a decline in throughput (Victor 2008). Similarly, Matthews *et al.* (2000) found no evidence that moderate decoupling led to absolute reduction in resource throughput, and Wijkman and Rockström (2012, p. 152) concluded the same. Most recently, Victor and Jackson (2015) note that while there has been some 'relative decoupling', any serious absolute decoupling is not evident.

So the evidence to date would suggest that it is impossible to *fully* decouple economic growth from physical environmental impact. Thus, while some forms of positive increase in GDP that don't rely on population and increased throughput could occur under an SSE (though these could more properly be called 'economic development'), talk of '100 per cent decoupling' may just be wishful thinking that allows 'business as usual' growth to continue. Daly (1991) believed it was an illusion to think that growth could continue by becoming ever less materially intensive and service-oriented, and Czech (2013) concurs. Welzer (2011) concludes that the decoupling debate maintains the illusion that we can 'just make minor adjustments'.

In contrast to the green, circular and blue economies, there also exists a number of other discourses or movements that take a clearer stance with respect to population and consumption growth (and are closely related to SSE). These include 'degrowth', 'post-growth', 'transition' and 'voluntary simplicity' movements. Like the SSE, they are currently largely marginalized from mainstream economic and political debates, but have all seen increasing academic and public interest in recent years (Charonis 2012; Pirgmaier 2012). We can only briefly discuss them here (for degrowth, see Perey in this volume).

As the name suggests, degrowth, at its core, aims at economic downsizing, particularly for developed economies (D'Alisa et al. 2014). Kallis (2011) defines sustainable degrowth as 'a socially sustainable and equitable reduction (and eventually stabilisation) of society's throughput'. An international conference on economic degrowth was first held in 2008 and there have been three more since. For many proponents of degrowth, the SSE is seen as the endpoint of a degrowth pathway, and thus they are consistent with each other. For example, the First International Degrowth Conference specifically stated in its final declaration that '[o]nce rightsizing has been achieved through the process of degrowth, the aim should be to maintain a "steady state economy" with a relatively stable, mildly fluctuating level of consumption' (FICED 2008, p. 318).

The post-growth movement has similar concerns to SSE and degrowth, and particularly focuses attention on positive visions of an economy no longer dependent on economic growth (D'Alisa et al. 2014). The emphasis is as much on well-being and quality of life benefits of moving away from growth dependency as it is on the ecological benefits. The title of Tim Jackson's popular book, *Prosperity without Growth* (Jackson 2009), captures the spirit of the movement. In a similar vein, some post-growth researchers distinguish their work from the SSE and degrowth in that they seek to identify and build on what's already working, rather than focusing on what is not (Hinton and Maclurcan 2014).

With a focus on resilient and self-sufficient local communities in response to climate change and peak oil, the Transition Movement shares many of the sentiments of the SSE, degrowth and post-growth. However, it has a stronger grassroots, practice-based flavour and it targets people wishing to improve their local community (for example, through local renewable energy or food projects) rather than one of public policy diagnosis and advocacy. The transition movement originated in Great Britain and Ireland in the 2000s, and is a development of the permaculture concept (Connors 2010). Rob Hopkins has pioneered the 'Transition Towns' concept (originally in Totnes in England and Kinsale in Ireland), and his Transition Towns manual (Hopkins 2008) and the Transition Network (www.transitionnetwork.org/) have helped spread the movement throughout the world.

Finally, focusing on human well-being as well as environmental sustainability, the voluntary simplicity movement has taken aim at the consequences of high-consumption, materialistic lifestyles and advocates a 'downshifting' or just 'simple

TABLE 10.1 Comparison of economic models

	Key promoters	Goals	Areas of focus	Example strategies and policies	Key points present in SSE not found here
Green Economy	UNEP, OECD, World Bank, IMF, Green Economy Coalition, Global Green Growth Institute, Green Growth Knowledge Platform.	Improved human well-being and social equity, while significantly reducing environmental risks and ecological scarcities.	Many sectors, including agriculture, cities, fisheries, forests, green buildings, industry, renewable energy, tourism, transport, waste management and water; Macroeconomic models assessing impact of green investment.	Improving environmental rules and regulations, strengthening market and legal infrastructure, employing market-based mechanisms, phasing out fossil fuel subsidies, redirecting public investment and greening public procurement.	Fails to discuss population Fails to question endless growth, in fact argues that it is a 'new engine of growth' Fails to strongly question consumerism
Circular Economy	Ellen MacArthur Foundation, European Commission, World Economic Forum, Project MainStream.	To create a model of industrial production that is less wasteful and more restorative, where components and materials can be reused many times.	Industrial production and practices of consumption; Service economy business models; Collaborative consumption.	Legislation on areas such as waste prevention targets and incentives around eco-design to promote products that are easier to reuse, remanufacture and disassemble; Data improvements to track and recover resources; Provide consumers with more information about product lifetimes; Extend minimum legal warranties; Lower taxes on repair service activities.	Fails to discuss population Fails to question endless growth as key ideological problem Fails to strongly question consumerism as an ideology

Blue Economy	Gunter Pauli, Club of Rome, Zero Emissions Research and Initiatives.	Redesign business and industrial structures that focus on the interconnectedness of systems and synergies between environment, economy and society.	Industrial activities; Entrepreneurship; Local economy, environment and communities.	Open-source movement bringing together concrete case studies; Collaborative projects.
Steady State Economy	Herman Daly, Centre for the Advancement of the Steady State Economy, Dietz and O'Neill (2013)	To create a zero material growth economy which features stable population and stable consumption that remains at or below carrying capacity.	Economy wide resource use; Population growth; Income distribution; Monetary and financial systems; Secure and meaningful employment; New forms of business and social enterprises; Well-being and consumerism; National goals and measures of progress.	Caps and quotas to limit resource use and waste production; Reduce incentives for having large family sizes; Distribute income and wealth equitably through taxes and minimum income requirements; Local currencies and restructuring of financial institutions; 'Work-life balance' policies; Support Cooperatives and new legal structures for firms such as Benefit Corporations.

Fails to discuss population
Fails to question endless growth as key ideological problem
Fails to strongly question consumerism as an ideology

living' as a pathway towards a more just and sustainable society (Alexander 2011). Of course, the notion of 'simple living' is not a new one and various religious and secular traditions have advocated such ideas across history. But unlike some earlier movements, recently formed organizations such as the Simplicity Institute (simplicityinstitute.org) and Simplicity Collective (simplicitycollective.com) make clear that they are not advocating living like ascetic monks, nor necessarily escaping to distant communes. Rather, they are suggesting that we reexamine our relationships with material possessions, the planet, ourselves and each other.

Conclusion

The variety of alternative ideas and models mentioned in this chapter point to an increasingly widespread view that the current structure of both the economy and society is *broken* and requires significant transformation. This chapter has provided an overview of three recent, prominent models of such transformation and has compared them to the older (and broader) concept of the steady state economy.

All four approaches share a common vision: one of improving the quality of life and well-being of humanity, while respecting the planetary ecological carrying capacity. However, we have also shown that there are important cleavages between the green, circular and blue economies, on the one hand, and the steady state economy approach on the other. Namely, the former are primarily based around the idea of *ecological modernization*: the idea that innovations can decouple economic growth from ecological constraints. While these new models do include advocating *social* innovations such as collaborative consumption, in addition to *technological* innovations, in presenting a vision of a future economy and society, the deeper lifestyle questions of whether we can continue to have growth in personal consumption and population are mostly ignored (or are assumed to not pose a problem in a decoupled economy). The green, circular and blue economies singularly fail to address the issue of population (presumably due to its contentious nature). They also singularly fail to challenge consumerism and overconsumption. Similarly, they also fail to challenge the 'endless growth myth' (see Washington in this volume). However, these approaches clearly can be very useful in terms of lowering throughput, a key aim of an SSE.

Therefore, proponents of the steady state economy, who agree on the vital importance of efficiency and waste minimization in production, product design and utilization of goods and services, would do well to learn and embrace many of the innovative ideas that have been spurred by these new models. However, they should also be concerned as to whether the popularity of these discourses may also be suppressing a vital set of complementary concerns that are voiced in the SSE discourse. Given the thin evidence (or lack thereof) to date of the viability of an 'absolutely decoupled' economy, the need for critical debate on the sanity, ethics or feasibility of the endless growth mantra is clear. As Kopnina notes in this volume, the circular economy can be subverted. So can the green and blue economies – to support a 'business as usual' growth approach. This is arguably why they have become far more popular than the steady state economy, which challenges endless growth. In conclusion, we would suggest that while the strategies in the green, circular and blue economies are all useful, they tackle *less than half the problem*. They fail to consider population growth and overconsumption (driven by advertising). As such, we do not believe these more recent economies can replace the broader (and more ecologically realistic) focus of the steady state economy.

References

Alexander, S. (2011) 'The voluntary simplicity movement: Reimagining the good life beyond consumer culture', *The International Journal of Environmental, Cultural, Economic and Social Sustainability*, 7(3), pp. 133–150.
Anderson, R. (1999) *Mid-Course Correction: Toward a Sustainable Enterprise: the Interface Model*, Atlanta, GA: Peregrinzilla Press.
Boulding, K. E. (1966) 'The economics of the coming spaceship earth', in H. Jarrett (ed.), *Environmental quality in a growing economy*, Baltimore: Johns Hopkins University Press, pp. 3–14.
Braungart, M. and McDonough, W. (2008) *Cradle to Cradle: Remaking the Way We Make Things*, London: Vintage Books.
Charonis, G-K. (2012) 'Degrowth, steady state economics and the circular economy: three distinct yet increasingly converging alternative discourses to economic growth for achieving environmental sustainability and social equity', World Economics Association Conferences, 21–24 October 2012.
Connors, P. (2010) 'Transitioning communities: community, participation and the Transition Town movement', *Community Development Journal*, 46(4), pp. 558–572.
Costanza, R., Alperovitz, G., Daly, H., Farley, J., Franco, C., Jackson, T., Kubiszewski, I., Schor, J., and Victor, P. (2013) 'Building a sustainable and desirable economy-in-society-in-nature', in *State of the World 2013: Is Sustainability Still Possible?*, ed. L. Starke, Washington: Island Press, pp. 126–142.
Czech, B. (2013) *Supply Shock: Economic Growth at the Crossroads and the Steady State Solution*, Canada: New Society Publishers.
D'Alisa, G., Demaria, F., and Kallis G. (eds) (2014) *Degrowth: A Vocabulary for a New Era*, London: Routledge.
Daly, H. (1991) *Steady State Economics*, Washington, DC: Island Press.
Daly, H. (2008) 'A steady-state economy: A failed growth economy and a steady-state economy are not the same thing; they are the very different alternatives we face', Think Piece for the Sustainable Development Commission, UK, 24 April 2008, see: http://steadystaterevolution.org/files/pdf/Daly_UK_Paper.pdf
Dietz, R. and O'Neill, D. (2013) *Enough is Enough: Building a Sustainable Economy in a World of Finite Resources*, New York: Berrett-Koeler Publishers.
EC (2015) Moving towards a circular economy. Available at http://ec.europa.eu/environment/circular-economy/index_en.htm
Ehrlich, P., Ehrlich, A., and Holdren, J. (1977) *Ecoscience: Population, Resources, Environment*, New York: WH Freeman and Co.
EMF (2012) Towards a circular economy: Economic and business rationale for an accelerated transition, Isle of Wight, UK: Ellen Macarthur Foundation. Available at: www.ellenmacarthurfoundation.org/business/reports/ce2012

FICED (2008) *Conference Proceedings of the First International Conference on Economic De-Growth, Paris, 2008.*
Friedman, T. (2013) 'Welcome to the sharing economy', *New York Times*, 21 July, 2013. See: http://www.nytimes.com/2013/07/21/opinion/sunday/friedman-welcome-to-the-sharing-economy.html?pagewanted=all&_r=0
Hinton, J. and Maclurcan, D. (2014) 'A post-growth event: Free money day – What is the difference between post-growth and degrowth?', *Degrowth Web Portal*. See: http://www.degrowth.de/en/2014/09/a-post-growth-event-free-money-day/ (accessed 1/9/15)
Hopkins, R. (2008). *The Transition Handbook: From Oil Dependency to Local Resilience.* Totnes: Green Books.
Jackson, T. (2009) *Prosperity without Growth*, London: Routledge.
Jewell, C. (2014) 'Martin Blake: Into the Blue Economy', *The Fifth Estate*, 14 April 2014. Available at http://www.thefifthestate.com.au/business/innovators-fringe-elements/martin-blake-into-the-blue-economy/60907
Kallis, G. (2011) 'In defence of degrowth', *Ecological Economics*, 7(5), pp. 873–880.
Matthews, E., Amann, C, Bringezu, S., Fisher-Kowalski, M., Hutler, W., Kleijn, R., Moriguchi, Y., Ottke, C., Rodenberg, E., Rogich, D., Schandl, H., Schutz, H., Vandervoet, E., and Weisz, H. (2000) *The Weight of Nations: Material Outflows from Industrial Economies*, Washington, DC: World Resources Institute. Available at: http://pdf.wri.org/weight_of_nations.pdf
Næss, P. (2011) 'Unsustainable Growth, Unsustainable Capitalism', *Journal of Critical Realism*, 5(2), pp. 197–227.
OECD (Organisation for Economic Cooperation and Development) (2011) *Towards Green Growth: A Summary for Policymakers May 2011*, Paris: OECD. See: http://www.oecd.org/greengrowth/48012345.pdf
OECD (2012) *Green Growth and Developing Countries: A Summary for Policymakers*, Paris: OECD.
Pauli, G. (2010) *The Blue Economy*, Boulder, CO: Paradigm Publishers.
Pirgmaier, E. (2012) 'Alternative Economic and Social Concepts', Growth in Transition Future Dossier No. 3., Austrian Federal Ministry of Agriculture, Forestry, Environment and Water Management. See http://www.growthintransition.eu/wp-content/uploads/WiW-Dossier_Alternative_Economic_and_Social_concepts_en.pdf
Raouf, M. A. and Luomi, M. (2015) 'Introduction' in M. A. Raouf and M. Luomi (eds) *The Green Economy in the Gulf*, London: Routledge.
SEEA (2012) *System of Environmental-Economic Accounting 2012: Central Framework.* New York: United Nations, European Commission, Food and Agriculture Organization of the United Nations, International Monetary Fund, Organisation for Economic Co-operation and Development, World Bank.
Stahel, W.R. (2006) *The Performance Economy*, London: Palgrave-MacMillan.
Stahel, W. R. and Reday, G. (1976) *Jobs for Tomorrow: The Potential for Substituting Manpower for Energy*, Report to the Commission of the European Communities (Brussels), New York: Vantage Press.
UNEP (2011) *Towards a Green Economy: Pathways to Sustainable Development and Poverty Eradication*, New York: United Nations Environment Programme. See: www.unep.org/greeneconomy

UNESCAP (United Nations Economic and Social Commission for Asia and the Pacific) (2015) 'Green growth and green economy'. See: http://www.unescap.org/our-work/environment-development/green-growth-green-economy/about

UN (2012) 'Blue economy concept paper'. See: https://sustainabledevelopment.un.org/content/documents/2978BEconcept.pdf

UNSD (United Nations Sustainable Development) (2015a) 'Green growth'. See: https://sustainabledevelopment.un.org/index.php?menu=1447

UNSD (2015b) 'Green economy in the context of sustainable development and poverty eradication'. See: https://sustainabledevelopment.un.org/topics/greeneconomy

van den Bergh, J. (2000) *Themes, Approaches, and Differences with Environmental Economics*, Tinbergen Institute Discussion Paper 2000–080/3, Tinbergen Institute, Rotterdam.

Victor, P. (2008) *Managing without Growth: Slower by Design, not Disaster*, Cheltenham: Edward Elgar.

Victor, P. and Jackson, T. (2015) 'The problem with growth', in L. Starke (ed.), *2015 State of the World Report, Confronting Hidden Threats to Sustainability*, Washington, DC: Worldwatch Institute, pp. 37–50.

von Weizsäcker, E., Hargroves, K., Smith, M., Desha, C. and Stasinopoulos, P. (2009) *Factor 5: Transforming the Global Economy through 80 per cent Increase in Resource Productivity*, London: Earthscan.

Washington, H. (2015) *Demystifying Sustainability: Towards Real Solutions*, London: Routledge.

WCED (World Commission on Environment and Development) (1987) *Our Common Future*, London: Oxford University Press.

WEforum (World Economic Forum) (2015) 'Favorable alignment of enablers, Box 2'. See: http://reports.weforum.org/toward-the-circular-economy-accelerating-the-scale-up-across-global-supply-chains/favourable-alignment-of-enablers/

Welzer, H. (2011) *Mental Infrastructures: How Growth Entered the World and Our Souls*, Berlin: Heinrich Boll Foundation.

Wijkman, A. and Rockström, J. (2012) *Bankrupting Nature: Denying Our Planetary Boundaries*, London: Routledge.

World Bank (2007) *World Development Indicators 2007*, Washington, DC: World Bank.

World Bank (2012) *Inclusive Green Growth: The Pathway to Sustainable Development*, Washington, DC: World Bank.

11

SUSTAINABLE, EQUITABLE, SECURE

Getting there?

Frank Stilwell

UNIVERSITY OF SYDNEY

Introduction

As a political economist, I embrace the notion of a steady state economy (SSE) because it focuses attention on the economic arrangements that are necessary for living sustainably as a whole society. SSE, both as an analytical concept and a social aspiration, is not free of tensions and difficulties – but what is? Its central contribution is in raising questions about how the economy needs to be reorganised. It directs our gaze to what would be required in moving beyond a rapacious relationship with nature towards one that is more harmonious. Concurrently, it challenges mainstream economic views that regard environmental issues only as 'externalities' that need to be addressed before resuming the 'business as usual' of endless economic growth. SSE gives us a valuable way of looking at economic activities, their social purposes and ecological relationships.

This chapter considers some key challenges thrown up by modern capitalism and explores whether SSE principles can be translated into effective political economic practice and policies. It places particular emphasis on issues of economic security and equity, alongside the environmental issues to which proponents of SSE usually give primary attention. It reasons that achieving security and equity are necessary accompaniments to sustainability, which is interpreted as 'longevity with sufficiency' (Daly 2014, p. ix).

The structure of the chapter reflects the view that any program to drive political economic change requires critique, vision, strategy and organisation. Indeed, these four elements are crucial for the success of any social movement. We need a clear critique of the current political economic arrangements; a vision of a preferred alternative; a strategy for getting from here to there; and one or more organisational vehicles to take us on the journey. Are these not always the elements necessary for bringing about social change if we seek to be mistresses/masters of our own destiny in a continuously troublesome world? The general necessity of critique, vision, strategy and organisation was posited in one of my previous publications (Stilwell 2000) and it seems particularly appropriate here. It directs our attention to what characteristics an SSE must have if it is to be more than a 'pipe dream' and to become a basis on which societies are actually organised.

Critique

The political economic problems that generate the need for change are all too familiar. Unemployment and poverty persist despite substantial economic growth. The economic growth itself tends to be sporadic, boom periods being interspersed with recessions. Even when economies are expanding, the outcome does not seem to be reliably happier societies. There is increasing recognition that growth for growth's sake is not ultimately fulfilling. Nor is it sustainable, given the limits imposed by finite resource endowments and the environmentally degrading consequences of current patterns of production and consumption. The conventional assumptions of mainstream economic theory need to be fundamentally reconsidered in these circumstances (see, for example, Perry and Primrose 2015).

The problems arising from the economy's unsustainable relationship to nature are fundamental. Any reader of this volume will be aware of at least some of these stresses. They are manifest as recurrent problems of resource depletion, pollution and other forms of environmental degradation. Ever since the early 1970s when the Club of Rome's research team (Meadows *et al.* 1972) produced its original calculations of the unsustainable trends in population, industrial production, pollution and depletion, there has been no excuse for ignorance about the environmental limits to growth. The precise nature of the cause–effect relationships and the severity of the limits remain matters of contested judgment (Higgs 2014, ch.4) but nature has the ultimately decisive voice. The evidence of climate change shows the potentially catastrophic consequence of failure to heed the earlier warnings. So too does the evidence that ecological footprints created by existing patterns of production and consumption are far larger than the capacity of the planet to sustain those volumes of economic activity. Economic optimists continue to assert that further technological progress can create 'fixes' for these problems, but time is evidently not on their side. We are living beyond our environmental means and the payback date cannot be indefinitely deferred.

Other current problems are more straightforwardly socio-economic, in both their causes and effects. The problems of economic instability and insecurity are cases in point. To a significant extent, the former cause the latter: the economy's roller-coaster ride of booms and slumps generates perpetual insecurity. Businesses prosper when times are good but then fail because of changed market conditions. Workers get jobs and then lose them, often through no fault of their own. The underlying reasons lie in the systemic instability of the capitalist economy. Capitalism's fundamental feature is production for profit, but the conditions for continuing prosperity are themselves vulnerable to myriad problems of resource depletion, market saturation, industrial disputation and excessive financial speculation.

Even in 'good' times, economic insecurity has become the norm. Increasing proportions of workers are employed on casual and short-term contracts, giving rise to what some commentators call the *precariat* – people for whom employment security is not achievable (Standing 2011). Even middle-class people with reasonably steady incomes now face additional uncertainties because of the 'risk shift' that has occurred in recent decades. Privatisation of public enterprises and services has resulted in households having to manage complex financial matters relating to personal health insurance, education fees and superannuation investments while also having to make previously unsought choices between different utility and communications service providers (Allon 2012). The economic security that most of us need as a basis for reliable social existence seems more elusive, despite increased overall economic prosperity.

Interacting with all these problems are the consequences of economic inequality. We live in an era in which neoliberal ideologies and political practices have seemingly relegated egalitarian concerns to a lowered social priority. Increased inequality in the distribution of income and wealth has become a major feature in most nations around the world, other than in South America. Some politicians and right-wing commentators evidently do not regard this as a problem. Like economic insecurity, inequality has its advocates among people of a neoliberal inclination who claim that inequality is a necessary stimulus for economic effort and enterprise. Empirical evidence to support this view remains elusive, however. And one must ask how much inequality would be justified on those neoliberal grounds? Perhaps a skilled craftsman needs a higher income than a labourer if there is to be sufficient incentive to acquire the craft skills in the first place. Perhaps an enterprising businessperson warrants a higher income than those s/he employs if s/he is particularly innovative or risk-taking. But the necessary or socially acceptable income relativities are always debatable.

In practice, the economic inequalities have grown enormously over the last two decades, particularly the gulf between the incomes of senior managers and their employees. The rapid increase in the ratio of CEO incomes to workers' median wages has little connection to measured productivity, but it has been a significant contributor to the sharply rising share of income going to the richest one percent of households (Piketty 2014, ch.9; Leigh 2013, ch.3).

What is particularly troubling about the trend to increased economic inequality is its connection with the intensity of a wide range of social problems. British epidemiologists Wilkinson and Pickett (2009) have documented the statistical links between income inequalities and indicators of poor physical and mental health, obesity, crime, prison incarceration and various other social disorders. Their research shows that the problems are generally more pronounced in highly unequal countries (with the USA often being the leading case) than in more egalitarian countries (like Japan and the Scandinavian nations). Moreover, the severity of the problems is more strongly correlated with economic inequality than with overall average incomes. In other words, the reduction of social problems would more likely be achieved by policies of *redistribution* than by the pursuit of further economic growth.

Supplementing this evidence on the link between economic inequality and social problems are somewhat similar findings on reported levels of happiness in different countries. The correlation between average incomes and reported happiness appears notably weak. Many nations have got richer over recent decades without their people in general becoming happier, according to surveys of self-reported well-being (Wilkinson and Pickett 2009, pp. 6–10). Admittedly, 'happiness' is a concept that may have different meanings in different national/cultural contexts. However, perhaps we should not be too surprised at the evidence on the disappointing results of economic growth. When a very poor person gets richer, there is a predictable improvement in her or his well-being but, beyond a certain point, the association tends to fall away. Indeed, isn't the point of economic progress to improve people's well-being by eradicating poverty, thereby enabling them to spend their time in more fulfilling pursuits beyond the narrowly materialistic? To pursue yet more income at the expense of those broader social purposes is ultimately counterproductive.

These findings have strong echoes of the case for a steady state economy made in the nineteenth century by the political economist and philosopher John Stuart Mill (1848). They also resonate with the arguments for a basic citizens' income put forward early in the twentieth century by the renowned mathematician and philosopher Bertrand Russell (1917). The shared ambition to make the economy serve society, rather than the other way round, seems remarkably sensible in retrospect. What has gone wrong in the meanwhile? One answer is that concerns for more balanced social progress have receded from view as capital accumulation has become the overriding economic goal. Moreover, the attempts that governments in many countries made to rein in economic inequality during the three decades after the Second World War have since been jettisoned in favour of neoliberal policies that encourage and facilitate widening inequalities.

Political economists have analysed these issues in detail. David Harvey's writing, for example, is particularly useful in showing the diverse manifestations of contradictions that are deeply embedded in the capitalist system (Harvey 2014). For our current purpose it is sufficient to note that major problems of economic insecurity and inequality co-exist with the ecologically unsustainable character of the current economic system; that these problems are *interlinked*; and that they are *not solvable by further economic growth*.

Vision

So what is to be done? As a society, we need to restructure the economy so that, instead of being 'geared for growth', it operates within environmental limits, distributes its fruits equitably and creates conditions in which people can lead more secure lives. This is not to argue that the economy and economic concerns are unimportant. Rather, the point is that *maximising* economic variables (profits, incomes, capital accumulation) should be replaced by *optimising*, which is a process of seeking balance between diverse, interrelated goals. The emphasis would then be on blending the satisfaction of basic economic needs with the pursuit of broader goals of personal and social development, advance of scientific knowledge and cultural enrichment, allowing people adequate time and space for their engagement in whatever forms of culture and creativity are personally fulfilling.

There are two principal ways in which we can extend these considerations of 'the vision thing' (as US President George W. Bush notoriously called it). One is to more fully elaborate on the admirable features of the preferred social order (e.g. an SSE), thereby hoping to convince more people of its desirability. This requires fuller consideration of the processes, mechanisms and institutions by which such a society would function. The other approach is more dialectical, focusing on how the tensions within any social order contain the seeds of change that can produce better outcomes.

The former approach has value. One may draw a parallel with commercial advertising campaigns that offer commodities as solutions to consumers' personal problems. The potential hazards that advertisers parade for this purpose are almost unlimited, including body odour, 'lifeless' hair, and clothes that have not come out of the wash sparkling clean. Fears of personal inadequacy or social ridicule are stimulated, quickly followed by the promise that these personal problems will disappear once the marketed products are purchased and used. Marketing an SSE is rather different. Here the hazards are societal rather than purely individual; and the threats are all too real but insufficiently widely understood. Indeed, the possibility of a different social order is so far beyond most people's personal experiences that it is hard to imagine or grasp. Selling commercial fixes for personal problems is so much more straightforward than promoting awareness of the need for broader societal change.

Yet societal change does occur. Indeed, it is constantly occurring, although we do not usually move smoothly from one social state to another. This is where the dialectical aspect enters the story. Dialectics involves change generated by conflict and contradiction. Understanding change therefore needs consideration of how the tensions shape the responses and likely outcomes. This is an important point to make in the context of developing an SSE vision, because it is out of the contradictions of the present that the possibilities of a different future are created.

The dialectical aspect of the desired shift to an SSE can be illustrated by drawing on key ideas in the work of US political economist James O'Connor (2011). Drawing on Marxian political economic analysis, O'Connor identifies the primary contradiction within a capitalist economy as that between capital and labour. Both capital and labour are essential for the production of goods and services but they have a rivalrous relationship that creates ongoing class conflict. This is manifest in continuing struggles over the application of technology, the changing conditions of work, the level of wages and the distribution of income between wages and profits. The resulting social struggles produce the potential for change to a different political economic system in which these tensions may be resolved. On this reasoning, it is the character of the primary contradiction – between capital and labour – that creates the distinctively class-based politics driving systemic change. There is nothing inevitable about this, of course, as is obvious in modern societies where the labour movement has been more concerned in practice with ameliorative than transformative political economic strategies.

What makes the story more directly relevant to the prospects for an SSE is O'Connor's argument that a second contradiction has developed within capitalism, layered on top of the primary contradiction. This is the contradiction between capital and nature. As capital draws on natural resources to sustain its own needs for expansion, the quality of the physical environment becomes a major arena of stress. The character of social and political conflicts changes accordingly. Greater emphasis comes to be placed on contestations over 'the commons', over patterns of land use and urban development, and over the provision of public services including public transport, public housing and environmental protection. The political economic vision takes on a correspondingly green hue.

Recognising the interacting character of the two political economic contradictions – between capital and labour and between capital and nature – enables us to see future possibilities more clearly. It highlights the structural imperative to transform the socio-economic system into one that is both classless and operates responsibly within environmental constraints. To achieve this requires a 'red-green' synthesis, combining the best elements of socialism and ecological sustainability. More modestly, it may be seen as recognising the necessary interdependence of the values of social justice and environmentalism.

Perhaps we are getting a little ahead of our story here, by looking at the politics of transition rather than keeping the focus purely on 'the vision thing'. It is helpful to consider these connections, however, because the vision can never be wholly separated from the politics of change. What we aspire to is shaped by that from which we seek to escape, by what needs to be changed, and by our experiences in the process of generating that change.

A key question in this context is whether focusing on problems of insecurity and inequity, as advocated in this chapter, makes the goal of sustainability easier or harder to identify and achieve. At first sight it would seem to make it harder, because the achievement of multiple goals – security, equity and sustainability – looks more difficult than targeting a single goal. But deeper reflection suggests otherwise. Because insecurity, inequity and unsustainability are interconnected problems, the resolution of any one of them is more likely to occur as the result of a simultaneous attack on them all. This is the rationale for developing a broad vision of a society that is secure, equitable and more sustainable. Indeed, this is the essence of a progressive steady state economy.

Strategy

So how do we get from here to there? Evidently, it cannot be easy. Imagining a desirable future does not directly deliver it, of course, and logical reasoning is seldom decisive in real-world politics. The currently dominant political economic ideologies, emphasising individualism, competitiveness and the universal benefits of growth, are not conducive to thinking in terms of the cooperative features of a steady state economy, nor of the politics of collective action to achieve it. Even more problematic are the vested interests based in the existing economic arrangements that can be expected to resolutely oppose any challenge to the status quo. As the historian R.H. Tawney memorably said, you can peel an onion layer by layer but you cannot skin a tiger paw by paw. The vested interests in a growth-oriented and environmentally rapacious system are not about to spontaneously reform it, irrespective of the range and intensity of current social and environmental problems.

Thinking strategically about what is to be done requires attention to both the temporal and spatial dimensions of political action. The notion of 'radical reform' is useful in this context. Radical reforms address immediate problems but also pave the way for more fundamental socio-economic transformations. As Andre Gorz (1999, p. 8) puts it, 'the task of politics here is to define immediate strategic objectives, the pursuit of which meets the urgent needs of the present, while at the same time prefiguring the alternative society that is asking to be born'.

Erik Olin Wright's analysis of 'envisioning real utopias' is also useful in this context (Wright 2010, 2015). Wright argues that transformative politics in the current era cannot sensibly be constructed in traditional left terms of 'smashing' the state or the capitalist system. Rather, it must combine elements of 'taming capitalism' (through strong social democratic reforms) and 'eroding capitalism' (through building non-capitalist institutions that have the potential to grow and eventually displace the currently dominant ones). It is the connection between these strategic components – the short term and long term, the localised and the generalised – that is crucial.

Time and space are key coordinates of these political processes. The *temporal* dimension is the more immediately obvious. Anyone who has ever been involved in seeking political reforms knows the importance of timing, particularly the timing of short-, medium- and long-term proposals for change. An impatient view, common among some deeply concerned environmentalists, is that anything less than immediate comprehensive action is likely to be 'too little, too late' for dealing with a complex and awesome problem such as climate change. Notwithstanding its merits as a statement of likely outcomes and as a call for urgent action, this view can be politically paralysing. The proponents of radical reform must also have a Plan B in their inside pockets. Otherwise there is no strategy for dealing with the inevitable resistance from vested interests and people willing to shift only incrementally from the status quo. Perhaps we should sensibly think of three stages for a comprehensive transformation to an SSE: a short-term strategy (focusing on the next five years), a medium-term strategy (five to twenty years) and a long-term strategy (unfolding over a twenty-year time horizon and beyond).

Turning from the temporal dimension to the *spatial* dimension of radical reform, we need to consider the geographical scales at which progress towards an SSE can most effectively be made. Some say the scale has to be worldwide, because the ecological challenge ultimately impacts globally. Others say radical reform is better targeted at nation-states, since that is the scale at which our existing democratic institutions mostly have their jurisdiction. Yet others extol the virtues of localism, because it is at the decentralised scale that grassroots activism has strongest traction and can produce the most clearly tangible outcomes.

At each of the three scales the conditions seldom seem propitious. Globally, most of the major political economic institutions – such as the International Monetary Fund, the World Bank and the World Trade Organisation – are imbued with neoliberal economic ideologies and work in tandem with transnational corporations whose interests are inexorably tied to capital accumulation and economic growth. Nationally, the formally democratic institutions are bedevilled by their short-term orientation, resulting in government policies that merely manage the status quo or make small variations thereto. Meanwhile, activities that are restricted to a local scale often seem to be 'a drop in the ocean' compared to what is needed for a more thoroughgoing and systemic transformation.

My personal judgment is that the best prospects for overcoming the barriers to comprehensive progress are through combining and coordinating action at all three scales. In other words, the fusion of progressive internationalism, defensive nationalism and alternative localism can foster the necessary transition to an SSE. For example, government policies that embody a defensive nationalism can be useful in standing against global capitalist political economic interests. As citizens, we can and should stand firm in our opposition to 'investor-state dispute settlement' mechanisms in so-called 'free trade' agreements that threaten the capacity of national governments to legislate for progressive social and environmental policies. Such forms of resistance can be internationally coordinated, linking into social movements operating at broader spatial scales. Although environmental activism – and, more generally, social struggle around the 'second contradiction' identified by O'Connor – is usually national or local in origin, there is no general need for it to remain spatially bounded. There is the continual prospect of 'going global'. The use of modern information and communications technologies to mutually inform and inspire social movements is an important tool in this process.

Organisation

Having organisational vehicles with clear goals and adequate resources is the fourth and final element for achieving the radical changes needed for progress towards an SSE. It is the lack of any such vehicle which sceptics and opponents of SSE often use to ridicule the movement as unrealistic and ineffective – and which proponents of SSE themselves privately bemoan. Yet, some important building blocks are already in place and more can be developed.

The Center for the Advancement of a Steady State Economy (CASSE) is an important starting point. Stimulated by key thinkers, most obviously Herman Daly, it has developed as a global network of people working to disseminate ideas and promote policies conducive to a growing movement supporting SSE principles.

There is no shortage of intellectuals expressing similar concerns in many parts of the world. In Australia, for example, an excellent report, *Addicted to Growth* (Washington 2014), helped to highlight the issues, as did two major conferences held in 2014 which were attended by hundreds of concerned citizens, scientists and activists. Nor is there any lack of progressive political engagement with environmental issues: such concerns regularly energise grassroots political activists. The growth of environmentally-concerned non-governmental organisations (NGOs) has been prodigious, notwithstanding (or perhaps because of) disappointments about the lack of clear progress at official international conferences on climate change prevention.

What would it take for the politics of seeking SSE to shift from margin to mainstream? Currently, the greatest potential rests with Green parties. Not all explicitly embrace the SSE goal, but the values are generally well aligned. Concerns with equity and social justice mingle with and strengthen the long-standing commitments to environmental protection. So if SSE is defined as including the goals of economic security and equity, as I have argued it should be, Green parties become a natural organisational vehicle for its pursuit. They are local or national in character but have the capacity to develop significant links as a global movement. They blend social democratic reform and grassroots activism, explicitly adapted for the challenges of the modern era. As they gain further parliamentary representation and influence, they can help to get progressive policies more prominently on the mainstream political agenda. Embedding sustainability, security and equity into all aspects of public policy becomes the next step. Equally important are the extra-parliamentary aspects of Green party politics: education and campaigning in the broader community are essential activities whatever the extent of parliamentary representation. If the major parties 'steal' the Greens' policies, so much the better.

It would be nice to conclude this chapter by saying something stirring like 'combining critique, vision, strategy and organisation ensures success'. Unfortunately, creating progressive political economic change is seldom so neat, nor so easy in practice. Pragmatically, however, contributions can be coordinated and momentum can be built. Environmentally and socially concerned intellectuals play crucial roles in these processes: pioneers such as Herman Daly, Fritz Schumacher, Manfred Max Neef, Paul Elkins and Arne Næss have done so, together with numerous other important contributors, such as Lester Brown, Tim Jackson, Brian Czech, Peter Victor, Jonathan Porritt, Jorgen Randers, Clive Hamilton and Ted Trainer. Progressive think tanks are significant players too, despite not being as well funded by corporate sponsors as the pro-growth outfits of the political right. So too are green left media organisations and journalists who take issues of sustainability seriously, albeit predictably less well financially backed than the media organs of corporate irresponsibility. Even on a playing field that is far from level, the game is still open and is gathering pace.

Longer lessons: work, war and love

Much work needs to be done to bring the SSE alternative to prominence and fruition. Intellectual work, educational work, political interventions and movement building are all important aspect of this process. And there are important allies whose participation is essential for success. A broad swath of working people has to be convinced that an SSE will provide adequate jobs, incomes, infrastructure and services – and that the transition process can be managed to avoid unemployment resulting from structural economic change. The owners and managers of small and medium-sized enterprises need to be assured that there will be an important role for them in a steady state economy if they can adapt the nature of goods and services they provide to be more ecologically sustainable. Philanthropists need to feel that the transition to an SSE is a direction of socio-economic change worthy of their support. Governments need to be persuaded, whether explicitly Green parties hold the balance of power or not, that their policies should aim at enhancing sustainability, security and equity. All these elements are important in creating the necessary paradigm shift.

When preparing for war, societies mobilise their resources to face the external threats. They engage in systematic planning for this purpose, identifying what economic activities need to be curtailed and shifting freed-up resources to serve the new social purposes. The challenge of transitioning from a 'gobble-gobble' growth economy to a steady state economy has some similar characteristics, although the threats to be faced are internally generated in this case. Faced with the need for rapid mobilisation and deployment of resources, *planning* is imperative (Spies-Butcher and Stilwell 2009). There must be planning to phase out coal mines and to promote the use of renewable energy sources instead. There must be planning to reduce dependence on private motoring and unsustainable long-distance air travel and shipping movements, while implementing more local production for local consumption. There must be planning to develop more 'green jobs' and the necessary workforce skills (Pearce and Stilwell 2008). These are all planning processes that do not rely primarily on market mechanisms as drivers of change. Market-based policies such as carbon pricing may play some role in fostering the economic transitions, but by no stretch of the imagination can they suffice (as argued more fully in Stilwell 2012).

Turning from war to love, other lessons may be learned from thoughtful contributors such as Charles Birch (1993) and Tim Flannery (2011) who have emphasised the problems that result from failure to adequately respect and care for each other and nature. Concern with the personal values and behaviours that generate adverse environmental impacts is also a distinctive feature of the recent papal encyclical *Laudato Si* (on Care for Our Common Home) which departs significantly from the prevailing anthropocentrism in church doctrine (Pope Francis 2015). These are pertinent reminders that making the SSE transition is not just a *technical* task – of creating an alternative economic plan. Neither is it just an *institutional design* task – of developing institutions to carry out transitional programs.

Nor is it just a *political process* – of sequencing policy initiatives, dealing with predictable sources of opposition and maintaining broad public support. All these elements are necessary, of course, but so too is a *cultural shift* – from individualism, wasteful competition and endless consumerism to broader social and environmental respect and responsibility. As Flannery (2010: p. 280) has written, 'if we do not strive to love one another, and to love our planet as much as we love ourselves, then no further human progress is possible here on Earth'.

References

Allon, F. (2012) 'Home Economics: The Management of the Household as an Enterprise', *Journal of Australian Political Economy*, No. 68, Summer, pp. 128–148.

Birch, C. (1993) *Regaining Compassion for Humanity and Nature*, Sydney: UNSW Press.

Daly, H. (2014) *From Uneconomic Growth to a Steady State Economy*, Cheltenham: Edward Elgar.

Flannery, T. (2011) *Here On Earth: An Argument for Hope*, Melbourne: Text Publishing.

Gorz, A. (1999) *Reclaiming Work: Beyond the Wage-Based Society*, London: Polity Press.

Harvey, D. (2014) *Seventeen Contradictions and the End of Capitalism*, London: Profile Books.

Higgs, K. (2014) *Collision Course: Endless Growth on a Finite Planet*, Cambridge, MA: MIT Press.

Leigh, A. (2013) *Battlers and Billionaires: The Story of Inequality in Australia*, Victoria: Redback, Collingwood.

Meadows, D.H., Meadows, D.L., Randers, J., and Behrens, W.B. (1972) *The Limits to Growth: A Report for the Club of Rome's Project on the Predicament of Mankind*, London: Earth Island.

Mill, J.S. (1965 [1848]) *Principles of Political Economy*, New York: Augustus M. Kelley.

O'Connor, J. (2011) 'Environmental Crisis: An Eco-Marxist Perspective', in G. Argyrous and F. Stilwell (eds.), *Economics as a Social Science: Readings in Political Economy*, 3rd Edition, Melbourne: Tilde University Press, pp. 202–206.

Pearce, A. and Stilwell, F. (2008) 'Green Collar Jobs: Employment Aspects of Climate Change Policies', *Journal of Australian Political Economy*, No 62, December, pp. 120–138.

Perry, N. and Primrose, D. (2015) 'Heterodox Economics and the Biodiversity Crisis', *Journal of Australian Political Economy*, No. 75, Winter, pp. 133–152.

Piketty, T. (2014) *Capital in the Twenty-First Century*, Cambridge, MA: Belknop Press.

Pope Francis (2015) *Laudato Si (on Care for Our Common Home)*, Encyclical Letter of the Holy Father, The Vatican. See: http://w2.vatican.va/content/francesco/en/encyclicals/documents/papa-francesco_20150524_enciclica-laudato-si.html

Russell, B. (1917) *Roads to Freedom*, London: George Allen and Unwin.

Spies-Butcher, B. and Stilwell, F. (2009) 'Climate Change Policy and Economic Recession', *Journal of Australian Political Economy*, No. 63, Winter, pp. 108–125.

Standing, G. (2011) *The Precariat: A New Dangerous Class*, London: Bloomsbury Academic.

Stilwell, F. (2000) *Changing Track: Towards a New Political Economic Direction for Australia*, Sydney: Pluto Press.

Stilwell, F. (2012) 'Marketising the Environment', *Journal of Australian Political Economy*, Summer, pp. 108–127.

Washington, H. (2014) *Addicted to Growth*, Sydney: CASSE. See: http://www.ies.unsw.edu.au/sites/all/files/AddictedtoGrowthweb.pdf

Wilkinson, R.G. and Pickett, K. (2009) *The Spirit Level: Why More Equal Societies Almost Always Do Better*, London: Allen Lane.
Wright, E.O. (2010) *Envisioning Real Utopias*, London: Verso.
Wright, E.O. (2015) How to be an anti-capitalist today, *Jacobin*, online at https://www.jacobinmag.com/2015/12/erik-olin-wright-real-utopias-anticapitalism-democracy/

12

THE GENUINE PROGRESS INDICATOR

An indicator to guide the transition to a steady state economy

Philip Lawn

FLINDERS UNIVERSITY

Introduction

Currently, there are many high-GDP countries which generate levels of real output that cannot be ecologically sustained (Global Footprint Network 2011). At the same time, there are impoverished, low-GDP countries which desperately need to increase the basic goods and services available to a large percentage of their citizens. Thus, while there are high-GDP countries that need to reduce the physical scale of their economies – a process referred to as 'degrowth' (Martinez-Alier 2009) – most low-GDP countries need a healthy dose of GDP growth before stabilising their economies at a desirable physical scale.

Unfortunately, pontificating about the need for some countries to degrow and others to limit expansion of their economies sheds no light on the problem of *when* to degrow or when to stop growing. Advocates of the steady state economy therefore need to answer the following questions: (i) how much should high-GDP countries reduce the scale of their economies?; and (ii) how much GDP-growth should poor countries engage in before stabilising the physical scale of their economies? There are further questions that arise even after these questions have been adequately answered, such as how can high-GDP and low-GDP countries prevent absolute poverty levels from rising as they either degrow their economies or restrict further growth of them? I'll leave this to a later stage of the chapter where I will briefly outline some suggested strategies.

Much of this chapter sets out to argue the case for a Genuine Progress Indicator (GPI) – an indicator still in need of further refinement – to guide the transition to a steady state economy. In doing this, I will not only explain why an economic indicator is required to assist in this transitional process, but why an alternative to GDP (and other suggested economic indicators) is vital.

Don't get me wrong. The most crucial thing is to ensure the economies of all nations, and the world generally, operate within ecological limits. To know whether the physical scale of national economies is ecologically sustainable requires biophysical indicators, not economic indicators. However, as we shall see, there is an 'economic' limit to growth as well as an 'ecological' limit, and the former exists at a scale much smaller than the latter. It may be essential for economies to be ecologically sustainable, but a sustainable scale is not necessarily a desirable scale per se. Since lower-than-anticipated levels of economic welfare can drive people to undertake ecologically-destructive practices, considerations of the economic welfare generated at a particular economic scale cannot be overlooked.

Ecological and economic limits to growth

From a strictly biophysical perspective, one fact is indisputable – the production of physical goods (producer goods as well as consumer goods) requires the ongoing input of low-entropy matter and energy, otherwise referred to as 'natural resources' (Georgescu-Roegen 1971). Because of the First Law of Thermodynamics – the Law of Conservation of Matter-Energy – the quantity of matter-energy embodied in the natural resources used to produce a given quantity of real goods must at least equal the quantity of matter-energy embodied in the real goods produced (Daly 1996). To be anything less would amount to the creation of matter-energy, which is impossible. Ergo, the production of a given quantity of real goods requires the input of a minimum quantity of natural resources (Ayres and Kneese 1969; Perrings 1987).

Because of the Second Law of Thermodynamics – the Entropy Law – the production process must entail some waste. That is, some of the matter-energy embodied in the low-entropy resources used in production is immediately transformed into high-entropy waste, which means only some of the matter-energy previously embodied in the natural resources continues to remain as low-entropy matter and energy embodied in the real goods produced. Thus, because of the Entropy Law, the quantity of matter-energy embodied in the natural resources used to produce a given quantity of real goods must exceed the quantity of matter-energy embodied in the actual goods produced (Georgescu-Roegen 1971). Following production, the matter-energy embodied in real goods is eventually and entirely transformed into high-entropy waste, either very rapidly (the consumption of non-durable goods) or slowly (the physical depreciation of durable goods) (Daly 1991). Most of this 'consumption' waste and initial 'production' waste exits the economy and returns to the natural environment. All of the waste energy returns to the natural environment because the Entropy Law forbids the recycling of energy. Not all waste matter immediately returns the natural environment because some of it can be captured and reconcentrated into low-entropy matter (materials recycling). However, the recycling of matter requires the input of additional low-entropy energy. Consequently, recycling only makes sense if the energy required to recycle matter is less than the energy expended to source virgin low-entropy matter.

The role of technological progress is an important factor, but is also limited by the first and second laws of thermodynamics (Peet 1992). What technological progress does *and only does* from a biophysical perspective is reduce the waste associated with the production process. If production is technically 50 per cent efficient, it implies that half of the matter-energy embodied in the natural resources used in production ends up physically embodied in the real goods produced. The remaining half immediately becomes high-entropy waste. Should technological progress increase the technical efficiency of production to 75 per cent, three-quarters of the matter-energy ends up as physical goods and one-quarter as waste. Clearly, technological progress of this magnitude would result in a 50 per cent increase in the quantity of real goods produced from a given quantity of natural resource inputs. Alternatively, it would allow the production of the same quantity of real goods from 33 per cent less resource inputs.

Of course, the technical efficiency of production must always be something less than 100 per cent. What's more, as technical efficiency rises, further increases become more difficult and more costly to achieve.

What does all this mean in terms of the physical scale of economic systems? For an economy to physically grow, the quantity of real goods being added to the existing stock of goods must exceed the quantity of real goods being consumed or depreciated through use (i.e. destroyed). A steady state economy exists when the production of new goods equals the quantity of goods being destroyed. As for degrowth, it occurs when the latter exceeds the former.

Because growth invariably involves the increased production of real goods[1], the quantity of natural resources required to make this possible almost always rises in unison. I say 'almost always' because it is possible for technological progress to reduce natural resource inputs if the percentage increase in the technical efficiency of production exceeds the percentage increase in the quantity of real goods produced. For two reasons, these circumstances are likely to be very short-lived. First, the technical efficiency of production tends to increase incrementally and by very small rates – indeed, often by lower rates than the rate of growth in real output. Secondly, as explained, there is a thermodynamic limit to increases in technical efficiency that, when obtained, become more difficult to achieve. Australia is a good example. As Figure 12.1 shows, despite an increase over the 1980–2010 period in the technical efficiency of production (as measured by the ratio of real GDP to energy consumption), Australia's total energy consumption rose over the same period because of the overwhelming 'scale effect' of its rising real GDP.

As economic activity proceeds, it generates various benefits. The great majority of these benefits exist in the form of welfare benefits enjoyed from directly consuming goods and services and from using or operating durable goods. Other welfare benefits are derived from the public capital provided by governments (e.g. museums and art galleries) and from meaningful forms of employment. Over a century ago, Fisher (1906) described these benefits as 'psychic income' – the subjective satisfaction that emerges in the stream of human consciousness from

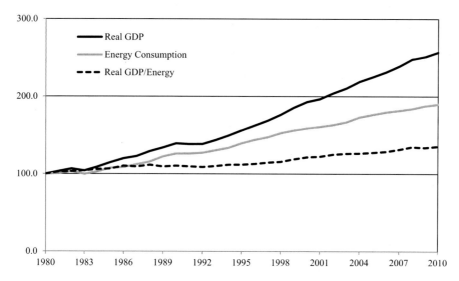

FIGURE 12.1 The scale effect of rising real GDP on Australia's energy consumption. (Note: Real GDP, total energy consumption (E), and the real GDP/E ratio have been set to an index value of 100 for 1980.)

consumption and other benefit-yielding endeavours. Whilst economic activity generates benefits, the production of new goods comes at a cost. Some of these costs are social costs, such as the cost of unemployment and the cost of crime and family breakdown caused by the pressure from having to grow and maintain the economy (Leipert 1986). Many social costs also arise because of people's reactions to the stigma attached to involuntary non-participation, which is often caused by unemployment and various forms of discrimination. Other costs are ecological, such as the cost of resource depletion, excessive pollution and the loss of ecosystem services. If, for convenience, we separate out the social costs from the ecological costs and subtract the former from psychic income, we arrive at 'net psychic income' – the uncancelled benefits of economic activity.[2] This leaves the ecological costs as the uncancelled costs of economic activity – an unsurprising inference given that all economic activity begins with the extraction of natural resources and concludes with the insertion of high-entropy wastes into the natural environment (Daly 1979).

As an economic system physically grows, one would expect the uncancelled benefits of economic activity to increase at a diminishing rate, which is represented by the uncancelled benefits (UB) curve in Figure 12.2. The shape of the UB curve reflects the widely accepted principle of diminishing marginal benefits. Nothing controversial here. Conversely, one would expect the uncancelled costs of economic activity to rise at an increasing rate, as represented by the uncancelled costs (UC) curve in Figure 12.2. The reason for this is that there is a general tendency to exploit the best grades and most accessible natural resources first. Hence, the need to dig deeper, pump further and travel longer distances to access

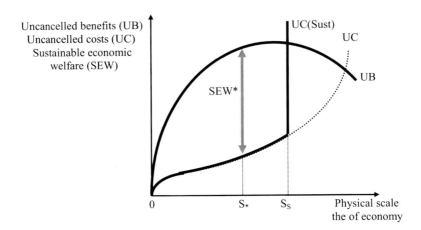

FIGURE 12.2 The economic welfare generated by a growing economy

what are usually poorer quality natural resources increases the marginal cost of resource extraction. At the same time, more waste places increasing pressure on natural waste sinks, while an additional hectare of the natural environment transformed for human utilitarian purposes becomes increasingly costly in terms of the ecosystem services lost. Again, there is nothing controversial about this assertion.

Assuming that ecological sustainability is a desirable social objective, we can assume that the UC curve is vertical at the *maximum sustainable scale*, which is also denoted by S_S in Figure 12.2. The maximum sustainable scale constitutes the largest physical scale of the economy that can be sustained by a throughput of matter-energy (i.e. input of resources and output of wastes) that does not exceed the natural environment's regenerative and waste assimilative capacities. Hence, S_S constitutes the ecological limit to growth.

It is important to understand that presenting the UC curve as a vertical line does not mean that the uncancelled costs of economic activity are infinite at S_S – it merely symbolises a 'line in the sand' that should never be transgressed.

Figure 12.2 indicates that there is a range of physical economic scales that are ecologically sustainable. Essentially, any economy between zero and S_S is technically sustainable. However, only one of these scales maximises a nation's economic welfare. This scale – the so-called optimal macroeconomic scale – is denoted by S_* and exists where the vertical difference between the UB and UC curves is at a maximum.

Interestingly, growth of the economy up to S_* increases a nation's economic welfare, but growth beyond S_* reduces it. For this reason, physical expansion of a national economy up to S_* can be considered 'economic' growth, whereas expansion beyond S_* can be regarded as 'uneconomic' growth – a significant departure from the standard definition of economic growth, but one that should be adopted by all advocates of a steady state economy. The important point to note here is that any growth that increases a national economy to a physical scale between S_* and S_S is uneconomic *despite* being ecologically sustainable. This dispels the mainstream belief that a phase of growth that is ecologically sustainable is necessarily desirable. Given the nature of the UB and UC curves, Figure 12.2 also indicates that there is an economic limit to growth (S_*) that is arrived at well before the ecological limit is reached (S_S).

Of course, the UB and UC curves in Figure 12.2 would not remain stationary. Technological progress and well-targeted policy measures have the capacity to shift the UB curve upwards and the UC curve downwards and to the right.[3] Upward shifts of the UB curve can be achieved by qualitatively improving the stock of goods that make up the economy (i.e. by increasing their use value) and through policies that reduce social costs, such as the cost of unemployment. Income redistribution policies can also shift the UB curve upwards given that the marginal benefits of consumption of the poor are higher than the marginal benefits of the rich. Hence, without having to grow the economy, the aggregate consumption benefits of a nation can be increased by redistributing income from the latter to the former (Robinson 1962).

As explained earlier, technological progress can reduce the natural resources expended to produce a given quantity of real goods. By doing this, technological progress can reduce the uncancelled costs of economic activity, which can shift the UC curve downwards. Since technological progress of this type would also increase the maximum sustainable scale of a national economy, it can also shift the vertical section of the UC curve to the right. However, for reasons outlined above, shifting the UC curve in this manner is severely limited by the first and second laws of thermodynamics.

Provided it remains possible to shift the UB curve upwards and the UC curve downwards and to the right, it is possible to increase a nation's economic welfare without having to grow the economy. It therefore follows that operating a steady state economy need not preclude development if development is defined as a *transformational process* that increases a nation's economic welfare.

Crucially, the limits imposed by the first and second laws of thermodynamics on the beneficial shifts of the UC curve imply two things. Firstly, since continued growth must eventually result in the economy surpassing its maximum sustainable scale, the transition to a steady state economy is a long-run necessity. Secondly, many of the welfare increases that are likely to be obtained whilst operating at a steady state economy will come from qualitative improvements in physical goods, reduced social costs and a more equitable distribution of income and wealth. Only in the short- to medium-term could we expect welfare increases from advances in the technical efficiency of production and a more productive stock of natural capital.

Assuming that the optimal macroeconomic scale is the most desirable scale to operate an economic system, what kind of indicator would best guide the transition to a steady state economy? Given the above, it would be an indicator that identifies, separates and measures the major benefits and costs of economic activity (Daly 1991; Lawn 2007). In other words, it would be indicator that can measure a nation's economic welfare. Presumably, if economic welfare is increasing as a national economy expands, this suggests that the economy is smaller than the optimal scale and that further growth is desirable. Should the increase in economic welfare begin to slow as the economy continues to expand, this suggests that the optimum is being approached and that the nation should initiate a transition to a steady state economy. As for a country that has exceeded its optimal scale, this would be identified by a decrease in economic welfare as the economy physically grows. A country in this position would need to implement a combination of policies to orderly reduce the physical scale of the national economy as well as protect the most vulnerable from its possible side-effects. To ascertain whether such action is effective, the same indicator could again be employed since, if the policies being implemented are succeeding, the economic welfare of the nation should again start rising as the economy returns to the optimum.

Indicators of the ecological and economic limits to growth

Although my focus in this chapter is on an economic indicator to guide the transition to a steady state economy, it would be remiss of me to overlook biophysical indicators that reveal where an economy is with respect to its maximum sustainable scale (S_S). This is particularly so given that everything should be done to avoid growing the economy to a physical scale that cannot be ecologically sustained.

Many biophysical indicators have been constructed in recent times to meet the growing need for an indicator of ecological sustainability. They include the Human Appropriation of Net Primary Production (HANPP) (Vitousek *et al.* 1986); the Environmental Sustainability Index (Yale 2005); Material Flow Accounts (Perman *et al.* 2003); and the Ecological Footprint (Wackernagel and Rees 1996). Despite some criticism (see van den Berg and Verbruggen 1999; Lenzen and Murray 2001; Patterson 2006), many believe that the Ecological Footprint is the best indicator of the physical presence of an economic system, which is invariably compared to a nation's biocapacity to determine whether its economy is sustainable. The Ecological Footprint estimates the land area *required* to generate the resources, absorb the wastes and provide the ecosystem services needed to produce a given quantity of real output (Wackernagel and Rees 1996; Wackernagel *et al.* 1999; Global Footprint Network 2011). The biocapacity, on the other hand, estimates the land area *available* to provide the very same source, sink and life-support services. If a nation's Ecological Footprint exceeds its biocapacity, this indicates that its economy is exceeding its maximum sustainable scale (i.e. is suffering an ecological deficit).

A study by the Global Footprint Network in 2003 estimated that 80 of 140 countries had an ecological deficit, and that the global economy as a whole was operating beyond its maximum sustainable scale to the tune of 40 per cent (Global Footprint Network 2006). Given that the economic limit to growth is reached prior to the ecological limit, it is not surprising that a recent study also indicated that the global economy has long surpassed its optimal scale (Kubiszewski *et al.* 2013).

Gross Domestic Product (GDP)

Turning now to a suitable economic indicator to guide the transition to a steady state economy, perhaps it is best to start with an assessment of real GDP in view of its widespread use as an indicator of national well-being. GDP is a monetary measure of the goods and services produced by *domestically-located* factors of production. Real GDP, as opposed to nominal GDP, involves a correction for price changes so that GDP reflects changes in the physical quantity of goods produced. Evidence of the changing physical volume of economic activity is still of some value, just as it was when GDP was devised to account for a nation's annual product during World War II (Kuznets 1941). But it falls well short of being an adequate measure of national income and shorter still as an indicator of national well-being.

National income is best defined as the maximum amount that a nation can consume over a year and still be in a position to consume at least as much in the following year and every year thereafter (Hicks 1946; Daly 1996). For GDP to be an accurate measure of national income, it must be possible for a nation to consume its entire GDP and be able to consume the same quantity of goods and services in the following year. This, however, is not remotely possible because much of what a nation produces in a given year is required to replace worn out capital goods (e.g. plant, machinery and equipment) as well as maintain the productive capacity of the labour force (e.g. education and training). Another large proportion of GDP is also designed to defend the economy against the negative side-effects of economic activity itself. Because defensive measures cannot prevent some damage to the economy's productive capacity, a further portion of GDP is required to rehabilitate productive factors, including human beings who are physically injured or mentally scarred by work. Finally, any component of GDP that involves the depletion of natural capital (e.g. forests, fisheries and ore deposits) undermines the capacity of the natural environment to provide the natural resources needed for future production. All up, GDP massively *overstates* a nation's national income.

Sustainable Net Domestic Product (SNDP)

It has been suggested that GDP should be adjusted to take account of its shortcomings. Daly (1996) has recommended the following subtractions from GDP to obtain a better indicator of national income – what Daly refers to as Sustainable Net Domestic Product (SNDP):

$$SNDP = GDP - \text{depreciation of } K_h - DRE - \text{depletion of } K_n \qquad (1)$$

where:

- SNDP = Sustainable Net Domestic Product
- GDP = Gross Domestic Product

- Kh = human-made capital
- DRE = defensive and rehabilitative expenditures
- Kn = natural capital

Although such an adjustment to GDP is commendable, for two main reasons, SNDP fails to serve as an adequate measure of economic welfare[4]. First, because GDP measures the goods and services that a nation must produce to accumulate and maintain a particular stock of welfare-providing goods, GDP is, in effect, an indicator of national cost (Boulding 1966). This renders SNDP an indicator of 'sustainable' national cost. For obvious reasons, the latter is a more useful indicator than the former. However, the latter's failure to explicitly measure and separate the benefits and costs of economic activity rules it out as an adequate measure of economic welfare.

Genuine Savings (GS)

A key sustainability requirement is the need to keep productive capital intact (Hartwick 1977; Pearce and Turner 1990; Daly 1996; Lawn 2007). In response, some analysts have developed stock-based indicators. One of these is an indicator referred to as Genuine Savings, which can be estimated by using the following formula (Pearce and Atkinson 1993):

$$GS = \text{Investment} - \text{NFB} - \text{depreciation of Kh} - \text{depletion of Kn} \qquad (2)$$

where:

- GS = Genuine Savings
- NFB = net foreign borrowing
- Kh = human-made capital
- Kn = natural capital

Not unlike SNDP, a measure of Genuine Savings also suffers from various shortcomings. While Genuine Savings is designed to provide a useful indicator of sustainability, there are many who believe that keeping a combined stock of capital intact is insufficient because of the unique and non-substitutable qualities of both human-made and natural capital (Daly 1996; Lawn 2007). The problem with Genuine Savings is that it assumes that these two forms of capital are substitutable. For example, Genuine Savings can remain positive, even as the stock of natural capital declines, if there is sufficient investment in human-made capital. Yet if human-made capital and natural capital are non-substitutable forms of capital, as studies demonstrate they are (Lawn 2007), a positive value for GS can misleadingly imply sustainability.

Notwithstanding this deficiency, Genuine Savings also reveals nothing about a nation's economic welfare. It cannot therefore provide any guide as to where a country should stabilise the physical scale of its economy to maximise national well-being.

The Genuine Progress Indicator (GPI)

The Genuine Progress Indicator (GPI) is an indicator designed to measure but separate the benefits and costs of economic activity. Originally called an Index of Sustainable Economic Welfare (ISEW) (Daly and Cobb 1989), and built on earlier work by Nordhaus and Tobin (1972) and Zolotas (1981), the GPI involves subtracting the costs from the benefits of economic activity to obtain a measure of economic welfare (Lawn 2003, 2007; Redefining Progress 1995).

There are some critics of the GPI who argue that the GPI has no theoretical basis, or is simply theoretically flawed (Neumayer 1999; Harris 2007; Brennan 2013). This is not true. The GPI has not been constructed out of thin air, but has been built on the principles laid down by Fisher (1906) concerning the distinction between income and capital (Lawn 2003, 2008b, 2013). For example, by treating the production of durable consumption goods as an activity designed to replace worn out existing goods and therefore generate welfare benefits in future years, the GPI does not include it as a current welfare benefit. However, it adds the welfare generated by existing durable goods (i.e. recent production), including public capital, which GDP and a measure of SNDP do not. Also included in the GPI are the welfare benefits provided by non-paid household and volunteer work – two major benefits overlooked in standard national accounts.

The GPI also deducts various social costs – the costs of unemployment, crime and family breakdown – as well as a range of environmental costs, such as the cost of non-renewable resource depletion; the cost of deforestation; the cost of land degradation; the cost of various forms of pollution; and the cost of long-term environmental damage (e.g. climate change).

One other important inclusion in the GPI is a correction made to consumption-related welfare caused by changes in the distribution of income. The correction is made so that a more even distribution of income leads to an upward adjustment of consumption-related welfare. On the other hand, a redistribution of income from the poor to the rich results in a downward adjustment to this welfare item.

It is common for the various benefit and cost items used to calculate the GPI to be loosely presented in a table with the value of the GPI as the sum total. As Table 12.1 reveals, for neatness and to support the theoretical basis of the GPI, I prefer to categorise the items as either 'psychic income', 'psychic outgo', or 'environmental cost' items, with a subtotal for 'net psychic income' and 'lost natural capital services'. Normally the values of each item are presented for each year of a given study period (see Lawn 2000). For convenience, I have simply provided the values for Australia for the year 2010.

TABLE 12.1 Items used to calculate the Genuine Progress Indicator (GPI) for Australia, 2010

Uncancelled benefits account	$	$
Psychic income items		
Private consumption and services from consumer durables	595,505	
Index of income distributional (DI) (1962 = 100.0)	137.5	
Weighted Consumption (Consumption ÷ DI × 100)	432,962	
Public consumption expenditure	194,967	
Benefits yielded by public infrastructure	43,160	
Services provided by non-household labour	294,341	
Services provided by volunteer labour	38,235	
Total psychic income		1,003,665
Psychic outgo items		
Defensive and rehabilitative expenditures	−156,250	
Cost of unemployment	−18,845	
Cost of crime	−11,530	
Cost of family breakdown	−4,234	
Cost of overwork	−10,689	
Disamenity cost of air pollution	−1,643	
Foreign debt	−47,967	
Total psychic outgo		−251,157
Net psychic income (Uncancelled benefits)		**752,508**

Uncancelled costs account	$	$
Lost environmental source function items		
Cost of non-renewable resource depletion	−57,011	
Cost of land degradation	−21,679	
Excessive water use	−18,350	
Cost of depleted timber stocks	245	
Cost of depleted fish stocks	−547	
Lost environmental sink function items		
Cost of air pollution (environmental element)	−6,570	
Cost of urban wastewater pollution	−5,215	
Cost of solid waste pollution	−6,174	

Lost environmental life-support function items		
Cost of lost wetlands	−11,947	
Cost of long-term environmental damage	−24,352	
Lost natural capital services		v151,601
Ecosystem Health Index (EHI) (1962 = 100.0)		88.1
Uncancelled costs (Lost natural capital services ÷ EHI × 100)		**−171,990**

Genuine Progress Indicator (GPI)	$	$
GPI		**580,518**
Australian population (thousands of people)		22,065
Per capita GPI		**26,309**

Notes: Except for the per capita GPI, all monetary values are in millions of 2004-05 dollars
DI and EHI are single index values determined in relation to a base year of 1962
Fish stocks increased in 2010. Hence, the positive value for cost of depleted fish stocks

GPI results and their implications

The initial estimates of the GPI were conducted on industrialised nations in the 1990s (Diefenbacher 1994; Moffat and Wilson 1994; Redefining Progress 1995; Rosenberg and Oegema 1995; Jackson and Stymne 1996; Jackson et al. 1997; Stockhammer et al. 1997; Guenno and Tiezzi 1998). Only more recently have GPI studies been performed on poorer countries (Lawn 2008a; Wen et al. 2008; Clarke and Shaw 2008; Nguyet Hong 2008). The early studies in the 1990s revealed a consistent and disturbing pattern (see Figure 12.3). They showed that although the GPI tends to rise in accord with GDP when GDP levels are low, at some point the GPI begins to fall as a nation's GDP continues to increase. It turns out that this critical point is usually in the order of US$20,000 per capita (2000 prices). These results led Max-Neef (1995) to put forward a 'threshold hypothesis' – a postulation that when the per capita GDP of a nation exceeds a particular level, the per capita GPI is likely to decline.

What these early GPI results and Max-Neef's conclusion intimate is that most industrialised countries have *surpassed* their optimal macroeconomic scale (Lawn 2007). That is, high-GDP countries have grown their economies to a point where further growth is pushing up environmental and social costs faster than it is boosting economic benefits. For many of these countries, the threshold point was reached in the early to mid-1980s, although, in the case of the USA, UK, and Australia, it was reached in the mid-1970s.

Had these countries been using the GPI to guide the economic process rather than real GDP, would they have done anything differently? They may not, but at least the GPI would have indicated that the time had come to make the transition to a steady state economy and to focus, not on further growth, but on qualitative

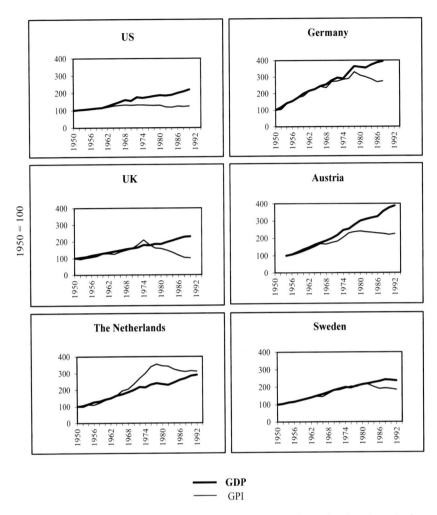

FIGURE 12.3 A comparison of the GDP and GPI for six industrialised nations (Jackson and Stymne 1996)

improvement, distributional equity, greater efficiency and natural capital maintenance. Not only would it have led to increased levels of economic welfare, it would have prevented many nations from exceeding their maximum sustainable scale. Why? Because they would have ceased growing their economies at the economic limit to growth, which, as we have seen, is well short of the ecological limit.

Now that many high-GDP countries are well *beyond* their optimal scale, the GPI is still of considerable value because it can help guide countries back to the optimum. Nevertheless, simply shrinking the economy through a process of degrowth will not suffice and could prove counterproductive if conducted injudiciously. There will be a need for a measured approach – best conducted through quantitative restrictions on the rate of resource throughput – with a significant emphasis on the redistribution of income and wealth to shield the most vulnerable in society from a likely decline in the quantity of goods available for consumption. The restriction in resource throughput would probably best be implemented through a cap-auction-trade system that would limit the rate of resource use/waste generation and ensure an adequate price signal is established to encourage a more efficient use of the incoming resource flow (Daly 1991; Lawn 2007). The ensuing destruction of some private-sector spending power caused by higher resource-use costs and charges on various forms of pollution would provide room for governments to support the poor, which they could do by reducing marginal tax rates on low incomes (better known as ecological tax reform) (Daly 1996; Lawn 2007). Cap-auction-trade systems would also free up real resources to support a Job Guarantee scheme that could achieve low levels of unemployment, if not full employment, even as real GDP declines (Mitchell and Muysken 2008; Lawn 2009).

The GPI would be useful in these circumstances because its value would presumably rise if the degrowth process was performed well, but decline if it was not. Even in the former case, the GPI would help nations to determine when to cease the degrowth process in order to stabilise the economy at something approximating the optimal scale (Lawn 2006).

As for low-GDP nations still in need of further GDP growth, they would be well advised to employ the GPI in the way that high-GDP nations should have employed an indicator of economic welfare in the 1960s and 1970s, had one been available. They should continue with GDP-growth – albeit growth that is as equitable and efficient as possible – so long as the GPI is rising and prepare for an orderly transition to a steady state economy once GDP-growth starts to slow the increase in the GPI.

Having said this, it is worth highlighting that the per capita GPI of both China and Thailand have already begun to fall even though their per capita GDP is much less than the US$20,000 per person threshold experienced by high-GDP countries (Lawn and Clarke 2008). The reason for this, it seems, is that the marginal cost of growth for these so-called growth 'late-comers' is much higher than it was for high-GDP nations in the 1950s and 1960s. This is because the world is now 'full' and the best and the most accessible of the world's material and energy resources have been exhausted by high-GDP countries, which has left poorer grade resources for low-GDP countries to fuel their current and future growth. Waste sinks are also fully if not over-committed, thus making the cost of waste generation much more expensive in the twenty-first century.

At the same time, many low-GDP nations have been adopting export-oriented strategies, which means they are not consuming as much of their own real output as high-GDP nations were when they were rapidly growing some 50–60 years ago. Also suppressing the welfare contribution of consumption in low-GDP countries has been the huge disparity in income growth of rich and poor citizens – a phenomenon not experienced by high-GDP countries in the post-World War II growth boom. Hence, the marginal benefits of GDP-growth for many low-GDP nations have not been as high as they were for high-GDP nations during the same stage of their economic development. In the end, the low marginal benefits together with the high marginal costs of growth have meant that the latter has been exceeding the former much earlier in the economic development process. Consequently, the economic welfare of some low-GDP countries has been levelling off or declining, despite per capita GDP being below US$10,000 – indeed, around US$5,000 (2004 prices) in the case of China and US$7,500 (2004 prices) in Thailand.

This evidence doesn't mean that the GPI should be rejected or that low-GDP countries should blindly grow their economies. After all, the costs of growth don't vanish just by being ignored. But it does mean that high-GDP countries have an even greater obligation to degrow their economies – which is in their best interests anyway – to provide low-GDP nations with the 'ecological space' to enjoy a phase of welfare-increasing growth.

Concluding remarks

All nations need to make the transition to a steady state economy – high-GDP countries immediately, which will require many of them to engage in a degrowth process; and low-GDP countries eventually, albeit they need to ensure that whatever GDP-growth they undertake it is as equitable and efficient as possible. Knowing whether there is a need to degrow the national economy and how much, or alternatively, when to cease expanding it, requires the careful monitoring of an indicator of economic welfare. Unfortunately, measures of real GDP and adjusted measures of national income and genuine savings fail in this regard. The GPI, as an indicator explicitly designed to measure a nation's economic welfare, does not.

Although the GPI is theoretically sound, more needs to be done to improve the methods employed to estimate some of the benefit and cost items used in its calculation. There is also a need to establish a standardised list of benefit and cost items and a consistent set of estimation methods (Lawn 2005, 2013). Despite its imperfections, the GPI should be used to guide the transition to a steady state economy, if only because it is better to be vaguely right than precisely wrong on a matter as crucial as the physical scale of a nation's economy and the economic welfare it generates. As an aside, but also of great importance, the GPI can confer significant weight to the case for a steady state economy – a reality that advocates of a steady state economy should not ignore.

Notes

1   It is possible for the quantity of real output to fall as the economy physically expands by reducing the rate of consumption and depreciation faster than the rate at which the production of new goods is reduced.
2   We can consider net psychic income as the uncancelled benefits of economic activity because it represents the monetary value of the benefits that remain after all intermediate transactions have cancelled out (Daly 1979).

3 Bad public policy can also result in the undesirable shifts of the UB and UC curves despite technological progress. This has occurred in the case of Australia (see Lawn 2000).
4 Daly is well aware of this shortcoming of SNDP, which is why he established the Index of Sustainable Economic Welfare (ISEW), a forerunner to the Genuine Progress Indicator (GPI) (see Daly and Cobb 1989).

References

Ayres, R. and Kneese, A. (1969) 'Production, consumption, and externalities', *American Economic Review*, vol. 59, pp. 282–297.

Boulding, K. (1966) 'The economics of the coming spaceship Earth', in H. Jarrett (ed.), *Environmental Quality in a Growing Economy*, Baltimore: John Hopkins University Press, pp. 3–14.

Brennan, A. (2013) 'A critique of the perceived solid conceptual foundations of the ISEW and GPI – Irving Fisher's cognisance of human-health capital in net psychic income', *Ecological Economics*, vol. 88, pp. 159–166.

Clarke, M. and Shaw, J. (2008) 'Genuine progress in Thailand: A systems-analysis approach', in P. Lawn and M. Clarke (eds.), *Welfare in the Asia-Pacific: Studies Using the Genuine Progress Indicator*, Cheltenham, UK: Edward Elgar, pp. 260–298.

Daly, H. (1979) 'Entropy, growth, and the political economy of scarcity', in V. K. Smith (ed.), *Scarcity and Growth Reconsidered*, Baltimore: John Hopkins University Press, pp. 67–94.

Daly, H. (1991) *Steady-State Economics*, Second Edition, Washington, DC: Island Press.

Daly, H. (1996) *Beyond Growth*, Boston: Beacon Press.

Daly, H. and Cobb, J. (1989) *For the Common Good*, Boston: Beacon Press.

Diefenbacher, H. (1994) 'The index of sustainable economic welfare in Germany', in C. Cobb and J. Cobb (eds.), *The Green National Product*, New York: University America Press, pp. 215–245.

Fisher, I. (1906) *Nature of Capital and Income*, New York: A. M. Kelly.

Georgescu-Roegen, N. (1971) *The Entropy Law and the Economic Process*, Cambridge, MA: Harvard University Press.

Global Footprint Network (2006) *National Footprint Accounts, 2006*. See: www.footprintnetwork.org

Global Footprint Network (2011) *National Footprint Accounts, 2011*. See www.footprintnetwork.org

Guenno, G. and Tiezzi, S. (1998) *An Index of Sustainable Economic Welfare for Italy*, Working Paper 5/98, Milan: Fondazione Eni Enrico Mattei.

Harris, M. (2007) 'On income, sustainability, and the 'microfoundations' of the GPI', *International Journal of Environment, Workplace, and Employment*, vol. 3, no. 2, pp. 119–131.

Hartwick, J. (1977) 'Intergenerational equity and the investing of rents from exhaustible resources', *American Economic Review*, vol. 65, no. 5, pp. 972–974.

Hicks, J. (1946) *Value and Capital*, Second Edition, London: Clarendon Press.

Jackson, T., Laing, F., MacGillivray, A., Marks, N., Ralls, J. and Stymne, S. (1997) *An Index of Sustainable Economic Welfare for the UK, 1950–1996*, Guildford: University of Surrey Centre for Environmental Strategy.

Jackson, T. and Stymne, S. (1996) *Sustainable Economic Welfare in Sweden: A Pilot Index, 1950–1992*, Stockholm: Stockholm Environment Institute.

Kubiszewski, I., Costanza, R., Franco, C., Lawn, P., Talberth, J., Jackson, T., and Aylmer, C. (2013) 'Beyond GDP: Measuring and achieving global genuine progress', *Ecological Economics*, vol. 93, pp. 57–68.

Kuznets, S. (1941) *National Income and its Composition: 1919–1938*, New York: National Bureau of Economic Research.

Lawn, P. (2000) *Toward Sustainable Development: An Ecological Economic Approach*, Boca Raton: CRC Press.

Lawn, P. (2003) 'A theoretical foundation to support the Index of Sustainable Economic Welfare (ISEW), Genuine Progress Indicator (GPI), and other related indexes', *Ecological Economics*, vol. 44, pp. 105–118.

Lawn, P. (2005) 'An assessment of the valuation methods used to calculate the Index of Sustainable Economic Welfare (ISEW), Genuine Progress Indicator (GPI), and Sustainable Net Benefit Index (SNBI), *Environment, Development, and Sustainability*, 7, pp. 185–208.

Lawn, P. (2006) 'Using the Fisherian concept of income to guide a nation's transition to a steady state economy', *Ecological Economics*, vol. 56, no. 3, pp. 440–453.

Lawn, P. (2007) *Frontier Issues in Ecological Economics*, Cheltenham, UK: Edward Elgar.

Lawn, P. (2008a) 'Genuine progress in India: some further growth needed in the immediate future but population stabilisation needed immediately', in P. Lawn and M. Clarke (eds.), *Welfare in the Asia-Pacific: Studies Using the Genuine Progress Indicator*, Cheltenham, UK: Edward Elgar, pp. 191–227.

Lawn, P. (2008b) 'Response to "On income, sustainability, and the 'microfoundations' of the GPI"', *International Journal of Environment, Workplace, and Employment*, vol. 4, no. 1, pp. 59–81.

Lawn, P. (2009) 'Final thoughts on reconciling the goals of ecological sustainability and full employment', in P. Lawn (ed.), *Environment and Employment: A Reconciliation*, Oxfordshire, UK: Routledge, pp. 345–379.

Lawn, P. (2013) 'The failure of the ISEW and GPI to fully account for changes in human-health capital – a methodological shortcoming not a theoretical weakness', *Ecological Economics*, vol. 88, pp. 167–177

Lawn, P. and Clarke, M. (eds.) (2008) *Welfare in the Asia-Pacific: Studies Using the Genuine Progress Indicator*, Cheltenham, UK: Edward Elgar.

Leipert, C. (1986) 'From gross to adjusted national product', in P. Ekins (ed.), *The Living Economy: A New Economics in the Making*, London: Routledge & Kegan Paul, pp. 132–140.

Lenzen, M. and Murray, S. (2001) 'A modified ecological footprint method and its application to Australia', *Ecological Economics*, vol. 37, no. 2, pp. 229–255.

Martinez-Alier, J. (2009) 'Socially sustainable economic de-growth', *Development and Change*, vol. 40, no. 6, pp. 1099–1119.

Max-Neef, M. (1995) 'Economic growth and quality of life', *Ecological Economics*, vol. 15, pp. 115–118.

Mitchell, W. and Muysken, J. (2008) *Full Employment Abandoned: Shifting Sands and Policy Failures*, Cheltenham, UK: Edward Elgar.

Moffat, I. and Wilson, M. (1994) 'An index of sustainable economic welfare for Scotland, 1980–1991', *International Journal of Sustainable Development and World Ecology*, vol. 1, pp. 264–291.

Neumayer, E. (1999) 'The ISEW – Not an index of sustainable economic welfare', *Social Indicators Research*, vol. 48, pp. 77–101.

Nguyet Hong, V. X., Clarke, M., and Lawn, P. (2008) 'Genuine progress in Vietnam: The impact of the Doi Moi reforms', in P. Lawn and M. Clarke (eds.), *Welfare in the Asia-*

Pacific: Studies Using the Genuine Progress Indicator, Cheltenham, UK: Edward Elgar, pp. 299–330.

Nordhaus, W. and Tobin, J. (1972) 'Is economic growth obsolete?', in *Economic Growth*, The National Bureau of Economic Research, Fiftieth Anniversary Colloquium, New York: Columbia University Press.

Patterson, M. (2006) 'Selecting headline indicators for tracking progress to sustainability in a nation state', in P. Lawn (ed.), *Sustainable Development Indicators in Ecological Economics*, Cheltenham, UK: Edward Elgar, pp. 421–448.

Pearce, D. and Atkinson, G. (1993) 'Capital theory and the measurement of sustainable development: An indicator of weak sustainability', *Ecological Economics*, vol. 8, pp. 103–108.

Pearce, D. and Turner, R. K. (1990) *Economics of Natural Resources and the Environment*, London: Harvester Wheatsheaf.

Peet, J. (1992) *Energy and the Ecological Economics of Sustainability*, Washington, DC: Island Press.

Perman, R., McGilvray, Ma. Y. and Common, M. (2003) *Natural Resources and Environmental Economics*, Third Edition, Harlow: Pearson.

Perrings, C. (1987) *Economy and Environment: A Theoretical Essay on the Interdependence of Economic and Environmental Systems*, Cambridge: Cambridge University Press.

Redefining Progress (1995) *The Genuine Progress Indicator: Summary of Data and Methodology*, Oakland, CA: Redefining Genuine Progress.

Robinson, J. (1962) *Economic Philosophy*, London: C. A. Watts & Co.

Rosenberg, K. and Oegema, T. (1995) *A Pilot ISEW for the Netherlands 1950–1992*, Amsterdam: Instituut Voor Milieu – En Syysteemanalyse.

Stockhammer, E., Hochreiter, H., Obermayr, B., and Steiner, K. (1997) 'The index of sustainable economic welfare (ISWE) as an alternative to GDP in measuring economic welfare: The results of the Austrian (revised) ISEW calculation 1955–1992, *Ecological Economics*, vol. 21, pp. 19–34.

van den Berg, J. and Verbruggen, H. (1999) 'Spatial sustainability, trade, and indicators: An evaluation of the ecological footprint', *Ecological Economics*, vol. 29, no. 1, pp. 61–72.

Vitousek, P., Ehrlich, P., Ehrlich, A. and Matson, P. (1986) 'Human appropriation of the products of photosynthesis', *BioScience*, vol. 36, pp. 368–373.

Wackernagel, M., Onisto, L., Bello, P., Callejas Linares, A., Lopez Falfan, S., Mendez Garcia, J., Suarez Guerrero, A. I., and Suarez Guerrero, Ma. G. (1999) 'National natural capital accounting with the ecological footprint concept', *Ecological Economics*, vol. 29, no. 3, pp. 375–390.

Wackernagel, M. and Rees, W. (1996) *Our Ecological Footprint: Reducing Human Impact on the Earth*, Gabriola Island: New Society Publishers.

Wen, Z., Yang, Y. and Lawn, P. (2008), 'From GDP to GPI: Quantifying thirty-five years of development in China', *Genuine Progress in the Asia-Pacific: Studies Using the Genuine Progress Indicator*, Cheltenham, UK: Edward Elgar, pp. 228–259.

Yale Center for Environmental Law and Policy, Center for International Earth Science Information Network, and World Economic Forum (2005) *2005 Environmental Sustainability Index*, New Haven: YCELP.

Zolotas, X. (1981) *Economic Growth and Declining Social Welfare*, New York: New York University Press.

13

CAPITALISM AND THE STEADY STATE

Uneasy bedfellows

Joshua Farley

UNIVERSITY OF VERMONT

Introduction

The impact of human activity on the global environment has become so profound that many scientists argue we have now entered a new geological epoch, the Anthropocene (Steffen *et al.* 2011; Crutzen 2002). Human-induced environmental changes may pose an existential threat to human civilization (see Washington in this volume), and few scientists believe that 'business as usual' can continue indefinitely. The economic system has played an important role in causing the problems we face, and changes to the system must play an important role in their solutions.

Continuous economic growth has driven excessive resource extraction, fossil fuel consumption and land use change, and hence has been the dominant cause of our environmental problems. Solving these problems requires that we transition to a non-growing, steady state economy, in which throughput or social metabolism (i.e. the rate of resource extraction, energy use and waste emissions) must be non-increasing. Earlier generations of economists foresaw the inevitability of a steady state economy (Mill 1848; Keynes 1991), but society has made no progress towards achieving it. There is now significant evidence that the economy has exceeded its maximum sustainable scale, and 'degrowth' – a reduction in the physical size of the economy – is now required (see Perey in this volume). However, those who cannot meet their basic needs require additional consumption, and we certainly cannot ask them to sacrifice their well-being for the sake of unborn future generations. If the economy must shrink or growth must end, then the issue of a just distribution of our finite wealth and resources becomes extremely important.

Capitalism is defined by the online Merriam Webster dictionary as

> an economic system characterized by private or corporate ownership of capital goods, by investments that are determined by private decision, and by

prices, production, and the distribution of goods that are determined mainly by competition in a free market.

(http://www.merriam-webster.com/dictionary/capitalism)

It is currently the dominant economic system on the planet, though almost all countries limit capitalism to certain economic activities, while relying on the public sector, strict regulations, or hybrid models for others. Neoliberalism is an economic philosophy that seeks to allow unregulated capitalism to control virtually all economic activity. An important question is the degree to which a steady state economy is compatible with capitalism, or whether society must develop new economic institutions to achieve ecological sustainability and social justice. This chapter explains why a steady state economy is completely incompatible with neoliberalism, and at best an uneasy bedfellow with capitalism. Section 2 explains in greater detail why we require a steady state economy. Section 3 explains why mainstream (capitalist) economists fail to recognize the need for a steady state economy, and Section 4 why competitive free markets are particularly ill-suited to attaining one. The steady state requires economic institutions based on *cooperation*. Section 5 shows that humans have evolved to be extremely cooperative and even altruistic, hence capable of solving these problems, but only if we adopt appropriate economic institutions. The chapter concludes that building new institutions that stimulate *cooperation* will be more effective than trying to force the steady state economy into a capitalist framework.

The steady state economy: paradigm and goals

The argument for a steady state economy is currently associated with ecological economics (EE), and emerges unavoidably from the core paradigms and goals of that field (Daly and Farley 2010). Three core paradigms concern the nature of the ecological economic system. First, the economy is a physical subsystem of the finite global ecosphere (Georgescu-Roegen 1971). Second, the economy and ecosphere are in a continuous process of co-evolutionary change (Gowdy 1994; Norgaard 1994). Third, the ecological economic system is highly complex and non-linear, subject to emergent properties, surprise, positive and negative feedback loops, thresholds of abrupt, often irreversible change, and hence profound uncertainty (Meadows 2008). A fourth core paradigm views humans as a highly social animal. The basic unit of analysis therefore must be persons-in-community heavily influenced by social norms, and deeply concerned about fairness and the welfare of others (Daly and Cobb 1994).

Both the economy and the ecosphere that sustains it are subject to the laws of physics and ecology. From physics we know that it is impossible to make something from nothing. Earth is a thermodynamically-closed system: solar energy can flow in and heat out, but matter cannot in any appreciable amount. All economic production therefore requires the physical transformation of raw materials provided by nature. When a renewable resource is depleted more rapidly than it can regenerate, over time the resource stock must decline to zero. Humans decide how fast to extract raw materials and energy and convert them into economic products. Any continuous use of non-renewable resources must ultimately result in their economic exhaustion, meaning that the costs of extracting remaining stocks will exceed their benefits. Energy is required to do work. Our only significant sources of energy are finite stocks of fossil fuels and radioactive minerals, and finite flows of solar energy in its various forms, including wind and hydro (Georgescu-Roegen 1975). Fossil fuels currently account for approximately 81.7 percent of total primary energy supply for the global economy and nuclear 4.8 percent. Though renewable energy use is growing rapidly, wind, solar, hydro, geothermal and lesser sources account for only 3.5 percent of supply, with biofuels and waste making up the remaining 10 percent (IEA 2014). While the solar energy striking the Earth's surface is enormous relative to human energy consumption, it is diffuse and difficult to store.

It is also impossible to make nothing from something, and total entropy increases. This means that fossil fuel and nuclear energy inevitably generate waste emissions and waste heat, which return to the environment as pollution. All economic products inevitably wear out, break down or fall apart, and are either recycled or return to the environment as waste. One hundred percent recycling is likely impossible (Georgescu-Roegen 1971, but see Ayres 1999 for an alternative viewpoint). If the flow of waste continuously exceeds the ecosystem's absorption capacity, the waste must accumulate as an ever-larger stock. Ecosystems have had little time to evolve the capacity to absorb wastes such as new human-made compounds, particularly those made from non-renewable resources, which are therefore particularly problematic.

From ecology we know that the ecosphere is a complex, evolving system. Much of the raw material we extract and convert into economic products alternatively serves as the structural building blocks of ecosystems (see Washington in this volume). Other economic activities such as agriculture and infrastructure simply replace natural ecosystems. A particular configuration of ecosystem structure is capable of capturing solar energy flows to generate ecosystem services, including many that are essential for the survival of humans and all other species (MEA 2005; Kumar 2010). Ecosystem services are provided at a rate over time that is determined by the health and size of the ecosystem that generates them; the ecosystem is not physically transformed into the services it provides. When the economy transforms ecosystem structure into economic products, the inevitable result is the loss of ecosystem services. Among these services is the capacity to regenerate renewable resources, and this capacity typically decreases as the ecosystem is degraded. Waste emissions in excess of absorption capacity further diminish the capacity of ecosystems to generate essential services (Daly 2007; Farley and Costanza 2010).

For any given technology, economic growth (as measured by economic activity[1]) will increase the use of throughput. Up to certain physical limits, a more efficient technology (i.e. one that uses fewer raw materials and less energy per unit of output) can achieve a given level of economic activity with less throughput. One problem is that in practice, efficiency improvements often lead to greater resource use, not less (Polimeni *et al.* 2008). A more serious problem is the nature of exponential growth. Over the past several decades, the greatest rate of decrease in energy intensity per unit of GDP was 1.87 percent annually between 2004–2008 (Enerdata 2015), a period during which oil prices approximately tripled (British Petroleum 2014). Achieving the IPCC recommendation of reducing greenhouse gas emissions by 80 percent by 2050 would require a nearly 5 percent annual reduction[2] in the absence of economic growth, but a nearly 8 percent annual reduction if the global economy were growing at a modest 3 percent per annum. Over longer time periods, the absurdity of continuous economic growth becomes obvious. One dollar invested in the year zero at 5 percent interest would now be worth a ball of gold (at $1300 per ounce) the size of the solar system beyond the orbit of Pluto.[3] Continuous exponential growth of any physical subsystem of our finite planet is clearly impossible. Technological advances can potentially improve the quality of what we produce with no discernible limit, but not the quantity.

Economics must consider what is normatively desirable as well as what is biophysically possible. The paradigm of persons-in-community who care about others, including future generations, coupled with biophysical limits, leads to the conclusion that ecological sustainability must be a central goal of ecological economics. At its most basic, an activity is sustainable when we can keep doing it into the indefinite future. A sustainable economic system cannot continuously extract renewable resources faster than they regenerate, or the resource stocks will fall to zero. It cannot continuously emit waste faster than it is absorbed, or waste stocks and the harm they cause will grow indefinitely. It cannot extract essential non-renewable resources (such as fossil fuels) faster than we develop renewable substitutes. Furthermore, resource extraction, waste emissions and land use change cannot be allowed to threaten the capacity of ecosystems to generate essential services (Daly 1996). If ecological sustainability is a desirable goal, the only solution is a steady state economy, in which throughput and human populations are non-growing and within the capacity of Earth's ecosystems to sustain them indefinitely (Daly 1991). Abundant evidence suggests we are already exceeding sustainable throughput by a significant margin (Catton 1982; Wackernagel *et al.* 2002; Rockström *et al.* 2009).

Sustainability is a question of intergenerational distribution, yet it makes little sense to worry about the well-being of future generations without worrying about the well-being of those alive today. A second goal of ecological economics is therefore the just distribution of wealth and resources (Daly 1992). Private ownership of resources created by nature or society as a whole is likely to be unjust; such resources should instead be owned in common by all humans, present and future (Bollier 2002; Raffensperger *et al.* 2009; Farley *et al.* 2015).

Following Herman Daly, most ecological economists would add efficient allocation as the third economic goal, subordinate to sustainability and justice (Daly 1992). Daly defines efficiency as the ratio between economic services gained and ecosystem services sacrificed (Daly and Farley 2010). Capitalism assumes that free markets are inherently efficient, and will optimally allocate ecosystem structure between economic products and ecosystem services as long as we account for all ecological costs (Simpson *et al.* 2005; Pearce and Turner 1990). In reality however, the capitalist economy presents numerous obstacles to achieving a steady state economy, and we cannot simply assume the two are compatible.

Capitalist perspectives on the steady state

Capitalism is more of an ideology than a practice, since, as pointed out previously, there are no *purely* capitalist economies. The basic tenets of capitalist ideology, and hence its perspective on the steady state, emerge from the paradigm and goals of neoclassical economics (NCE), the mainstream economic theory. Rather than acknowledging limits to physical growth of the economy, the NCE paradigm stresses built-in mechanisms that overcome any limits. Its goals implicitly make growth the greatest good, and failure to grow – hence a steady state economy – the greatest threat. The emergence of these perspectives deserves elaboration.

Prior to the Great Depression and the development of GDP in the 1930s, NCEs paid little attention to economic growth, which only became a focus of economic theory in the 1940s and a political goal in the 1950s (Yissar 2013). The 1940s also saw growing concern over limits to growth (Osborn 1948; Hubbert 1949), leading the government to commission a study – dominated by economists – on material limits to growth (PMPC 1952). The conclusion of this study, and of NCE in general, was that growing scarcity of any resource would trigger a price increase, reducing demand, increasing supply, and spurring the development of substitutes. While individual resources could become scarce, near perfect substitutability between resources would overcome general limits to growth (Barnett and Morse 1963; Solow 1973, 1974). Attention to environmental degradation and the loss of natural amenities raised concerns about ecological limits to growth (Carson 1962; Meadows *et al.* 1972), with the additional problem that such amenities were frequently non-excludable, and hence had no price to signal scarcity (Ayres and Kneese 1969; Daly 1973). Again however NCE concluded that the price mechanism and technological progress could still overcome any limits to growth as long as we created mechanisms for internalizing ecological costs into prices (Simpson *et al.* 2005; Pearce and Turner 1990). NCE in fact became quite scornful of any discussion of limits to growth or of a steady state economy (Yissar 2013; Solow 1972, 1973; Beckerman 1995), and has largely ignored it. Even today, most economic analysis assumes growth is inevitable. For example, the IPCC assumes a baseline growth rate of 1.6–3 percent per year in the absence of climate change, with the expectation that consumption would increase seven-fold by 2100 (IPCC 2014).

Faith in the price mechanism to solve environmental problems arises from the NCE failure to acknowledge complexity. NCE models the economy as an equilibrium system in which human behavior is consistent and predictable, and prices always function as a negative feedback loop that balances supply and demand. The entire field is based on 'methodological individualism', which attributes all social phenomena to the actions of individuals and ignores the potential for emergent properties (Keen 2011). Similarly, there is virtually no acknowledgement that ecosystems also exhibit thresholds, significant time lags between cause and effect, emergent properties and surprise (Gowdy and O'Hara 1995; Farley 2008). This vision of a simple linear world underlies capitalists' claims that the 'prophets of ecological doom' (e.g. Malthus 1798; Daly 1977; Meadows et al. 1972; Ehrlich 1968; Ehrlich and Ehrlich 1981) have all been proven wrong (Solow 1972; Simon 1996; Beckerman 1995).

Within the NCE vision, a steady state economy is not only unnecessary, but also undesirable. Distilled to its essence, the central goal of NCE is to allocate factors of production towards the economic products with the greatest monetary value, then to distribute these resources towards those individuals who value them most, as measured by willingness to pay, thus maximizing monetary value (Frank and Bernanke 2003). In the words of one neoliberal economist, 'wealth rather than happiness [is] the criterion for an efficient allocation of resources' (Posner 1985, p. 88)[4]. Over time, the goal is more wealth, hence continuous economic growth. Belief in continuous progress, which capitalists define as ever increasing consumption, has been a central tenet of Western philosophy since the enlightenment. Finally, there is abundant empirical evidence that when capitalist economies fail to grow, the result is widespread unemployment and poverty. From this perspective, economic growth is a moral imperative (Friedman 2006). In summary, the neoclassical and hence capitalist perspective on the steady state is that it is both unnecessary and intolerable.

Conflicts between capitalism and the steady state

Given the absence of any *purely* capitalist economy, and the innumerable varieties of hybrid economies undergoing continuous evolutionary change, it is difficult to determine whether or not some form of capitalism could be compatible with a steady state economy. Some serious problems, however, suggest major incompatibilities: the drive for capital accumulation, the nature of money as interest bearing debt, the failure of capitalist economies to price non-excludable resources, and the failure of prices to efficiently allocate non-rival resources.

The central goal of capitalism is to accumulate more capital by investing money or other financial assets in activities that generate a positive rate of return. Most investments are debt-financed, and thus require a rate of return greater than the interest rate (Hudson 2012; Farley et al. 2013). Capital accumulation can be the result of increased economic production or redistribution of existing capital, but neither of these is compatible with a steady state. Furthermore, most money is loaned into existence by banks as interest-bearing debt, and is destroyed when that debt is repaid. This conflicts with a steady state economy in three important ways. First, it creates a tendency to systematically 'discount the future' (and hence sustainability) because money now can pay down interest bearing debt or be loaned at interest, and is hence worth more than money later (Lietaer et al. 2012). Even harvesting a species to extinction can be profit maximizing if that species grows more slowly than a debt or investment opportunity (Daly and Farley 2010). Second, if the money supply is not increasing, there will not be enough money available to pay back existing principal plus interest. When loans are not being repaid, banks will not make new loans, but will continue to collect (to the best of their ability) outstanding debt, resulting in a smaller money supply, economic contraction, layoffs, and poverty. Money as interest-bearing debt forces a capitalist economy to choose between inherently *un*sustainable continuous growth and misery (Robertson 2012; Dietz and O'Neill 2013; Lietaer *et al.* 2012; Soddy 1935; Daly 1980). Third, since interest rates and growth rates of capital almost always exceed economic growth rates, capitalism systematically increases economic inequality (Piketty 2014; Farley *et al.* 2013). In a non-growing economy, increasing inequality increases poverty. Curiously, NCE theory has little to say on these topics because its central models are based on a barter economy in which money is neutral and there is no way to accumulate and invest surplus value (Gowdy 2009; Keen 2011).

A central goal of the steady state economy is to ensure the continued provision of life-sustaining but frequently non-excludable ecosystem services, ranging from climate regulation to pollination. Non-excludable resources cannot be effectively priced, since individuals can use them whether or not they pay. Capitalists are therefore likely to ignore them in their economic decisions. Many economists claim that the monetary value of such impacts can be objectively calculated – which is highly contentious – then integrated into market prices, leading to their optimal provision (Pearce and Turner 1990; Baumol and Oates 1989). However, virtually all resource extraction and waste emissions cause negative externalities. An army of technocrats would need to estimate the monetary values of these externalities. Feeding them back into the price mechanism (e.g. through taxes) would inevitably require political compromises. Since market prices are constantly changing in response to changes in supply and demand, this would be an endless process. Capitalists idealize the market because it allows individuals to freely satisfy subjective individual preferences (Stigler and Becker 1977; Hayek 1945), yet so-called market solutions to the problem of non-excludable resources require collective decisions, centralized information and a central authority. Another option is to declare public or common ownership of resources created by nature, including waste absorption capacity, then allot or auction off the renewable increment to the private sector (Farley *et al.* 2015), but public ownership of the means of production is socialism.

Furthermore, even if ecological costs could be internalized into markets, market allocation in an unequal world can be quite perverse. By many accounts, the greatest current threat to the global ecosystem is agriculture (Rockström *et al.* 2009; Tilman *et al.* 2011; Kumar 2010), so if food prices reflected their full ecological costs, they would be much higher. When drought, speculation and ethanol production doubled the price of staple grains in 2007 and 2008 (Lagi *et al.* 2011; FAO *et al.* 2011), citizens of rich countries scarcely noticed, primarily because food accounts for only a small share of the average household budget, and staple grain prices for much less. For example, where wheat accounts for only 5 percent of the cost of a loaf of bread, doubling its price barely affects the price of bread. When wheat prices tripled between 2006 and 2008, US consumption actually increased slightly (USDA 2013). In many poor countries, on the other hand, people may spend 50 percent or more of their income on food, largely in the form of unprocessed staple grains (Anker 2011; Seale *et al.* 2003). In response to the 2007–2008 food crisis, poor people dramatically reduced their consumption, causing a major increase in malnutrition and hunger (FAO 2009). In an unequal world, markets may allocate the most important resources towards those who need them least, and raising prices to reduce ecological degradation would force those who contributed least to the problem to make the biggest sacrifices to solve it (Farley *et al.* 2014).

Capitalism may be even less appropriate for non-rival resources. Take the example of information. Though knowledge actually improves through use, capitalism uses patents to make it excludable in order to incentivize innovation. However, using prices to ration access to these technologies reduces their use, and hence their value. The main input into any new technology is existing information, and the cheapest way to develop new technologies is to make that information open access (Kolata 2010, Benkler 2004). Once a useful new technology has been developed, making the underlying information freely available to all maximizes its value. However, in the absence of price rationing, capitalism will not supply non-rival resources. Furthermore, unregulated capitalism provides no incentives to produce technologies that provide or protect public goods. The viability of the capitalist growth model relies on endless technological innovation, which capitalism may paradoxically inhibit. Most scientists work for salaries, and there is no reason to believe they would work less hard when paid by the public sector. Public investment to provide collectively owned non-rival resources reduces costs and increases benefits relative to capitalist approaches (Farley and Perkins 2013; Kubiszewski *et al.* 2010).

In summary, markets deal very poorly with issues of ecological sustainability and just distribution. Herman Daly has long made the case that these problems must be solved before the markets can be trusted (Daly 1973, 1992). Most solutions require collective provision and ownership of nature and knowledge, removing them from the capitalist economy. The growing importance of sustainability and justice would seem to relegate capitalism to a shrinking role in a hybrid economy.

Prisoner's dilemmas and cooperation

Capitalism may work reasonably well for rival and excludable resources, as long as resource extraction and waste emissions are well within the ecosphere's limits. However, as soon as economic activity threatens to degrade non-excludable ecosystem services and exceed ecological thresholds, important decisions must be made at the social level. Many of the most serious problems confronting our transition to a steady state economy, ranging from climate change and overpopulation to depletion of oceanic fisheries, can be modeled as 'prisoner's dilemmas' (Hardin 1968; Nowak and Highfield 2011). A prisoner's dilemma occurs when universal cooperation or altruism generates the best outcome for society as a whole, but regardless of others' choices, self-regarding behavior generates the best outcomes for the individual. Selfish individuals reason that whether everyone else reduces greenhouse gas emissions or no one else does, they are better off as individuals not reducing them. NCE theory and capitalism are based not only on the assumption that people are *inherently selfish* (they care only about their own utility generally measured by their own consumption, though enlightened self-interest will lead them to help someone else if it rebounds in their favor), but also that everyone pursuing their own self-interest generates the greatest good for the greatest number (Keen 2011; Graafland 2009; Gowdy 2009). However, even enlightened self-interest breaks down for prisoner's dilemmas, which can only be solved through cooperation[5] (Axelrod 1984; Nowak and Highfield 2011).

Natural selection is driven by competition between individuals, which supports the NCE view on human behavior, unless specific mechanisms are at work. Fortunately, humans may be the only species that exhibits all five mechanisms that have been shown conducive to the evolution of cooperation: reciprocity, indirect reciprocity, kin selection, proximity and multi-level selection (Nowak 2006). Perhaps the most interesting of these mechanisms is multi-level selection (MLS), which occurs when variation, differential survival, and retention of traits operate at different levels. Within a group, selfish individuals will outcompete altruistic ones. At this level, evolution favors selfishness. However, in any type of prisoner's dilemma situation, cooperation yields higher payoffs to the group than selfishness. A group dominated by altruistic individuals facing prisoner's dilemmas will have greater survival of offspring than one dominated by selfish individuals. If the advantages of cooperation are adequate, there is homogeneity within a group and heterogeneity between groups, then competition between groups will favor the evolution of altruism and cooperation. Cooperative individuals, both humans and of other species, can learn to detect and exclude defectors, reducing the within group advantage of selfish behavior. The dark side of group selection is that it does not promote cooperation with those outside the group (Wilson 2007; Wilson and Wilson 2007). Nonetheless, though group level selection has come to dominate individual level selection only a few times in evolutionary history to produce eusocial or ultrasocial[6] species, such as humans, ants and termites, these few species have become the dominant animals on earth, as measured by biomass, population size and impacts on their environment (E.O. Wilson 2012; Gowdy and Krall 2015). MLS can also explain how prokaryotes may have cooperated to form eukaryotes, how unicellular eukaryotes cooperated to form multicellular life, how individuals within a species cooperate in groups, and even how different species can cooperate to form ecosystems (Margulis 1970; Wilson and Wilson 2007).

Cultural evolution can create norms and institutions that reinforce cooperative, altruistic behavior or competitive, selfish behavior. It can also help extend the definition of the group from hunter–gatherer societies of 150 individuals to countries of over one billion individuals, for which citizens will altruistically sacrifice their lives. One widely studied mechanism that promotes cooperation is known as altruistic punishment, in which individuals suffer a loss to their own fitness in order to punish non-cooperators (hereafter defectors). This punishment reduces or eliminates the benefits of defection, and can make cooperation a dominant strategy even for selfish individuals. The group as a whole benefits from the sacrifice of the punisher. Punishing individuals who fail to punish defectors increases the likelihood that defectors will be punished, and further promotes cooperation (Boyd and Richerson 1992; Boyd et al. 2003; Henrich and Henrich 2007). For most of human history, we lived as hunter-gatherers in highly egalitarian societies with the cultural norm of ostracizing individuals who tried to take more than their fair share of food or other resources, when ostracism often meant death (Sober and Wilson 1998). Cooperation has also been shown to stimulate production of the powerful neurotransmitter oxytocin, which stimulates feelings of reward and pleasure and also further cooperation in a positive feedback loop (Kosfeld et al. 2005; Gordon et al. 2011). Research in behavioral economics (Bowles and Gintis 2002, 2004; Boyd et al. 2003; Gintis et al. 2005), biology (Nowak and Highfield 2011; E.O. Wilson 2012), political science (Axelrod 1984), psychology (Kahneman 2011), evolution (Sober and Wilson 1998; D. Wilson 2007), anthropology (Henrich and Henrich 2007) and other fields provide convincing theoretical and empirical evidence that humans *are* capable of highly cooperative, pro-social behavior.

Unfortunately, the theory and practice of capitalism seems to make people *less* cooperative, less socially oriented, less empathic, and more selfish. In prisoner's dilemma situations, economists and economics students are less likely to cooperate than non-economists (Frank et al. 1993; Marwell and Ames 1981). Providing monetary rewards for contributing to the public good can undermine people's intrinsic motivation to do so, in essence making them more selfish (Frey 1992; Frey and Jegen 2001; Reeson and Tisdell 2008; Bowles 2008). People who are wealthy or simply primed to think about money become less social, more selfish, less likely to offer help, less likely to solicit help from others, and they are less empathic, less honest and less moral, but also more favorable to free market economics and more likely to justify inequality (Vohs et al. 2006, 2008; Caruso et al. 2013; Piff et al. 2012). Capitalism and neoliberalism, together with the policies and cultural traits that have emerged around them, appear to undermine the cooperative behaviors required to achieve a steady state economy.

Conclusions

Economics is frequently defined as 'the allocation of scarce resources among alternative competing ends'. This definition suggests a clear order in which economic analysis must proceed: identify the desirable ends, identify the scarce resources, and only then determine what allocative mechanisms are appropriate. Arguably, the free market was appropriate when the main economic goal was to increase material consumption in a fossil fuel economy on an empty planet, characterized by abundant natural resources and resilient ecosystems. Human activity on an increasingly full planet now threatens basic life support functions essential to human civilization and even survival, while material consumption has reached unprecedented levels. Sustaining resilient global ecosystems that continue to generate these functions has become far more important than ever greater consumption. Unless we accept blind faith in technological progress as a solution, we must achieve a steady state economy. It will likely be impossible to achieve a steady state economy without a more just distribution of resources.

Achieving a just, steady state economy will unquestionably require cooperation, not competitive self-interest. The changes required of a capitalist economy to make it compatible with a steady state are immense, and are incompatible with the attributes that make a capitalist economy desirable. Rather than trying to shoehorn the steady state into the capitalist economy, we should instead be striving to create institutions that stimulate cooperation. Excellent possibilities include revitalized cooperatives (Alperovitz 2005, 2013), reclaiming the commons (Raffensperger *et al.* 2009; Bollier and Helfrich 2012; Weston and Bollier 2013; Barnes 2006; Farley *et al.* 2015), and explicit resource rights for future generations and/or other species (e.g Earth jurisprudence) (Brown 2008; Burdon 2011). It may be that once we have achieved ecological sustainability and just distribution, the market will be able to allocate resources efficiently without undermining these higher order goals. Until then, however, capitalism and the steady state are unlikely bedfellows.

Notes

1. Gross Domestic Product is intended as a measure of economic activity, but it is at best a rough approximation. For example, it is well established that when the supply of an essential resource decreases by one percent, the price increases by more than one percent. This means that, perversely, the contribution of any essential resource to GDP will increase as the supply decreases (Farley 2008).
2. The equation for the annual rate of reduction required to achieve an 80 percent total decrease over 35 years is $r=\ln(0.2)/35=4.6$ percent.
3. Calculated by author.
4. Though this quote comes from a period when Posner was a neoliberal economist of the Chicago School, it's important to note that he was one of vanishingly few neoclassical economics who viewed the 2008 financial crisis as a failure of capitalism and hence evidence that core tenets of neoclassical theory were wrong. See Posner (2009) for more details.
5. Cooperation here follows Nowak's (2006) definition in the evolutionary sense of 'selfish replicators forgoing some of their reproductive potential to help one another' (p. 1560). It more practical terms, it means cooperating in a prisoner's dilemma setting, even though non-cooperation offers greater rewards to the individual regardless of what others do.
6. Both the terms eusocial and ultrasocial have been used to describe humans, ants and termites, which are arguably the most social species on the planet. See Gowdy and Krall (2015) for a detailed distinction between the two terms.

References

Alperovitz, G. (2005) *American Beyond Capitalism: Reclaiming Our Wealth, Our Liberty, and Our Democracy*. Hoboken: John Wiley and Sons.

Alperovitz, G. (2013) *What Then Must We Do? Straight Talk about the Next American Revolution*. White River Junction, VT: Chelsea Green Publishing.

Anker, R. (2011) 'Engel's Law around the World 150 Years Later', Working Paper Series, University of Massachusetts Political Economy Research Institute Number 247.

Axelrod, R. M. (1984) *The Evolution of Cooperation*. New York: Basic Books.

Ayres, R. U. (1999) 'The Second Law, the Fourth Law, Recycling and Limits to Growth', *Ecological Economics*, 29:473–484.

Ayres, R. and Kneese, A. (1969) 'Production, Consumption, and Externalities', *The American Economic Review*, 59:282–297.

Barnes, P. (2006) *Capitalism 3.0: A Guide to Reclaiming the Commons*. San Francisco: Berrett-Koehler Publishers.

Barnett, H. and Morse, C. (1963) *Scarcity and Growth: The Economics of Natural Resource Availability*. Baltimore, MD: John Hopkins University Press.

Baumol, W. and Oates, W. (1989) *The Theory of Environmental Policy*. Cambridge, MA: Cambridge University Press.

Beckerman, W. (1995) *Small Is Stupid: Blowing the Whistle on the Greens*. London: Duckworth.

Benkler, Y. (2004) 'Commons-Based Strategies and the Problems of Patents.' *Science*, 305 (5687):1110–1111. doi: 10.1126/science.1100526

Bollier, D. (2002) *Silent Theft: The Private Plunder of our Common Wealth*. New York: Routledge.

Bollier, D. and Helfrich, S. (eds.) (2012) *The Wealth of the Commons: A World Beyond Market and State*. Amherst, MA: Levellers Press.

Bowles, S. (2008) 'Policies Designed for Self-Interested Citizens May Undermine "The Moral Sentiments": Evidence from Economic Experiments', *Science*, 320 (5883):1605–1609.

Bowles, S. and Gintis H. (2002) 'Behavioural Science – Homo reciprocans', *Nature*, 415 (6868):125–128.

Bowles, S. and Gintis, H. (2004) 'The Evolution Of Strong Reciprocity: Cooperation in Heterogeneous Populations', *Theoretical Population Biology*, 65 (1):17–28.

Boyd, R., Gintis, H., Bowles, S., and Richerson P. J. (2003) 'The Evolution of Altruistic Punishment', *Proceedings of the National Academy of Sciences of the United States of America*, 100 (6):3531–3535.

Boyd, R. and Richerson, P. (1992) 'Punishment Allows the Evolution of Cooperation (or Anything Else) in Sizable Groups', *Ethology and Sociobiology*, 13 (3):171–195. doi: http://dx.doi.org/10.1016/0162-3095(92)90032-Y

British Petroleum (2014) *Statistical Review of World Energy*, Full Report. See: http://www.bp.com

Brown, P. (2008) *Right Relationship: Building a Whole Earth Economy*. San Francisco: Berret-Koehler.

Burdon, P. (ed.) (2011) *Exploring Wild Law: The Philosophy of Earth Jurisprudence*. Mile End, South Australia: Wakefield Press Pty Ltd.

Carson, R. (1962) *Silent Spring*. Boston: Houghton Mifflin.

Caruso, E., Kathleen, M., Vohs, D., Baxter, B., and Waytz, A. (2013) 'Mere exposure to money increases endorsement of free-market systems and social inequality', *Journal of Experimental Psychology: General*, 142 (2):301–306.
Catton, W. (1982) *Overshoot: The Ecological Basis of Revolutionary Change*. Champaign, IL: University of Illinois Press.
Crutzen, P. (2002) 'Geology of mankind', *Nature*, 415:23.
Daly, H. (ed.) (1973) *Toward a Steady-State Economy*. San Francisco: W. H. Freeman and Co.
Daly, H. (1977) *Steady-State Economics: The Political Economy of Bio-physical Equilibrium and Moral Growth*. San Francisco: W. H. Freeman and Co.
Daly, H. (1980) 'The Economic Thought of Frederick Soddy', *History of Political Economy*, 12 (4):469–488.
Daly, H. (1991) *Steady State Economics: 2nd edition with new essays*. Washington, DC: Island Press.
Daly, H. (1992) 'Allocation, distribution, and scale: towards an economics that is efficient, just, and sustainable', *Ecological Economics*, 6 (3):185–193.
Daly, H. (1996) *Beyond Growth: the Economics of Sustainable Development*. Boston, MA: Beacon Press.
Daly, H. (2007) *Ecological Economics and Sustainable Development, Selected Essays of Herman Daly*. Edited by Jeroen C.J.M. van den Bergh. Northampton, MA: Edward Elgar.
Daly, H. and Cobb, Jr., J. (1994) *For the Common Good: Redirecting the Economy toward Community, the Environment, and a Sustainable Future*. 2nd ed. Boston: Beacon Press.
Daly, H. and Farley, J. (2010) *Ecological Economics: Principles and Applications*. 2nd ed. Washington, DC: Island Press.
Dietz, R. and O'Neill, D. (2013) *Enough Is Enough*. San Francisco: Berret-Koehler.
Ehrlich, P. (1968) *The Population Bomb*. New York: Sierra Club/Ballantine Books.
Ehrlich, P. and Ehrlich, A. (1981) *Extinction: The Causes & Consequences of the Disappearance of Species*. New York: Random House.
Enerdata (2015) Global Energy Statistical Yearbook 2015. See: https://yearbook.enerdata.net/
FAO (2009) *The State of Food Insecurity in the World 2009*. Rome: FAO.
FAO, IFAD, IMF, OECD, UNCTAD, WFP, The World Bank, the WTO, IFPRI and UN HLTF (2011) *Price Volatility in Food and Agricultural Markets: Policy Responses*. See: http://www.worldbank.org/foodcrisis/pdf/Interagency_Report_to_the_G20_on_Food_Price_Volatility.pdf
Farley, J. (2008) 'The Role of Prices in Conserving Critical Natural Capital', *Conservation Biology*, 22 (6):1399–1408.
Farley, J., Burke, M., Flomenhoft, G. Kelly, B., Murray, D., Posner, S., Putnam, M., Scanlan, A., and Witham, A. (2013) 'Monetary and Fiscal Policies for a Finite Planet', *Sustainability*, 5 (6):2802–2826.
Farley, J. and Costanza, R. (2010) 'Payments for Ecosystem Services: From Local to Global', *Ecological Economics*, 69 (11):2060–2068.
Farley, J., Costanza, R., Flomenhoft, G., and Kirk, D. (2015) 'The Vermont Common Assets Trust: An Institution for Sustainable, Just and Efficient Resource Allocation', *Ecological Economics*, 109 (0):71–79. doi: http://dx.doi.org/10.1016/j.ecolecon.2014.10.016
Farley, J., Filho, A., Burke, M., and Farr, M. (2014) 'Extending Market Allocation to Ecosystem Services: Moral and Practical Implications on a Full and Unequal Planet', *Ecological Economics*, 117:244–252. doi: http://dx.doi.org/10.1016/j.ecolecon.2014.06.021

Farley, J. and Perkins, S. (2013) 'Economics of Information in a Green Economy', in *Building a Green Economy*, edited by R. Robertson. East Lansing, Michigan: Michigan State University Press, pp. 83–100.
Frank, R. and Bernanke, B. (2003) *Principles of Microeconomics*. 2nd ed. New York: McGraw Hill.
Frank, R., Gilovich, T., and Regan, D. (1993) 'Does Studying Economics Inhibit Cooperation?', *Journal of Economic Perspectives*, 7 (2):159–171.
Frey, B. (1992) 'Pricing and regulating affect environmental ethics,' *Environmental and Resource Economics*, 2 (4):399–414. doi: 10.1007/BF00304969
Frey, B. and Jegen, R. (2001) 'Motivation Crowding Theory', *Journal of Economic Surveys*, 15 (5):589–611.
Friedman, B. (2006) 'The Moral Consequences of Economic Growth', *Society*, 43 (2):15–22. doi: 10.1007/BF02687365
Georgescu-Roegen, N. (1971) *The Entropy Law and the Economic Process*. Cambridge, MA: Harvard University Press.
Georgescu-Roegen, N. (1975) 'Energy and Economic Myths', *Southern Economic Journal*, 41 (3):347–381.
Gintis, H., Bowles, S., Boyd, R., and Fehr, E. (2005) (eds.) *Moral Sentiments and Material Interests: The Foundations of Cooperation in Economic Life*. Cambridge, MA: MIT Press.
Gordon, I., Martin, C., Feldman, R., and. Leckman, J. (2011) 'Oxytocin and social motivation', *Developmental Cognitive Neuroscience*, 1 (4):471–493. doi: 10.1016/j.dcn.2011.07.007
Gowdy, J. (1994) *Coevolutionary Economics: The Economy, Society and the Environment*. Boston: Kluwer.
Gowdy, J. (2009) *Microeconomic Theory Old and New: A Students Guide*. Stanford, CA: Stanford University Press.
Gowdy, J. and Krall, L. (2015) 'The Economic Origins of Ultrasociality', *Behavioral and Brain Sciences*, April, 1–63.
Gowdy, J. and O'Hara, S. (1995) *Economic Theory for Environmentalists*. Boca Raton, FL: St. Lucie Press.
Graafland, J. (2009) 'Self-Interest', in *Handbook of Economics and Ethics*, edited by Jan Peil and Irene van Staveren. Edward Elgar, pp. 477–483.
Hardin, G. (1968) 'The Tragedy of the Commons', *Science*, 162 (3859):1243–1248.
Hayek, F. (1945) 'The Price System as a Mechanism for Using Knowledge', *American Economic Review*, 35 (4):519–530.
Henrich, J. and Henrich, N. (2007) *Why Humans Cooperate: A Cultural and Evolutionary Explanation, Evolution and Cognition*. New York: Oxford University Press.
Hubbert, M. (1949) 'Energy From Fossil Fuels', *Science*, 109:103–109.
Hudson, M. (2012) *The Bubble and Beyond*. USA: ISLET.
IEA (2014) *2014 Key World Energy Statistics*. Paris: International Energy Agency.
IPCC (2014) *Climate Change 2014: Synthesis Report*. Contribution of Working Groups I, II and III to the Fifth Assessment Report of the Intergovernmental Panel on Climate Change. Core Writing Team, R.K. Pachauri and L.A. Meyer (eds.). Geneva, Switzerland: IPCC.
Kahneman, D. (2011) *Thinking, Fast and Slow*. New York: Farrar, Straus and Giroux.
Keen, S. (2011) *Debunking Economics – Revised and Expanded Edition: The Naked Emperor Dethroned?* New York: Zed Books.
Keynes, J. M. (1991) *Essays in Persuasion*. New York: Norton.

Kolata, G. (2010) 'Sharing of Data Leads to Progress on Alzheimer's', *New York Times*, 12 August 2010, A1.

Kosfeld, M., Heinrichs, M., Zak, P., Fischbacher, U., and Fehr, E. (2005) 'Oxytocin Increases Trust in Humans', *Nature*, 435 (7042):673–676.

Kubiszewski, I., Farley, J., and Costanza, R. (2010) 'The Production and Allocation of Information as a Good That Is Enhanced with Increased Use', *Ecological Economics*, 69 (6):1344–1354.

Kumar, P. (ed.) (2010) *The Economics of Ecosystems and Biodiversity: Ecological and Economic Foundations*. London and Washington: Earthscan.

Lagi, M., Bar-Yam, Y., Bertrand, K., and Bar-Yam, Y. (2011) *The Food Crises: A Quantitative Model of Food Prices Including Speculators and Ethanol Conversion*, New England Complex Systems Institute. See: http://ssrn.com/abstract=1932247 or http://dx.doi.org/10.2139/ssrn.1932247

Lietaer, B., Arnsperger, C., Goerner, S., and Brunnhuber, S. (2012) *Money and Sustainability – The Missing Link*. Axminster: Triarchy Press.

Malthus, T. (1798) *An Essay on the Principle of Population, as It Affects the Future Improvement of Society; with Remarks on the Speculations of W. Godwin, M. Condorcet and Other Writers*, 3rd ed. London: J. Johnson.

Margulis, L. (1970) *Origin of Eukaryotic Cells: Evidence and Research Implications for a Theory of the Origin and Evolution of Microbial, Plant, and Animal Cells on the Precambrian Earth*. New Haven: Yale University Press.

Marwell, G. and Ames, R. (1981) 'Economists free ride, does anyone else?: Experiments on the provision of public goods, IV', *Journal of Public Economics*, 15 (3):295–310. doi: http://dx.doi.org/10.1016/0047-2727(81)90013-X

MEA (2005) *Living beyond Our Means: Natural Assets and Human Wellbeing, Statement from the Board*. New York: Millennium Ecosystem Assessment, United Nations Environment Programme (available www.millenniumassessment.org).

Meadows, D. (2008) *Thinking in Systems: A Primer*. White River Junction, VT: Chelsea Green.

Meadows, D., Meadows, D., Randers, J., and Behrens, W. (1972) *The Limits to Growth: A Report for the Club of Rome's Project on the Predicament of Mankind*. New York: Universe Books.

Mill, J. S. (1848) *Principles of Political Economy with Some of Their Applications to Social Philosophy*. London: John W. Parker. Original edition, 1909. Reprint, 2009.

Norgaard, R. (1994) 'The Coevolution of Environmental and Economic Systems and the Emergence of Unsustainablility', in *Evolutionary Concepts in Contemporary Economics*, edited by Richard W. England, pp. 213–225. Ann Arbor: University of Michigan Press.

Nowak, M. (2006) 'Five Rules for the Evolution of Cooperation', *Science*, 314 (5805):1560–1563.

Nowak, M. and Highfield, R. (2011) *Super Cooperators: Altruism, Evolution, and Why We Need Each Other to Succeed*. New York: Free Press (Simon Schuster).

Osborn, F. (1948) *Our Plundered Planet*. Boston: Little, Brown and Company.

Pearce, D. and Turner, R. (1990) *Economics of Natural Resources and the Environment*. Hertfordshire, England: Harvester Wheatsheaf.

Piff, P. K., Stancato, D. M., Cote, S., Mendoza-Denton, R., and Keltner, D. (2012) 'Higher Social Class Predicts Increased Unethical Behavior', *Proceedings of the National Academy of Sciences of the United States of America*, 109 (11):4086–4091. doi: 10.1073/pnas.1118373109

Piketty, T. (2014) *Capital in the 21st Century*. Cambridge, MA: Harvard University Press.

PMPC (1952) *Resources for Freedom: A Report to the President. Volume I: Foundations for Growth and Security, The President's Materials Policy Commission*. Washington, DC: United States Government Printing Office.

Polimeni, J., Mayumi, K., Giampietro, M., and Alcott, B. (2008) *The Jevons Paradox and the Myth of Resource Efficiency Improvements*. Sterling, VA: Earthscan.

Posner, R. (1985) 'Wealth Maximization Revisited', *Notre Dame Journal of Law, Ethics and Public Policy*, 2:85–105.

Posner, R. (2009) *A Failure of Capitalism: The Crisis of '08 and the Descent into Depression*. Cambridge, MA: Harvard University Press.

Raffensperger, C., Weston, B., and Bollier, D. (2009) *Define and Develop a Law of the Ecological Commons for Present and Future Generations, in Vermont Law School*. Climate Legacy Initiative Recommendation No. 1.

Reeson, A. and Tisdell, J. (2008) 'Institutions, Motivations and Public Goods: An Experimental Test of Motivational Crowding', *Journal of Economic Behavior & Organization*, 68 (1):273–281. doi: http://dx.doi.org/10.1016/j.jebo.2008.04.002

Robertson, J. (2012) *Future Money: Breakdown or Breakthrough?* Totnes, Devon: Green Books Ltd.

Rockström, J., Steffen, W., Noone, K. Persson, A., Chapin, F., Lambin, E., Lenton, T., Scheffer, M., Folke, C., Schellnhuber, H., Nykvist, B., de Wit, C., Hughes, T., van der Leeuw, S., Rodhe, H., Sorlin, S., Snyder, P., Costanza, R., Svedin, U., Falkenmark, M., Karlberg, L., Corell, R., Fabry, V., Hansen, J., Walker, B. Liverman, D., Richardson, K., Crutzen, P., and Foley, J. (2009) 'A Safe Operating Space for Humanity', *Nature*, 461 (7263):472–475.

Seale Jr., J., Regmi, A., and Bernstein, J. (2003) *International Evidence on Food Consumption Patterns*. Electronic Report: Economic Research Service.

Simon, J. (1996) *The Ultimate Resource 2*. Princeton, NJ: Princeton University Press.

Simpson, D., Toman, M., and Ayres, R. (eds.) (2005) *Scarcity and Growth Revisited: Natural Resources and the Environment in the New Millennium*. Washington, DC: Resources for the Future.

Sober, E.T. and Wilson, D. (1998) *Unto Others: The Evolution and Psychology of Unselfish Behavior*. Cambridge, MA: Harvard University Press.

Soddy, F. (1935) *The Role of Money; What It Should Be, Contrasted with What It Has Become*. New York: Harcourt, Brace and Co.

Solow, R. (1972) 'Notes on "Doomsday Models"', *Proceedings of the National Academy of Sciences of the United States of America*, 69 (12):3832–3833. doi: 10.2307/62096

Solow, R. (1973) 'Is the End of the World at Hand?', *Challenge*, 16 (1):39–50. doi: 10.2307/40719094

Solow, R. (1974) 'The Economics of Resources or the Resources of Economics', *American Economics Review*, 2:1–14.

Steffen, W., Grinevald, J., Crutzen, P., and McNeill, J. (2011) 'The Anthropocene: Conceptual And Historical Perspectives', *Philosophical Transactions of the Royal Society A: Mathematical, Physical and Engineering Sciences*, 369 (1938):842–867.

Stigler, G. and. Becker, G. (1977) 'De Gustibus Non Est Disputandum', *American Economic Review*, 67 (2):76–90. doi: 10.2307/1807222

Tilman, D., Balzer, C., Hill, J. and Befort, B. (2011) 'Global Food Demand and the Sustainable Intensification of Agriculture', *Proceedings of the National Academy of Sciences*, 108 (50):20260–20264. doi: 10.1073/pnas.1116437108

USDA (2013) Wheat data. See: http://www.ers.usda.gov/data-products/wheat-data.aspx. Uulb42RdXyU

Vohs, K., Mead, N., and Goode. M. (2006) 'The Psychological Consequences of Money', *Science*, 314 (5802):1154–1156. doi: 10.1126/science.1132491

Vohs, K., Mead, N., and Goode, M. (2008) 'Merely Activating the Concept of Money Changes Personal and Interpersonal Behavior', *Current Directions in Psychological Science*, 17 (3):208–212.

Wackernagel, M., Schulz, N., Deumling, D. Linares, A., Jenkins, M., Kapos, V., Monfreda, C., Loh, J., Myers, N., Norgaard, R., and Randers, J. (2002) 'Tracking the Ecological Overshoot of the Human Economy', *Proceedings of the National Academy of Sciences*, 99 (14):9266–9271. doi: 10.1073/pnas.142033699

Weston, B. and Bollier. D. (2013) *Green Governance: Ecological Survival, Human Rights, and the Law of the Commons*. New York: Cambridge University Press.

Wilson, D. (2007) *Evolution for Everyone: How Darwin's Theory Can Change the Way We Think about Our Lives*. New York: Delacorte Press.

Wilson, D. and Wilson, E.O. (2007) 'Rethinking the Theoretical Foundations of Sociobiology', *The Quarterly Review of Biology*, 82 (4):327–348. doi: doi:10.1086/522809

Wilson, E.O. (2012) *The Social Conquest of Earth*. New York: Liveright Publishing Corporation.

Yissar, R. (2013) 'Neoclassical Economic Theory and the Question of Environmental Limits to Growth, 1950–1975', Master's Thesis, Porter School of Environmental Studies, Tel Aviv University.

SECTION 4
Ethics and a message from the future

14

SUSTAINABLE DEVELOPMENT VS. SUSTAINABLE BIOSPHERE

Holmes Rolston III

COLORADO STATE UNIVERSITY

In sustainability debates, there are two poles, complements yet opposites. Economy can be prioritized, with the environment contributory to economics at the center. This is sustainable development, an approach widely advocated by the United Nations. At the other pole, a sustainable biosphere model demands a baseline quality of environment. The economy must be worked out within such quality of life in a quality environment. This is advocated by the Ecological Society of America. People and their Earth have entwined destinies; that past truth continues in the present and will remain a pivotal concern in the new millennium. What we most ought to develop and sustain is a sense of respect for this wonderland planet.

The United Nations Conference on Environment and Development entwined its twin concerns into 'sustainable development'. No one wants unsustainable development, and sustainable development has for the two decades since Rio remained the favored model. The duty seems unanimous, plain, and urgent. Only so can this good life continue. Over 150 nations have endorsed sustainable development. The World Business Council on Sustainable Development includes 130 of the world's largest corporations.

Proponents argue that sustainable development is useful because it is a wide-angle lens. The specifics of development are unspecified, giving peoples and nations the freedom and responsibility of self-development. This is an orienting concept that is at once directed and encompassing, a coalition-level policy that sets aspirations, thresholds, and allows pluralist strategies for their accomplishment.

Critics reply that sustainable development is just as likely to prove an umbrella concept that requires little but superficial agreement, bringing a constant illusion of consensus, glossing over deeper problems with a rhetorically engaging word. Seen at more depth, there are two poles, complements yet opposites. Economy can be prioritized, the usual case, and anything can be done to the environment, so long as the continuing development of the economy is not jeopardized thereby. The environment is kept in orbit with economics at the center.

Develop! Develop! Develop! One ought to develop (since that increases social welfare and the abundant life), and the environment will constrain that development if and only if a degrading environment might undermine ongoing development. The underlying conviction is that the trajectory of the industrial, technological, commercial world is generally right – only the developers in their enthusiasm have hitherto failed to recognize environmental constraints.

If economics is the driver, we will seek maximum harvests, using pesticides and herbicides on land, a bioindustrial model, pushing for bigger and more efficient agriculture, as long as this is sustainable. This will push to the limits the environmental constraints of dangerous pesticide and herbicide levels on land and in water, surface and ground water, favoring monocultures, typically of annuals, inviting soil erosion and invasive species. The model is extractive, commodification of the land. Land and resources are 'natural capital'.

At the other pole, the environment is prioritized. A 'sustainable biosphere' model demands a baseline quality of environment. The economy must be worked out within such a policy for environmental quality objectives (clean air, water, stable agricultural soils, attractive residential landscapes, forests, mountains, rivers, rural lands, parks, wildlands, wildlife, renewable resources). Winds blow, rains fall, rivers flow, the sun shines, photosynthesis takes place, carbon recycles all over the landscape. These processes have to be sustained. The economy must be kept within an environmental orbit. One ought to conserve nature, the ground-matrix of life. Development is desired, but even more, society must learn to live within the carrying capacity of its landscapes. The model is land as community.

Sustainable. Sustainable, but sustainable what? 'Sustainable' is an economic but also an environmental term. The Ecological Society of America advocates research and policy that will result in a sustainable biosphere. 'Achieving a sustainable biosphere is the single most important task facing humankind today' (Risser *et al.* 1991). The fundamental flaw in 'sustainable development' is that it sees the Earth as resource, as commodity only. The underlying conviction in the sustainable biosphere model is that the current trajectory of the industrial, technological, commercial world is generally wrong, because it will inevitably overshoot. The environment is not some undesirable, unavoidable set of constraints. Rather, nature is the matrix of multiple values; many, even most of them, are not counted in economic transactions. In a more inclusive accounting of what we wish to sustain, nature provides numerous other values (aesthetic experiences, biodiversity, sense of place and perspective), and these are getting left out. The *Millennium Ecosystem Assessment* explores this in great detail. Though it is an anthropocentric document, it does insist that we depend heavily on ecosystem services.

A central problem with contemporary global development is that the rich grow richer and the poor poorer. Many fear that this is neither ethical nor sustainable. The rich and powerful are always ready to exploit both nature and people. This forces the poor as well as the rich to over-exploit nature, and brings escalating environmental degradation, more tragedy of the commons, with instability and collapse. Such issues come under another inclusive term, 'environmental justice'.

For thousands of years of human history, we have been pushing back limits. Especially in the West, we have lived with a deep-seated belief that life will get better, that one should hope for abundance, and work toward obtaining it. Develop! Develop! Develop! Economists call such behavior 'rational'; humans will maximize their capacity to exploit their resources. Moral persons will also maximize human satisfactions, at least those that support the good life, which does not just include food, clothing, and shelter, but an abundance, more and more goods and services that people want. Such growth is always desirable. We have built development into our concept of human rights: a right to self-development, to self-realization. Such an egalitarian ethic scales everybody up and drives an unsustainable world. When everybody seeks their own good, there is escalating consumption. But equally, if one seeks justice and charity, when everybody seeks everybody else's good, there is, again, escalating consumption. But this continually pushes the system toward its limits.

Many will say, if you wish to know what policy to sustain, you should ask an ecologist. Ecology is strikingly like medical science. Both are therapeutic sciences. Ecologists are responsible for environmental health, which is really another form of public health. Health is not just skin-in; it is skin-out too. One cannot be healthy in a sick environment. Health is something that is easy to advocate and the criteria seem to be scientific. That helps move us toward sustainable development.

But ecologists have no special competence in evaluating whether to give priority to economic development or to conserving nature beyond what ecology is required for human development. A people on a landscape will have to make value judgments about how much original nature they have, or want, or wish to restore, and how much culturally modified nature they want, and whether it should be culturally modified this way or that. Ecologists may be able to tell us what our options are, what will work and what will not, what is the minimum baseline health of landscapes. But there is nothing in ecology per se that gives ecologists any authority or skills at making these further social decisions, whether to feed more people or save the tigers. Science does not enable us to choose between diverse options, all of which are scientifically possible.

I can equally substitute the word 'economics' for 'science'. Economists have no special competence in evaluating what rebuilding of nature a culture desires, or how far the integrity of wild nature should be sacrificed to achieve this. Economists, like the ecologists, may be able to tell us what our options are, what will work and what will not. But there is nothing in economics per se that gives economists any authority or skills at making these further social decisions. What the sciences may teach us is how to get more x out of y, but they do not teach whether we ought to. After four centuries during which science and economics have progressively illuminated us about how we can transform nature into the goods we want, the value questions raised in economics, too, are as sharp and as painful as ever.

Humans are not well equipped to deal with the sorts of global level problems we now face. The classical institutions – family, village, tribe, nation, agriculture, industry, law, medicine, even school and church – have shorter horizons. We are genetically driven to care for children, grandchildren. Far-off descendants and distant races do not have much biological hold on us. Across the era of human evolution, little in our behavior affected those remote from us in time or in space, and natural selection shaped only our conduct toward those closer. Further, we have also made such conduct moral. Care for your children; help your neighbors. So we have a biological legacy coupled with a moral legacy that endorses continuing development on our local and national landscapes. Global threats require us to act in massive concert of which we are incapable. If so, humans may bear within themselves the seeds of their own destruction. More bluntly, more scientifically put: our genes, once enabling our adaptive fit, will in the next millennium prove mal-adaptive and destroy us.

Is there any hope? There are some good signs. Humans can sometimes get larger frames of reference. The European Union has transcended national interests with surprising consensus about environmental issues. Kofi Annan, Secretary General of the United Nations, praised the Montreal Protocol, with its five revisions, widely adopted (191 nations) and implemented as the most successful international agreement yet. All the developed nations, except the United States and Australia, have signed the Kyoto Protocol. The Convention on International Trade in Endangered Species of Wild Fauna and Flora (CITES) has been signed by 112 nations. There are over 150 international agreements (conventions, treaties, protocols, etc.), registered with the United Nations, that deal directly with environmental problems (United Nations Environment Programme 1997; Rummel-Bulska and Osafo 1991). So there is some evidence that we can make these larger collective visions work.

One of the concerns of the Millennium Ecosystem is that we do not have any theoretical basis to alert us to impending dangers, especially as it affects the poor. There are many thresholds, trigger points, uncertainties. If you are always pushing a system toward its limits, and you do not know the danger zones, then you are likely to crash. We need to think of ourselves more globally.

People and their Earth have entwined destinies; that past truth continues in the present, and will remain a pivotal concern in the new millennium. Humans can move past thinking of themselves as local citizens, even as national citizens, and reach this more inclusive sense of worldwide entanglements. To get there from here, start by thinking how the air does move around the globe, that the climate is a set of complex interconnections. That will lead us to connecting sustainable development with a sustainable biosphere. We are moving in the direction of thinking of ourselves as residents on Earth, of the biosphere as a living community of life.

Sustainable development is impossible without a sustainable biosphere. The fundamental flaw in sustainable development, we earlier said, was in seeing Earth as resource only. Now we further see that first priority flaw as moral. Ecologists, economists – and ethicists and theologians – alike need to learn this: There is something morally naïve about living in a reference frame where one species takes itself as absolute and values everything else as a resource to be developed, even if we phrase it that we are taking ourselves as primary and everything else as secondary. The vision we need even beyond a sustainable biosphere is respect for life, even reverence for life.

Develop! Develop! Maximize development! Is that the future of life on Earth? Maybe what you want to develop and sustain is a sense of respect for this wonderland planet.

(The editors would like to thank Jack Lee and Ria University Press for permission to publish this paper, originally from Lee, J. (ed.) (2010) *Sustainability and Quality of Life*, Palo Alto CA: Ria University Press, ISBN: 978–0-97434724–9).

References

Risser, P. G., Lubchenco, J., and Levin, S. (1991) 'Biological Research Priorities – A Sustainable Biosphere', *BioScience*, vol 47, pp. 625–627.

Rummel-Bulska, I. and Osafo, S. (eds.) (1991) *Selected Multilateral Treaties in the Field of the Environment, II*, Cambridge: Grotius Publications.

United Nations Environment Programme (1997) *Register of International Treaties and Other Agreements in the Field of the Environment*, Nairobi: United Nations Environment Programme.

15

A MESSAGE FROM THE FUTURE ABOUT THE STEADY STATE ECONOMY

Geoff Mosley

CASSE AUSTRALIA

Introduction

I want you to imagine that I am a time traveller coming back from the future to tell you about our steady state economy. Hopefully this will help you with your goal setting and give you some idea about what will need to be transformed and what we disposed of. When I have explained how we live, I think you will conclude that every major facet of our lives is very different from yours. The biggest difference though is that ours has a good chance of survival. That is because we have a way of life that is, in every way, in close harmony with the environment. It is important, I believe, to also let you know that what I am going to describe extends across the whole globe.

Above all, we live within the Earth's limits. This means, first, that we have fitted ourselves into the environment in a manner that utilises natural processes providing food, water and energy in a non-disruptive way. Second, we also live in harmony with each other in a fully cooperative way. This is essential because there is none of the competition, greed and dominance of some over others and constant resort to warfare that is a major cause of environmental depletion and social disharmony in your way of life. I will describe the main features of our 'steady state' way of life: our values, our food, water, energy and transport systems, and our social organisation including our settlement patterns and governance arrangements.

The steady state economy of the late twenty-third century

Values – a new ethic

Our main aims are to live contentedly, sustainably and cooperatively. We seek and enjoy a good life rather than material accumulation and privilege. We live by an 'eco-centric' worldview and see ourselves as belonging to the Earth, rather than the

Earth belonging to us and do not see ourselves as superior to other living things. Similarly, our attitude of non-superiority applies to our view of other human beings. In our classless society, all people are regarded as equal and treated equally throughout their lives and this has brought obvious benefits in terms of health, education, satisfying work, knowledge, lifestyle skills and involvement in governance. The community, not individuals, owns and regulates the land and its resources, and we feel bonded to our family, our community and our neighbourhood. Private ownership of land and resources has been fully replaced by cooperative ownership and organisation at the local community level. Education includes learning about the world and its history, but we gain most satisfaction from learning about the places where we live and passing that knowledge on to others.

Supply of food, energy and water

The underlying principles concerning our access to food, energy, water, housing and other materials are those of *sustainability and self-sufficiency*. Every community is responsible (to the maximum extent possible) for supplying themselves with the basic necessities of food, energy and water and for providing health and education services from the places where they live. This means of course that, being in direct contact with their environments, people have a very close understanding of their character and potential and how to use them sustainably and also, as a result of that, have a great respect for them. The kinship between people and their environment has been re-established. The people who have the most to lose from resource depletion are now in charge. Water is drawn from rooftops and other sources where people live. Fruit and vegetables are major crops, and due to (as a result of reliance on local production) organic management (including permaculture type practices) and use of waste from humans and animals, there is no industrial-scale agriculture and no use of industrial fertilisers and pesticides. We gain satisfaction from supplying most of our own food needs. Energy supply is from local renewable sources. Being decentralised, we do not have the vast energy grids of your day. House building and repair is carried out by those who live in them, and the days of paying off debts to banks for loans are long gone. Goods are designed to have a long life and be capable of being recycled. There has been major recycling of materials left over from the huge abandoned cities of the past. Needless to say, we did not arrive fully at our steady state destination until we had repaired the serious environmental damage of the past and adjusted our populations and their consumption to sustainable levels.

Trade

With communities being largely self-reliant there is little need for trade in commodities. Where it does occur it is largely between adjacent regions of the same country and on an exchange basis. Exploitation of resources and labour by means of the market, international trade and competition are all things of the past.

Populations, settlement patterns and quality of life

Population levels and settlement patterns are largely determined by the character and carrying capacity of the different localities in which people live. Hence most settlements are small in scale. The alienation of people from the environment that was created by living in large cities is a thing of the past. People work where they live. We have a settlement hub in each region for the purposes of technology development, manufacturing, governance, health, education and the arts. In these larger (but not very large) towns we have cooperatively-run community gardens. In our socially inclusive communities all are treated equally. There are no superiority distinctions made with regard to the nature of the work people do and there is a considerable amount of job sharing. Cooperation in performing tasks and in creative activities is normal but there are no private companies for this purpose. Overall, people live more simply than they did in the economic growth-driven societies of the past. With all basic needs met, people and cooperation have replaced competition as a major goal; people have richer and more creative lives. In addition, because we no longer have an economy based on the goals of endless economic resource and population growth, and because we do not have economic and social inequality, the world's overall population and consumption of resources is massively reduced compared with what it once was (roughly a quarter of 2000 AD levels). The global population of 1.5 billion is the sustainable level suggested by Daily *et al.* (1994) – they got it right. It took a long time for this adjustment to be made.

Trade and transport

With most communities and regions being self-reliant in terms of the supply of the basic necessities, there are no major longer-distance supply chains for the transport of commodities. People work in their local area and public transport along with cycling and walking are the main forms of transport and the connections between localities and regional hubs are largely by these means. Air and sea travel is by means of publicly owned planes and ships. There is a considerable amount of human travel both within and between countries for a number of purposes including recreation, education, health, governance and creativity. People travel to learn and take pleasure from the differences between places, the wonders of the natural world and the ways in which different communities relate sustainably and creatively to their environments. Internships in different regions and countries are common, and usually on an exchange basis.

Governance and security

Our governance is based on the fundamental principles of self-government and direct participatory democracy. Every person has a voice and a say in the planning and management that concern him or her. At the local community level, people assemble and vote on measures and issues and choose delegates for regional assemblies. The same approach of voting and choosing delegates is used for representation at the national and international assemblies. Any national issue is put to a vote of the whole national population after discussion in the various assemblies. The scope of the assemblies at the various geographic levels has been determined so that they only deal with relevant matters. For instance, at the international level the matters discussed relate to global-scale environmental changes and threats and include the management of the global commons. The universal acceptance of the sustainable use of resources on a self-sufficiency basis eliminated the resource struggles between communities and nations, including the use of the military to secure access to resources and territories.

The economy

Private ownership of land and resources has been replaced by community ownership and the communities (through their individual and collective efforts) are responsible for the supply of all goods and services. People do not aspire to accumulate wealth and to live in better conditions than their fellows. In our steady state economy, all people are guaranteed the same standard of living. As a result, when we made these changes there was no need to continue the past practices of allowing private individuals or groups to either make investments for profit (creating additional costs) or take out loans and create debts. Money and the market in our world are purely for their original purpose of facilitating transactions, and we have no private banks making money out of the interest on loans.

The transformation

How it happened

Although the end result was good, I am sorry to have to tell you that the transformation to the universal steady state economy I have described was far from easy and took a long time to achieve. I am sure this will not surprise you because you will surely be well aware of the likely consequences if you continue for very much longer doing things the way you currently do. The problem is that certain things are ingrained in your economy and society. This includes an absolute dedication to economic and population growth, and a reliance on military force (including the maintenance of nuclear weapons arsenals) as a major method of resolving disputes between nations and groups over territory and resources. The basic fault in your system is that it is dependent upon perpetual growth. Even in your day if you asked people, 'Do you believe that on a finite planet you can continue to grow physically forever?' they said, 'No!', yet your neoclassical economy was based on this impossibility. To get to our society in the future we had to confront this absurdity and move past it.

Looking back on your time from the position of a totally different mindset, it is obvious that your commitment to economic and population growth was equivalent to a religion, even though it was becoming increasingly obvious that this was mainly for the benefit of the most powerful. The majority of the population was in effect powerless, and most environmental groups were timid in their approach, focusing on protests and on individual damage limitation (mitigation) and adaptation measures rather than major system change. Only a dramatic rapid shift in both economic and political systems could have avoided this situation and the dominance of the endless growth philosophy (combined with the control of the economy and society by these vested interests) made that a bridge too far. The response of your society to this challenge, reactive rather than proactive, dealing with symptoms rather than the cause, was completely inadequate in relation to both the nature and the scale of the problem.

Things had to change but they did not, and the outcome of these convergences of growing populations, increasing demand for resources and growing reliance on warfare as a control mechanism was dire. There were also the persistent distractions of inadequate stand-alone solutions such as improvements in technology based on techno-centrism, the idea that technology could solve everything. Hence, for the remainder of the twenty-first century, on a hitherto unknown scale, the globe was ravaged by further depletion of resources, civil unrest (including mass migration of refugees fleeing social and economic disruption) and escalating warfare. Chomsky and Polk (2013) had foreseen the likelihood of this catastrophic situation, drawing attention to the main problems of human survival. Their call for action went unheeded. Kunstler (2005) also foresaw this period of collapse, lasting for several hundred years, as the outcome of a combination of resource scarcity, poor planning, nuclear war and environmental degradation. For his prescient history of the period 1914–1991, Eric Hobsbawm (1994) chose the title *Age of Extremes* and closed his book on a sombre but realistic note, saying, 'Our world risks both explosion and implosion. It must change … and the price of failure, that is to say, the alternative to a changed society, is darkness'.

Unfortunately, the message failed to get through and it was only after a century of extremes, literally picking up the pieces, that some parts of society in the early twenty-second century began to see the appeal of the steady state economy as the obvious alternative basis for an entirely new way of life and developed strategies to move to it. The underlying cause, your certain-to-fail economy, was finally recognised. Fortunately, the efforts of those visionary enough to describe the faults and develop a completely different approach (e.g. Daly, 1991, 1996, 2008) had not been forgotten and indeed some of you had battled on all through the long period of the great disruption, never giving up. Not forgotten either was the example of the tremendous achievements of the national park systems established across the Earth for the common good.

There was no quick way of dealing with the conditions left behind by these catastrophic events and there were several alternatives. Kunstler (2008) had also presented a convincing imaginary picture of the efforts different communities were using to try to survive after resources had run out and the economic growth-oriented way of life had collapsed, such as self-sufficiency/localism and recycling of materials. Amongst the alternatives was the anarcho-syndicalism approach that had briefly come to life during the Spanish Civil War and had been described by Orwell (1938).

There was no sudden switch, and different parts of the global society took different amounts of time to convert to the steady state economy alternative, assisted of course by agreement amongst nations that this was the most environmentally friendly way, and it took the whole of the twenty-second century for the steady state way to become the universally adopted way. That of course was by no means the end of the steady state evolution because for many decades a high priority had to be given to environmental rehabilitation and to population stabilisation, and this last objective required matching numbers to the long-term carrying capacity of each geographic unit. As a result it was another hundred years before these legacy problems were overcome, making a total of nearly three hundred years between your time and the steady state economy I have described.

Was it remarkable that individuals and communities were able to regain those skills of living that had been lost as most people had become dependent on the large-scale production of goods from factories and industrial agriculture often produced at a great distance from where they were consumed? Some thought so, but others referred back to the sudden changes in society that had been necessary when past wars had put a stop to these long-distance supply lines. Also, it was soon discovered that those who had managed to survive by growing their own food and by engaging in community activities such as food growing and building walking and cycling trails were able to pass on their knowledge to others. The development of travel for the purpose of learning more about the world and the different ways people had developed their own versions of the steady state economy (related to the particular circumstances of their lands) was another important facilitator.

Looking back: what we learned from the past

When our historians looked back at how the steady state economy evolved in your time they found several works that were prescient in terms of describing the flawed situation of seeking endless economic growth in a finite world and, most importantly, others that were beginning to map out the way to the major alternative that became our steady state economy.

With regard to recognition of the looming problem of overpopulation, the most important contribution was made by Paul Ehrlich in *The Population Bomb* (1968). Daily *et al.* (1994) suggested an optimum population size for the Earth of 1.5–2 billion. The most influential publication dealing with the adverse impacts humans were having on the physical environments of Earth was *The Limits to Growth* (Meadows *et al.* 1972), a report for the Club of Rome. It was updated by Meadows *et al.* (2004) and by Randers (2012). Wackernagel and Rees (1996) had developed a more precise measure of the human impact in their book *Our Ecological Footprint*.

An important part of the move to a steady state economy was the realisation that capitalism could have no part in it. In fact, nothing illustrates so well the difference between our and your systems as our complete rejection of capitalism. Capitalism is defined in the Shorter Oxford English Dictionary (1984) as 'the condition of possessing capital or using it for production; a system of society based on this, dominance of private capitalists'. The free market and Neoliberalism were integral facilitators of the economic growth-driven system of your time. It depended on economic growth, competition and the making of profit for its very existence. As Speth (2008) put it, the capitalist economy to the degree that it is successful is '*inherently*' an exponential growth economy'. Capitalism was closely associated with both globalisation and the dominance of the market in government decision-making. In the capitalist market a few people exercised enormous power, and it helped to create and maintain social inequality. Since it depended for its very existence on never-ending economic growth, it could not possibly have a place in a steady state economy.

Capitalism was a beneficiary of the globalisation of trade involving the foreign ownership and development of resources such as fossil fuels in distant places, destroying the nexus between people and their lands. The capitalist owners of land and resources had little or no feeling of responsibility for the long-term future of the lands and inhabitants of the places they were exploiting. Their overriding objective was maximisation of production for profit. Settlement patterns were strongly influenced by market forces. Capitalism placed short-term money values on things of intrinsic value, resulting for instance in the deforestation of water catchments and the destruction of the habitat of indigenous wildlife to supply distant markets. Capitalism was in effect economic colonialism and seriously obstructed efforts to move to the sustainable use of land and resources and to self-sufficiency by interfering with local and national control of resources. Short-term profits were viewed as more important than the future. We decided that it was far better for control of the land and its resources to be exercised by the people who live there and who have a better knowledge of it and have a greater stake in its future. Also, just as the economic and social class system was closely interlinked with capitalism, it was realised that full equality was an essential necessity for our steady state economy.

The recognition that capitalism contained an intrinsic flaw and that it had adverse effects on all aspects of human and other life on Earth developed traction in the nineteenth century and played a major role in the development of alternatives. In 1933, during the middle of the Great Depression, economist John Maynard Keynes pinpointed the defects of the free global market and recommended its replacement with *national self-sufficiency*. This of course was to become a fundamental part of the move to a steady state economy. In the early twenty-first century, the analysis of capitalism's particular economic and social defects continued, an example of many critics being Naomi Klein (2014), who focused on its link with climate change, and Thomas Picketty (2014), who wrote about capitalism's contribution to inequality. In 2014 Oxfam International summarised the extreme nature of this inequality with the information 'that almost half the world's wealth is now owned by just one per cent of the population' (Oxfam 2014).

Historical roots of the steady state economy

The pioneer of what became the steady state economy concept was John Stuart Mill, who in his 1848 book *Principles of Political Economy* described an alternative 'stationary state of population and capital'. Rachel Carson's book *Silent Spring* (1962), although concerned specifically with the adverse impact of pesticide use, had the effect of attracting wider public interest in environmental matters. More recently Nicholas Georgescu-Roegen (1971) explained the critical role of entropy. Then there was economist Herman Daly, a winner of the 2014 Blue Planet Prize, who was described in the nomination as 'the preeminent exponent of the steady state economy the main alternative to the prevailing economic growth paradigm'. It was Daly (e.g. Daly 1991, 1996 and 2008) who, from the late 1960s, further developed Mill's insightful idea towards the type of economy that prevails in our lives today – in your future. It was also his efforts that inspired the formation by Brian Czech in 2004 of the Center for the Advancement of the Steady State Economy (CASSE). CASSE was the main international advocate of the switch to a steady state economy, and of how the change to this very different economy could be made. Amongst the many publications about the need for a major system change and the necessary transformation measures were books by Czech (*Supply Shock* (2013)), and Dietz and O'Neill (*Enough is Enough*) 2013)). Now, at last, the emphasis was not only on what was wrong with society but on what was a *feasible alternative*.

In parallel movements, several organisations worked for simpler ways and sustainability focusing their efforts on promoting transformative measures such as the 'Deep Ecology Movement', 'Transition Towns' and 'Voluntary Simplicity', one of the leading proponents in Australia being Ted Trainer (2010). Haydn Washington (2015) helped to identify the pitfalls and clear away the mystification surrounding the sustainability concept.

Largely missing from the discussion in the twentieth and early twenty-first centuries were attempts to visualise a conservation-based sustainable economy in operation. You were far more likely to be aware of dystopias such as the totalitarian world of Orwell's *Nineteen Eighty-Four* (1948) and the population-controlled society of Huxley's *Brave New World* (1932), both of which had relevance to the discussion of alternative futures. An exception to this vacancy was Alexander's *Entropia* (2013), which provided an imaginary but useful account of a flourishing simple way of life on a small Pacific island. Washington (2014) devoted a large part of *Addicted to Growth* to what it would be like to live in a steady state economy. Assadourian (2013) produced a vision of what life in a sustainable USA could look like in 2100 if we started to make major shifts in our economic, political and cultural systems right away. However, your society failed to do that.

A major problem was the distraction caused by partial solutions such as the challenges represented by 'decoupling' measures as discussed by a Panel of the United Nations Environment Programme (UNEP 2011a) and in the 'green economy' proposed by UNEP (2011b). Rather than wishful thinking about absolute decoupling, what was most needed was *a major paradigm shift*. The plain truth is that partial solutions are only of value if they are related to and part of a comprehensive move to an overall sustainable system. Decoupling was essentially a 'damage limitation approach' which unfortunately had the effect of assisting those who wanted to continue with ever increasing economic and population growth – acting as a licence to keep on growing. The irony of this was that Jevons (1865) had exposed the contributions of efficiency measures to continuing growth in consumption and production in 1865 to such an extent that the effect became known as the 'The Jevons Paradox'. Other examples of partial solutions included more intensive agriculture, more intensive living in high-rise buildings, a move to nuclear energy and the use of genetic engineering. It was only in the aftermath of the global environmental disaster that the need for the fundamental and comprehensive approach of the steady state economy was not only recognised but also acted on.

Looking back, the truly amazing aspect of the discussion of the alternative of a steady state economy in your time was that it was often described by people living in a world ravaged by resource exploitation, overpopulation, gross levels of inequality and more or less continuous warfare as being either 'utopian', an 'extreme solution' or 'too difficult to achieve'. These views are as clear an indication of any of the major obstacles your society has to overcome. They show the need of those recommending the steady state solution to explain *how* it can be achieved over time by a number of transformative steps including its elevation to a major alternative in political discourse and decision-making.

Conclusion

If we had not made this change to a steady state economy, the prospects for the long-term survival of humanity would have been bleak. In our time we have adapted our way of life to the biophysical limits of the Earth and its dynamic equilibrium, and achieved full equality for all. In doing so, we have an altogether more sustainable and more satisfying way of life.

(This chapter represents the views of the author, whereas CASSE takes no position regarding models of political economy. CASSE's focus is on the macroeconomic policy goal, recognizing that various cultures and countries are suited to achieve that goal via alternative systems of political economy.)

References

Alexander, S. (2013) *Entropia: Life Beyond Industrial Civilisation*. Melbourne: Simplicity Institute.
Assadourian, E. (2013) 'Choose Your Future: A Vision of a Sustainable America in 2100'. *E-Magazine,* March–April 2013: 26–30. See: http://erikassadourian.com/wp-content/uploads/2013/08/America-in-2100-E-Magazine-2013.pdf
Carson, R. (1962) *Silent Spring*. Boston: Houghton Mifflin.

Chomsky, N. and Polk, L. (2013) *Nuclear War and Environmental Catastrophe*. New York: Seven Stories Press.

Czech, B. (2013) *Supply Shock. Economic Growth at the Crossroads and the Steady State Solution*. Gabriola Island, British Colombia: New Society Publishers.

Daily, G. C., Ehrlich, A. H., and Ehrlich, P. R. (1994) 'Optimum Human Population Size', *Population and Environment: A Journal of Interdisciplinary Studies*, 15(6): 469–475.

Daly, H. E. (1991) *Steady-State Economics* (2nd edition). Washington, DC: Island Press.

Daly, H. E. (1996) *Beyond Growth: The Economics of Sustainable Development*. Boston: Beacon Press.

Daly, H. E. (2008) 'A Steady-State Economy: A Failed Growth Economy and a Steady-State Economy Are Not the Same Thing; They Are the Very Different Alternatives We Face', Think Piece for the Sustainable Development Commission, UK, 24 April 2008. See: http://steadystaterevolution.org/files/pdf/Daly_UK_Paper.pdf

Dietz, R. and O'Neill, D. (2013) *Enough Is Enough. Building a Sustainable Economy in a World of Finite Resources*. New York: Berrett-Koeler Publishers.

Ehrlich, P. R. (1968) *The Population Bomb*. New York: Ballantine Books.

Georgescu-Roegen, N. (1971) *The Entropy Law and the Economic Process*. Cambridge, MA: Harvard University Press.

Hobsbawm, E. (1994) *Age of Extremes: The Short Twentieth Century 1914–1991*. London: Michel Joseph.

Huxley, A. (1932) *Brave New World*. London: Chatto and Windus.

Jevons, W. S. (1865) *The Coal Question: An Inquiry Concerning the Progress of the Nation and the Probable Exhaustion of Our Coal Mines*. London: MacMillan and Co.

Keynes, J. M. (1933) 'National Self-Sufficiency', *Yale Review*, 22(4): 755–769.

Klein, N. (2014) *This Changes Everything: Capitalism vs. the Climate*. New York: Simon and Schuster.

Kunstler, J. H. (2005) *The Long Emergency: Surviving the Converging Catastrophes of the Twenty-First Century*. New York: Grove/Atlantic.

Kunstler, J. H. (2008) *World Made by Hand*. New York: Grove.

Little, W., Fowler, H., and Coulson, J. (1984) The Shorter Oxford English Dictionary on Historical Principles. Revised and edited by C. T. Onions, Third Edition, Volume 1 A-Markworthy. Oxford: Clarendon Press.

Meadows, D. H., Meadows, D., Randers, J., and Behrens, W. (1972) *The Limits to Growth*. New York: Universe.

Meadows, D. H., Meadows D., and Randers, J. (2004) *The Limits to Growth: The 30-Year Update*. White River Junction, VT: Chelsea Green Publishing.

Mill, J. S. (1848) *Principles of Political Economy with Some of their Applications to Social Philosophy*. London: J. W. Parker.

Orwell, G. (1938) *Homage to Catalonia*. London: Secker and Warburg.

Orwell, G. (1948) *Nineteen Eighty-Four*. London: Secker and Warburg.

Oxfam International (2014) *Oxfam Briefing Paper 178 – Working for the Few: Political Capture and Economic Inequality*. Oxford: Oxfam.

Picketty, T. (2014) *Capital in the Twenty-First Century*. Cambridge, MA: Harvard University Press.

Randers, J. (2012) *2050: A Global Forecast for the Next 40 Years*. White River Junction, VT: Chelsea Green Publishing.

Speth, J. G. (2008) *The Bridge at the End of the World: Capitalism, the Environment and Crossing from Crisis to Sustainability*. New Haven and London: Yale University Press.

Trainer, T. (2010) *The Transition to a Sustainable and Just World*. Canterbury, NSW: Envirobook.

UNEP (United Nations Environment Programme) (2011a) *Decoupling Natural Resource Use and Environmental Impacts from Economic Growth. A Report of the Working Group on Decoupling to the International Resource Panel*. Nairobi: United Nations Environment Programme.

UNEP (2011b) *Towards a Green Economy: Pathways to Sustainable Development and Poverty Eradication*. Nairobi: United Nations Environment Programme.

Wackernagel, M. and Rees, W. (1996) *Our Ecological Footprint: Reducing Human Impact on the Earth*. Gabriola Island, British Colombia: New Society Publishers.

Washington, H. (2014) *Addicted to Growth*. Sydney: CASSE NSW. See: https://steadystatensw.wordpress.com/2014/10/14/addicted-to-growth-booklet/

Washington, H. (2015) *Demystifying Sustainability: Towards Real Solutions*. London: Routledge.

SECTION 5
Policy for change

16

DEGROWTH AS A TRANSITION STRATEGY

Robert Perey

UNIVERSITY OF TECHNOLOGY SYDNEY

Since the beginning of the industrial revolution environmentalists have drawn attention to the coming ecological crisis as one of the significant consequences of this transformational societal change. The emerging field of 'degrowth' is a new movement addressing the issues of this ecological crisis and its potential disruptive impact for organisational and societal sustainability. Degrowth strongly criticises the logics that underpin today's economic systems and continues a long trend of drawing societal attention to the ecological limits of growth that constrain humanity's cultural practices and activities.

In recent times limits to growth of our current economic activities have been recognised as a significant barrier to the progress of capitalism as we understand this system today (see Farley in this volume). Awareness of the limits of natural systems underpinning our economy was prompted by the Club of Rome research publication *Limits to Growth* (Meadows *et al.* 1972), which despite early criticism of its modelling has proved to be an accurate predictor of the problems we face today (Turner 2008).

The degrowth project

Degrowth signifies, first and foremost, a *critique of growth*. It calls for the abolishment of economic growth as a social objective. Beyond that, degrowth signifies a desired direction, one in which societies will use fewer natural resources and will organise and live differently than today (Latouche 2009; D'Alisa *et al.* 2015). 'Sharing', 'simplicity', 'conviviality', 'care' and the 'commons' are primary significations of what this society might look like (Kallis *et al.* 2015, p. 3).

Degrowth – understood as a voluntary transition towards a contraction-based economy in line with ecological limitations and greater social equity – is a call for a radical break from traditional growth-based models, and has already made its mark on ecological economics and political theory. As Foster (2011, p. 5) notes,

> As valuable as the degrowth concept is in an ecological sense, it can only take on genuine meaning as part of a critique of capital accumulation and part of the transition to a sustainable, egalitarian, communal order; one in which the associated producers govern the metabolic relation between nature and society in the interest of successive generations and the earth itself.

Degrowth is a socio-political project (Latouche 2009) that has a universal aim of creating societies that cooperatively exist within the limits that the ecological systems, on which we depend, can support. Whilst the term is recent, the crystallisation of this idea goes back some fifty years to the claim put forward by Georgescu-Roegen (1971) that the economic system that dominates the modern world is unsustainable because its logic of perpetual linear growth is a physical impossibility. Georgescu-Roegen argued that all economic systems had to account for the natural environment as a self-organising system that did not have the capacity to provide endless raw materials and resources for human consumption, nor have the capacity to absorb and integrate humanity's endless growth of waste. An implication of his reasoning for societies, if they failed to rectify their economic systems' relationships with the natural environment, is that they would falter and possibly collapse. This new approach led to Georgescu-Roegen developing a new framework/theory of bioeconomics (Gowdy and Mesner 1998) that formed the foundation for the new field of ecological economics, from which emerged Daly's advocacy of the steady state economy (1991, 1996) and degrowth (Latouche 2009).

Degrowth is a term that is deliberately designed to disrupt entrained patterns of socio-economic thinking, it is a 'missile concept' (Fournier 2008) to stimulate exploration of alternatives to economic growth. An explicit aim of the degrowth movement is to recreate societies that are radically different to current modern understandings of how societies should be structured and function (Latouche 2009). In doing this, Latouche argues that degrowth goes beyond modernity and challenges the spirit of capitalism. The concept of degrowth does not openly advocate anti-capitalism; it does, however, raise questions about the deficiencies of capitalism and whether new forms of capitalism (see for example Andreucci and McDonough 2015) can function within the ecological limits of the One Earth boundary.

One of the interpretations circulating about the degrowth project is that it is aimed principally at the developed world, because the disparities between developed and developing worlds mean the latter is allowed some modest growth to improve their lot. This particular interpretation is one that mirrors the logic of sustainable development and is used to justify the growth of the developing world before this group engages with any form of economic or socio-political constraint (Redclift 1987). Proponents of degrowth argue that this logic of permitting the developing world to continue to grow to reach a level of material wealth that corresponds to that of current developed economies is a false logic, one that remains trapped in the growth paradigm. For the degrowth project, '[t]he word "development" is toxic. No matter which adjective we use to dress it up' (Latouche 2009, p.10), and its current widespread usage remains attached to the defence of the development and growth of the consumer society.

Degrowth is an important discourse that continues to gain international stature. Over the last half-decade there have been four international degrowth conferences: Paris 2008, Barcelona 2010, Venice 2012 and Leipzig 2014. The movement also spawned regional gatherings such as the Degrowth in the Americas conference held in Montreal in May 2012. These conferences promote a strong interaction amongst academics, activists and practitioners to explore solutions to current ecological and economic structural societal problems, and to rethink what a truly prosperous world beyond growth would be.

In the next section I introduce recent non-academic assessments of the socio-economic system that draw attention to the structural problems that consumer capitalism poses for our economy. A conclusion advocated by all of these authors is the need to create and implement post-consumer-capitalist economic systems.

Crises in capitalism

The aftermath of the financial crisis of 2008/2009, the recent Eurozone crisis, faltering outlooks of economic growth and debt levels of the public and private sectors (unmatched since 1929) cast doubts on the success story of the capitalist system that has come to dominate most of the world's economic policies and activities. At the same time, the ecological crisis of overuse of natural resources, climate change, desertification, loss of biodiversity, peak oil and an ever-increasing ecological footprint appears to be tightly connected with the evolution of consumer capitalism, particularly its 'dark side' (for example Banerjee's (2008) theory of necrocapitalism), and the way it dominates present-day business logic.

Consumer capitalism, the strategy to maintain and expand the productivity of the industrial system immediately after the Second World War, is the economic interpretation/understanding that dominates our societies today. The principles of consumer capitalism were calculated and simple: increase the sales of goods by limiting their lifespan. The enactment of this logic would continue to drive the engine of growth, and a philosophy of happiness and contentment was built around this model. Designers took pride in creating obsolescence into the things they made. In addition to material obsolescence, societies have now also manufactured 'social obsolescence' through the vicissitudes of fad and fashion (Whiteley 1987).

Whilst consumer capitalism continues to dominate societal behaviour, there are an increasing number of people questioning whether this system can continue, albeit with incremental changes, or whether it needs to be disbanded. In parallel to the ecological crisis there are a succession of economic crises that many people are arguing are indicative of impending systems failure. For example, Gilding (2011), *The Great Disruption*; Naomi Klein (2013) in 'How Science is Telling us all to

Revolt'; Jeremy Leggett (2013) in 'An Oil Crash is on its Way and We Should be Ready'; and Satyajit Das (2015) in *A Banquet of Consequences* all argue a need for change to fundamental social-economic-political systems due to the ecological crisis that is now upon us.

The important thread running through these texts is 'risk blindness' (Leggett 2013) or a failure of sense-making. Leggett talks of risk blindness as a human psychological flaw, and Klein draws on the observations of scientists to the increasing level of not recognising the risks in climate collapse (for example) that 'business as usual' generates. Leggett argues that the risk of being affected by a 'carbon bubble' is a certainty and has both economic and ecological factors that are being equally ignored by decision-makers. Ecologically there is the issue of climate change and the problems of carbon gases warming the atmosphere. Economically the issue is that we have gone beyond 'peak oil' and in many respects 'peak gas' and what we are currently facing is extraction of oil and gas that is increasingly uneconomical as we are now having to draw on reserves that are more difficult to exploit. These two factors combined (difficult access and environmental damage) will create a shift in social support for fossil fuel miners, users and their political supporters. This will result in system collapse and Leggett's prediction for this is in the near future – 'a few years'.

Gilding's text is based firmly in the Limits to Growth tradition set by Meadows *et al.* (1972) but he has used different language to describe the crisis: 'the great disruption'. He argues that the current economic model has exceeded the capacity of the Earth – the limits are physical not philosophical – and there is a high risk of social and economic collapse. He considers that a system design change is needed and that it can be achieved if we accept that there is a problem. We need to recognise the sense-making cues and organise promptly to deal with this crisis – and in doing so change the discourse in academia and popular outlets. An important argument he makes is that collectively we will not see the small signs until systems collapse – this lack of sense-making is in part bolstered by a 'good life' that is still to be had.

Finally, Das (2015) critically analyses the modern economic environment. He argues that the engine of growth has faltered and whilst governments know what needs to be done, none are acting for fear of being electorally punished. There needs to be unpopular structural change, and politicians are aware that people do not wish to recognise that their cornucopia of consumption has come to an end. Growth cannot continue indefinitely, and what we are seeing now are the consequences of this myopic adherence to the oracle of growth. His reasons include demographic changes, reduction in productivity, increasing scarcity of natural resources, the impact of human-induced climate change, and the rising inequality within and between nations. He too forecasts a radical crash, in the not too distant future, that will have long-term life-changing consequences.

The analyses of these four observers are posed much more dramatically than most academic arguments. They argue essentially that our economic model of growth has exceeded the capacity of the Earth and that the tipping points for each of their areas of analyses have already passed. Gilding and Das believe that 'their' tipping point was about the time of the recent global financial crisis 2008/2009 and that we are already in a state of high risk of social and economic collapse, which will lead to chaos. The limits they all talk about are physical not philosophical and others, like McKibben (2011), concur that sustainability issues no longer require prevention – it is too late – but adaptation by businesses and other institutions.

The conclusion of many, including the advocates of degrowth (for example Swift 2014), is that capitalism is broken and at best in need of repair, but more than likely will need to be replaced.

Degrowth in the future

To tackle the challenge of the ecological crisis, organisations and societal institutions adopt one of two strategies. The first strategy, and by far the most popular among policy makers and captains of industry, is eco-efficiency for 'green growth'. Eco-efficiency may be situated in the dominant paradigm of sustainable development within the market system of free enterprise and a growing base of capital (the 'business as usual' paradigm). More fuel-efficient cars, or cars with alternative engine technologies (like hydrogen fuel cells or batteries) are examples of this strategy. However, the limitations of this strategy are apparent since Jevons gave his analysis of the 'Rebound Effect' (Polimeni *et al.* 2008). The other strategy, and by far the least popular, is *limiting growth*, creating sufficiency and focusing on services to meet consumer demands rather than products themselves. This strategy has the tendency for less or 'small is beautiful' and the economic ideal is that of a 'steady state economy': fewer products, less material throughput, maintaining a scale of economic activities that are in line with the limits of a finite planet.

Degrowth is not an attempt to stimulate negative growth or static growth but a move to replace growth both conceptually and materially with different language and assumptions about what constitutes a good life, business practices and societal measures of well-being and success.

The theme for the third international conference on Degrowth for Ecological Sustainability and Social Equity held in Venice in September 2012 was 'The Great Transition: Degrowth as a Passage of Civilisation'. The following quote taken from the conference website captures key issues explored in the chapter:

> There is a lot of concern about the label degrowth in part because it misrepresents the ideas and in part because it challenges the foundations of capitalism and the unchallenged assumption that growth is a reality that must be maintained if human social systems are to function and prosper. The language of living simpler lives and downscaling production and consumption challenge the assumptions of what it means to live a good life. The challenge is to consumer capitalism and as with all human systems the challenge is to those who materially gain from the status quo.

Among the challenges for organisations and societal institutions posed by degrowth is the need to radically alter some of the assumptions and values that shape the role and processes of business. Degrowth is not simply about reducing growth rates, it is about replacing growth as the indicator of success for human endeavour. To stimulate the transition to a post-growth society, degrowth aims to '…open up a space for the inventiveness and creativity of the imagination' (Latouche 2009, p. 9).

Social imaginary

The 'social imaginary' is both a concept and a practice, which Castoriardis (1987, p.3) contends is an all-encompassing enabling structure for the organisation of society:

> The imaginary of which I am speaking is not an image of. It is the unceasing and essentially undetermined (social-historical and psychical) creation of figures/forms/images, on the basis of which alone there can ever be a question of 'something'. What we call 'reality' and 'rationality' are its works…

Taylor (2004) also argues that the social imaginary is more than a set of ideas. It is what enables the practices of society and is both defined by and at the same time defines the moral order of society. It is a dynamic discursive practice through which humans create and represent their collective life, that is:

- the way [people] 'imagine' their social surroundings, and … it is carried in images, stories, legends, etc.
- shared by large groups of people, if not the whole society.
- that common understanding which makes possible common practices, and a widely shared sense of legitimacy (Taylor 2004, p. 24).

Taylor's modern social imaginary (2004) – a shared system of meanings that captures the imaginations of individuals and shapes their social groupings and society – is characterised by two facets that have had a powerful formative effect on modern societies: the central place assigned to the economic in our private and public lives, and the importance of equality in our social and political lives that is a fundamental value shaping our decisions and actions. The dominance of the 'economic' as the hegemonic imaginary may be seen in the organisational and political responses to the Global Financial Crisis that started in 2008. Despite counter narratives such as sustainability, the response and interpretation of GFC events appears to have been a reversion to 'business as usual' approaches to the global capital crisis and strengthening of neo-liberal economic models (Jessop 2012).

I argue that the social imaginary that frames our decision making needs to fundamentally change from one grounded in economics to one grounded in ecology – we need to create an *ecological imaginary* to replace the economic imaginary if we are to successfully transition to a post-growth society.

Degrowth aims to remove the 'modern social imaginary's' automatic association 'of growth with better' (Kallis et al. 2015, p.5) and one of the emerging actions in the degrowth movement is to explore other 'ontologies' or 'cosmologies' to facilitate this shift. For example, Thomson (2011) comments on the possibilities of synthesising the aims and ideals of degrowth with the Latin American paradigm of 'buen vivir' or 'good living', which draws on a plurality of indigenous cultures, and takes a non-Western approach to re-creating their social imaginary in innovative ways to overcome the failures of the capitalist system.

It is this process of imagining our world (and creating our world through our processes of imagination) that the degrowth project anchors on (Latouche 2009, 2015). Degrowth aims to decolonise the imaginary's automatic association 'of growth with better' (Kallis et al. 2015, p.5).

Degrowth world

The degrowth project calls for a radical reinvention of society at all scales. It means 'building convivial societies that are autonomous and economical in both the [developed] and the [developing worlds]' (Latouche 2009, p. 32). To trigger the process of degrowth, Latouche sets out eight interdependent principles, for what he foresees as 'the virtuous circle of quiet contraction'. These are:

- *Re-evaluate* – the values that shore up competition and replace these with values that support co-operation. This challenges the hegemony of consumerism and the focus on self-interest. It also allows the relationship with the natural environment to change from one dominated by control over to one framed by obligations to.
- *Re-conceptualise* – understanding reality in a different way, which allows us to redefine concepts such as wealth and poverty, and how to share the natural abundance of nature's resources.
- *Restructure* – re-designing the variety of structures, material and social, to propagate and support the new values system – processes of organising and institutionalising.
- *Redistribution* – this is a consequence of restructuring and applies equitable distribution of wealth in all its forms across all societies, developed and developing, and within societies. This will dampen and remove the behaviours associated with conspicuous consumption and an important 'new' value here is 'taking less' instead of 'taking more'.
- *Relocalise* – this is a change of direction in economic and political terms from centralisation to decentralisation. The emphasis is on re-establishing the importance of local production of food and commodities and the establishment of local processes of decision making for political and social needs.

- *Reduce/ Reuse/ Recycle* – are processes already underway in the sustainability movement and should be strengthened. They are important actions to reduce the quantity of materials we utilise and diminish the rate and quantity of resources we extract from the ecological environment, and improve the quality of commodities to increase their longevity and reduce their ecological footprint.

Degrowth is a program of economic democratisation grounded in a belief that material growth needs to be replaced by an economy of sufficiency. Such a transition requires significant changes, for example, dramatic reduction in global trade, taxation geared to radical redistribution of wealth and controlling resource extraction (material flow) to operate within ecological systems constraints.

Proponents of degrowth re-imagine a society fundamentally different to that shaped by consumer capitalism, a society that seems counter-intuitive and will initially garner resistance, but one they argue will provide increased well-being for all people and all life on this planet. Their restructuring of society for a degrowth future commences with the following core ideals which should emphasise *prioritising the local* in everything we do. This includes our places of work, our supply of food, and our access to services and skills that are readily accessible from our homes. This is coupled with a moral imperative to eliminate poverty and destitution through a redistribution of capital in all its forms.

Applying the principles outlined above, degrowth scholars and practitioners (see for example Kallis *et al.* 2015; Latouche 2009; Swift 2014) set out some of the changes that should form the foundations for a degrowth society:

- Quality of life measured in human relationships immersed in a culture of conviviality, not life measured in the quantity of consumer capital.
- Prioritising the local in everything. This includes decision-making, the provision of energy, food and the disposal/reuse/recycling of waste. The aim is a high level of community self-sufficiency.
- Reducing working hours and implementing a social wage to guarantee income to everyone. Associated with a guaranteed income is an expansion of community defined volunteer work.
- Allocating resources democratically within and across communities.
- Revitalising political life by extending the practices of direct democracy at the community level and extending this into the organisation.

The application of these principles is intended to stimulate the creativity involved in constructing a new social imaginary. All of these principles engage and challenge the underlying assumptions and values that constitute the economic moral order of 'the modern social imaginary' that Taylor (2004) presented – privileging of the individual; everything meaningful is able to be assigned a fiscal exchange value; and a belief that growth has no constraints.

Degrowth is thus arguably more than simply a transition phase to a 'beyond growth' economy. It recognises that the shift in the social imaginary requires fundamental changes to the value systems we organise by, and that this requires moral growth if we are to successfully create a post-growth world. Kerschner (2010, p. 549) captures this potential and the possibilities that the degrowth movement offers:

> Degrowth movements and writers have gone a long way already, when promoting social justice, solidarity … 'joy of life'…the pursuit of 'relational good' rather than material goods and the cultivation of human relationships … However this may not go far enough and other immaterial endeavours such as 'love' or 'compassion'… Which appear to be too esoteric even for the revolutionary spirit of the degrowth community, might have to be called upon as well.

References

Andreucci, D. and McDonough, T. (2015) 'Capitalism', in D'Alisa, G., Demaria, F., and Kallis, G. (eds), *Degrowth: A Vocabulary for a New Era*, New York: Routledge, pp. 59–62.

Banerjee, S. B. (2008) 'Necrocapitalism', *Organization Studies*, vol. 29, no. 12, pp. 1541–1563.

Castoriadis, C. (1987) *The Imaginary Institution of Society*, Cambridge: Polity Press.

D'Alisa, G., Demaria, F., and Kallis, G. (2015) *Degrowth: A Vocabulary for a New Era*, New York: Routledge.

Daly, H. E. (1991) *Steady-State Economics* (2nd ed.), Washington, DC: Island Press.

Daly, H. E. (1996) *Beyond Growth: The Economics of Sustainable Development*, Boston: Beacon Press.

Das, S. (2015) *A Banquet of Consequences: How We Consumed Our Own Future*, Melbourne: Viking.

Foster, J. B. (2011) 'Capitalism and Degrowth: An Impossibility', *Theorem Monthly Review*, vol. 6, pp.1–6. See: http://monthlyreview.org/2011/01/01/capitalism-and-degrowth-an-impossibility-theorem

Fournier, V. (2008) 'Escaping from the Economy: The Politics of Degrowth', *International Journal of Sociology and Social Policy*, vol. 11, no. 12, pp. 528–545.

Georgescu-Roegen, N. (1971) *The Entropy Law and the Economic Process*, Cambridge, MA: Harvard University Press.

Gilding, P. (2011) *The Great Disruption: Why the Climate Crisis Will Bring on the End of Shopping and the Birth of a New World*, New York: Bloomsbury Press.

Gowdy, J. and Mesner, S. (1998) 'The Evolution of Georgescu-Roegen's Bioeconomics', *Review of Social Economy*, vol. 56, no. 2, pp. 136–156.

Jessop, R. (2012) 'Economic and Ecological Crises: Green new deals and no-growth economies', *Development*, vol. 55, no. 1, pp. 17–24.

Kallis, G., Demaria, F., and D'Alisa, G. (2015) 'Introduction: Degrowth', in D'Alisa, G., Demaria, F. and Kallis, G. (eds), *Degrowth: A Vocabulary for a New Era*, New York: Routledge, pp. 1–17.

Kerschner, C. (2010) 'Economic Degrowth vs. Steady-State Economy', *Journal of Cleaner Production*, vol. 18, no. 6, pp. 544–551.

Klein, N. (2013) 'Naomi Klein: How Science Is Telling Us All to Revolt', *Castlemaine Independent News*, 30 October 2013.

Latouche, S. (2009) *Farewell to Growth*, Cambridge: Polity.

Latouche, S. (2015) 'Imaginary, Decolonisation of', in D'Alisa, G., Demaria, F., and Kallis, G. (eds), *Degrowth: A Vocabulary for a New Era*, New York: Routledge, pp. 117–120.

Leggett, J. (2013) 'An Oil Crash Is on Its Way and We Should Be Ready', *New Scientist*, vol. 2941, pp. 28–29.

McKibben, B. (2011) *Earth: Making a Life on a Tough New Planet*, New York: Random House Digital, Inc.

Meadows, D. H., Meadows, D., Randers, J., and Behrens III, W. (1972) *The Limits to Growth: A Report to The Club of Rome*, New York: Universe Books.

Polimeni, J. M., Mayumi, K., Giampietro, M., and Alcott, B. (2008) *The Jevons Paradox and the Myth of Resource Efficiency Improvements*, London: Earthscan.

Redclift, M.R. (1987) *Sustainable Development: Exploring the Contradictions*, London: Methuen and Co.

Swift, R. (2014) *S.O.S. Alternatives to Capitalism*, Oxford: New Internationalist Publications.

Taylor, C. (2004) *Modern Social Imaginaries*, London: Duke University Press.

Thomson, R. (2011) 'Pachakuti: Indigenous Perspectives, Buen Vivir, Sumaq Kawsay and Degrowth', *Development*, vol. 43, no. 4, pp. 448–454.

Turner, G. M. (2008) 'A Comparison of *The Limits to Growth* with 30 Years of Reality', *Global Environmental Change*, vol. 18, no. 3, pp. 397–411.

Whiteley, N. (1987) 'Toward a Throw-Away Culture: Consumerism, "Style Obsolescence" and Cultural Theory in the 1950s and 1960s', *Oxford Art Journal*, vol. 10. no. 2, pp. 3–27.

17

STRATEGIES FOR TRANSITION TO A FUTURE BEYOND GROWTH

Mark Diesendorf

UNSW AUSTRALIA

Introduction

Before embarking upon a journey we must choose a destination. Human society embraces over seven billion journeys, and each person has their own needs, aspirations and visions. No individual can determine the future of human society, although throughout history several have had major influences for a period, most with selfish, power-hungry goals and destructive impacts. If we are to nudge social, political and economic institutions towards the creation of a better world for the majority of humans and other species, the first step is to develop a vision, or visions, that many people can share. This chapter starts by offering a vision of an ecologically sustainable, socially just society, hereinafter called a 'sustainable society', for consideration and discussion.

Consistent with the theme of this book, the emphasis of this chapter is on one important aspect of such a sustainable society: a future economic system that has no biophysical growth, that is, no growth in human population and in the use of energy, materials and land. Furthermore, degrowth in the use of energy, materials and land is implemented, initially in the developed world. It is an economy that respects the finite biophysical capacity of Earth (Jackson 2009; Daly and Farley 2010; Dietz and O'Neil 2013; CASSE website). For brevity we call it a steady state economy (SSE), although the focus is on the biophysical economy, not the monetary.

We do not have to assume that there is no growth of socio-economic activity in an SSE. Despite the lack of biophysical growth, an SSE is one in which there can be growth in human knowledge, innovation in technology and the arts, ethics and social organisation. Indeed, such qualitative growth may be essential for transitioning to an SSE. There must also be quantitative growth in environmentally sound industries, technologies and services to the detriment of environmentally destructive ones.

After sketching the vision of sustainable society and an SSE that is one of its foundations, this chapter outlines some strategies that may help achieve it.

Sustainable society

In a sustainable society, social justice or equity is defined here as 'equal opportunity for all in terms of basic needs such as food, shelter, health, education, personal security, an unpolluted environment, social support and participation in social decision-making'. The case that ecological sustainability and social justice are inextricably entwined is set out by Sachs (2002). He argues that the notion that, on a finite planet, everyone can become continuously and endlessly richer in material terms is a scientifically impossible fantasy. Since there are billions of low-income people who desperately need to increase their economic activity, and the planet and its resources are finite, the rich must contract their economic activity so that the poor can expand theirs (Trainer 1985; Sachs 2002).

Furthermore, in order for everyone on this planet to have a material standard of living equivalent to that of the average North American, it would require the land of five Earths to provide the resources we use and to absorb our wastes (GFN 2015). Therefore we must aim for not only a clean and fairer economy, but also a lean economy (Sachs 2002). Many economists and decision-makers, and even some environmentalists, are in a state of denial about this. Contrary to scientific understanding, they maintain the fiction of development through economic growth for all, supported by the well-known metaphors of the eternally growing cake and the perpetually 'rising tide lifting all boats'. In reality, the size of the cake is limited by the size of the oven and the rising tide overflows the harbour (Sachs 2002).

An additional requirement on a sustainable society and its SSE is that social justice should not entail everyone being equal in a state of extreme poverty. A sustainable society must offer a better quality of life for all, better than is described for Planet Anarres in Ursula K. LeGuin's novel, *The Dispossessed* (Le Guin 1974).

The foregoing discussion suggests that a sustainable society is one that develops according to the following key sustainable development principles or objectives, condensed and modified from Australia's National Strategy for Ecologically Sustainable Development or ESD (Commonwealth of Australia 1992):

- To enhance individual and community well-being.
- To provide for equity (equal opportunity in the basics) between and within generations.
- To protect biological diversity and maintain essential ecological processes and life-support systems.
- To apply the Precautionary Principle, namely: 'Where there are threats of serious or irreversible environmental damage, lack of full scientific certainty should not be used as a reason for postponing measures to prevent environmental degradation.'

Although these principles can be interpreted and applied in different ways by different interest groups, they offer a useful starting point for discussion and action. Concepts like 'green economy' and 'ecological sustainability' are inevitably contestable, just like justice, democracy and freedom. Contestability is not a valid reason for avoiding them. Partly through discussion and debate of such concepts we can find pathways towards their achievement in spirit and real substance.

To assert the primacy of ecological sustainability and social justice over economic activity and thus obtain a strong concept of sustainability, the above principles avoid trade-offs between ecological sustainability and the demands of an unstable and destructive economic system. Furthermore, the principle 'to enhance individual and community well-being' should be sufficient to make it clear that an ecologically sustainable society is not a failed growth economy. Diesendorf (2000) has proposed the following definition of strong sustainable development that makes the priorities explicit:

> Sustainable development comprises types of social and economic development that protect and enhance the natural environment and social equity.

Thus environmental protection and social justice become constraints on development, avoiding trade-offs against economic development. 'Development' is not equated to 'economic growth'. Instead it is to be interpreted as 'qualitative improvement in human well-being' and 'unfolding of human potential', descriptions attributed to ecological economist Herman Daly. In poor countries, part of sustainable development may include economic growth, but in rich countries it must entail a reduction in economic activity (or 'degrowth'), especially in environmentally damaging and socially unjust activity.

The above definition of strong sustainable development is different from, but consistent with, Pearce's concept of 'strong' sustainable development based in environmental economics, which requires natural capital not to decrease, in contrast to 'weak' sustainable development, which only requires total (natural plus human-made) capital not to decrease (Pearce *et al.* 1989, Chapter 2). Weak sustainable development allows human-made capital to substitute for natural capital, leading to the destruction of the natural environment and so eventually to the end of human civilisation.

Like the above strong definition of sustainable development, the following definition by Griggs *et al.* (2013) avoids trade-offs between the natural environment, which is our life-support system, and economic development:

> Sustainable development . . . [is] development that meets the needs of the present while safeguarding Earth's life-support system, on which the welfare of current and future generations depends.

This strong definition builds upon and strengthens the well-known Brundtland definition, which assumes endless economic growth (WCED 1987, p.8):

> Humanity has the ability to make development sustainable – to ensure that it meets the needs of the present without compromising the ability of future generations to meet their own needs. ... But technology and social organization can both be managed and improved to make way for a new era of economic growth.

The definitions of strong sustainable development by Diesendorf (2000) and Griggs et al. (2013) both recognise that the economy is a subset of the environment and so ecological sustainability acts as a constraint on the types of socio-economic development permitted. Although social justice is not mentioned explicitly in the Griggs et al. (2013) definition, it enters in the next step of their framework, which combines the Millennium Development Goals, which focus on reducing extreme poverty in poor countries, with conditions necessary to assure the stability of Earth's systems, to form a set of six Sustainable Development Goals. The authors mention in passing that 'none of this is possible without changes to the economic playing field' (Griggs et al. 2013, p. 307), but do not pursue that any further.

The earlier chapters and the books on SSE cited in the introduction to this chapter make the case that the existing economic system is one of the principal drivers of unsustainable development and indeed a threat to the future of human civilisation and biodiversity. This can also be seen by application of the identity $I = PAT$ that disaggregates environmental impact I into the product of population P, affluence (i.e. consumption per person) A and technological impact T (Ehrlich and Holdren 1972). In the original identity affluence is defined as GDP per person and technological impact is defined as environmental impact per unit of GDP, and so

$$I = P \times (GDP)/P \times I/(GDP)$$

Although this relationship just says $I = I$, the disaggregation of I into PAT is useful because each term on the right-hand-side may be addressed with different policies: to stop population growth; stop growth in consumption per person; and clean up polluting technologies.

There are many possible variations of the original identity. For instance, if I represents the CO_2 emissions (a proxy for their impact) by energy generation E, then we can write (Diesendorf 2002):

$$I = P \times E/P \times I/E$$

In this example, affluence is measured by energy use per person E/P, which can be reduced by improving energy efficiency and conservation without necessarily diminishing quality of life, and technological impact by CO_2 emissions per unit of energy use, which can be reduced by replacing fossil fuels by renewable energy.

To make the original $I = PAT$ identity more compatible with our biophysical definition of SSE, we can replace the monetary GDP with a biophysical version, such as used by Turner (2011) and Turner et al. (2013).

Vision of a sustainable society and an SSE

There are a number of visions of future societies, some of them quite unpleasant. For example, Gilding (2011) sees an imminent 'great disruption' that others would call a 'collapse of industrial society' followed by the 'great awakening', the rapid emergence of an enlightened society that addresses climate change and other global problems. While a potential collapse is already unfolding, historical experiences, such as the French Revolution, the collapse of the Soviet Union and the collapse of several pre-industrial societies (Diamond 2005) do not inspire confidence in the likelihood of a 'great awakening'.

This chapter envisages a transition to a sustainable society through a series of minor disruptions, environmental, social and economic. It too may have low credibility in the eyes of many, but the alternative is to give up, retreat to a remote region, build a self-sufficient, fortified farm and try to ride out the coming socio-economic collapse. The majority of the world's people have no prospect of such a personal future in a rural, gated Garden of Eden. The only choice for most of us is to engage in a political struggle for a quasi-orderly transition to a sustainable society. Hence the following vision and scenario for a sustainable society must be taken seriously. It may be of debatable credibility, but it's all we've got.

In practical terms, what would a sustainable society look like in, say, 2050? Here again there are choices. The huge human population of this planet preempts the possibility of a general retreat from cities to self-sufficient rural areas. While I agree with Trainer (1985) that 'the rich must live more simply so that the poor may simply live', his 'simpler way', based on small, anarchistic, local communities (Trainer 2010) is not well defined and does not explain how we can have the benefits of industrial society while abandoning industry and infrastructure that can only be built by the combined efforts of a nation or state. Therefore I postulate a future industrial society that has cities where most people live, universities, hospitals, high-rise buildings, electricity grids, water supplies, railways, Internet and pharmaceuticals. However, the means by which these facilities and services are provided will be very different.

A crucial question is: can an SSE maintain full employment? In conventional economic thinking, nearly full employment is maintained by economic growth. However, Victor (2008, 2012) used a macroeconomic econometric model of the Canadian economy to explore this question. He compared a business-as-usual (BAU) scenario with several other scenarios with low- or no-growth economies measured in terms of GDP per capita. In the scenario where economic growth was terminated and no other policies were changed, unemployment increased greatly, confirming that a (monetary) SSE cannot be a failed growth economy. However, other scenarios, each with several different policies as well as no growth, selective growth or degrowth, showed that nearly full employment is possible while CO_2 emissions are reduced. The additional policies included a shorter working week, population stabilisation and changing the trade balance by increasing local industries instead of imports.

A different approach, by Turner (2011), used a biophysical model of the Australian economy called the Australian Stocks and Flows Framework and obtained similar results. The framework is essentially an input-output model for the physical processes underlying the monetary economy. It tracks stocks of materials, energy, employed people, livestock, physical capital (buildings, machinery) and land; flows are treated as changes in stocks. The biophysical model finds, consistent with the macroeconomic model of Victor (2008), that unemployment is determined by population and its age structure, length of working week, labour productivity and economic activities requiring labour. By adjusting these variables, Turner (2011) shows that it is possible to obtain a biophysical SSE with 5 per cent unemployment while reducing environmental impacts in terms of CO_2 emissions and water consumption.

This initial modeling is encouraging; however, it shows that the SSE requires careful design and hence greater government intervention than maintaining BAU until it collapses. Both macroeconomic and biophysical modeling are relevant, because at present growth in the economy is correlated with growth in the use of materials and energy (e.g. Schandl and West 2012). We next consider the case studies of transitions to sustainable energy and to more sustainable cities.

Vision of an energy future in 2050

Energy use is one of the fundamental drivers of industrial society. In the sustainable society energy use will be far more efficient and some wasteful energy services will be constrained, with the result that per capita energy use will be much lower than in today's USA and even possibly today's Denmark. A sustainable energy system comprises a combination of energy supply by renewable sources and demand reduction through a combination of energy efficiency (i.e. having the same energy services while using less energy), energy conservation (having fewer energy services) and 'smart' electricity supply-demand systems that can adjust demand in real time as well as supply. A genuinely sustainable energy system will substitute renewable energy and demand reduction for fossil fuels, not supplement them. Thus a sustainable energy system can be lean.

Renewable energy systems are green, because, with two exceptions, they emit no greenhouse gas emissions during operation and, once the raw materials are mined and the technologies are manufactured with renewable energy, they will have no life-cycle emissions either. (The exceptions are hydro-electric dams that flood extensively vegetated valleys and so can become substantial methane emitters, and some sources and uses of biomass to produce bioenergy.) Renewable energy done well is also very low in air and water pollution. Wind and solar photovoltaics (PV) use no water during operation. Although wind farms can span large areas, they only occupy 1–2 per cent of land spanned (Denholm et al. 2009) and this is usually agricultural land. Crops grow and animals graze between the turbines. Rooftop solar occupies no land. In renewable energy supply most land occupied per unit of energy generated results from large dams and on-ground solar power stations. However, depending on the energy mix, the area occupied can be much less than that of a fossil-fueled system with open-cut coalmines. Renewable energy systems will last as long as the sun remains stable – billions of years.

Renewable energy is evolving simultaneously on three scales: small-scale local, especially rooftop solar PV; medium-scale systems, including microgrids, for communities, industrial parks, etc.; and large-scale grid-connected electricity supply. The small- and medium-scale systems allow households, community groups, small and medium-sized enterprises, schools and hospitals greater autonomy in their energy supply and so potentially can strengthen social capital and social equity. Even large-scale systems such as wind and solar farms can be owned by cooperatives and other community-based organisations (Hicks and Ison 2014).

Renewable energy and energy efficiency can also provide economic benefits, by increasing local employment and capping energy prices once the initial investments have been made. In many parts of the world electricity from rooftop solar PV is actually cheaper than electricity from the grid purchased at retail prices during the daytime. In a few parts of the world wind farms and on-ground solar PV power stations are beginning to compete without subsidies with conventional power stations (Diesendorf 2015).

Despite these favourable characteristics, vigilance is needed to ensure that renewable energy is not implemented in ways that foster an unsustainable growth economy. Imagine, for instance, giant satellites in space beaming huge quantities of solar energy to earth; or multinational corporations clearing native forests in order to build gigantic solar farms or to plant palm trees to produce biodiesel – the latter has already been happening in Malaysia and Indonesia. Another issue that needs attention is to ensure that components of renewable energy systems are designed for reuse and recycling, and that substitutes are found for materials in short supply, such as the rare earth elements used in the generators of wind turbines. It's the responsibility of sustainable energy proponents and developers to pressure decision-makers to ensure the energy sector becomes sustainable in all ways.

In the future sustainable society most energy is delivered in the form of renewable electricity. This is a big change from the present system, where most heat is supplied by burning gas or coal directly and most transport runs on oil. However, in transforming to renewable energy, it will be easier and more efficient to supply most heat with electric heat pumps, supplemented at low temperatures by direct solar heating, and most transport, both public and private, by electric vehicles, supplemented by active transport.

Already in 2015 there are credible scenario studies for 80–100 per cent renewable electricity for many regions of the world. A number of these are based on hourly computer simulations spanning 1–8 years of large-scale electricity supply-demand systems and most are based on commercially available renewable energy technologies. They include studies of the whole world (Jacobson and Delucchi 2011; Delucchi and Jacobson 2011), the USA (Mai et al. 2012; Jacobson et al. 2015), Europe (Heide et al. 2011; Rasmussen et al. 2012; Palzer and Henning 2014) and Australia (Elliston et al. 2013, 2014; AEMO 2013).

Reliability of large-scale renewable electricity supply is achieved by (Mai *et al.* 2012; Elliston *et al.* 2013, 2014):

- Having a mix of variable renewable energy (e.g. wind and solar PV) and flexible, dispatchable[1] renewable energy sources (e.g. concentrated solar thermal with thermal storage, biofuelled gas turbines and hydro with dams);
- geographic dispersion of renewable energy power stations assisted by a few new major transmission links;
- demand management assisted by 'smart' meters and switches in a 'smart' grid.

Vision of future cities and their transport systems

Cities are congregations of people who live close to one another for the purposes of social life, employment, business, higher education, entertainment, medical and hospital care, and more. Our urban scenario recognises the value of cities, especially compact ones with nodes of high population density, where citizens have easy access to these facilities. This scenario avoids the damage that urban sprawl inflicts on the natural environment, society and economy (Newman and Kenworthy 1999; Newman *et al.* 2009).

In the cities of the future sustainable society, most trips are taken by a mix of electric public transport and active transport. Where car or truck trips are required, electric vehicles are used. To facilitate this change in travel mode and behaviour, cities have been renovated to restructure them into a hierarchy of population clusters that reduces the need for trips by private cars. At the top level the city is composed of a number of transit cities, whose town centres are linked together by fast heavy rail. Each transit city contains, in addition to its town centre, a number of local centres. Within a transit city, people travel between local centres and between the town centre and local centres by bus, light rail or cycling. Housing is concentrated around public transport nodes (White *et al.* 1978; Newman and Kenworthy 1999, 2006).

As in the case of energy, this approach would make our cities more environmentally sound, leaner in terms of transport use and fairer in terms of providing an excellent transport system for all people. Our scenario emphasises the social and economic values of cities and the environmental value of the hinterland. Hence it concentrates the urban population in nodes and protects the hinterland.

Cities taken in isolation from their hinterland cannot be entirely sustainable, although their environmental impacts can be greatly reduced. Cities have insufficient space to produce most food, energy and industrial raw materials. The alternative of allowing a 'city' to become a gigantic suburb, where every household has its own big garden, ideally producing all its own food, would sprawl over vast areas, losing many of the benefits of a city and destroying the natural environment of the hinterland.

Other key issues in brief

The demand for raw materials in our future sustainable society has been greatly reduced by designing products to be reusable and recyclable. There is much less mining and very little solid waste. Materials are chosen to be of low toxicity and most can be produced with low energy inputs. A high-energy exception, aluminium, is almost entirely recycled. In the steel industry iron ore is reduced to iron by using carbon in biomass produced sustainably, instead of coal.

Future forest cover is much greater than in 2016, the increase being composed of both young native forests and plantations on some of the land previously used for agriculture. Paper use has been greatly reduced. Plantation forests are used extensively to produce timber, replacing most concrete, bricks and steel in low- and medium-rise buildings.

Much agricultural land has been freed up for timber and bioenergy by a shift towards low-meat and no-meat diets. Changing the trend of the early twenty-first century towards eating more meat has been the most difficult part of the scenario. Although agriculture is still far from a sustainable industry, the increased use of perennial crops instead of annual and organic alternatives to conventional fertilisers (e.g. sewerage, human urine, crop residues, municipal waste, biological nitrogen fixation) has helped reduce the environmental impacts and energy use of agriculture.

Strategies and policies for transitioning to a sustainable society

At this point it is necessary to emphasise the distinction between the goal of an ecologically sustainable and socially just sustainable society, shortened to 'sustainable society', and the process or pathway towards the goal, ecologically and socially just development, shortened to 'sustainable development' (Diesendorf 2000), the topic of this section.

Developing and discussing a vision of a sustainable society is just the first step in the sustainable development process (Diesendorf 2000). In the words of aviator Antoine de Saint-Exupery, 'As for the future, your task is not to foresee it, but to enable it'. Since governments are generally influenced by vested interests, especially large corporations, recommending government policies is not sufficient, although necessary. We also need strategies for households and community groups to transform themselves while simultaneously organising to pressure governments to take effective action (Diesendorf 2009). We also need intergovernmental actions, but because agreements are so difficult to achieve among nearly 200 countries, the main emphasis here is on countries, states/provinces, cities and local communities. Thus overall strategy combines top-down and bottom-up actions.

This section outlines strategies for transforming energy and urban planning/transport and then more general strategies and policies for transforming the economic system into an SSE.

Energy strategies

There is an old saying that 'to every complex problem there is a simple solution… and it is wrong'. No single policy measure is sufficient to drive the transition from fossil fuels to renewable energy and energy efficiency. This is partly due to the diversity of barriers to change, partly to the fact that energy policy affects many sectors of the economy and partly to the great diversity of sustainable energy technologies and measures at different stages of maturity and various scales of manufacture and use (Diesendorf 2014, pp.199–200).

Pricing, e.g. a carbon price, is necessary, or at least very important, because it internalises some of the external (e.g. environmental and health) costs of making and using a technology and sends a message to investors – from households to multinational corporations – that it is financially risky to invest in e.g. an electric resistance hot water heater or a new coal-fired power station. Furthermore, a carbon price applied 'upstream' to the major greenhouse polluters flows 'downstream' to all economic transactions, affecting energy, materials, transport, buildings, land use, etc. In this way it is more efficient and effective than a piecemeal approach. A carbon price raises revenue that governments can use to assist the transition and compensate workers who become unemployed as a result of the transition.

Pricing can assist in reducing the use of polluting technologies, but it doesn't automatically provide the alternatives. The energy market is nothing like the idealised perfect market of conventional economics. Neither producers nor consumers have complete information. If they did, every home and business would be highly energy efficient, because there is still huge cost-effective potential in countries like the USA and Australia (McKinsey and Company 2009; ClimateWorks 2015). Furthermore, the market frequently fails to provide essential infrastructure such as transmission lines and railways. Indeed, the market operates best at the margin and is generally very weak in implementing long-term strategies unless guided by government legislation and other institutions.

Therefore, for national and state/provincial governments, a multiplicity of mutually reinforcing policies is needed to drive the transition. The broad types of policy are (Diesendorf 2014):

- targets for renewable electricity and heat and for energy efficiency;
- economic instruments, such as a carbon price, feed-in tariffs, tradeable certificate schemes, reverse auctions, low-interest loans, grants, fees, rebates and feebates (RMI 2008), and fair pricing of grid electricity;
- laws, regulations, standards and labelling;
- research, education, training and information;
- institutional change, such as creating energy service companies to replace energy supply companies;
- planning and design of towns, precincts, buildings and consumer products;
- seeding grants and facilitating legislation for the development of community sustainable energy projects.

The market does not automatically provide a fair distribution of goods or a fair distribution of costs of a socio-technical transition. For example, carbon pricing falls most heavily upon the poor, unless governments direct some of the revenue raised to compensate them. In Australia in 2012, the former Labor Government compensated low-income earners for its (temporary) emissions trading scheme by raising the income tax threshold from $6,000 to $18,200 p.a. (Webb 2011, see appendix). However, it overlooked the unemployed and only gave a token increase to pensioners.

Other actors will also need new policies. For instance, the electricity industry will need to develop new business models that are compatible with distributed generation. At present the standard business model of electricity distributors and retailers is collapsing in countries where rooftop solar PV and energy efficiency are growing substantially, to the extent that demand on the grid is declining (Diesendorf 2014).

Community groups will need to act on two fronts: to develop their own community-owned renewable energy projects on small and medium scales and to campaign to achieve the necessary government policies.

Urban planning and transport strategies

Carbon pricing, which increases the costs of motor vehicle fuel, can motivate reduced car and truck use, provided governments fund the alternatives: railways, buses, bicycle paths, pedestrian paths and the initial charging points for electric vehicles. Urban renovation is essential to increase population density around public transport nodes and along public transport routes, gradually transforming cities into the hierarchical structures described in the vision section, where the need for car transport of any kind, fossil or renewable, is greatly reduced. This entails a change in planning laws and may also require changes in the way state/provincial governments raise revenue: e.g. in Australia, a large source of income for this level of governments is stamp duty, a tax paid by people who buy a house. This discourages people from moving house and hence slows the restructuring of urban form.

General policies for SSE

To nudge society towards sustainability we must implement strategies and policies to clean up industries and technologies while reducing total throughput, stabilise the planet's human population and reduce biophysical consumption per person, as suggested by the identity $I = PAT$. We must do it an a way that is fairer (i.e. protects social equity), is economically efficient, taking into account the full environmental, health and social costs of the socio-technical system, and improves human well-being as measured by indicators such as happiness and life satisfaction.

The seven mutually reinforcing policy directions proposed by Dietz and O'Neill (2013) are compatible with these goals:

1. Limit resource use and waste production.
2. Stabilise population.

3. Distribute income and wealth equitably.
4. Reform monetary and financial systems.
5. Change the way we measure progress.
6. Secure full employment.
7. Rethink how businesses create value.

Limiting resource use and waste production could be initiated by the rich countries, but ultimately must involve global caps covered by international agreements. There is little point in controlling the resource use and pollution from making and using a gizmo if the number of gizmos sold keeps increasing. The model of Contraction and Convergence introduced in the context of transitioning to equal per capita greenhouse gas emissions (GCI 2015) could be extended to cover all resource use. Indeed, the rich countries must move onto ecologically sustainable, socially just, transition pathways while simultaneously assisting developing countries. On a national scale, brakes on the consumption society can be applied by means of tighter controls on advertising potentially harmful products and by legislating for extended producer responsibility.

Stabilising population must be addressed in both rich and poor countries. It is important for rich countries, because of their high per capita consumption: e.g. an additional person in the USA or Australia has much higher per capita greenhouse gas emissions than an additional person in the rural areas of India or China. In poor countries successful population stabilisation depends on education of women and poverty alleviation in general (see Engelman in this volume). This requires long-term programs with substantial aid funding by the rich countries.

Distributing income and wealth more equitably goes beyond setting a dole or minimum wage. It could also involve setting maximum incomes, either directly, or indirectly through progressive income tax, and closing tax loopholes. An inheritance tax or a wealth tax could also be introduced.

Reforming monetary and financial systems: These systems, which let us down again and again, as demonstrated recently by the Global Financial Crisis (GFC), must be brought under control. The challenge is to create a system that fosters productive investments, such as in renewable energy technologies and public transport, while discouraging the current system where the vast majority of financial transactions are simply unproductive gambling on the stock market. Australia rode out the GFC quite well, partly because it had stricter controls on financial institutions than the USA and several European countries. It recently raised the reserve requirements for lending by financial institutions to 25 per cent. Even higher reserve requirements should be set, possibly to 100 per cent, with special provisions for exemptions for essential infrastructure that is compatible with ecological sustainability and social justice. To further reduce financial speculation, a tax on international financial transfers, sometimes known as a Tobin Tax, could be implemented.

To *change the way we measure progress* new indicators such as the Genuine Progress Indicator can be utilised (see Lawn in this volume). There is nothing sacrosanct about GDP, which misleadingly counts all economic activity, both benefits and costs, as positive.

To assist in *securing full employment* in an SSE, we can set shorter working weeks to share the work around and encourage more local production of goods and services (Dietz and O'Neill 2013). Local production would be assisted by carbon pricing, which would make international freight transport more expensive.

Rethinking how businesses create value will lead to new business models that are less likely to foster growth than shareholder-owned corporations. Instead of trying to sell a product in the form of a material object, they would sell a service or lease a product. In so doing they would retain ownership of the equipment that provides the service and take responsibility for supplying, maintaining and recycling it. This would foster high-quality, long-life equipment and savings in materials and energy (Dietz and O'Neill 2013). Types of business that foster environmental and social equity goals for its members and the local community should be encouraged: e.g. the cooperative, which has a democratic decision-making structure, with each member having one vote. Community organisations should propose and lobby governments to pass laws and regulations to foster these business models that create value that is not limited to consumer goods and services.

With these modifications and constraints, the new economic system could be considered to be a constrained type of capitalism (Daly 1991). Markets would still exist, but they would be shaped to serve the majority of people instead of large corporations and other vested interests.

Note

1   A 'dispatchable' power station is one that can generate electricity on demand.

References

AEMO (Australian Energy Market Operator) (2013) 100 percent renewables study – modelling outcomes. See: http://www.climatechange.gov.au/reducing-carbon/aemo-report-100-renewable-electricity-scenarios

CASSE (Center for the Advancement of the Steady State Economy). See: http://steadystate.org

ClimateWorks (2015) Australia's energy productivity potential. See: http://climateworks.com.au/sites/default/files/documents/publications/climateworks_energy_productivity_report_20150310.pdf

Commonwealth of Australia (1992) *National Strategy for Ecologically Sustainable Development*. Canberra: AGPS.

Daly, H.E. (1991) *Steady-State Economics*. 2nd edition. Washington, DC: Island Press.

Daly, H.E. and Farley, J. (2010) *Ecological Economics: Principles and Applications*. 2nd edition. Washington, DC: Island Press.

Delucchi, M.A. and Jacobson, M.Z. (2011) 'Providing all global energy with wind, water, and solar power, Part II: Reliability, system and transmission costs, and policies'. *Energy Policy* vol. 39, pp. 1170–1190.

Denholm, P., Hand, M., Jackson, M., and Ong, S. (2009) *Land-Use Requirements of Modern Wind Power Plants in the United States*. Technical report NREL/TP-6A2–45834. Golden, CO: National Renewable Energy Laboratory.

Diamond, J. (2005) *Collapse: How Societies Choose to Fail or Survive*. London: Penguin.

Diesendorf, M. (2000) 'Sustainability and sustainable development'. In: Dunphy, D., Benveniste, J., Griffiths, A., and Sutton, P. (eds) *Sustainability: The Corporate Challenge of the 21st Century*. Sydney: Allen and Unwin, pp.19–37.

Diesendorf, M. (2002) 'I = PAT or I = BPAT?'. *Ecological Economics* vol. 42, p. 3.

Diesendorf, M. (2009) *Climate Action: A Campaign Manual for Greenhouse Solutions*. Sydney: UNSW Press.

Diesendorf, M. (2014) *Sustainable Energy Solutions for Climate Change*. London: Routledge-Earthscan and Sydney: NewSouth Publishing.

Diesendorf, M. (2015) *100 Per Cent Renewable Electricity for South Australia*. Adelaide: Conservation Council of South Australia. See: http://www.conservationsa.org.au/images/100_Renewables_for_SA_Report_-_Dr_Mark_Diesendorf_-_web_version.pdf

Dietz, R. and O'Neill, D. (2013) *Enough Is Enough: Building a Sustainable Economy in a World of Finite Resources*. San Francisco: Berrett-Koehler Publishers.

Elliston, B., MacGill, I., and Diesendorf, M. (2013) 'Least cost 100 per cent renewable electricity scenarios in the Australian National Electricity Market'. *Energy Policy* vol. 59, pp. 270–282.

Elliston, B., MacGill, I., and Diesendorf, M. (2014) 'Comparing least cost scenarios for 100 per cent renewable electricity with low emission fossil fuel scenarios in the Australian National Electricity Market'. *Renewable Energy* vol. 66, pp. 196–204.

Ehrlich, P.R. and Holdren, J. (1972) 'A *Bulletin* dialogue on "The Closing Circle": Critique'. *Bulletin of the Atomic Scientists* vol. 28, no. 5, pp. 18–27.

GCI (2015) Global Commons Institute. See: http://www.gci.org.uk/contconv/cc.html

GFN (2015) Global Footprint Network. See: http://www.footprintnetwork.org/en/index.php/GFN/

Gilding, P. (2011) *The Great Disruption*. London: Bloomsbury Press.

Griggs, D., Stafford-Smith, M., Gaffney, O., Rockström, J., Öhman, M.C., Shyamsundar, P., Steffen, W., Glaser, G., Kanie, N., and Noble, N. (2013) 'Sustainable development goals for people and planet'. *Nature* vol. 495, pp. 305–307.

Heide, D., Greiner, M., von Bremen, L., and Hoffmann, C. (2011) 'Reduced storage and balancing needs in a fully renewable European power system with excess wind and solar power generation'. *Renewable Energy* vol. 36, pp. 2515–2523.

Hicks, J. and Ison, N. (2014) Community energy in Europe. See: http://www.embark.com.au/display/public/content/Community+energy+in+Europe;jsessionid=BA1E17ECDE44D51F0B5BA27CF3CF49B3

Jackson, T. (2009) *Prosperity without Growth*. London: Earthscan.

Jacobson, M. and Delucchi, M.A. (2011) 'Providing all global energy with wind, water, and solar power, Part I: technologies, energy resources, quantities and areas of infrastructure, and materials', *Energy Policy* vol. 39, pp. 1154–1169.

Jacobson, M., Delucchi, M.A., Bazouin, G., Bauer, Z.A.F., Heavey, C.C., Fisher, E., Morris, S.B., Piekutowski, D.J.Y., Vencilla, T.A., and Yeskooa. T.W. (2015) '100 per cent wind, water, and sunlight (WWS) all-sector energy roadmaps for the 50 US states'. *Energy and Environmental Science* vol. 8, pp. 2093–2117. DOI: 10.1039/c5ee01283j

Le Guin, U.K. (1974) *The Dispossessed*. New York: HarperPrism.

Mai, T., Wiser, R., Sandor, D., Brinkman, G., Heath, G., Denholm, P., Hostick D.J., Darghouth, N., Schlosser, A., and Strzepek, K. (2012) *Renewable Electricity Futures Study*. Technical report TP-6A20-A52409. Golden, CO: National Renewable Energy Laboratory. See: http://www.osti.gov/bridge

McKinsey and Company (2009) 'Unlocking energy efficiency in the US economy'. See: http://www.mckinsey.com/client_service/electric_power_and_natural_gas/latest_thinking/unlocking_energy_efficiency_in_the_us_economy

Newman, P., Beatley, T., and Boyer, H. (2009) *Resilient Cities: Responding to Peak Oil and Climate Change*. Washington, DC: Island Press.

Newman, P. and Kenworthy, J. (1999) *Sustainability and Cities: Overcoming Automobile Dependence*. Washington, DC: Island Press.

Newman, P. and Kenworthy, J. (2006) 'Urban design to reduce automobile dependence'. *Opolis: An International Journal of Suburban and Metropolitan Studies* vol. 2, no. 1, Art.3. See: http://repositories.cdlib.org/cssd/opolis/vol2/iss1/art3

Palzer A. and Henning, H.M. (2014) 'A comprehensive model for the German electricity and heat sector in a future energy system with a dominant contribution from renewable energy technologies – Part II: Results'. *Renewable and Sustainable Energy Reviews* vol. 30, pp. 1019–1034.

Pearce D., Markandya, A., and Barbier, E. (1989) *Blueprint for a Green Economy*. London: Earthscan.

Rasmussen, M.G., Andresen, G.B., and Greiner, M. (2012) 'Storage and balancing synergies in a fully or highly renewable pan-European power system'. *Energy Policy* vol. 51, pp. 642–651.

RMI (2008) *Feebates: A Legislative Option to Encourage Continuous Improvements to Automobile Efficiency*. Boulder, CO: Rocky Mountain Institute. See: http://www.rmi.org/Knowledge-Center/Library/T08–09_FeebatesLegislativeOption

Sachs, W. (2002) 'Ecology, justice and the end of development'. In: Byrne, J., Glover, L., and Martinez, C. (eds) *Environmental Justice. Discourses in International Political Economy – Energy and Environmental Policy, Vol. 8*. New Brunswick and London: Transaction Publishers, pp. 19–36.

Schandl, H. and West, J. (2012) 'Material flows and material productivity in China, Australia and Japan'. *Journal of Industrial Ecology* vol. 16, pp. 352–364.

Trainer, T. (1985) *Abandon Affluence*. London: Zed Books.

Trainer, T. (2010) *The Transition to a Sustainable and Just World*. Sydney: Envirobooks.

Turner, G.M. (2011) Consumption and the environment: impacts from a system perspective. In: Newton, P.W. (ed.) *Landscapes of Urban Consumption*. Collingwood: CSIRO Publishing pp. 51–70.

Turner, G.M., Elliston, B., and Diesendorf, M. (2013) 'Impacts on the biophysical economy and environment of a transition to 100 per cent renewable electricity in Australia'. *Energy Policy* vol. 54, pp. 288–299.

Victor, P. (2008) *Managing without Growth: Slower by Design, Not Disaster*. Cheltenham, UK and Northampton, MA: Edward Elgar.

Victor, P. (2012) 'Growth, degrowth and climate change: A scenario analysis'. *Ecological Economics* vol. 84, pp. 206–212.

WCED (World Commission for Environment and Development) (1987) *Our Common Future*. Oxford: Oxford University Press.

Webb, R. (2011) *Securing a Clean Energy Future: Some Economic Aspects*. See: http://www.aph.gov.au/About_Parliament/Parliamentary_Departments/Parliamentary_Library/pubs/rp/rp1112/12rp05

White, D., Sutton, P., Pears, A., Mardon, C., Dick, J., and Crow, M. (1978) *Seeds for Change: Creatively Confronting the Energy Crisis*. Melbourne: Conservation Council of Victoria and Patchwork Press.

CONCLUSION: THE ENDLESS GROWTH MYTH

Simplicity and complexity

Haydn Washington and Paul Twomey

UNSW AUSTRALIA

At the heart of this book is both simplicity and complexity. The simplicity is that on a finite planet, endless physical growth *is* actually impossible. When one raises this question with an audience, in our experience we have yet to find anyone who puts up their hand up to argue that endless physical growth is possible forever. To believe otherwise denies reality – yet this is actually the assumption that Western society and orthodox economics still operate under. A child can tell you it is not possible, yet our leaders and governments and august neoclassical academic faculties of economics still maintain that not only is endless physical growth possible, it is indeed even considered *praiseworthy*. At the government and business level, society still proceeds with the mantra of endless growth.

That there are still many parts of the world that are still in need of material growth to reduce poverty and meet basic needs such as food, clothing and shelter cannot be questioned. However, to confuse this imperative of targeted growth with acceptance of continued endless global physical growth is a gross error. In particular, the argument that growth-for-all is needed to 'trickle down' to the poor has been shown to be unconvincing (Layard 2005; Picketty 2013). Furthermore, as many writers in the volume have revealed, the cumulative damages from growth are readily apparent and are only getting worse for our planet's wealth of life, and hence the society that depends on this.

The current endless growth economy is thus, at the most fundamental level, a *delusion*, a very dangerous one that is the key cause of the environmental crisis, and is blocking society from reaching any meaningful sustainability (as the introduction discusses). Hence this is why we desperately need to find a sustainable 'future beyond growth'. Environmental scientists (e.g. Ehrlich and Ehrlich 1991) and scholars (e.g. Catton 1982; Brown 2011) and ecological economists such as Herman Daly (1991, 1996) have been pointing this out for decades, yet orthodox economics and governments remain in denial of ecological limits. *It is time for change.*

So what of the 'complexity'? The complexity lies in knowing what to do to turn things around. So deeply ingrained in society is the 'endless growth' myth (and the neoliberal reverence for the free market) that those in power simply refuse to enter into dialogue about the impossibility of endless growth. Mostly they deny it is even an issue. Growth is seen as inherently 'good', and anyone who questions it is 'not good' – even portrayed as morally evil.

The complexity in this vital topic is thus finding a way to gain a meaningful dialogue about ecological limits, a degrading biosphere caused by endless growth, and the key drivers of overpopulation and overconsumption. How do we mainstream a rational debate as to how we might all live *meaningful lives of well-being* – without destroying the planet and the ecosystem services that support our society?

Such a debate is not just a question of science – the science is well and truly 'in' (and has been in for thirty years at least), just getting more and more certain, and more and more disturbing (MEA 2005). It is also more than just a question of 'economics' (although there are many problems to be resolved to create a steady state economy). Rather, the debate must also include questions of ethics and the value given to nature and life, both current and of the future. It is also a question of psychology and sociology – how does one deal with society's deep denial and resistance to imagining prosperity without the growth economy? Thus it is also a question of education – how does one educate to move past the 'growth is always good' mantra, towards a realisation that a steady state economy is actually rational and, potentially, the basis of a better society? And of course it's also a question of politics: how do we get our governments – which are addicted to growth – to quit the habit? So there is a great deal of complexity as to how to 'move beyond growth' – but the key is *dialogue*: we have to talk about this.

The breadth of the problems of the growth economy is extensive, hence the breadth of the topics this book has sought to cover. Some have consequently only received cursory attention. The book has examined in the introduction why the growth economy is broken, because it is the key cause of *un*sustainability and a worsening environmental crisis (Washington). It's looked at what a steady state economy actually *is* (Magnus-Johnston) and the relationship of the steady state economy to the circular, blue and green economies (Twomey and Washington). It has talked about the related issue of degrowth (Perey). It has looked at the stocks and flows framework of Turner (Chapter 9) to assess the biophysical sustainability of Australia. It has looked at the relationship between an SSE and economic stability, social equity and ecological sustainability (Stillwell). It has looked at the GPI as a guide to the transition to a steady state economy (Lawn). Joshua Farley has tackled the difficult issue of how capitalism relates to an SSE, and to what extent they are 'uneasy bedfellows'. The book has also covered the difficult issues of overpopulation and overconsumption (see below). It has also discussed ethics (Rolston) and what future generations might have to say about the current path we are on (Mosley).

There are other key areas that perforce were only referred to in passing. One key issue in this category is equity and equality of income – now rapidly worsening in most countries (as the Gini coefficient shows). Wilkinson and Pickett (2010) in

The Spirit Level successfully demonstrated how inequality of income is bad for societal health. The usual argument advanced by orthodox economists in defence of the growth economy is that growth provides a 'bigger cake' to share all round, or 'a rising tide raises all boats'. In other words, if the economy keeps growing, the claim is that it will 'trickle down to the poor' and inequality will improve – except it hasn't happened. Inequality is *getting worse* (Dietz and O'Neill 2013). And this is weakening social capital at exactly the time when we need it to be strong so as to begin the transition to an SSE. As Wilkinson and Pickett observe, improving equality of income is really a prerequisite for a SSE, and we accept the need to acknowledge the truth of this. However, it has not proven possible to cover everything in this book, so we acknowledge that this key aspect deserved greater discussion than it was given.

The key drivers of overpopulation and overconsumption

Apart from the general endless growth economy, humanity has another related taboo it doesn't like talking about – *overpopulation*. Many books on sustainability and environmental studies shy away from this contentious issue. The UN, likewise, avoids it in most of its reports. It is interesting that the World Commission on Environment and Development in *Our Common Future* (WCED 1987) *did* discuss the importance of stabilising population. However, the UN and the OECD, and most international governmental organisations, have been singularly silent since then regarding overpopulation. Indeed, they do not acknowledge that the Earth is past its ecologically sustainable human population. UNEP (2011) in its 'green economy' document fails to discuss the need to stabilise (and then reduce over time) the world's population to an ecologically sustainable level. Interestingly, as the chapter on the green, blue and circular economies (Twomey and Washington) notes, the advocates of these alternate economies also all fail to discuss population stabilisation.

Almost every government likewise fails to talk about stabilising population. Indeed, most not only don't have national policies to reach an ecologically sustainable population, rather they *actively encourage* further population growth. How could they not – when they remain addicted to endless growth? More people means more consumers and more tax payers, and this is seen as a plus (not a dangerous minus). The impact they cause is simply silently ignored. This is typically done by sleight-of-hand phrases such as 'sustainable growth' and '100 per cent decoupling'. Feeding a growing population (when soils are eroding, water resources declining and climate change impacting strongly (Brown 2012)) is similarly defended through phrases such as the 'sustainable intensification' of food production. All these phrases sound good, but are weakly grounded in any evidence (and are effectively signs of denial). They are 'magic bullet' phrases that allow us to think that all will be well. Yet all is not well, and more and more people being added to the world is making things far worse.

So we are gratified to have four chapters about overpopulation in this book. The first, by Herman Daly, situates why a stable and sustainable population is a key aspect of an SSE. If we are to accept the reality of ecological limits, then a sustainable economy cannot be based on an endlessly increasing population. As Hulme (2009) notes, if there is a 'safe' level of greenhouse gases to avoid runaway climate change, then 'is there not also a desirable world population?' There are a variety of such figures for an ecologically sustainable population, and all are far below the world's current population, as several chapters note. Ian Lowe builds on this insight, arguing that our population needs to become *better* – not bigger. We editors, as Australians living in the OECD country with the highest population growth rate in the OECD (1.4 per cent in 2014, the majority of which is due to immigration), appreciate his insight into the Australian situation. In particular, Lowe explains that Australia could stabilise its population (already almost certainly beyond the ecologically sustainable level) by reducing net overseas immigration to 70,000 a year (a figure that still allows room for a substantial humanitarian refugee intake).

We are especially happy to have an updated chapter by Robert Engelman of the Worldwatch Institute on how we can stabilise our population to stop short of 9 billion. These are humane and non-coercive strategies, mostly centred around education for young women, and providing family planning and contraceptives. The final chapter in the population section is by Eileen Crist on 'Choosing a planet of life'. She reminds us that we live on a simply amazing world that we should respect and protect. When we editors were children, our world was teeming with life, which is now in major decline due to the endless growth myth operating in regard to human numbers. She eloquently raises the ethics of overpopulation, and how it drives a fundamental *un*sustainability that is destroying the well-being of the rest of life on Earth. Of course, that means it also destroys *our own* well-being, and also that of future generations. She also aptly describes the deep anthropocentrism inherent in our society, amounting to 'human supremacy'.

Of course, given the reality of the entity $I = PAT$ (see Washington and Diesendorf chapters), overpopulation and overconsumption are entwined. Like Siamese twins, you cannot consider one without the other, as shown in the section on throughput and overconsumption. Erik Assadourian of the Worldwatch Institute explains that the West's 'shop 'til you drop' consumer culture was actually a *deliberate construct* created in the 1950s in the United States. At that time in society, 'thriftiness' was the accepted norm, one the automobile, fast food and pet industries worked hard to change, as they sought to build the current consumer culture. US society was thus engineered to become the 'consumer' society, and this was then exported by globalisation to the rest of the world. It became embedded in most cultures, supported by the $500 billion a year spent on advertising around the world. However, if it was deliberately constructed, then it can also be deliberately *de*constructed. The reality of our ecological crisis demands this. If we are to reduce throughput of resources (a key aspect of an SSE), then we must confront consumerism. Interestingly, the green, blue and circular economies fail to be critical of consumerism (Twomey and Washington in this volume), while the SSE and its advocates do confront consumerism.

Kopnina looks at 'sustainable business' in the context of the circular economy, showing that (like many terms in academia) the circular economy can be *subverted* to promote 'business as usual' growth. Simon Michaux's chapter is directly about throughput of non-renewable resources – mining. He shows that we are rapidly approaching 'peak mining', where many factors are pushing us to step down from high resource use. Peak mining in many ways is thus a good thing, aiding the move to lower throughput of resources, and encouraging us to be less wasteful in those resources we do extract.

Capitalism

Few terms evoke such a powerful response as 'capitalism'. Proponents proclaim various virtues of capitalism, including the promotion of freedom of choice, rewarding effort and innovation, and suggest that there are no viable (successfully demonstrated) alternative systems. Opponents point to various problems of capitalism, including wealth inequality, social alienation, economic instability, a voracious appetite for material resources and a lack of regard for environmental damage.

Debate over these merits and faults, however, is often made difficult by the fact that there are many varieties of capitalism, which can have profoundly different outcomes. Farley here concludes that the currently dominant neoliberalism – characterised by minimal (or no) regulation of markets and promotion of market relations into new areas of society – is incompatible with an SSE. He also lists several reasons why capitalism and an SSE are uneasy bedfellows. A most interesting discussion in Farley's chapter is the problem of the worldview and ideology of capitalism. Capitalism extolls individualism and competition – not cooperation and sharing. The SSE, however, *requires* that we cooperate (indeed humanity has arguably survived due to our ability to do so). Hence, Farley convincingly shows that the ideas behind capitalism, while not totally incompatible with an SSE, make it far harder to move to an SSE quickly. Farley also reminds us that no society actually is *100 per cent* capitalistic (even the USA). So it may be a matter of changing the balance somewhat. The rise of cooperatives and not-for-profit businesses indicates that it may also be how one structures corporations (which many, like Sukhdev (2013), argue must now evolve to support sustainability).

However, this does not necessarily mean capitalism is completely 'the enemy'. As key writers on the SSE, such as Herman Daly (1991, 1996), Brian Czech (2013) and Dietz and O'Neill (2013) have noted, there are other *types* of capitalism, and some may be made compatible with the interests of environmental sustainability and social well-being.

Various authors in this book have proposed changes that can be part of a reformed economic system. For example, most agree that regulatory instruments that tax the 'bads' in society (such as a carbon tax or price), and the removal of all subsidies to fossil fuels, are rather obvious and sensible reforms. However, even modest attempts so far to introduce a carbon price or reduce fossil fuel subsidies have been meet with furious resistance from incumbent fossil fuel interests (as we

Australian editors know too well as we saw the creation of a modest carbon price in Australia, only to be removed by a new government after a major fear campaign).

Changes in the value orientation of corporations to include in their mission the interests of all major stakeholders – customers, employees, investors, communities, suppliers, and the environment – is another proposal for a more 'conscious' form of capitalism (Mackey and Sisodia 2013). The growing interest in 'benefit corporations' or B-corps (Cordes 2014) and 'not-for-profit' businesses (Maclurchan and Hinton 2016) shows that changes to business enterprises *is* possible and *is* happening.

Thus, the key problem is arguably not capitalism per se – but the *dominance of neoliberalism* and the bias towards unregulated markets. While markets are powerful devices for allocating goods and services, they are not perfect and certainly do not deserve the almost god-like status many have given them. They can and should be regulated in the interests of society and the nature that supports our societies.

Denial

Perhaps nothing is so odd in regards to humanity's predicament as humanity's tendency to *deny* difficult issues. Indeed, we are sure that there are many people out there who will deny most of the content of this book, along with most of the environmental science compiled over the last three decades. Like the proverbial ostrich that Pliny the Elder wrote about, society continues to stick its head in the sand. Denial is simply fascinating, and one of us (Washington and Cook 2011; Washington 2014a, 2015) has written about humanity's ability to 'flick a switch in our brain' and simply ignore something that is deeply worrying. We call ourselves *Homo sapiens*, but in reality we could be called *Homo denialensis*.

To move to a future *beyond growth* requires major change, and let's face it – change is worrying, it's something we fear, and fear is not a good motivator. When we are afraid, we tend to freeze up, to distract ourselves with other things (such as the latest sport or weather), to blame others (its someone else's fault), to fool ourselves with just how smart we are (techno-centrism will solve everything) or to come up with a conspiracy theory (all those scientists are just saying this to get research funding). Most commonly, society's denial is expressed in *silence* (Zerubavel 2006). As university lecturers who teach, and in our speaking engagements with the community, we find again and again that *people simply do not know* the full extent of the environmental crisis, nor have they thought about the ethics of what society is doing. One of us (Washington) remembers asking a student class if nature had 'intrinsic value', a right to exist for itself. One very worried student came up to him later and asked: 'Why have I never thought about this before? Why has nobody ever asked me about this before?' It's an excellent question. The answer is because society rarely talks about ethics – yet we should, and if we are ever to become sustainable, we must.

However, there are signs that the denial dam *is* breaking. The most heartening is that more and more people are questioning endless growth – and looking for more rational and intelligent ways to live their lives. As noted in the preface, this book has arisen from the 2014 Fenner Conference on the Environment (held in Sydney at UNSW). Its title was 'Addicted to Growth?' and it brought together thinkers from around the world to discuss our growth addiction, and talked about ways to move beyond this – especially the steady state economy. A third of the audience was under thirty, and they were so *happy* that at last someone was *talking about this* and calling out that the Emperor truly may not have on any clothes. The Fenner Conference is sponsored by the Australian Academy of Sciences, so the fact that this august body would approve a conference on this theme demonstrates just how much awareness has grown on the problematics of endless growth. We don't believe that five years previously the Academy would have approved such a topic, yet in 2014 they did (as it has become clearer that endless growth is rapidly degrading the Earth) – so change *is* thankfully happening.

Dialogue

Dialogue is what this book aims at – we have to talk about this issue to create change. The 2014 Fenner conference in Australia was a great start, as are the degrowth conferences that have been held around the world (see Perey in this volume). Dialogue is the *enemy of denial*. It helps us see the elephants in the room. If we can see the elephants, then we can really think about them, we can apply our rational mind and consider whether our actions are sensible. Hence, breaking denial can allow humanity's co-intelligence (Atlee 2003) and creativity to come into play, where we can solve problems. If we talk about this problem, then we may be able to create cracks in the denial dam that lead to it eventually bursting.

We do not pretend that this book is 'definitive'. In many ways, the authors of its chapters are only feeling their way towards a rational and sane economic and social system that is no longer dependent on the rapacity of endless growth. Some of the ideas and solutions here will work, others will be superseded by ideas better suited to both society's needs and the evolving reality we face. If society can rationally and respectfully have a dialogue about this topic, then it may prove possible to make an orderly transition to a post-growth society. If we cannot, then we face a grimmer prospect of the growth imperative pushing us into the abyss of systemic collapse, as Diamond (2005) has eloquently explained (though this may well happen in stages (Greer 2008)).

As the editors of this book, we find the dialogue in these chapters positive and refreshing. The authors don't necessarily agree on all aspects of the prognosis or proposed solutions. Nor should they, as the SSE and its component parts are not a mantra or dogma, but a rational response to the impossibility of endless growth. However, these authors all share a recognition that things are not well, and cannot go on as they are.

The ethics of economics

In any discussion of a long-term sustainable economy, ethics cannot be ignored. It makes us consider what is really important, what we really value. It is interesting also to note the spectrum of views regarding ethics. Even we editors have slightly different takes on ethics. Washington takes a strong eco-centric stand (like Crist and Rolston in their chapters). He agrees with Daly (1991), who has observed:

> It is widely believed by persons of diverse religions that there is something fundamentally wrong in treating the Earth as if it were a business in liquidation.
>
> *(p. 248)*

For humanity is indeed in the process of liquidating the living world at an accelerating rate (Washington in this volume). The environmental crisis is rapidly worsening, to the extent that by 2100 we face the appalling prospect that we may cause the extinction of two-thirds of life on Earth (Raven et al. 2011). Growth is not the answer (though almost all governments keep insisting it is) – it is the *cause*. Endless growth is not making things better, but far worse. Washington relates to the statement of Daly and Cobb (1994), who

> find it hard to suppress a cry of anguish, a scream of horror. We humans are being led to a dead end, we are living by an ideology of death and accordingly we are destroying our own humanity and killing the planet.
>
> *(p. 21)*

This is not 'polemic' or 'hyperbole', but rather it's the literal truth, borne out by the flood of environmental data coming in. Washington agrees with what Crist (2012) has observed, the scale of what we are doing, the sheer 'moral evil' is almost unimaginable.

Washington feels it's not just a new Earth ethics (Rolston 2012) we need, but a new eco-centric worldview of ecological harmony (Næss 1989). Changing our worldview (or paradigm) is a key solution, for as Donnella Meadows (1997) concluded:

> People who manage to intervene in systems at the level of a paradigm hit a leverage point that totally transforms systems … In a single individual it can happen in a millisecond. All it takes is a click in the mind, a new way of seeing.
>
> *(p. 84)*

Twomey does not disagree with the substantive ethics of such a position. Rather, from a pragmatic perspective, he sympathises with those who believe that the likelihood of success in dealing with the many issues discussed in this book will be greater if one takes a pluralistic position on environmental ethics (e.g. Light and

Katz 1996). That is, one that is inclusive of a range on value positions and normative and meta-ethical systems. This can include stances that are anthropocentric and non-anthropocentric, realist and anti-realist, mainstream ethical traditions (e.g. Kantian ethics, utilitarianism, virtue ethics) and other schools of environmental ethics (e.g. eco-centrism, deep ecology).

Seeking common ground in shared policy *goals* and *objectives* can characterise a unity that is more productive in interactions with those who formulate economic and environmental policy. Crucially, Twomey feels this pluralistic perspective can include people who have difficulties accepting some of the metaphysical and even religious foundations associated with some versions of the new environmental ethics (O'Neill *et al.* 2008). Thus, for example, whether one opposes a strip mining project for reasons of enlightened self-interest (e.g. aesthetic, recreational, cultural, climate security for future generations) or whether it is because one believes that the land is sacred and imbued with objective 'intrinsic value' – the goal of preventing the mine is the same. In practice, the overwhelmingly dominant motivational element of environmental advocacy, policy and law to date has been to advance human interests (Minteer 2009). Kopnina (2012) is more critical of pluralism, as is Washington (2015).

Of course, there is no guarantee that these different values and motivations will align. A well-known optimistic perspective in this regard is that of Norton (1991), who argues for what he calls 'the convergence hypothesis', which is the view that anthropocentrism and non-anthropocentrism will recommend the same environmental policies. However, this is still hotly debated (Minteer 2009; Rolston 2012).

In conclusion then, both editors feel that in regard to economics, ethics must become a central discussion point. Arguably we cannot reach a sustainable and just society via an SSE unless ethics is highlighted in our discussion. If economics is to be returned to serving society (rather than the other way around) – then it must be.

A time for transformation

The final section is on 'policy for change', where Perey discusses how degrowth is a necessary transition strategy, and Diesendorf discusses how society might be transformed to an SSE. There are many things we can do, and many of the first steps are actually in common with those proposed for the green economy and circular economy. For example, we need to put a price on carbon, get rid of subsidies for fossil fuels, encourage renewable energy quickly, and radically reduce the waste and throughput of resources in Western society. However, concurrently we need to *stabilise population* (and Engelman explains how to do this in non-coercive and humane ways). Washington (2014b) also details many other ideas for 'small and easy' steps towards an SSE. Of course, we cannot pretend that the full blueprint of a transformation to an SSE is fully mapped out here. That is why we need dialogue. We need to work through to the best way forward.

A key problem here is that most of the mainstream economic departments in universities and elsewhere *will not take part* in such a dialogue. Ecological economists of course will do so, but mainstream orthodox economists still remain in denial, and many of their books don't even mention the SSE. Even UNEP (2011) in its 'green economy' doesn't mention the SSE or the many writings of Herman Daly and others. This situation was highlighted in the 2014 Fenner conference 'Addicted to Growth?', where most UNSW faculties attended – *except* for the economics faculty. This lack of engagement with the topic by university economic faculties remains a serious problem. We hope this obstacle may now rapidly disappear, and we urge everyone (especially academics) to encourage such a dialogue.

One chapter here is a message from the future (Mosley), which is written from the perspective of one of our descendants returning to tell us how society reached the SSE of their time. This is a vision by a long-time CASSE advocate in Australia. The chapter suggests that society had to go through a period of collapse before it moved on to a sustainable future with an SSE, where population was ecologically sustainable, equity was far better, and throughput of resources was much lower. We editors wish to point out that we do not believe that such a collapse is *inevitable*, as our problems are still solvable – if we break the denial dam and move rapidly to solutions, key among which is the SSE. However, we cannot argue the likelihood of collapse if we stay with our endless growth economy, and an overpopulated and overconsuming world. Humanity is indeed on a collision course (Higgs 2014) with our life-support systems. As the original *Limits to Growth* study showed long ago (Meadows *et al.* 1972), without change, collapse is likely to happen by the middle of this century. The data coming in today doesn't push this date backwards, rather it suggests it may be sooner. *Unless we change*.

Neither we, nor the authors of the chapters, believe it will be easy to reach a steady state economy. There are powerful interests ranged against such a change – multi-national corporations, governments, the majority of the media, and even much of the education system. They insist we *must* keep growing, and if one listens to any media source, one is bombarded daily with such views, that growth is good and must continue forever. Scholars of the SSE such as Herman Daly have been writing and lecturing about the SSE since the 1970s. Mostly the message frustratingly has seemed to fall on deaf ears. Most of the public still believe the economy *must* grow, that there is no alternative. Many also don't want to talk about overpopulation or overconsumption. Indeed, some are proud that they like to 'shop 'til they drop'. There are thus many barriers we face to finding a path to a future beyond growth.

We recognise the difficulties, but we most certainly do not advocate either apathy or despair. It is neither hopeless nor too late. As Paul Ehrlich has noted, there are thresholds in human behaviour when cultural evolution moves rapidly: 'When the time is ripe, society can be transformed virtually overnight' (in Daily and Ellison 2002, p. 233). Nobody foresaw the collapse of the Soviet Union and the fall of the Berlin Wall even a few months beforehand. There are times when society *does* change rapidly to a new path, and this is one tipping point we desperately do need. Are we close to that tipping point? It's hard to see such points before they happen (as the Soviet Union collapse showed). However, *change is happening*, more and more people are questioning the endless growth mantra. More people are talking about solutions that avoid the endless growth mindset. There is more dialogue about this now than there has ever been before, and that is a very good thing. Dialogue is the enemy of denial. Given most people actually *do* recognise that endless growth is impossible on a finite planet, that reality is starting to move into the realm of social discussion. However, we can all help to speed this up (and we encourage *you* to be part of this). Certainly, we have further to go, and sure there is great urgency, for we need to change things immediately. However, when enough of us change our worldview, when enough of us call for a steady state economy – then governments, business, the media and the education system will follow. To quote the wisdom of Gandhi: 'You must be the change you wish to see in the world'.

References

Atlee, T. (2003) *The Tao of Democracy: Using Co-Intelligence to Create a World That Works for All*, Manitoba, Canada: The Writers Collective.

Brown, L. (2011) *World on the Edge: How to Prevent Environmental and Economic Collapse*, New York: Norton.

Brown, L. (2012) *Full Planet, Empty Plates: The New Geopolitics of Food Scarcity*, New York: Norton.

Catton, W. (1982) *Overshoot: The Ecological Basis of Revolutionary Change*, Chicago: University of Illinois Press.

Cordes, C. (2014) 'The rise of triple-bottom-line businesses', in *State of the World 2014: Governing for Sustainability*, ed. L. Mastny, Washington, DC: Island Press, pp. 203–214.

Crist, E. (2012) 'Abundant Earth and the population question', in *Life on the Brink: Environmentalists Confront Overpopulation*, eds. P. Cafaro and E. Crist, Athens, GA: University of Georgia Press, pp. 141–151.

Czech, B. (2013) *Supply Shock: Economic Growth at the Crossroads and the Steady State Solution*, Vancouver, British Columbia: New Society Publishers.

Daily, G. and Ellison, K. (2002) *The New Economy of Nature: The Quest to Make Conservation Profitable*, Washington, DC: Island Press.

Daly, H. (1991) *Steady State Economics*, Washington, DC: Island Press.

Daly, H. (1996) *Beyond Growth: The Economics of Sustainable Development*, Boston: Beacon Press.

Daly, H. and Cobb, J. (1994) *For the Common Good: Redirecting the Economy toward Community, the Environment, and a Sustainable Future*, Boston: Beacon Press.

Diamond, J. (2005) *Collapse: Why Societies Choose to Fail or Succeed*, New York: Viking Press.

Dietz, R. and O'Neill, D (2013) *Enough Is Enough: Building a Sustainable Economy Is a World of Finite Resources*, San Francisco: Berrett-Koehler Publishers.

Ehrlich, P. and Ehrlich, A. (1991) *Healing the Planet: Strategies for Resolving the Environmental Crisis*, New York: Addison-Wesley Publishing Company.

Greer, J. M. (2008) *The Long Descent: A User's Guide to the End of the Industrial Age*, Vancouver, British Columbia: New Society Publishers.

Higgs, K. (2014) *Collision Course*, Cambridge, MA: MIT Press.

Hulme, M. (2009) *Why We Disagree About Climate Change: Understanding Controversy, Inaction and Opportunity*, Cambridge: Cambridge University Press.

Kopnina, H. (2012) 'Education for sustainable development (ESD): The turn away from "environment" in environmental education?', *Environmental Education Research*, vol. 18, no. 5, pp. 699–717.

Layard, R. (2005) *Happiness: Lessons from a New Science*, New York: Penguin Press.

Light, A. and Katz. E. (1996) 'Introduction: Environmental pragmatism and environmental ethics as contested terrain', in *Environmental Pragmatism*, eds. A. Light and E. Katz, New York: Routledge, pp. 1–18.

Mackey, R. and Sisodia, R. (2013) *Conscious Capitalism: Liberating the Heroic Spirit of Business*, Cambridge, MA: Harvard Business Review Press.

Maclurchan, D. and Hinton, J. (2016) *How on Earth: Flourishing in a Not-for-Profit World by 2050*, White River Junction, VT: Post Growth Publishing.

MEA (2005) *Living Beyond Our Means: Natural Assets and Human Wellbeing, Statement from the Board, Millennium Ecosystem Assessment*, New York: United Nations Environment Programme (UNE). See: www.millenniumassessment.org

Meadows, D. (1997) 'Places to intervene in a system: In increasing order of effectiveness', *Whole Earth*, Winter 1997, pp. 78–84.

Meadows, D., Meadows, D., Randers, J., and Behrens, W. (1972) *The Limits to Growth*, Washington, DC: Universe Books.

Minteer, B. (2009) 'Unity among environmentalists? Debating the values–policy link in environmental ethics' in *Nature in Common? Environmental Ethics and the Contested Foundations of Environmental Policy*, ed. B. Minter, Philadelphia: Temple University Press, pp. 3–17.

Næss, A. (1989) *Ecology, Community and Lifestyle*, Cambridge: Cambridge University Press.

Norton, B. (1991) *Toward Unity among Environmentalists*, New York: Oxford University Press.

O'Neill, J., Holland. A., and Light, A. (2008) *Environmental Values*, Oxon, UK: Routledge.

Picketty, T. (2013) *Capital in the Twenty-First Century*, Cambridge, MA: Harvard Belknap Press.

Raven, P., Chase, J., and Pires, J. (2011) 'Introduction to special issue on biodiversity', *American Journal of Botany*, vol. 98, pp. 333–335.

Rolston III, H. (2012) *A New Environmental Ethics: The Next Millennium of Life on Earth*, London: Routledge.

Sukhdev, P. (2013) 'Transforming the corporation into a driver of sustainability', in *State of the World 2013: Is Sustainability Still Possible?*, ed. L. Starke, Washington: Island Press, pp. 143–153.

UNEP (2011) *Towards a Green Economy: Pathways to Sustainable Development and Poverty Eradication*, New York: United Nations Environment Programme. See: www.unep.org/greeneconomy

Washington, H. (2014a) 'Denial as a key obstacle to solving the environmental crisis', in Goldie, J. and Betts, K. (eds) *Sustainable Futures: Linking Population, Resources and the Environment*, Australia: CSIRO Publishing, pp. 159–166.

Washington, H. (2014b) *Addicted to Growth*, Sydney: CASSE NSW. See: https://steadystatensw.wordpress.com/2014/10/14/addicted-to-growth-booklet/

Washington, H. (2015) *Demystifying Sustainability: Towards Real Solutions*, London: Routledge.

Washington, H. and Cook, J. (2011) *Climate Change Denial: Heads in the Sand*, London: Earthscan.
WCED (World Commission on Environment and Development) (1987) *Our Common Future*, London: Oxford University Press.
Wilkinson, R. and Pickett, K. (2010) *The Spirit Level: Why Equality is Better for Everyone*, London: Penguin Books.
Zerubavel, E. (2006) *The Elephant in the Room: Silence and Denial in Everyday Life*, London: Oxford University Press.

INDEX

anthropocentrism: academia, in 6; church doctrine, change in 155; convergence hypothesis 247; human supremacy 6, 242; nature = resources 6; society, in 50, 242; worldview, as 6

biodiversity: ecosystem energy flow 2; ecosystem services 4–6, 178; extinction crisis 2, 46–7, 53, 70–1, 97, 101, 109, 182, 246; human dependence on nature 2–6; keystone species 3; nutrient cycles 3
blue economy: case study focus 135; comparison with other economic models 136–8; novel ways to create value 135; resource efficiency 135; systemic focus 135; waste minimization 135

capitalism: blind faith in technology 186; blocking sustainability 183; broken 217; capital and labour 150; challenges 146; competitive free markets and SSE 177; constrained 235; consumption, ever-increasing 181; contradictions in 149; cultural evolution 184; definition 176; discounting the future 181; ecological factors, ignoring of 181; economic colonialism 206; economic insecurity 148; eroding 152; growth as 'greatest good' 180; growth required to repay debt 181; ideology, as 180; inequality, increases 148, 182; limitations on 177; methodological individualism 180; no pure capitalist economies 180; persons in community 179; production for profit 147; public goods, failure to protect 183; prisoner's dilemma 183–4; self-interest, based on 184; SSE, compatibility with 177, 180–1, 186; SSE, seen as threat 180–1; SSE, uneasy bedfellow with 176, 186, 240, 243; substitutability ideology 180; taming 152; technical innovation, requirement for 183; vs cooperation 177, 185; vs. public sector 177; *see also* neoliberalism
CASSE (Center for the Advancement of a Steady State Economy) xxi–xxiii; 153; 207; 223; 248
circular economy: business, explaining to 79; business, ignorance of 78; closed loop 72, 102; 'cradle to cradle', relation to 71; certification systems, problems of 72; consumerism, failure to challenge 137; decoupling, support for 138; eco-efficiency can allow bad design 71; Ellen Macarthur Foundation 72–4, 130, 133–4, 138, 140; explanation 133; focus on industry and business 136; go beyond

mainstream sustainability 78; greenwash, risk of 74, 80; 'in the cloud' 72; 'new engine of growth' 72; population, ignoring 74, 137; relationship to green economy 133; resource efficiency strategy 29–30; service provision in 134; sharing economy, and 134; subversion, risk of 72–3, 76, 80; 'waste = food' principle 72

cooperation: commons, reclaiming 186; cooperatives 186; Earth jurisprudence 186; essential for SSE 186; evolution of 184; mechanisms for 184; resource rights 186; stimulation needed 186

consumerism: automobile industry 63; B-corporations 65; Big History 66; biocapacity 61; cultural norms, changing 67; culture of sustainability 62; fast food industry 64; Green Flag program 66; myth-building in 66; natural, feeling 61; North Face 67; Patagonia 65–7; pet food industry 63; re-engineering cultures 61; resistance to consumerism 63; solutions to 10–11; thriftiness 63, 242; transcending limits 61; Transition movement 66

decoupling: absolute 138; 100% 138; illusion, as 138; possible, is it? 138; strategy of 'slowing down not stopping' 138; throughput, failure to decrease 138

deep ecology 207, 247

degrowth: alternatives to growth 214; bioeconomics 214; capitalism, new forms of 214; critique of growth 213; evidence of need for 176; degrowth society 220; development, criticism of 215; economic democritisation 220; economic downsizing 139; future prospects 217; indicators of success, changing 218; pathway to SSE 139; risk blindness 216; social change 213; social equity 213, 220; virtuous circle of contraction 219; *see also* social imaginary

denial: barrier to SSE 244; blocking sustainability 8; breaking denial dam 9, 244–5; delusion, as 8; dialogue enemy of 245; driver of unsustainability 7; 'elephant in the room' 8; found in those opposing regulation 8; historical examples 8; *Homo denialensis* 8; 'magic bullet' phrases in 241; need for fair and lean economy, of 224; planetary crisis, of 80, 239; prosperity without growth, of 240; orthodox economists, in 248; silence in 8; stupid things, believing in 7

development: concept of human rights 197; failure of institutions 198; ideology of 197

Earth, Rights of the 65

ecological economics: ecological sustainability central goal 179; end of growth-based approach 89; definition 103; difference to environmental economics 103; bioeconomics in 214; fantasy, not 10; just distribution of wealth 179; scale of economy 136; SSE within 103, 179; transdisciplinary nature 103

economics: conventional 100; development in 24; environmental 103, 136, 225; laissez-faire 8; neoclassical xxii, 10, 97, 99–103, 106, 109, 180–1, 186, 203, 239; orthodox 26; physical science, and 101; serving society 11; sufficiency focus needed 20; *see also* blue economy; *see also* circular economy; *see also* degrowth; *see also* ecological economics; *see also* green economy; *see also* steady state economy

ecosystem services 4–6, 178

environmental crisis: nature of 1–2; growth as cause 7, 239–40; denial in society 8; population as driver 21; circular economy as possible solution 76; ignorance of extent of 244; rapidly worsening 246

ethics: entwined destinies 198; future 200; hope 198; larger frames of reference 198; making decisions 197; thinking globally 198; sustainable biosphere = key goal 198; residents of Earth 198; resourcism, problem of 198–9; respect for life 199

Factor 4 and Factor 5 30, 112, 130, 138

future: message from 201; trade in 201; population in 202; governance in 202;

transformation to reach 203; learning from past 205; need for moral growth 221

Genuine Progress Indicator (GPI): calculation of 168; definition 167; GDP, alternative to 158; GDP and energy consumption 161; GDP vs. GPI 170; guide to transition to SSE 172; implications of GPI 169; improving 172; uncancelled benefits/ costs of economic activity 161–2

green economy (UNEP): comparison with other models 136–8; definition 131; green growth 130,132; growth focus 142; population, ignoring 142; tackling only half the problem 143; *see also* circular economy

growth: definition 98; delusion, as 239; endless 1, 7–9, 74, 137, 140–3, 204, 214, 239–246, 249; growthism 20, 74; 'magic pudding' analogy 1; problems of 1–2

I = PAT 98, 112, 137, 226, 233, 242
indicators, biophysical 164
Interface carpets 134

life, choosing a planet of 43, 46
Limits to Growth 25, 75, 90–1, 112, 123, 126, 147, 159, 164, 180, 205, 213, 216, 248

myth, endless growth 239

neoliberalism: definition 177; dominance in major economic institutions 153; incompatible with SSE 177; reducing egalitarianism 148

overconsumption, *see consumerism*
overpopulation, *see population*

peak mining: Australia, in 85; causes of 85; 'change is upon us' 89; evolution of civilization 91; finite planet 83; industrial transformation 90; Limits to Growth 90–1; low resource use = practical path 92; metal production and consumption 84; ore deposit grade, declining 85–6; peak coal 88; peak gas 87; peak oil 86; peak resource use 83; peak total energy 88; symptom of unsustainability 92

policies: birthrates, lowering 52; capitalist 185, 215; climate change 61; economic systems, in 129, 140–1; effective political 146; electricity production 233; environmental 153, 247; human rights 40; low growth modelling 227; market-based 153; mutually reinforcing 232; neoliberal 149, 185; physical scale, reducing 164; population 40–1, 52, 137, 226, 241; progressive 154; redistribution 149, 163; rewarding extra children 38; scope of 136; 'simple and easy', problems with 74; social costs, reducing 163; SSE, for 106, 153, 231, 233; status quo 153; sustainability, enhancing 155; tailoring to find solutions 98

population: adjust to ageing 39; appropriate sexuality education 37; better not bigger 21; carrying capacity 48; catastrophe, as 43; contraceptives 35; 'coercion' myth 51; demographic transition 18; dissipative structures 17; economic impacts of 26; education for all 36; ending financial incentives for 38; ending growth of 34; family planning 35; gender bias 37; feeding 10 billion 46; forecast = self-fulfilling prophecy 43; impact of 44; impact of strategies 40; longevity with sufficiency 20; Malthus 48; migration 24; myths about 25; net migration 19; optimism 44; overlooked issue 30; selective blindness 30; solutions to 10, 35–39; stabilising 27, 52–3; strategies 35–9; sustainable population 24, 53; wisdom of limitations 46

renewable energy: 66, 72, 133, 135, 139–40, 155, 178, 226, 228–30, 232–4, 247
resourcism 6, 198–9

Index 255

sharing economy 134
simplicity and complexity 239
social imaginary: concept and practice 218; ecological imaginary 219; growth ≠ better 219
solutions: addressing overpopulation and overconsumption 241; challenge of reaching SSE 248; denial, breaking dam 244; ; denial, dealing with 244; dialogue, enemy of denial 245; dialogue, meaningful 245; economic faculties, failure to enter dialogue 238; need for new ethics of economics 246; neoliberalism, breaking dominance of 244; time for change 239; transformation needed 247; *see also* strategies for transition
steady state economy (SSE): cultural shift needed 156; definition 100; dematerialization 105–6, 112, 115; debt reduction 107; ecological economics, within 103; efficiency vs. sufficiency 104; efficient allocation 100; environmental economics, difference to 103; fair distribution 100; growth debate 97; growth in what? 98; growth vs. well-being 99; growth = environmental degradation 105; happiness and GDP 100; increasing work flexibility 107; key initiatives 106; Keynes 104; limiting income inequality106; material use by society 99; measurement of 101; Mill's 'stationary condition' 104; optimal scale 100–1; reforming banks 107; roots of 207; scale 100; simplicity, shift to 108; strategies, temporal 152; systematic planning 155; techno-optimism 97; thermodynamic irreversibility 101; ; *see also* decoupling; *see also* degrowth; *see also* steady state economy, physical path to; *see also* thermodynamics
steady state economy, physical path to: Australian Stocks and Flows Framework (ASFF) 113; challenge of 126; strategies needed 126; feasibility of reaching SSE 123; outcomes of alternative scenarios 119; reduction in consumption 119; role of consumption 116; scenario settings 120; simulating a healthy economy 115; simulating economy's physical activity 113; simulating standard growth paradigm 116–8; working week, shorter 121
strategies for transition: distributing income equitably 234; employment 227–8; energy policies 232; general policies for SSE 233; limiting resource use 234; new indicators 235; reforming financial systems 234; securing full employment 235; renewable energy future 228–230; rethinking how business creates value 235; stabilizing population 234; sustainable agriculture 231; sustainable cities 230; sustainable society 224, 227; transport 230, 233
sustainable biosphere 195
sustainable business: avoidance of population issue 75–6; business-as-usual growth 72; case study, Netherlands 77; circular economy in business, making it work 79; circular economy 'in the cloud' 76; 'cradle to cradle' 71; closed loop systems 71–2; Ellen Macarthur Foundation 72–4, 130, 133–4, 138, 140; global north vs south 75; 'simple and easy' approach 74; solutions 80; subversion, risks of 73,76; supply chains 74,78; waste = food principle 73; *see also* circular economy
sustainable development: discussion of 225–6; economics as driver 196; extractive model of 196; illusion of consensus 195; inequality rising 196; not same as sustainability 9; vs. land as community 196
sustainable net domestic product 165
sustainability: barriers to 7; capitalism and 181; challenges 76; closed loop 72; 'cradle to cradle' in 78; cultures of 59, 62, 65, 67; denial blocking 8; desirable social objective 162; eco-efficiency in 71; ecological economics, central goal of 179; economic 10–11; economic models in 136; ecological 10; economic growth incompatible 74; education 66;

entwined with social justice 224; Factor 5 in 138; failure of markets in 183; growth economy as barrier to 240; indicators 164–6; intergenerational distribution in 179; key relevance of overpopulation 21; longevity with sufficiency 20, 146; meaningful 239; new economic institutions in 177; not same as sustainable development 9; population, avoidance of issue 240; public policy, in 154; sustaining the unsustainable 70; strategies 126; system analysis of 113; voluntary simplicity in 139; *see also* unsustainability

systems thinking 112

Thermodynamics, Laws of 101–2, 159–160, 163, 177
Transition movement 10, 66, 139, 207

unsustainability, drivers of 6

worldview 6, 92, 200, 243, 246, 249